CHIEF OF STAFF

About the Author

Gavin Barwell was appointed Downing Street chief of staff to former prime minister Theresa May in the immediate aftermath of the general election in June 2017. He remained in post until she stood down as prime minister in July 2019. Now sitting in the House of Lords, he was the MP for Croydon Central from 2010 until 2017 and served as a government minister from 2013 to 2017.

GAVIN BARWELL

CHIEF OF STAFF

NOTES FROM DOWNING STREET

Atlantic Books
London

First published in hardback in Great Britain in 2021 by
Atlantic Books, an imprint of Atlantic Books Ltd.

Copyright © Gavin Barwell, 2021

1   3   5   7   9   10   8   6   4   2

A CIP catalogue record for this book
is available from the British Library.

Hardback ISBN: 978 1 83895 412 3
E-book ISBN: 978 1 83895 413 0

Printed in Great Britain by CPI Group (UK) Ltd, Croydon CR0 4YY

Atlantic Books
An imprint of Atlantic Books Ltd
Ormond House
26–27 Boswell Street
London
WC1N 3JZ

www.atlantic-books.co.uk

To Mum and Dad, for giving me the best start in life
any child could ask for. I miss you every day, Dad,
and wish you could have seen where the journey ended.

And to Karen, for all the sacrifices and support
every step of the way. You complete me.

CONTENTS

'The real proof of whether you understand something is whether you can explain it to someone else clearly and simply.'

BILL GATES

INTRODUCTION

I agonised over whether to write this book for over a year, because I knew that doing so would bring back painful memories. If it is, in part, the story of Theresa May's inability to secure support for her Brexit deal, it is also the story of my failure, because – whatever other roles the chief of staff to the prime minister may have – their primary responsibility is to keep their boss in office. Whenever I've said this to friends and colleagues, they have sought to console me with some variant of 'no one could have done more'. But kind words cannot disguise the truth: it was my job to keep Theresa May in Number 10 and help her 'get Brexit done', and I couldn't find a way to do it. Revisiting that failure was not an inviting prospect. I also thought it would be unfair to Boris Johnson to publish anything until he had negotiated and ratified his Brexit deal. And finally, I was conscious that there was no point writing something unless I was prepared to be honest about what I think, even if that risks upsetting people who I admire and enjoyed working with.

I eventually concluded that the case for telling my story outweighs those considerations. The last two years of the May government were among the most turbulent and important in modern British political history. The existing accounts are second-hand, at best partial and at worst get important details wrong. As Theresa May's chief of staff, I was with her when she negotiated her Brexit deal, met Donald Trump, learned about the poisoning of Sergei and Yulia Skripal in Salisbury, made the decision to authorise the use of military force in

Syria, took the call from Boris Johnson in which he told her that he was resigning from her cabinet, met Jeremy Corbyn to try to break the Brexit logjam and made the decision to stand down as leader of the Conservative Party. Apart from Theresa herself – and, at the moment, at least, she has no plans to write her own memoirs – there is no one better qualified to describe what went on behind the scenes and to give an insight into what motivated this most private of prime ministers. Subsequent events – Boris Johnson's decision to withdraw the whip from a number of his senior colleagues, his attempts to prorogue parliament, his willingness to break international law, the slow realisation of what his Brexit deal means for trade both with the EU and between Great Britain and Northern Ireland – and potentially for the future of the United Kingdom – have prompted a reassessment of Theresa and what she was trying to achieve, reinforcing the case for telling my story.

However, this book is not just an account of those two years. There has been huge interest in Dominic Cummings, the person who was effectively my successor, and the dysfunctionality of the Number 10 operation Boris Johnson has put in place. I am uniquely placed to give an insight into how the country is run from behind that famous black door.

I have only censored myself in four regards. First, there are things that it would be damaging to national security for me to reveal. Second, people sometimes told me things in confidence or agreed to meet me on the condition that I would keep the fact of our meeting confidential; I have respected those confidences. Third, I have not revealed what was agreed at meetings of the cabinet or its committees except where those decisions have subsequently been made public, nor have I quoted what ministers said at those meetings except in relation to discussions on Brexit, which were extensively leaked by many of the participants. I have drawn on such coverage, giving a particularly full account of two crucial meetings, the meeting in July 2018 that agreed the Chequers proposals and the meeting in November 2018 that agreed the deal. Details of both were leaked and dissected in the press. And fourth, when I've quoted other heads of government, I've been more relaxed about revealing what those who have since stood down from public office said than those who are still in post.

*   *   *

Theresa's key job as prime minister was to deliver Brexit, and she failed. However much time passes, that will always be the first line in any judgement on her premiership. But subsequent events have led to a reappraisal of what she was trying to achieve. The disagreement between her and Boris Johnson over Brexit boiled down to a philosophical difference and four arguments on which we can now reach a conclusion.

The philosophical difference concerned compromise. Theresa's view was that the referendum result was clear but close and that two of the four nations of the UK had voted to remain, so while we should leave, we should have a close relationship with the EU after we had left. Boris rejected any idea of compromise – if you didn't break completely free of the EU, he said, there was no point leaving.

The first argument was about whether leaving the European Union without a deal was a good outcome. Boris thought it was, or at least claimed to. Theresa's position was that while you have to be prepared to walk away from any negotiation if the proposed deal isn't good enough, leaving without a deal would not be a good outcome economically. But of greater concern to her was the risk that it could lead to the break-up of the UK, given the opposition to it in Scotland and Northern Ireland.

Second, setting aside the argument about whether no deal was a good policy, was it a viable one? If the government tried to leave without a deal, would parliament block it? Boris believed that if the party was led by someone who supported leaving without a deal, those in cabinet and on the backbenches who opposed it would fall into line. You could unite the parliamentary party and, with support from the DUP and a few 'Labour Leavers', win a vote. However, Theresa thought that those who opposed no deal felt just as strongly on one side of the argument as Boris did on the other.

Third, would the threat of leaving without a deal force the EU to shift its position? Boris believed that it would. Theresa was much more sceptical, in part because the EU had less to lose from no deal than the UK but mainly because they didn't regard it as a credible threat, given the parliamentary arithmetic and the Speaker John Bercow's willingness to bend parliamentary conventions.

Fourth, if parliament remained gridlocked, was going back to the country a credible strategy? Could the Conservative Party win a general election without having delivered Brexit? Boris was confident that he could. Theresa, coloured by her experience in 2017, was more sceptical.

We now know who was right on at least three of these questions. Boris Johnson was unable to force through no deal, thanks to the opposition of twenty-one Conservative MPs, including five members of Theresa's cabinet (Philip Hammond, David Gauke, Greg Clark, Rory Stewart and Caroline Nokes). In retaliation, he withdrew the whip from them and prevented some of them from standing as Conservative candidates at the election he was forced to call, effectively ending their political careers. Their ministerial experience – and that of others such as Sajid Javid, Jeremy Hunt and Julian Smith, who he has exiled to the backbenches – was sadly missed as the government struggled to respond to the COVID-19 pandemic.

The threat of leaving without a deal when Boris became prime minister did not extract any meaningful concession from the EU. Despite all the talk from his chief negotiator David Frost about how the May government had blinked at key moments, the truth is that the deal Boris agreed was 95 per cent Theresa's deal, with the 5 per cent that was new involving a concession by the UK. Boris went back to what the EU had wanted all along: special arrangements for Northern Ireland that created a partial border within our own country.

At the time, Boris hailed his deal as a triumph and denied that it meant a partial border down the Irish Sea, but the government was subsequently forced to admit that it would mean increased checks when goods move from Great Britain to Northern Ireland. Indeed, it turned out that what had been a great deal in the run-up to the December 2019 election was so problematic the following September that the government attempted to pass legislation to override parts of it in domestic law, doing grave damage to the UK's international reputation in the process. And now that the protocol is in partial operation, the effect is clear, both in terms of the difficulties it is causing businesses and the political unrest it has provoked. Things will be even worse if it is ever fully applied.

But if Boris was proved wrong about his ability to force through no deal and whether the threat of it would extract concession from the EU, he was proved right about his ability to win an election. The coalition he built, holding on to Conservative seats in the South and gaining Leave-supporting Labour seats in the Midlands, the North and in Wales, was the coalition Theresa was trying to assemble in 2017, but he ran a better campaign and benefited from the fact that in the intervening two years, Leave-supporting voters had witnessed parliament doing everything it could to block Brexit. The need for a large Conservative majority to get Brexit done was self-evident.

On the fourth question, we will never know what a no-deal exit would have meant for the future of our United Kingdom, but over the next few years we will discover the consequences of Boris Johnson's hard Brexit, and the omens are not good. Support for Scottish independence rose from the moment he became prime minister, driven by antipathy to him, opposition to his government's Brexit policy and the perceived relative handling of the COVID-19 pandemic by the UK and Scottish governments. Seventy-two of the 129 members of the Scottish parliament elected in May 2021 stood on a manifesto promising a second independence referendum. If the Scottish parliament was elected using the Westminster system, the

SNP would have won sixty-two of the seventy-three seats. The UK government is on strong ground arguing that it is not the right time for a second independence referendum – polls show Scottish voters want the immediate focus to be on recovery from the pandemic – but the democratic mandate for the question to be asked again at some point is clear.

A clear majority of MPs in the 2017–19 parliament would have preferred Theresa's compromise to the deal Boris negotiated – indeed, some have publicly said they regret not voting for it (most notably former Labour MP Gloria De Piero, who tweeted, 'I was an idiot for not voting for May's deal'). I will try to explain why things turned out the way they did and consider whether there is anything we could have done differently (spoiler alert: it's not all Gloria's fault).

* * *

With the exception of my first few days and last few weeks as chief of staff, I've chosen to tell this story thematically rather than chronologically. Such an approach obscures the constant jumping between issues that is a fundamental of the job, but breaking the role down gives a clearer sense of what it involves. Furthermore, it is easier to understand why the government struggled to agree a Brexit policy, negotiate a deal and secure parliamentary approval for that deal if Brexit is told as a single narrative without budgets, party conferences and various crises intervening.

With the exception of the first few months, the book is based on my contemporaneous notes. I started taking these in November 2017 and they eventually amounted to nine bound volumes. The entries are of varying detail. For some key meetings, they are a near-verbatim account of who said what. At the other end of the spectrum, I sometimes wrote something like 'Shit meeting on customs' with no explanation. For my first few months as chief of staff, and in relation to any key meetings that I didn't attend, I have spoken to former colleagues to ensure that my account is as accurate as possible. I am hugely grateful for their assistance, but will spare their blushes because some of them still work in government.

As any GCSE history student knows, it's important to understand the provenance of a source in order to interpret their account. But before I tell you about myself, here's an anecdote that should serve as a warning. When I was an MP, one of the things I most enjoyed was visiting schools to speak about being an MP. One of the questions I was frequently asked was a variant of 'Are you like us?' At first, I struggled to answer the question. I didn't want to insult the students' intelligence by pretending that I'd had as tough a childhood as some of them, but nor did I want them to think that I was so different from them that they couldn't aspire to be an MP. In the end, I found a way of answering the question that grabbed their attention and made them think. I gave them two answers and said that at the end of the session they could vote on which one they thought was true. The first was that I had gone to a private school then Cambridge University and had worked in politics all my adult life. The second was that I'd lived in Croydon all my life, both my parents had left school at sixteen and I was the first person in my family to go to university. At the end I would reveal that both stories were true. I'd tell them that while very few politicians will tell outright lies, most will bend the truth to give their audience a favourable impression of them. I'd add that the question they should ask was not 'Are you like us?' but 'Do you understand what it is like to be us?' That is a much tougher thing to judge.

So with the warning that I'm trying to paint the best picture of myself out of the way, what should you know about me? When I was eleven, I did very well in an exam and it changed my life, allowing me to go to a private school in Croydon called Trinity on a full scholarship. It gave me an outstanding education, but just as importantly, I met seven boys who remain my best friends thirty-seven years later. That close friendship group was crucial in helping me cope with the pressure during my two years in Number 10.

It was at school that I developed a love of debating that fostered an interest in politics. Many people make the mistake of thinking that being good at debating is all about public speaking. That's a part of it, of course, but it's just as important to be good at listening. In order to rebut an opponent's argument, you need to work out where the weaknesses are. I'd argue that an ability to listen is equally important in politics. Politicians need to understand the perspectives of those with different life experiences to them and to adjust their views accordingly. You might think there isn't much racism in Britain today, but if you're not from an ethnic minority background, are you able to judge? You might think people in London have life easy, but how do you know if you've never lived there? In this age of social media when too many people only hear from people like themselves, we're losing the ability to listen.

From Trinity, I got into Cambridge, where I studied natural sciences, specialising in theoretical physics. That scientific background has shaped my approach to politics. I have a distaste for blind faith in ideology, preferring to base my views on evidence. Several people in Number 10 commented that you could tell I was a scientist by training because my interventions in meetings tended to be logically structured ('I think we should go with option A for the following reasons . . .').

After I'd graduated, I had no idea what to do next. My roommate, worried that I'd drift into unemployment without his intervention, came back from the careers library with a bundle of random job adverts. The only one I didn't reject out of hand was a job in the Conservative Party's research department. He dragged me down to the computer room to write a CV and covering letter, and a couple of months later I'd been offered a job.

So began a career in politics. I did two years in CRD (working alongside one George Osborne), followed by two years as a political adviser in what was then the Department of the Environment and another year back in CRD, before switching over to the campaigning department, whose job it was to help Conservative candidates get elected. I ended up as the Conservative Party's chief operating officer, the most senior position at Conservative HQ. In 2010, I was elected as an MP and in 2013 I was appointed as a minister.

Finally, you need to understand my views on Brexit. I was never a rose-tinted supporter of the European project. In particular, I disliked the increasing extent to which power sat with unelected officials in the commission and with MEPs, who in the UK were largely anonymous in a way that MPs and councillors are not. But I always believed that whatever the EU's flaws, we were better off being part of the club, so when the referendum was called, I campaigned for Remain. I was upset at the outcome, which led to an ill-judged tweet the next morning, when I said that I was proud that my hometown had rejected the politics of hate and division. The comment was aimed at some of the disgraceful things Nigel Farage had said during the campaign, but when I looked back at it a couple of years later, after people started raising it with me as evidence of my hostility to Brexit, it read like it was directed at everyone who voted Leave and I could understand why people had taken offence. I might have been upset, but the referendum result was clear-cut, so from that moment I've believed that we should leave. However, given it was close and that two of the four nations of our United Kingdom had voted Remain, I thought we should do so in a way that brought people back together, delivering the key things Leave supporters voted for but maintaining a close relationship with the EU.

I am conscious that lots of people will disagree with my views about the May government and why things turned out the way they did. I cannot claim to be neutral, particularly on the topic of Theresa May, whose sense of duty, work ethic and resilience under the most extraordinary pressure I witnessed at first hand. But I have tried to give every side of the story, explaining why those who disagreed with her thought as they did as well as describing what motivated her. I hope that even those who disagree with my views will find my account of this turbulent period interesting. Above all, my aim is to give a unique insight into what is involved in being chief of staff to the prime minister, which I hope will be illuminating to everyone who cares about how our country is governed.

*   *   *

The role of chief of staff is a relatively recent innovation in British politics, an import from the US. The first person to do the job in the UK was Jonathan Powell, who became Tony Blair's chief of staff when Blair was leader of the opposition and held the role for the whole of his premiership. During his time in the job, Jonathan played a crucial role in the Northern Ireland peace talks that led to the Good Friday Agreement.

Gordon Brown, perhaps to differentiate himself from his predecessor, combined the role with that of principal private secretary (Bernard, for fans of *Yes, Prime Minister*). He appointed a civil servant, Tom Scholar, but that only lasted for six months, at which point a political adviser, Stephen Carter, took over the role. He lasted for less than a year, and no one held the title for the remainder of Brown's premiership.

Ed Llewellyn had the job for the whole of the Cameron premiership, having taken it on when David Cameron was leader of the opposition. During his time as chief of staff, Ed played a crucial role in the renegotiation of the terms of our membership of the EU which preceded the referendum. He was our ambassador in Paris while I was chief of staff and so the one predecessor I could easily turn to for advice.

When Theresa May became prime minister, she appointed Fiona Hill and Nick Timothy as co-chiefs of staff. They had both worked for her in opposition and at the Home Office, and, thanks in part to their work, she was in a strong political position when she called the 2017 general election. However, Fi and Nick were widely blamed for the disastrous 2017 campaign and, as I was to discover, they had fallen out with a number of senior cabinet ministers. They resigned two days after polling day and I was appointed shortly afterwards.

No one had the title for the first period of Boris Johnson's government, but Dominic Cummings was clearly carrying out many of the functions of the role. In the aftermath of his departure, Boris appointed Dan Rosenfield, a former civil servant who had had been principal private secretary to both Alistair Darling and George Osborne. After his appointment, there was a noticeable improvement in the effectiveness of the Number 10 operation.

As I discovered, there is no job description – what you do depends on what the prime minister wants, what the political situation demands and your skill set. A few weeks into the job, the prime minister asked me which of two outfits she should wear to a particular event. Like most husbands, I knew to say 'Yes' when asked 'Does this look nice on me?', but being asked to choose between two options was outside my comfort zone. In essence, a chief of staff is a human Swiss Army knife, but for those chiefs of staff who are political appointments rather than career civil servants, the core of the role is to be the prime minister's most senior political adviser and to manage the rest of the political team in Number 10 and, to a degree, political advisers across the government. Another key role is to tell truth to power. Very few people are prepared to say no to the prime minister or tell them something they don't want to hear. I can remember one occasion in Brussels where the European Council overran and a discussion on protecting the steel industry from dumping was postponed to the next morning. The prime minister had kept the morning free to spend some rare time with her husband Philip, so had arranged for one of the other heads of government to represent her views. As we prepared to leave, James Slack said to me that he thought it was a mistake for the prime minister to miss the discussion, and it turned out that everyone else agreed with him. 'Right,' I said, 'someone needs to tell the prime minister.' Everyone looked at me. It's fair to say that she wasn't best pleased, but once she'd calmed down, she thanked me for saying something.

I am, so far, the only chief of staff who had previously served as a minister. That prior experience was certainly useful, but there are two big differences between the two jobs. First, as chief of staff you have to be across everything the British state is doing, rather than one particular area of policy. You have to help the prime minister make decisions based on a précis of the issue and options available. There's no time to dig into the detail on every decision, which I often found uncomfortable. Second, as chief of staff you're not there to argue for your own views. You have no democratic mandate – your job is to advise the prime minister and then get the government machine to do whatever he or she decides. A few months into the job, I was given a wonderful history of the office of White House chief of staff called *The Gatekeepers*. It was full of great advice, but a particular quote from James Baker, who served as chief of staff to both Ronald Reagan and George H. W. Bush, has stuck with me:

> You are extraordinarily powerful when you are White House chief of staff. You may be the second most powerful person in Washington. But the minute you forget that your power is all vicarious from the president then you're in trouble.

The key word in the job title is 'staff', not 'chief'. To reinforce that point in my own and others' minds, I always addressed Theresa as 'prime minister' rather than by her first name during my time in Number 10, even when we were the only two people in the room. It was several months after she had stopped being prime minister before I finally got out of the habit, much to her amusement.

* * *

For two and a bit years, this incredible job took up virtually every waking hour of my life. I arrived at work before 6 a.m. and often stayed so late that it didn't make sense to commute home to Croydon. Sometimes I would stay with George Hollingbery, then an MP and the prime minister's parliamentary private secretary but now British ambassador to Cuba, who lived just off Parliament Square. Sometimes I would find somewhere else to crash for a few hours. Even when I wasn't at work, I spent much of the time glued to my mobile phone. While ministers are reasonably respectful about not disturbing the prime minister late at night or over the weekend, they're less bothered about disturbing the chief of staff.

During those two years, I saw pretty much every submission the prime minister saw. I could attend whichever of her meetings I wanted to, and I got to know the leaders of the opposition parties and a number of world leaders on a first-name basis (at least, they called me by my first name). It was exhausting and at times very stressful, but it was also the most amazing job I'll ever have. I hope this account gives a feel of what it was like.

CHAPTER 1

APPOINTMENT

On the morning of 18 April 2017, Clare Brunton, the civil servant who ran my ministerial office, told me that the prime minister had just announced that she was calling an early general election.

I had served as the member of parliament for Croydon Central for seven years and had been a government minister for three and a half years, first in a succession of roles in the whips' office and then as minister for housing and planning and minister for London at the Department for Communities and Local Government. I loved both being an MP and being minister for housing. Some people become MPs because they want to be ministers, but I would have been happy just representing the town where I've lived for almost all my life. And some ministers get appointed to a role for which they lack any relevant experience or passion – often, a prime minister will know who they want to promote and fit them in, rather than thinking about the gaps and identifying the best people to fill them. Perhaps Theresa May knew that I had worked in the old Department of the Environment on housing policy and that housing was a key issue in my constituency. Or perhaps I was just – not for the first or last time – incredibly lucky. Either way, there can't have been many people in the country who loved their job more than me.

I had a great relationship with my boss, Sajid Javid, the secretary of state for communities and local government. I worked with a fantastic team of civil servants, who shared our passion for transforming housing policy. The prime minister and her two chiefs of staff were supportive. The department had recently published a seminal white paper, *Fixing Our Broken Housing Market*, which for the first time acknowledged that we have a housing crisis and made the case that we needed to build more homes to buy *and* more homes to rent and to reform the planning system *and* the housing market. If things had turned out differently and I had held my seat, I would have been very happy to be kept in that job, ending the merry-go-round of housing ministers that so frustrates the sector.

The news that the prime minister was calling an early election was a hammer blow. At the 2015 election, I had managed to cling on to my seat by a wafer-thin majority of 165 votes, while similar London seats like Brentford and Isleworth, Ealing Central and Acton, Enfield North and Ilford North were lost to Labour. It was a gruelling campaign that had taken its toll. I was privately resigned to the fact that I was highly likely to lose next time because, like much of outer London, Croydon was changing demographically in a way that favoured Labour. The government's benefit cap was leading poorer families to move from inner to outer London, the area was becoming more ethnically diverse and home ownership was in decline. Nevertheless, I had hoped that having held on by my fingertips in 2015, I would have five more years as an MP and as a minister. The prime minister's announcement shattered that illusion. I had supported Theresa May in the leadership election, in part because I thought she was the best candidate to bring the party back together after the bitter experience of the referendum, but also because she had given a clear assurance that she would not call an early election.

I thought briefly about whether I wanted to put myself through another campaign, but at least this would be a short one. In any case, it is not in my nature to quit. I had clung on in 2015 with the help of an incredible group of Conservative councillors and activists in Croydon, who gave up hundreds of hours of their time to help get me re-elected. It was time to 'get the band back together'. I got on the phone and we assembled at my house that evening.

At first, things went well. We were miles ahead in the national polls. A small number of former Conservatives were staunch Remainers and unwilling to vote for us, but the majority of the Conservative vote was rock-solid and lots of lifelong Labour voters were also saying they intended to switch to us. Privately, senior Labour activists in Croydon told us they expected us to win by about 5,000 votes.

Normally, the national campaign in the weeks before polling day makes little difference – the polls when the election is called tend to be a pretty good predictor of the final result. But in 2017, the publication of the Conservative manifesto transformed the election. Among the proposals were plans to make people with assets of more than £100,000 pay for any care they required in old age, including that provided in their own home. It was quickly branded a 'dementia tax' by opponents. The manifesto also proposed scrapping the planned cap on care costs, abolishing the triple lock on the state pension, means-testing winter fuel payments and having a free vote on legalising fox hunting. These plans simultaneously unnerved our elderly supporters and put off many of those lifelong Labour supporters who had planned to vote for us. Theresa was right to want to address inter-generational unfairness. She was also right to think that people with significant assets should contribute more to the cost of their care. But whatever the merits of these policies, announcing detailed proposals in the middle of an election campaign, without any preparatory work to explain the problem she was trying to solve, was a terrible mistake.

It is also the starting point of this story, because Theresa's struggles over the next two years can be traced back to this manifesto. If these unpopular policies hadn't been included, she would have won a comfortable majority, leaving her in a stronger position within the Conservative Party and in the Brexit negotiations. Nick Timothy and Fiona Hill would have continued as her co-chiefs of staff, while I would probably have continued as the MP for Croydon Central and, I subsequently learned, would have been made a cabinet minister.

But from the moment the manifesto was published, I was in trouble. I knew I had lost when the exit poll was published at 10 p.m. on polling day. I was driving home after nearly twelve hours knocking on the doors of floating voters. The response had been as good as I could have hoped for – it felt like more people were voting for me than in 2015 – but everything rested on whether the Labour vote increased by even more. The exit poll was far better for Labour than anyone expected, predicting they would gain thirty-four seats and deprive the Conservatives of an overall majority.

When I got home, my wife and my mum tried to cheer me up, suggesting that the exit poll could be wrong or that Croydon Central could buck the national trend. But I knew they were clutching at straws – in recent elections, the exit polls had been very accurate. And if Labour were doing that well nationally, they had to be doing very well in London – no matter how good a local campaign we had run, Croydon Central would be a Labour gain. A little later, a call from my campaign manager and friend Jason Cummings, who was at the count, confirmed my fears. It was obvious as soon as the ballot boxes were opened that we were going to lose by a significant margin. In the end, we got 1,500 more votes than in 2015, but Labour increased their total by 7,000.

I went to the count shortly before the result was due to be declared and delivered a concession speech, congratulating the new MP Sarah Jones and thanking the people of Croydon for giving me the chance to serve them for seven years. I ended by saying that there was only one silver lining, which was that 'my wife Karen and my three boys will get more of my time that they so richly deserve'. How wrong I was.

I got home at about 6.30 a.m., physically shattered and emotionally drained. I had lost the job I loved in the most public way possible, rejected by the people in my home town. As a result, I would also lose the other job I loved: my role as housing minister. I had no idea what I would do next. All I knew was I really needed some sleep.

I woke up on Friday afternoon to hundreds of messages, some from friends saying how sorry they were and others from journalists asking me to comment on the Conservative campaign. I agreed to do three interviews the next day – *BBC Breakfast*, *Today* and an interview with Nick Robinson for an edition of *Panorama* that would go out a couple of days later.

When I emerged from New Broadcasting House, it was a lovely sunny day and central London was looking its glorious best. I decided to walk back to Victoria and reflect on what to do next, but I'd only gone a short way when my mobile rang. It was Gavin Williamson, the chief whip. After offering his sympathies, he started talking nineteen to the dozen about what a mess the party was in. I wasn't paying much attention – it didn't feel like my problem anymore – but then I heard him say something about me becoming chief of staff to the prime minister.

'What did you just say?'

'I've told her she should make you her chief of staff, but don't worry – it probably won't happen.'

After he rang off, I got a call from Julian Smith, one of my best friends in parliament and one of Gavin's key lieutenants in the whips' office. When he found out I was in central London, he suggested I come over to his flat near the City. We sat on his terrace and it became clear that, far from being some madcap idea of Gavin's, making me chief of staff was being actively considered. I then got a text message from the Number 10 switchboard saying that the prime minister wanted to speak to me.

I called my wife first. It was, after all, barely twenty-four hours since I'd stood on stage and promised Karen and the boys that they would see a lot more of me now that I was no longer an MP (when my appointment as chief of staff was announced, some wag tweeted the footage with the message '#politicians #promises'). I decided to introduce the idea gently:

'I've got some good news and some bad news.'

'What's the good news?'

'I think somebody is about to offer me a job.'

'And the bad news?'

'The job is chief of staff to the prime minister, so it's going to mean working even longer hours than before.' I filled her in on the surprise turn the morning had taken.

She immediately gave me her blessing. 'Politics is what you love and it's an amazing job – you have to take it. How long would you be doing it for?'

'I have no idea. It could only be a couple of days – there'll be a meeting of the parliamentary party early next week and they may want her to stand down. But if I can help her secure her position I could be doing the job for a few years.'

I suspect that she was at least as worried about it lasting for years as it lasting a few days. Politicians talk a lot about public service, and most of those I've met mean it – they want to change their local community and the country for the better. But there's another side to it, too, and here seems the right point to acknowledge it: we also do what we do because we enjoy it and, like any other high-profile job, it comes at some cost to our loved ones. Taking on a job like chief of staff to the prime minister is an act of public service but also a selfish act prioritising career fulfilment over other areas of your life. I am more grateful than I can put into words to Karen for the support she has given me throughout my career – and for the sacrifices she has made in her own career in order to do that. I hope to repay her now that I'm done with active politics.

I called the Number 10 switchboard and was put through to the prime minister, who began by saying how sorry she was that I had lost my seat. Then she told me she was in a bit of a hole. She needed to make some changes at Number 10; Nick Timothy and Fiona Hill would be resigning, and she would like to offer me their job.

Even though I'd been given some advance warning by Gavin and Julian, I was taken aback and didn't answer immediately. I suspect someone had told her that I had young children and might want to take a break from politics, because she quickly said that she would understand if I didn't feel able to do it. I reassured her that I would be honoured to accept the role, but that she ought to be aware that I had just recorded an interview with Nick Robinson in which I had made some criticisms of her recent campaign. That didn't change her mind, so we moved on to the logistics of announcing my appointment – at that point, Nick had agreed to resign but Fi had yet to do so. As the conversation drew to a close, I said, 'Prime minister, I think you are in a *big* hole, and I should probably come and see you right now. Are you in Downing Street?'

She was in her constituency home in Sonning, Berkshire. She suggested I get a train to Reading, where her husband, Philip, would pick me up.

I hadn't asked who had suggested my name and I never found out. In his account of Theresa's premiership, *May At 10*, Anthony Seldon attributes the idea to at least three people: the Cabinet Secretary Jeremy Heywood, Gavin Williamson and George Hollingbery. Whoever's idea it was, the logic was clear. The prime minister needed to rebuild relations with the parliamentary party, so it made sense to pick an ex-MP. It would be helpful to have someone who understood how government worked, so it made sense to pick an ex-minister. And it would also be helpful to have someone with knowledge of the Conservative Party outside parliament. I had worked in Conservative politics all my life, so I ticked all the boxes.

As I sat on the train, I thought about what lay ahead. I didn't know the precise responsibilities of the role, but I did know I would be replacing two people who had worked with the prime minister for years, not just in Number 10 but at the Home Office and in opposition. I, on the other hand, didn't know her very well. We'd served together as MPs for seven years, she'd come to campaign with me in Croydon Central a couple of times, I'd had one meeting with her in my time as housing minister and I'd worked in Conservative central office when she was party chairman. But you didn't see her in the tea room, smoking room or members' dining room at parliament as much as some other ministers. I needed to build a close relationship with her, and I needed to do it that afternoon. I needed to know why she thought the election had gone so disastrously wrong, and what she wanted to do to fix the situation. And I needed to know her views on pretty much everything; a chief of staff who can't speak for their boss is no use at all.

How could I possibly build that relationship and find out everything I needed to know in a few hours, particularly with a notoriously private politician who had just been through a bruising campaign and the huge shock of the election result? What could I use as an icebreaker? I sat on the train and came up with what, looking back on it now, was a pretty high-risk strategy. I drew up two lists: three things that Theresa May had done as a politician that had made me proud to be one of her colleagues and three things with which I strongly disagreed.

Philip met me at the station and drove me to their home. George Hollingbery, her parliamentary private secretary, was already there. When I deployed my icebreaker, I detected a slight narrowing of the prime ministerial eyes. 'What are the three things you disagreed with?' she asked.

'Well first, the vans telling illegal immigrants that they should go home or face arrest . . .'

A look of relief. They weren't her idea, she said – they'd been approved while she was away and she'd put a stop to them.

'Then there was that line in your conference speech that if you believe you are a citizen of the world, you are a citizen of nowhere.'

She was frustrated that people had taken that phrase out of context, she said. It was from a section of the speech that was making an argument about the obligations we have to one another that make British society work, and how people in positions of power were behaving as though they had more in common with elites in other countries than their fellow countrymen. The people she was criticising were people who didn't pay their fair share of tax, the people who paid themselves huge dividends despite knowing their company's pension scheme was about to go bust.

In which case, I countered, the line was badly worded, because people who hadn't read the whole speech would think she had been attacking people who thought of themselves as good global citizens. To me, that brought to mind the people in my constituency who were involved in Amnesty International, Christian Aid and Friends of the Earth – not global elites.

But it was my third example that sparked the strongest reaction: the moment in the recent election campaign when she had U-turned on the manifesto proposals on social care but then said that nothing had changed. She seemed surprised I had chosen this. 'What would you have said?' she asked.

'I would have admitted that it was a massive U-turn,' I replied, 'and said that strong leadership is about owning up when you've got something wrong rather than ploughing on regardless – and that if people vote for me on 8 June, they can rest assured that if I get something wrong, I'll put my hands up, admit it and put it right.' I wasn't in the room when she was being prepped for that press conference so can't say for certain, but from her reaction I sensed that no one had suggested that she take this line.

With some relief, I moved on to my list of things she had done that made me proud. I started with her reforms to stop the misuse of stop and search, an injustice that disproportionately impacted young black men, before moving on to her work on Hillsborough that finally brought justice for the victims and their families. It is rare in politics to receive tributes from your political opponents, but I remember Labour's Andy Burnham saying the cover-up 'persisted because of collusion between elites in politics, police and the media. But this home secretary stood outside of that . . . I express my sincere admiration and gratitude to her for the stance she has consistently taken in righting this wrong.' Her reforms of stop and search and her work on Hillsborough illustrate two of Theresa's best characteristics: an anger when she finds injustice and the stubbornness to take on the establishment and tackle it.

It was when I came to my third example that I hit the jackpot: 'The "country that works for everyone" speech you gave on the day you became prime minister.'

Her reaction was instantaneous. If anyone wanted to know what she believed in, she said, it was all in that speech. The election campaign should have been based on it. She should never have allowed herself to be talked into running a campaign she was deeply uncomfortable with, which presented her as an almost presidential figure.

This is why I had come to Sonning – to understand what motivated her and what she wanted to achieve in her remaining time in Downing Street. I had the answers I needed and, just as importantly, she had been in a better frame of mind than I had feared. She was upset, of course. But she wasn't blaming everyone else – she was furious with herself for letting the party down, and she was focused on making things better. Over time, I was to learn that this resilience is another of her greatest attributes, but encountering it for the first time on that Saturday afternoon, I was very encouraged. We had the fight of our lives on our hands, but she was clearly up for it – to keep her job, to secure the government, to deliver Brexit and to turn that speech from lofty rhetoric into policies that would change the country for the better.

One other positive came out of the meeting. At some point we were joined by JoJo Penn, the prime minister's deputy chief of staff. I didn't know her, but the prime minister spoke highly of her and I was keen that she stay on to ensure some continuity. Meeting her was almost as important as meeting the prime minister – and she too seemed up for the fight.

I had one last question of the prime minister: what did she want me to do? Was there a job description? No. 'You sit outside my office, attend whichever of my meetings you want to attend and give me advice. And I'd like you to focus on improving relations between Number 10 and the parliamentary party.' That was enough to be getting on with.

During the two years I served her, politicians and journalists would often say, 'She must be a nightmare to be chief of staff to – she's so difficult to get to know.' But from that first meeting, that was never my experience. I knew that – provided that she was among people she trusted – I could ask her whatever I needed to know. And just as important, I knew that she would allow me to speak my mind.

The first meeting established our relationship. With that done, I headed to Downing Street.

CHAPTER 2

STEADYING THE SHIP

Most chiefs of staff enter 10 Downing Street at a moment of triumph for their boss, who has either just won a general election or the leadership of the governing party. I was entering at a moment of crisis – Theresa's job was on the line.

Having called a snap election in the belief that she would increase her majority, she found herself five seats short of the number needed to win a confidence vote in the House of Commons. Thirty-three Conservative MPs, myself included, had lost their seats and many others had seen their majorities cut, with Theresa and her key aides being personally blamed. There had been little consultation about the disastrous manifesto, and her own performance in the campaign was attracting criticism.

But it wasn't just the election result. A brief statement, made outside Downing Street the day after the election, had made things worse rather than better. There was talk of providing certainty and leading the country forward, but there was no sense of contrition about those colleagues who had lost their seats or of her taking responsibility for what had gone wrong. As I was to find out when I spoke with her, it wasn't that the prime minister didn't feel these things – she was distraught that she had let everyone down – but the advice she received was primarily from the civil service, who were concerned about ensuring there wasn't a panic in the financial markets. It was Conservative MPs who would determine whether she kept her job, but the political advisers who should have tempered the civil servants' advice had either resigned or were traumatised by the result. And her instinct was to focus on the national interest, rather than the politics.

My immediate priority was to help the prime minister steady the ship, which meant doing three things: appointing a government; assuaging the anger and calming the fear of Conservative MPs; and doing a deal with the DUP, so that the government could command a majority in the House of Commons.

Appointing a government

The first job was to put a new government in place. The question was, would ministers continue to serve under Theresa or would some of them resign to try to precipitate a confidence vote? To a degree, that question had been answered before my appointment. On the Friday, when she asked Philip Hammond, Boris Johnson, Amber Rudd, David Davis and Michael Fallon to continue to serve as chancellor of the exchequer, foreign secretary, home secretary, secretary of state for exiting the European Union and defence secretary respectively, all of them agreed to do so.

The question now was whether to make any changes to her cabinet below these five top jobs. Both the chief whip Gavin Williamson and I felt that, given her vulnerability, the last thing she should do was to destabilise things further by sacking people, who might then become a rallying point for angry backbenchers. That meant there was only one gap, created by the fact that the talented minister for the Cabinet Office, Ben Gummer, had lost his seat.

My advice to her was that she needed to bring Michael Gove back into government. She was not particularly close to him – they had clashed during the Cameron government – and after his behaviour in the 2017 leadership election, she had felt able to leave him on the backbenches. But in the situation she found herself, he was too significant a figure to leave there, whether she got on with him or not. He was highly regarded by the media and, more importantly, had demonstrated his ministerial abilities at the Department for Education, developing and implementing a package of reforms to raise standards and narrow the attainment gap between children growing up in the most deprived parts of the country and those born in more affluent areas. His mistake had been that in his zeal to drive through his reforms as quickly as possible, he had failed to take enough of the teaching profession with him; conscious of his unpopularity among teachers, David Cameron moved him sideways to chief whip in the run-up to the 2015 election. I knew Michael well, having served as his parliamentary private secretary and then in the whips' office with him, and I felt he had learned from that experience. The question was, where to put him?

Before answering that question, the starting point of the post election reshuffle was to promote Damian Green from secretary of state for work and pensions to first secretary of state. The thinking here was clear: the prime minister was going to have to spend much of her time on Brexit, so it made sense to have a deputy to support her on domestic policy. She had known Damian since university, they had entered parliament at the same time and he had been one of her junior ministers when she was home secretary, so she trusted him completely.

That left a vacancy at Work and Pensions. There wasn't a lot of new policy work needed there – it was a question of bedding down Iain Duncan Smith's reforms and in particular addressing the problems with the universal credit system. We needed someone with the intellect to quickly master a technically complex policy area, and the prime minister chose to promote David Gauke from chief secretary to the Treasury. I had worked closely with him when I was the Treasury whip; as a middle-ranking minister at the Treasury, he had to do most of the grunt work getting bills and secondary legislation through parliament. I thought he deserved the promotion – he was always on top of his brief, popular with MPs and a safe pair of hands in the media. I remain a fan today – he's a huge loss to the Conservative Party.

David's promotion left a vacancy at chief secretary to the Treasury. Liz Truss was the first female lord chancellor and secretary of state for justice, but she had struggled in the role, coming in for criticism for not standing up for the judiciary when the *Daily Mail* had branded three judges 'enemies of the people' for ruling that the government needed parliament's approval to trigger Article 50. The prime minister wanted to move her but didn't want to sack her, so it was decided to make her chief secretary to the Treasury. Although it was technically a demotion, an economic portfolio was more to her taste.

The next decision was who to make lord chancellor. The prime minister decided to promote David Lidington, at that time the leader of the House of Commons. David had served as Europe minister throughout the Cameron government, and the hope was that his diplomatic skills and emollient style would rebuild bridges with the legal profession.

The final pieces of the jigsaw were making Andrea Leadsom, the secretary of state for the environment, food and rural affairs, leader of the house and giving Michael Gove her job. The Department for Environment, Food and Rural Affairs had a huge policy agenda (we would need our own agriculture and fisheries policies after we had left the EU and a new system of environmental governance), and the feedback was that Andrea was struggling. Policy development was one of Michael's strengths and it seemed fitting that, as one of the leading figures of the Leave campaign, he should develop the UK's new policies in these areas. Andrea took some persuading – she initially saw it as a demotion – but in time she developed a passion for her new role, helping to drive through reforms to tackle the bullying of parliamentary staff and progress the restoration and renewal of the Palace of Westminster. The finishing touch was to appoint Brandon Lewis, one of the up-and-coming members of the 2010 intake, as minister of state for immigration and invite him to attend cabinet.

This reshuffle would stand the test of time. Although Damian had to resign from government within six months, he and his successor David Lidington were pillars of support to Theresa over the next two years. David Gauke was a loyal and effective cabinet minister, both at DWP and when he succeeded David Lidington at Justice. Liz Truss proved better suited to chief secretary to the Treasury than lord chancellor. Andrea loyally supported Theresa until virtually the end of her premiership, despite her misgivings about the Brexit deal. Brandon would serve in cabinet for the remainder of Theresa's time as prime minister, later becoming party chairman. And despite their not having a particularly close personal relationship, no cabinet minister other than chief whip Julian Smith did more than Michael Gove to help Theresa try to sell her deal.

With the new cabinet appointed, a meeting of political cabinet took place on the Monday afternoon. Political cabinet is a cabinet meeting to discuss party political business. No civil servants are present and it can't take decisions about government policy. The agenda for this meeting was to discuss the election campaign, the talks with the DUP – which offered the only obvious prospect of a House of Commons majority – and the status of the 2017 manifesto. We weren't going to be able to deliver some of our promises given the parliamentary arithmetic, and there was a question about whether others should be dropped, given the feedback we had received on the doorstep. Philip Hammond understandably thought that if we couldn't deliver some of the manifesto commitments to reduce government spending, some of the spending commitments needed to go, too.

What became clear to me during this meeting was how angry many cabinet ministers were about the behaviour of my predecessors, with Sajid Javid particularly blunt about how he had been treated. I don't think those who aired their grievances felt that the prime minister was aware of the behaviour that had so upset them, but she had appointed Nick and Fi. The strength of feeling was underlined in my first meeting with Philip Hammond later that afternoon. I said it was clear that relations between Number 10 and cabinet ministers hadn't been as good as they should be and that the prime minister was keen for me to put that right. But before I could mention any of the things I wanted to discuss, he launched into a long account of how he had been treated. He clearly hadn't wanted to say all this in front of the whole cabinet, but he needed to get it off his chest.

The strength of feeling he and others expressed came as a real shock. Since I'd left the whips' office, I had fallen out of touch with what was happening across government. I'd been immersed in the detail of housing policy and had then spent every waking hour of the last two months trying to save my seat. It also didn't chime with my own experience. I didn't know Fiona very well – we had overlapped when we both worked for Conservative Campaign Headquarters years before, but while she was chief of staff I only had one meeting with her. I knew Nick much better. As with Fiona, we had worked together at CCHQ, but I also had quite a bit to do with him when he was chief of staff. In late 2016 and early 2017, we were trying to agree a white paper that would set out a new approach to housing policy. When we sent our proposals to Number 10 and other government departments for clearance, the Treasury wanted them changed in one direction and Number 10 wanted them changed in the opposite direction. Because Sajid didn't have a particularly good relationship with Number 10, I became the intermediary and met with Nick several times. I was impressed by his grasp of policy detail. He also knew the prime minister's mind – if he agreed something with you, you could be confident that she would sign it off. And although he had strong opinions, you could change his mind with good arguments. Whatever my own experiences, it was clear I had a big job on my hands if I was to restore relationships between Number 10 and the cabinet.

The 1922 Committee

But that was for the future. Shortly after political cabinet, the prime minister was due to address the 1922 Committee, the collective body of backbench Conservative MPs, in what would clearly be a make-or-break moment. I had started work on some speaking notes for her on Sunday morning. My former colleagues were angry, but they were also scared. Would the Conservative Party be able to reach an agreement with the DUP? If not, another general election – against a rejuvenated Jeremy Corbyn – was on the cards, in which more of them might lose their seats and which might result in Jeremy Corbyn becoming prime minister. Their anger needed to be assuaged, but their fear was helpful to the prime minister. The last thing they wanted was anything that would strengthen Labour's argument for another election.

It was clear that any repeat of Friday's tone would be fatal. The prime minister's colleagues needed to see how upset and angry with herself she was, how she blamed herself for the loss of those thirty-three colleagues. They needed to be reminded of her years of service to the party as an activist and councillor before she was an MP, that she knew how hard people had worked during the campaign. And they needed to know that she understood that the manifesto had been a disaster and that there needed to be a better relationship between the parliamentary party and Number 10. Only when she had left her audience in no doubt about her penitence could she make the case for stability, including gently making three points about the election result. First, although we had suffered a net loss of thirteen seats, she had got 2.3 million more votes than David Cameron in 2015 and increased the Conservative vote share by 5.5 percentage points. If we had managed to increase our share by that much after a lousy campaign, she should ask them, what might we have achieved with a decent one? The message here was that the campaign had been a disaster, but what she had been doing for the previous year was clearly working. Our handful of gains in the Midlands and the North, despite the national swing away from us, showed that a breakthrough in what is known as the 'Red Wall' was possible. Second, we should be pleased with the result in Scotland, where we had gained seats from the SNP. And third, the big increase in Labour's share of the vote wasn't just the result of us running a poor campaign; we, like much of the media, had underestimated Jeremy Corbyn's appeal and needed to take his threat much more seriously.

I gave the prime minister my speaking notes on Monday morning and she told me she liked them. For the second time in three days, I then took something of a risk, telling her that in half an hour I was going to come into the office and take the notes away. She needed to use that time to put my suggested line of argument into her own words. One of the main criticisms of her during the election campaign had been that she was robotic, trotting out rehearsed lines without any emotion. Theresa May isn't a performer like David Cameron. She can't just say any old line and make you feel like she means it, but she can be a very effective communicator when she believes what she's saying. And I felt that for this crucial speech, it was important that the words were authentic and not just the message.

Once she was happy with the speaking notes, a group of us discussed how she should handle the inevitable questions that would arise. The key one was how long she wanted to continue as prime minister. If she put a date on her departure, she would be a lame duck, as Tony Blair had discovered, but it would be tone deaf to imply that she intended to go on for years. Her colleagues might accept the need for stability, but few of them wanted her to lead the party into another election. She might be able to change their minds, but now was not the time for that debate. I suggested a formulation that struck a balance between ambition and humility: she would continue to serve as long as the party wanted her to.

The 1922 meets in Committee Room 14, the largest committee

room in the Palace of Westminster, but on this occasion there wasn't even standing room. I followed the prime minister in and stood just behind her. She started off by acknowledging that relations between Number 10 and the parliamentary party hadn't been close enough. Nick Timothy and Fiona Hill had stood down, and she had appointed me in her place. That got a huge cheer. Some of the people in that room would change their minds about whether my appointment had been a good thing over the next couple of years, but four days after losing my seat, it meant a lot to get such a warm response from my former colleagues.

From that moment, the prime minister knocked it out of the park. She talked about the good colleagues who had lost their seats, the activists who had worked so hard and how she had let them down. You could feel the mood of the room shifting. And then, fixing them with a stare, she said, 'I got us into this mess and I'm going to get us out of it.' When she'd finished speaking, Graham Brady took questions. It was obvious that the whips had encouraged loyalists to be supportive, but when she got the key question about how long she intended to remain as leader, she was pitch-perfect: she spoke about how she had served the party for most of her adult life and said she would go on serving as long as it wanted her to. It was authentic and powerful. When we reached the point when the prime minister was scheduled to leave, Graham Brady said something like 'The prime minister has to go now' and she corrected him, saying she was happy to answer any more questions. The subtext was clear: she planned to invest more time in her relationship with the parliamentary party,

As the meeting went on, she was able to get in some of the nuance about the election result. At the end, there was a prolonged banging of desks, which is how the 1922 shows its approval, that was audible to the mass of journalists outside. We had made it through the immediate crisis.

A deal with the DUP

If I had taken a lead in preparing the prime minister for her appearance before the 1922, Gavin Williamson took the lead in negotiating the deal with the DUP that would allow the government to continue in office.

The decision to seek an agreement with the DUP had been taken before I was appointed. The prime minister had spoken to their leader Arlene Foster on Friday morning and in her statement outside Number 10 had said 'we will continue to work with our friends and allies in the Democratic Unionist Party in particular'. Gavin had flown out to Belfast that afternoon, taking Alex Dawson, one of the most senior remaining political advisers in Number 10, with him, as well as two senior Cabinet Office civil servants.

Gavin offered the DUP a choice of what is known as a 'confidence and supply' agreement, where they would commit to supporting the government in tax and spending plans and confidence motions, but not necessarily on any other issues or – to the consternation of some back in Westminster – a full-blown coalition, where DUP ministers would be part of the government. That would mean they would have a say in determining government policy, but they would have to support all government policies. They quickly concluded that they didn't want to be committed to voting with the Conservative Party on everything, so the talks then focused on the confidence and supply option.

On Saturday afternoon, the message came back that the deal was nearly done. Such was the desperation in Number 10 to provide some stability that a statement was released to that effect. The DUP took umbrage at what they saw as an attempt to 'bounce them' and decided they were not in any hurry, forcing the government to delay the Queen's Speech. Eventually, the prime minister decided that things had dragged on long enough and scheduled the Queen's Speech for 21 June as a way of forcing the issue.

In the end, the agreement was signed on 26 June by the two chief whips, Gavin Williamson and Jeffrey Donaldson, in the presence of the prime minister and Arlene Foster. It was Gavin's finest hour, though he was ably assisted by Jonathan Caine, a political adviser who was steeped in Northern Irish politics, having worked for countless secretaries of state and shadow secretaries of state for Northern Ireland.

There are a number of things that are worth noting about the agreement. First, although it fell short of a full coalition, it went further than a simple confidence and supply agreement:

The DUP agrees to support the government on all motions of confidence; and on the Queen's Speech; the budget; finance bills; money bills, supply and appropriation legislation and estimates. In line with the parties' shared priorities for negotiating a successful exit from the European Union and protecting the country in the light of recent terrorist attacks, the DUP also agrees to support the government on legislation pertaining to the United Kingdom's exit from the European Union; and legislation pertaining to national security. Support on other matters will be agreed on a case-by-case basis.

Second, we had to make it clear that we would not proceed with two policies that had been in our manifesto:

Both parties have agreed that there will be no change to the pensions triple lock and the universal nature of the winter fuel payment.

This wasn't much of a concession – there was no appetite among Conservative MPs to proceed with either measure – but it reinforced Philip Hammond's argument that if we weren't going ahead with some of the savings from our manifesto, we couldn't go ahead with some of the spending commitments, either.

Third, the agreement provided the government with long-term stability: it would 'remain in place for the length of the parliament'.

Fourth, it sought to address two of the concerns we knew people would have about us doing a deal with the DUP: that it was inappropriate, given the government's obligation under the Good Friday/ Belfast Agreement (if you want to understand Northern Irish politics, a good starting point is that the two sides can't agree on the name of their peace agreement) to exercise its jurisdiction in Northern Ireland with 'rigorous impartiality' and that it would disincentivise the DUP from restoring the devolved institutions:

> The Conservative Party reiterates its steadfast support for the Belfast Agreement and its successors and, as the UK government, will continue to govern in the interests of all parts of the community in Northern Ireland . . . The DUP recognises the need for early restoration of inclusive and stable devolved government in Northern Ireland and affirms its commitment to agreeing the formation of an executive . . . The DUP will have no involvement in the UK government's role in political talks in Northern Ireland.

And finally, it was explicit about what the DUP were getting in return for their support: £1 billion over two years for public services and projects in Northern Ireland.

The deal came in for predictable criticism, and I felt uncomfortable about it myself. The concerns about its implications for the UK government's role under the Good Friday Agreement were understandable, although we had worked hard to address them. The concerns of those who feared that the DUP's views on social issues like same-sex marriage and abortion would exercise influence on the UK government's policy in these areas proved unfounded, but I was worried about the damage association with them would do to our brand. And giving Northern Ireland an extra £1 billion in return for the DUP's support wasn't exactly edifying, even if this kind of 'pork barrel' has always been a necessary part of politics.

But none of the critics were able to suggest a better alternative. The country needed a government, and the electorate had rejected a majority Conservative government but voted in such a way that it would be impossible to form a government without the Conservative Party. Who should we work with? There was no question of Labour, the Scottish nationalists or Plaid Cymru working with us, and nor would the Liberal Democrats, after the political price they paid for doing so in 2010. A Conservative–DUP arrangement was the only option. If we had failed to come to an agreement, it would have meant another election. That may have suited Jeremy Corbyn, but it's hard to see how weeks of political uncertainty would have been in the interests of the country – and there's no guarantee it would have led to a markedly different result.

The confidence and supply agreement, on top of the prime minister's performance at the 1922 Committee, secured the May government. It gave the DUP significant leverage – if they withdrew from the agreement, it meant an election. But they failed to recognise that the moment the Conservative Party had a leader who could call an election, it would no longer need the DUP. If Theresa was bound to the DUP, they were also bound to her.

The story of the confidence and supply agreement is one of two misjudgements. Theresa assumed that she could rely on DUP support for a Brexit compromise. The DUP assumed that any deal Boris Johnson negotiated would be more to their liking. We were both wrong.

CHAPTER 3

BUILDING A TEAM

In most departments, there are two or three political advisers and hundreds of civil servants; in Number 10, there is a more even split, with about forty political advisers in total.

I inherited a much depleted team. My predecessors Nick Timothy and Fiona Hill weren't the only people who had resigned: director of communications Katie Perrior and Lizzie Loudon, the prime minister's press secretary, had also left. The prime minister decided she wanted to make further changes, thanking John Godfrey, the head of her policy unit, and Chris Brannigan, the director of external relations, for their service. And Chris Wilkins, the director of strategy, and Will Tanner, the deputy head of the policy unit, both chose to move on. This left six of the most senior special adviser positions in Downing Street vacant. Once the prime minister's position was moderately secure, I needed to rebuild the team.

Experienced hands

Thankfully, some key people were committed to staying. First and foremost was JoJo, the deputy chief of staff. She was in shock from the election result and the departure of Nick and Fi, but once she decided to stay, she was 100 per cent committed, and I quickly discovered how invaluable she was. She knew the prime minister much better than me, having worked for her both in opposition and at the Home Office. A policy specialist, she played an important role in reading everything that was due to go to the prime minister. I couldn't attend the prime minister's meetings as well as my own while getting through all the material, so I tended to focus on submissions on Brexit, housing and a few other key issues, leaving much of the burden on JoJo. She had high standards, often sending things back for further work if she didn't think they were up to scratch. This was sometimes a frustration to civil servants and political advisers, but everyone admired her eye for detail and political judgement.

Anyone who has ever taken over a leadership position will know that there is inevitably an atmosphere of 'The king is dead, long live the king!' in your first few weeks in charge. Lots of people were keen to tell me how awful the previous regime had been and what a breath of fresh air I was. I was conscious of how awkward this must have been for JoJo, as well as others who had been in senior positions before the election. So in an early special adviser meeting, I gently pointed out that although mistakes had been made during the election campaign and the atmosphere in Number 10 hadn't been right, Theresa's dominant political position at the start of the campaign was proof that she and those working for her had got a lot of things right. I confirmed that JoJo would be continuing as deputy chief of staff and should be taken as speaking for me if I wasn't present. I wanted everyone to hear that, but particularly her.

Someone else who was keen to stay was Alex Dawson, who led the research, messaging and speech-writing team. My sense was that he had played an important role in pulling people together in the thirty-six hours between the election result and my arrival. By the time I got to Number 10 on the Saturday evening, he was on his way to Northern Ireland with Gavin Williamson. Thoughtful and calm under pressure, he played a key role in briefing the prime minister for PMQs over the next eighteen months. He also worked with me on strategy and was the driving force within Number 10 on what became the long-term plan for the NHS.

Another key figure who served for the whole of Theresa's

premiership was Denzil Davidson, her Brexit adviser. Denzil had been involved in the Conservative Party for years and earlier in his career would have been thought of as a Eurosceptic. While his views hadn't changed, the centre of gravity within the party had shifted and he now found himself on the 'soft Brexit' side of the argument. He had genuine expertise on this issue, having worked for successive shadow foreign secretaries and foreign secretaries and for Jonathan Hill when he was an EU commissioner.

Stephen Parkinson – universally known as Parky – was another constant. He was not technically a special adviser; he and his team were paid by the Conservative Party but based at Number 10 to provide a link between party and government. I knew he had felt shut out under the previous regime, and I suspect those feelings persisted to a degree after I took over. As more and more meetings began to leak, there was an understandable instinct to reduce attendance at meetings, and he was sometimes the victim of that. With hindsight, he should have been in the room more often – he had played an active role in the Leave campaign and would have been better able to make our case to that wing of the party if he had been more involved. He was uncomfortable with the prime minister's deal but very loyal to her, and he played a crucial role in winning the vote of confidence in her leadership in December 2018.

Last but not least was the head of the events and visits team Richard Jackson, universally known as Tricky. As the name implies, E&V were responsible for the logistics whenever the prime minister left Downing Street, whether for a foreign trip or a visit in the UK, and also for any events we held at Number 10. It was a large team, composed mainly of civil servants plus Tricky and two other political advisers. They had an uncanny ability to conjure pretty much anything out of thin air, from a boat to rescue Denzil when he was left behind on the other side of Gothenburg, to a charter plane when our RAF plane broke down.

As well as running the team alongside a civil servant, Tricky accompanied the prime minister for most trips, carrying her bag, making sure she got from A to B on time and reminding her of what was next on her agenda. A straight-talking Lancastrian, he was devoted to Theresa and to his team, many of whom regarded him as something of a father figure. He was also personally very supportive of me, with the exception of a time when he nearly left me in Tokyo with no passport or money, and a time in Sweden when, knowing I don't eat shellfish, he arranged a dinner that consisted of the world's largest platter of prawns and a single cube of cheese.

Tricky is also a larger-than-life figure, the life and soul of the party. When I look back on those two and a bit years, many of the moments that make me smile involve him. To spare his blushes, I will only recount three. The first took place on a visit to New York for a meeting of the UN General Assembly. We had left the UN building for a bilateral with President Trump in one of his hotels. Tricky had a golden rule when it came to visits: if you weren't in one of the cars when the prime minister was ready to leave, you would be left behind. On this occasion, Tricky and his opposite number were enjoying an upmarket buffet in a separate room while we were meeting with President Trump. When the bilateral ended, we were shown down to our cars. A couple of minutes later, Tricky messaged me: when was the meeting ending? I replied that we'd left a few minutes earlier – surely he hadn't missed the convoy? I'll never let him forget that one . . .

But it was to get even better when we left New York. I was in the lead car with the PM when Tricky called to say the minibus carrying him and half the team had broken down in the middle of a three-lane highway. Once we got to JFK, the prime minister and I cooked up a wind-up: I rang Tricky and said that if they weren't with us in half an hour, we would have to leave without them. At that point, he hailed down an NYPD patrol car, told them he worked for the British prime minister and promised the officers a photo with her if they could get them to the plane on time. As I said, that man could conjure pretty much anything out of thin air . . .

Finally, there was his infamous 'assault' on an EU Council official. When we arrived at a Council meeting, most of our team were shown to the UK delegation room, while the prime minister and Tricky went a different way, so she could give a short arrival statement. On this occasion, an official made the schoolboy error of trying to stop Tricky from going wherever the prime minister was going, and he responded with a handoff Mako Vunipola would have been proud of. The whole incident was caught on camera and we spent the remainder of the trip playing it back on ultra slow-mo.

New recruits

JoJo, Alex, Denzil, Parky and Tricky would form half of my senior team, but I urgently needed to fill the vacant slots.

I came into Downing Street with one clear view from my time in the whips' office, which was that Number 10 doesn't understand parliament. It normally isn't very interested, because in our system governments by definition have a majority in the House of Commons. It is different in presidential systems like the US – the government and legislature are elected separately, so it is possible for the president's party not to have a majority in Congress. The benefit of the American system is that it forces parties to work together, but the drawback is that you sometimes get gridlock. The benefit of our system is that governments have no excuses for not delivering; the drawback is that they normally have large majorities, so they can more or less do what they want between elections. However, it was clear that this government needed to take parliament very seriously – even with the confidence and supply agreement, we only had a tiny majority and would be vulnerable to even the smallest rebellions. In effect, we would be governing in coalition with parliament, so we needed a team in Number 10 whose sole focus was the government's legislative programme.

It turned out that my view was shared by some in the civil service.

Jeremy Heywood shared a proposal his team had been working on about setting up a legislative affairs team that would liaise with the whips' offices in parliament. We took this to the prime minister and got her approval.

I had an ideal candidate in mind to head the team. During my time in the whips' office, I had worked closely with James Marshall, who had served as special adviser to three successive chief whips. He'd previously been special adviser to the chief whip in the House of Lords, so he knew both ends of parliament. Unfortunately, Gavin Williamson was adamant that he could not work with him. Maybe he didn't want someone in Number 10 who knew parliamentary procedure as well as him. Whatever the reason, there was no point appointing someone who the chief whip was unwilling to work with.

Fortunately, there was another strong candidate: Nikki da Costa, who had worked for Patrick McLoughlin when he was chief whip. Patrick sung her praises, so I recommended to the prime minister that we offer her the job. Nikki was probably the most popular senior special adviser with the civil servants because of her obvious expertise, her willingness to pitch in and her habit of turning up to work each Friday morning with enough pastries to feed an army. It was a huge blow when she resigned over Brexit in the autumn of 2018. The prime minister and the team were devastated and it is encouraging that Boris Johnson has rehired her.

Having hired a director of legislative affairs, I was keen to find some other position for James. He met the prime minister and she decided to appoint him as head of the policy unit – his understanding of parliament would be useful in advancing her domestic legislative agenda. He probably had the most frustrating job of any of the senior team because he was constrained by the parliamentary arithmetic, Brexit and Philip Hammond: it was no good bringing forward radical domestic policies unless we were confident they would enjoy the support of pretty much every Conservative MP; for all that the prime minister was determined that Brexit should not drown out her domestic agenda, the harsh reality was that it took up increasing amounts of the government's bandwidth; and Philip Hammond's fixation on eliminating the deficit while retaining fiscal firepower in case of a no-deal Brexit made getting agreement for even relatively modest spending programmes a slow and painful process.

James bore these constraints with stoicism. He and his team came into their own in the run-up to party conferences, when even Philip Hammond acknowledged that we needed some domestic announcements; in the winter of 2019, when they drew up a draft manifesto in case we were forced to call an election to break the Brexit impasse; and in the last two months of Theresa's premiership when, unable to do anything more on Brexit, we were able to focus on domestic policy.

The other key appointment in the summer of 2017 was a new director of communications. Given that James Slack, the prime minister's official spokesman, came from a print background, the ideal candidate would have a broadcast background, as well as some knowledge of the Conservative Party. Damian Green recommended Robbie Gibb, brother of the schools minister Nick Gibb. Robbie had worked for Francis Maude when he was shadow chancellor and had gone on to forge a successful career at the BBC, where he was responsible for all its politics output. Like Nikki and Parky, he was also a Brexiteer, which would give us a more balanced top team.

Of all the nonsense written about me during my two years as chief of staff, the thing I found most bewildering was the suggestion that Robbie and I were at daggers drawn. We certainly came at Brexit from different starting points – he was a conviction Leaver, while I had campaigned for Remain. However, we got on well from day one and worked together to try to help the prime minister sell the compromise she believed in. He was more interested in the overall narrative than the policy detail and was probably at his happiest during the two or three weeks when we moved out of Number 10 and created a war room in the Cabinet Office and focused on trying to communicate our case. He put his heart and soul into trying to sell the deal, at the cost of some of his friendships with fellow Leavers, and I am proud to call him a friend.

Robbie recruited Paul Harrison to be the prime minister's new press secretary. Along with the prime minister's official spokesman, this is probably the hardest job in Downing Street. If you are head of the policy unit or director of legislative affairs, your job will consume a large part of your waking hours, but it won't follow you home. Those responsible for briefing the media, however, are never off-duty. Paul did the job during one of the most difficult periods without complaining about some of the threadbare lines he was given, and he always maintained a cheery demeanour.

The final member of the senior team wasn't recruited until nearly a year after the election. I had a number of meetings with business leaders over the summer of 2017 and was struck by their uniform view that the government was anti-business. Theresa was certainly more prepared to call out unacceptable practices than some previous Conservative leaders, but she was far more supportive than she was thought to be of the role of business, not just in creating prosperity and jobs but in delivering public services and helping to solve complex social problems. We needed someone to help build bridges, not least because we would need a strong business voice to help us sell any Brexit deal. The problem was finding the right person: someone sufficiently senior that they would be credible with the chairs and chief executives of major businesses, but willing to give up a well-paid private sector career to work for the government. It took time, but we eventually found the perfect candidate in William Vereker, who had run the global investment banking division at UBS. In a year and a bit in Number 10, he transformed the prime minister's engagement with business, to the benefit of her standing with business leaders and her understanding of their concerns.

In time, I added one more person to the senior team: James Johnson, who was responsible for our opinion research and so was indispensable to any discussion about strategy. I can think of few people in British politics who better understand the realignment that is currently taking place and what the Conservative Party needs to do to hold on to its existing support while winning over voters in the Red Wall.

Setting the tone

As well as rebuilding the senior team, I wanted to change the atmosphere among the political advisers. In my first few days, a number of people told me how bad things had been before the election. They complained about poor communication, a lack of access to the prime minister and a culture where people were afraid to speak out if they thought the government was getting something wrong. I can't claim to have solved the issue around access – there is only so much prime ministerial time to go around, and as meetings on Brexit started to leak, there was an inevitable instinct to reduce the cast list – but I hope that every special adviser felt that I made time to explain what was going on, answer questions and listen to suggestions.

I took my responsibilities as a manager as seriously as my work as an adviser. All special advisers across government ultimately report to the prime minister, although those working outside Number 10 regard their minister as their real boss. The best ones find a way to balance this dual allegiance, doing their minister's bidding while alerting Number 10 to any problems and working to try to resolve them. I reinstated fortnightly meetings of the special adviser team and when a minister left the government, I did my best to find alternative roles for those special advisers who wanted to carry on and who I felt had sought to work with rather than against Number 10.

I felt very strongly at the time – and still do, as I watch with despair the factionalism that seems endemic in Boris Johnson's Number 10 – that while Downing Street is inevitably a stressful place to work, it shouldn't be an unpleasant one. Walking through that famous door every morning and working at the heart of the government is an enormous privilege. People should look back on it as a career highlight, not a traumatic period when they were unable to do their job properly because they were shut out of key meetings or being briefed against. An effective Downing Street operation needs a diverse group of political advisers with different perspectives on what the government should do, because the prime minister needs to hear a range of views. But once the prime minister has made their decision, the adviser team needs to come together to implement and sell it.

The May government was characterised by increasingly bitter infighting among ministers, but I am proud that the Number 10 political team stuck together and fought for the prime minister's Brexit compromise and her vision of a country that works for everyone until the end.

CHAPTER 4

WORKING WITH SIR HUMPHREY

Most people think of Number 10 as the prime minister's home. That was its original purpose and there are flats in Number 10 and Number 11, although since Tony Blair's time, the prime minister has lived in the larger flat above Number 11, with the chancellor in the smaller flat above Number 10. But behind the famous façade, 10, 11 and 12 Downing Street are, in fact, one building. The chancellor has an office and a meeting room in the middle somewhere and the famous Cabinet Room and some state rooms are there for receptions and dinners, but the rest of the building is home to what is effectively a small government department, the office of the prime minister. The building has a Tardis-like quality, being much bigger than it appears from the outside – a couple of hundred people work behind that famous black door. Much like the Houses of Parliament, it is both an amazing and a lousy place to work: amazing because of the history that is all around you, lousy because its origins as a private home mean there are hardly any open-plan spaces where you can bring whole teams together – most people work in small crowded rooms.

When I arrived on that first Saturday, I was met by Peter Hill, the prime minister's principal private secretary. This would be a key relationship: the chief of staff is responsible for the political advisers and the private secretary is responsible for the civil servants, and they have to work together.

I spent the first few months (or in truth, the whole two years) bombarding Peter with questions. He was a font of knowledge – I assumed he'd been doing the job for some time and was shocked when I finally discovered that he'd only been appointed a few weeks before me. His background was in foreign policy, trade and national security. Immediately prior to his appointment, he had been the director of strategy at the Foreign Office, and he had worked with Theresa on security and counter-terrorism when she was home secretary and in Brussels for Peter Mandelson when he was EU trade commissioner. We complemented each other well: as an MP in a marginal seat, I had focused on domestic policy, because that was what my constituents were most concerned about. It seemed that during his time in the Foreign Office, Peter had built up a wardrobe for every micro-climate. Whenever we went abroad, I would be in my usual suit, perhaps with a coat if we were going somewhere cold; he would be like the Action Man I owned as a child. We had 'Alpine Pete' in Davos and 'Mediterranean Pete' in Florence, and he was constantly trying to wrangle a trip to Antarctica so he could show off 'Polar Pete'.

Unlike many of the people you meet in politics, Peter doesn't have a huge ego. He didn't feel the need to say something in every meeting, but when he did, he was prepared to speak truth to power. I suspect some of his predecessors would not have allowed me to do as much as I did, seeing me as a rival in the battle for the prime minister's ear. He also always knew exactly what to say to diffuse any tension. I tried my best to stay calm despite the pressure I was under, but there was one moment towards the end of Theresa's premiership when I finally cracked and lost it with three cabinet ministers. Having told them what I thought of them in my most colourful south London vernacular, I stormed out of the room. Peter followed me. I was expecting a lecture on how I couldn't speak to cabinet ministers like that, but instead he smiled and said, 'I've been waiting nearly two years for you to lose it with those people.' In short, I could not have asked for a more supportive colleague. In fact, he's one of those annoying people who's good at everything – he could have played professional rugby, he's Grade who-knows-what on some musical instrument and in his spare time oversaw various home improvement projects in Number 10. He now deservedly has lots of letters after his name and is the chief executive of the COP26 conference.

I don't remember too much about my first meeting with Peter. He showed me to my desk, which was immediately outside the door to the prime minister's office. This had one big advantage: it made me a literal gatekeeper. Provided I was at my post, no one could pop in to see the prime minister without me knowing about it. It meant I could stop ministers, officials or political advisers trying to stitch up a decision with the prime minister before a meeting or overturn a decision they didn't like after one. And Theresa was an easy prime minister to be chief of staff to – much easier, I suspect, than her successor. Not many people knew her mobile number, so she wasn't constantly getting private advice – and on the rare occasions when she did, she would always brief me about it.

I would discover, however, that the location of my desk had two disadvantages. First, people would congregate in the outer office before meetings, making it difficult to get work done. Second, the prime minister was adept at quietly opening the door to her office, so I might be in the middle of saying what I thought we should do about a particular issue – or very occasionally sharing a bit of gossip – only to hear her say, 'That's very interesting . . . when were you going to tell me?' over my right shoulder.

Peter mentioned on that first Saturday evening that I was entitled to a civil service private secretary and asked if there was anyone I'd like to be considered. It hadn't occurred to me that I would have a private secretary now I was no longer a minister, so I hadn't given the matter any thought – and in any case, I didn't know any of the officials in Number 10. I mentioned that Clare Brunton, my private secretary when I was housing minister, had been outstanding, and when I came into work on Monday, there she was. This was the first example of how being chief of staff to the prime minister was different from being a junior minister. On my first day as housing minister, I'd had to answer questions in the House of Commons and struggled with a mammoth briefing pack that, while impressive, was totally unusable. I asked if it was possible to have an iPad so the information was more accessible and was still waiting eleven months later. In this new job, if I said I wanted something, it happened almost instantly.

Requesting Clare as my private secretary was one of the best decisions I made. She's one of those very rare people who makes things happen, but in a way that doesn't put other people's noses out of joint. I could delegate things to her and be confident that they would get sorted. She instinctively knew when I was under the cosh and needed the diary clearing and when she could force me to focus on something that needed my attention. She quickly became one of the most popular people in the building because of her reputation as a problem solver. You could go to her with an issue and she would either help you resolve it or escalate it to me and make sure I dealt with it. She's only recently left Number 10, having proved as invaluable to Boris Johnson's government as she was to Theresa's.

One other person I met on that Saturday evening was to prove a huge support during my first year in Number 10: Jeremy Heywood. The Cabinet Secretary is the most senior civil servant in the country (Sir Humphrey, for *Yes, Prime Minister* aficionados, although Jeremy was nothing like him). I hadn't met him before, but knew him by reputation and during the short time we worked together, he proved to be everything people said: highly intelligent, a workaholic, a passionate defender of the civil service and a master of the machinery of government. His know-how would prove vital to overcoming Treasury resistance to the prime minister's desire to give the NHS a long-term financial settlement. He was one of the few people I could speak frankly to about the challenges I was grappling with – we had a one-on-one meeting most weeks – and he would occasionally invite me to his weekly meeting of permanent secretaries. After one such meeting, he messaged me to say, 'All my colleagues think you would make a great perm sec,' which will confirm some people's worst suspicions about me!

How Number 10 is organised

As I settled in, I began to get a handle on how Number 10 worked. The starting point is the private office, the civil servants who act as the link between Number 10 and government departments (apart from the Ministry of Defence, where the prime minister's military adviser performs that role). If the prime minister has a meeting with a cabinet minister, the relevant private secretary will take a note of the meeting and send a formal readout to that cabinet minister's principal private secretary afterwards, setting out what was agreed. If a cabinet minister writes to the prime minister seeking approval for a policy proposal, the relevant private secretary will collate views from across Number 10 and write a submission to the prime minister, setting out what the cabinet minister wants to do, what the views are in Number 10 and asking for a prime ministerial steer, which they will then relay back to the cabinet minister's principal private secretary. When I was housing minister, the secretary of state's office would regularly receive letters from Lorna Gratton, the private secretary responsible for the Department of Communities and Local Government. It was nice to finally meet the mysterious Lorna.

This system has one major strength, but a couple of drawbacks. On the plus side, there is always a written record of what was agreed, but it can be frustrating for ministers. Say the prime minister has asked you to take responsibility for the welfare system. You might spend several months working up policy proposals with your officials and send them to Number 10, only for some political advisers and civil servants to tell the prime minister why you've got it wrong without you getting the chance to respond. The other drawback is that it can be quite slow. When I was housing minister and we were trying to get clearance to publish a white paper setting out policies to fix our housing market, my boss Sajid Javid duly wrote to the prime minister and other cabinet ministers seeking collective agreement and received replies from Number 10 and the Treasury asking us to change the document in contradictory ways. I kept saying to my officials, 'Why can't we just get this Lorna Gratton and the officials advising the chancellor around a table and agree what we're going to do, rather than writing letters and waiting for a reply?'

I shared the prime minister's outer office with six other people: JoJo; Peter; his deputy Will Macfarlane, who was the private secretary responsible for the Treasury; the diary secretary; a third private secretary (whoever was responsible for whatever we were dealing with that day); and the duty clerk. There is always a clerk on duty, twenty-four hours a day, 365 days a year. They are an amazing group of people who make the whole place work, from ensuring everyone has their papers for that day's meetings, to liaising with their equivalents if the prime minister needs to speak to a foreign head of government.

Because of the layout of the building, everyone else is much further away from the prime minister. The communications team is based on the other side of the chancellor's office. They had the best office, consisting of the only large open-plan room and some smaller offices off it. On the civil service side, they were led by James Slack, the prime minister's official spokesman, who along with Paul Harrison, his political equivalent, had one of the hardest jobs in the building: briefing 'the lobby', the political journalists based at parliament. If you read a newspaper article and it quotes 'the prime minister's spokesman', that's James's successor answering a question at a lobby briefing. The first time I joined him for this was one of the most terrifying experiences of my life. As a Sheffield United fan, he was used to dealing with adversity, which may explain why he was able to do the job through the Brexit chaos and the start of the COVID-19 pandemic and his cheery demeanour – he would often start the prime minister's morning media briefing by saying, 'the papers really aren't too bad, all things considered.' I found him invaluable. As a former print journalist, he had an intuitive ability to predict how whatever line we were thinking of taking on a particular story would be received by the press.

There's one other team I need to mention: the remarkable Downing Street switchboard. If I needed to speak to someone, I would just call them and say, 'Could you get me so-and-so, please?' and they would call back once they had them on the line. I don't know if it's a true story or an urban legend, but the *Daily Mail* reported that a civil servant once phoned Switch wanting to speak to me, only they asked for Gary Barlow rather than Gavin Barwell. There's literally no one Switch cannot reach, so they duly put the civil servant through to a very bemused Take That frontman.

The weekly routine

Like many workplaces, Number 10 has both a weekly and an annual rhythm. When parliament was sitting, Theresa would spend the weekend either in her constituency or at Chequers, the manor house at the foot of the Chiltern Hills that serves as the prime minister's country home. She would come into London on a Monday morning and her day would start at 10.15, when James Slack would brief her on what was running in the media and get her steer on how he should respond to any difficult questions he anticipated at the lobby briefing. We would then run through her diary for the day, checking that she was happy with what was planned, before discussing anything else that needed an urgent decision.

She would stay overnight in Downing Street from Monday to Thursday, so on Tuesday, Wednesday and Thursday mornings the meeting was earlier, at 8.30. Attendance was quite large: between fifteen and twenty civil servants and political advisers who worked at

Number 10, plus the Cabinet Secretary, the prime minister's de facto deputy (Damian Green initially, then David Lidington) and the chief whip.

I quickly felt there were three problems with these meetings. First, they weren't very focused: when an issue came up – how to respond to a difficult story in the media or what to do about a vote in parliament that we might lose – there would be a long discussion where everybody gave their views. It wasn't a good use of the prime minister's time. I therefore put in place a staff meeting half an hour before the main meeting, where we could run through the issues on which we needed a decision from the prime minister and either agree unanimous advice or on a range of options to put to her. This helped make the meetings more effective.

Second, there were too many people in the room. Not only could they barely fit, but it meant that when something leaked – as happened far too often – it was difficult to establish who was responsible. I tried to slim down the cast list, but people were upset to be told they were no longer invited – in Downing Street, status is very much linked to face time with the prime minister. We ended up having one agenda with the whole group and a separate one with a smaller group. This did reduce the leaking, but as time went on and the prime minister's position became more vulnerable, more of the agenda moved into the smaller group and those who were excluded resented it. They could understand the need to slim down the meeting if there was a national security or personnel issue to discuss, but when it was about Brexit, they felt that they couldn't do their job properly if they weren't in the room.

Third, the meetings were too short-termist – what was in the media that morning or what was happening in parliament that day. There were understandable reasons for this – a government without a majority has to worry about every vote and the modern media has an insatiable appetite for news – but I thought we needed to try harder to resist it. We started using the Thursday meetings to look at 'the grid' – what the government was planning for the next couple of months. We invited Philip Hammond to these Thursday meetings, partly to make him feel more involved and partly because the Treasury not clearing things in time was a common cause of delays. If we gave him plenty of notice, it would hopefully ensure that any issues were resolved in time (spoiler: it didn't, but it did at least give us more notice when there was a problem). We also worked with the Cabinet Office's implementation unit to check whether the government was on course to meet its targets in certain policy areas and, if it wasn't, to try to identify what was going wrong. To the prime minister's frustration, we only managed this a few times because of the amount of time taken up by Brexit.

If the prime minister's day started with the morning meeting, it ended with work on the policy submissions, intelligence reports and draft speeches that had landed in her in-tray that day. She would only ever have the odd ten minutes here and there during the day to do any of this, so most of it would be collated during the day and given to her in one of the famous red boxes to work on overnight or over the weekend. Theresa wanted to understand all the detail when taking decisions, so was happy to do several hours of box work each night. Submissions would come to Peter, Will, JoJo and me during the day, and we could add covering notes if we wished. When the outer office got the box back the next day, they would circulate the prime minister's comments to the senior staff, so people could see not just what the prime minister had decided, but why.

A key moment in the working week was cabinet, which took place at 9.30 on a Tuesday morning. Formal meetings of the cabinet and its committees are different from informal ministerial meetings and political cabinet meetings. Whereas I could participate in the latter, only ministers can participate in the former. I sat away from the table, behind the prime minister and just to her right, from where I could pass notes to her or other ministers. Sometimes meetings would have a fairly thin agenda and only a few members would comment on each item; at other times, particularly when there was a key decision to take on Brexit, they were mammoth affairs, where every minister spoke at length.

Tuesday lunchtimes were a rare time in the week when I wasn't at the prime minister's side. One of the things she had asked me to focus on was improving relations with the parliamentary party, so each week I would invite ten or so Conservative MPs into Number 10 for an informal sandwich lunch. The idea was to give them an opportunity to raise whatever they liked. Some wanted to discuss the government's overall strategy, some wanted to talk about a particular policy area and some wanted to raise a constituency issue that they were struggling with. These lunches definitely made a difference at first, but as time went by, like everything else, they increasingly became dominated by Brexit.

Another weekly set piece was Prime Minister's Questions. I think most people would be surprised at how much time prime ministers spend preparing themselves for the half an hour (or more like fifty minutes, under Speaker Bercow) that they spend answering questions from MPs at midday each Wednesday. The prime minister has the advantage of having the last word, but the leader of the opposition chooses the subject matter, and Theresa would have an initial session on a Monday afternoon to try to work out which issues Jeremy Corbyn was most likely to ask about. We were normally able to predict what he would choose, but he did occasionally catch us out – for instance, just before the key Chequers cabinet meeting on Brexit and the day before the seventieth anniversary of the NHS, he chose to ask about bus services. The prime minister would have another session on Tuesday before devoting the whole of Wednesday morning to preparation, spending the last half hour alone while she ran through her lines.

You might not think this is the best use of a prime minister's time; I sometimes felt the same, but I will make two points in defence of it. First, the exchanges may not always be particularly edifying, but the fact that prime ministers are held to account in this way is important. Heads of governments in many other countries don't have to do this. Second, in the course of this prep, prime ministers will often discover that they are uncomfortable with the suggested answer to a particular question, which is a good indicator that there is something wrong with government policy. Without PMQs, the prime minister would inevitably focus on a few key areas of policy; the weekly session helps keeps them abreast of everything their government is doing.

For the first year or so of my time as chief of staff, I attended most of the prep sessions. They were led by Alex Dawson, who played the role of Jeremy Corbyn. My role was to think of the most difficult supplementary questions the prime minister might be asked. On one occasion, when stumped by a particularly awkward question, she smiled and said, 'Thank goodness you don't get to ask me questions.' To our relief, Jeremy Corbyn almost never asked the really tough questions, preferring a more polemic style that made for good social media clips.

Once PMQs was over, you knew you were more than halfway through the week. The prime minister normally had her audience with Her Majesty the Queen on a Wednesday evening. Peter Hill was the link between the government and the Royal Household, so he accompanied the prime minister to the palace – this was the one part of her week in which I had no involvement.

Most weeks, there was also a meeting of the National Security Council and a meeting with the home secretary, police and MI5 to discuss the terrorist threat, although they didn't have a set place in the diary. The NSC was established by David Cameron in 2010. Like cabinet, it is chaired by the prime minister, but it is composed of a mix of ministers and officials, including the national security adviser, the heads of the intelligence agencies and the chief of the defence staff.

It was rare for important votes to be scheduled on a Thursday – the whips try to keep MPs happy by giving them the option of returning to their constituencies early – so this was a good day for organising prime ministerial visits. Unless she was abroad, the prime minister would leave London on a Thursday night and spend Friday in her constituency. I didn't work closely with any of her predecessors, but my sense is that she was a more active constituency MP than them. She would regularly go out canvassing with activists, and she was fortified by conversations with her constituents on the doorstep and at community events: they were rarely hostile and convinced her that most people were less polarised on Brexit than MPs in Westminster.

In summary, when parliament was sitting, the first half of the week would be dominated by cabinet, NSC and PMQs, with the second half including constituency time and sometimes a visit. When parliament was in recess – roughly speaking, when schools are on holiday – things were easier. Recess was an opportunity for prime ministerial travel, and when she wasn't on foreign trips, Theresa would divide her time between Downing Street and the constituency, with the occasional holiday to recharge her batteries.

Between them, the regular drumbeat of morning meetings, cabinet, NSC, security briefings, PMQs, the weekly audience with Her Majesty, domestic visits and foreign trips took up a significant proportion of the prime minister's time. Once you added regular catch-ups with key ministers, with her chief Brexit negotiator Olly Robbins and with the policy unit to talk about domestic priorities, statements to the House of Commons, meetings with foreign heads of governments and receptions for charities that we hosted at Number 10, there was precious little time for things that were important but not urgent. And at any time, the entire diary could be turned on its head if something urgent cropped up, which happened quite a lot. If briefing the media is the toughest job in Number 10, managing the prime minister's diary comes a close second.

As time went on, Brexit began to squeeze out everything else. The prime minister spent increasing amounts of time with Olly and his team, with individual ministers or backbenchers, on trips to Brussels and other European capitals and at the despatch box updating the House of Commons.

Learning the lingo

Like any workplace, Number 10 had its own acronyms and terms; for example, there were COBRs (crisis meetings in the secure Cabinet Office Briefing Room) and diptels (what used to be known as 'diplomatic telegrams' – messages from our ambassadors around the world). A few weeks after I started, a meeting about bridges went into my diary. I wondered whether Boris had written to the prime minister suggesting yet another bridge, but there were no papers circulated in advance. When I got to the meeting, it turned out that 'bridge' is a code word for a plan made for the death of a senior member of the royal family, one of which – Operation Forth Bridge – sadly had to be put into effect with the death of Prince Philip in April 2021.

Security clearance

When I was appointed chief of staff, I had to undergo security clearance before I was granted access to classified material. As you would expect, this involved completing a long and intrusive questionnaire about every aspect of my personal life, some extensive checks to ensure I had answered honestly and a briefing about the material I would see – how to handle it, who I could discuss it with and where in the building it was safe to have such a discussion. The briefing ended with a warning about personal security: which countries I shouldn't holiday in, protocols when travelling abroad and video footage of an official who had been caught in a honey trap, with the warning 'If you're approached in a bar by an attractive woman who is not your wife, don't assume it's because of your good looks.'

I initially only had access to certain categories of material, but after a while I was invited to a meeting with two officials and informed that I would receive a broader range of material. I still smile when recall this meeting, despite the seriousness of what was discussed, because it was the one bit of direct performance feedback I received, albeit via an intermediary. I thought the prime minister was happy with the job I was doing – she appeared to value my advice – but it's not the kind of job where you get an annual appraisal. As the two officials were leaving, one of them turned and said, 'The prime minister asked us to let you know that your predecessors did not have access to this material.' I knew Theresa was incredibly cautious about which ministers got access to intelligence material; this was her way of letting me know that I was doing something right.

The loss of Jeremy Heywood

A few months after my appointment, Jeremy told me that he had recently been diagnosed with cancer. He was keen to keep on working – he felt it was good for him – and hoped the prime minister felt he was still able to do the job, even if he wasn't able to work at full capacity. I told him that the prime minister hadn't discussed it with me, no doubt waiting for him to tell me in his own time, but that I knew how much she valued his counsel. And I reassured him that I hadn't noticed anything – he may have felt he wasn't at full capacity, but by any normal standard, his output was phenomenal. I told him about my own experience (I had lymphatic cancer as a child) and we spoke about his options for treatment.

Just before Christmas in 2017, Jeremy wrote to the prime minister with bad news. His cancer, which had responded well to treatment over the summer, had spread. He was going to try gene-based therapy, but the chances were that he would have to give up working soon. His preference was to wait and see if the new treatment worked, but he understood if the prime minister wanted to make a change at the start of the new year, given that she would probably have to do so at some point in the near future.

The prime minister didn't want to lose Jeremy and could see how much he wanted to keep working. In the event, he was able to continue for a further six months. In June, he took a leave of absence and Mark Sedwill, the national security adviser, took over as acting Cabinet Secretary, volunteering to cover both jobs for a short period. I continued to exchange emails with him – you could tell when he was receiving chemotherapy, because you would receive a deluge of short emails while he was lying in the hospital with nothing else to do. It was great to still be able to get his advice and he was clearly desperate to know what was going on. In the early autumn of 2018, he was confident that he would be able to return to work. On 8 October, the prime minister asked Mark to continue covering both jobs until Easter 2019, at which point – if Jeremy was still not able to return – a decision would have to be made about a permanent replacement.

Sadly, less than two weeks later, Jeremy learned that his cancer had spread and he only had a few weeks to live. With the Brexit negotiations at their height, the prime minister decided that it was not the right time to recruit a replacement, so she appointed Mark as both Cabinet Secretary and national security adviser, with a view to separating the two jobs once Brexit was done. On 24 October, it was announced that Jeremy was retiring with immediate effect and that Mark was taking his place.

The next day I spoke to David Cameron, who was upset by the news about Jeremy and by the prime minister's decision to combine the roles. He saw the creation of the National Security Council and the position of national security adviser as an important part of his legacy and felt that Theresa was unpicking that reform. I understood why he felt as he did and tried – without much success, I fear – to reassure him that it was only temporary.

The prime minister nominated Jeremy for a life peerage and on 26

October he was made Baron Heywood of Whitehall. Five days later, the Queen promoted him to Knight Grand Cross of the Order of the Bath. He died on 4 November, aged just fifty-six. His death was not just a terrible loss for his wife Suzanne, their children and his wider family, but for the prime minister, at a time when she needed all the support she could get, and for the country as a whole. He believed in public service, in the power of government to do good and in the civil service he loved. I'm grateful that I got the chance to work with him, and only wish it could have been for longer.

Jeremy's loss was felt deeply across Number 10, and there was a moving all-staff meeting the next day. His funeral was held on 23 November in the Henry VII Chapel in Westminster Abbey, the chapel of the Order of the Bath, and it was one of the occasions when I felt imposter syndrome most strongly. I was shown to the second row of the chapel and sat behind the prime minister, David Cameron, Gordon and Sarah Brown and Nick Clegg as we listened to Jeremy's wife Suzanne give the most remarkable eulogy. A memorial service was held seven months later, also in Westminster Abbey. There were reflections from Gus O'Donnell, Jeremy's predecessor as Cabinet Secretary, from Tony Blair, Gordon Brown, David Cameron and Theresa, the four prime ministers he served, and from Nick Clegg. Theresa spoke movingly without notes and ended by suggesting that 'the legend of our brilliant civil service should be no longer the fictional Sir Humphrey but the true story of Sir Jeremy, the greatest public servant of our time.'

As I listened to this extraordinary array of people pay tribute to Jeremy, I felt for Mark, his successor. It is easy to take on a job, as I had, where your predecessor was perceived to have done a bad job, but it is harder when you take over from someone who was highly regarded – and doubly so when that person has tragically passed away. Mark was sufficiently self-confident to do the job in his own way. He had to delegate more, because the prime minister had asked him to do two big jobs simultaneously. He brought a greater expertise on foreign affairs and national security issues, but didn't have Jeremy's heft with the Treasury. Theresa and the civil service were lucky to have someone who was prepared to shoulder the burden of doing both jobs at such a difficult time.

CHAPTER 5

CRISIS MANAGEMENT

When asked by a journalist what was most likely to blow governments off course, former prime minister Harold Macmillan is alleged
to have replied, 'Events, dear boy, events.' Though governments can
strategise and plan announcements in an attempt to dominate the
news agenda, they are far more at the mercy of events than they let on.

In this chapter, I will cover three of the domestic crises that the
May government faced during my time as chief of staff: the Grenfell
Tower fire, the #MeToo allegations that engulfed a number of minis-
ters and the Windrush scandal.

Grenfell

In the early hours of 14 June 2017, a fire broke out in a fourth-floor
flat in the twenty-four-storey Grenfell Tower in North Kensington. It
would later be determined that the fire was caused by a faulty fridge
freezer. Firefighters arrived within five minutes to deal with what
should have been a routine incident, yet somehow the fire spread
rapidly up the outside of the building, across the roof and down the
other sides, enveloping the whole building. Seventy-two people died,
the biggest loss of life in a single incident in the UK since the Hillsborough disaster in April 1989.

Watching the horrific images in the prime minister's outer office
the next morning, everyone was wondering how this could possibly
have happened. Was there something specific about this building or

did it suggest a wider problem about the safety of tall buildings in the UK? In addition to supporting survivors, the families of the victims and the local community, we needed an urgent answer to this question.

This would have been a very difficult issue for the government however it had responded. The whole country was in shock, people in the local area were traumatised and understandably angry, and it was only a few days after the general election, so the prime minister's position was far from secure. However, the fact that she didn't meet with members of the local community when she visited Grenfell the next day made things even more difficult. She met with the commissioner of the London Fire Brigade Dany Cotton and members of Gold Command, the officials who were co-ordinating the emergency response, to check they had the resources they needed. She also walked around the base of the tower to thank members of the emergency services. She then went to Chelsea and Westminster Hospital, where she met some of the most seriously injured survivors, but that visit was off-camera.

The reason she didn't meet with members of the local community was that the Events & Visits team were advised that the necessary security arrangements would put too much strain on the police at a critical time. We should have insisted. When Jeremy Corbyn visited the site later that day, he was pictured meeting volunteers and people from the local community. A contrast would have been drawn in any case, but in the context of the recent election campaign, where the prime minister had been criticised for not engaging with the public, it was even more damaging.

It wasn't just the prime minister who was being criticised. I had been housing minister until a few days previously, and the media were asking why I hadn't done more to improve fire safety. I was in a difficult position. If I had still been a minister I could have answered questions, but as a political adviser I wasn't allowed to give interviews. There was one particularly awkward moment when a camera crew spotted me walking up Whitehall early one morning and filmed me ignoring their correspondent's questions. Hindsight is a wonderful thing, but I should have ignored the rules and answered the questions – the footage made me look indifferent to events, when the opposite was the case. Some of the things being said about me on social media – for example, that I had been warned that Grenfell Tower was unsafe and that I had sat on a report on fire safety – were untrue, but I am not going to mount a defence of what I did and didn't do here, because I owe my first account to the public inquiry that Theresa subsequently established. The consequence of this criticism was that I didn't accompany the prime minister in meetings with survivors, victims' families and residents – my presence would have made things even more difficult. As a result, much of what follows is based on my conversations with Liz Sanderson, who has been a political adviser to Theresa since she was home secretary and took the lead on Grenfell within Number 10.

Faced with criticism of her failure to meet members of the local community, Theresa did what she does best: absorbed the criticism and focused on getting the next decisions right. She set up the Grenfell Tower Recovery Taskforce, bringing together representatives from various government departments, the local council, the mayor of London's office and the local health trust. She initially chaired this herself before passing it to Sajid Javid, the secretary of state for housing, communities and local government. It continues to meet to this day. The government established a command centre under the leadership of John Barradell, chief executive of the City of London, supported by a number of other London borough chief executives. The Westway Sports Centre was transformed into an emergency community hub to help those who had lost everything get new driving licences, passports and whatever else they needed to carry on with their lives, as well as support from NHS staff, Citizens Advice and the Red Cross. An emergency fund was set up for Grenfell Tower residents, with every household receiving an initial payment of at least £5,500. One of the most urgent issues was trying to rehouse people. The fire had destroyed 151 homes, and many more had been damaged by smoke or water or had lost gas, heating and hot water.

On 16 June, the prime minister announced that there would be an independent judge-led inquiry into Grenfell, to get to the truth of what happened and who was responsible. She was determined that the victims and their families wouldn't have to wait for years, as the Hillsborough families had, to get justice. Later that day, she returned for a meeting with residents and survivors at St Clement's Church. The atmosphere was sombre, but they were pleased to see the prime minister. However, a large crowd of angry demonstrators gathered outside and Theresa's protection team advised her to leave. She was reluctant to do so but ultimately accepted their advice, promising that the meeting would be rearranged at the earliest opportunity. As soon as she got back to Number 10, she asked her office to invite every-one to Downing Street the next morning. Sixteen people attended, a mixture of local residents, volunteers and one survivor. They were angry about the fire and the chaos of the aftermath, as well as the years of neglect of social housing and the way the council had ignored their complaints and warnings. It was this meeting that convinced the prime minister that beyond helping those affected by the fire and understanding its cause and whether other buildings were at risk, the government needed to address the stigmatisation of social hous-ing, making sure that those who lived in such accommodation were listened to and treated with respect.

On the evening of 21 June, Theresa was back in North Kensington to visit a local resident's flat overlooking Grenfell Tower. She went onto the roof and a couple of residents told her what they saw that night. Seeing the tower up close and hearing their descriptions had a lasting impact on her. The speed with which the fire had spread up the outside of the tower had led experts to suspect that there was a prob-lem with the building's cladding, and the government had arranged to test other tower blocks as a precaution. On 22 June, the prime minister was due to give a statement on the government's response to parliament, which had just resumed sitting after the election. Shortly before she went into the chamber, she was informed that a number of these tests had revealed the cladding was combustible. What had been an unimaginable tragedy affecting the residents of one tower block in west London was turning into a crisis affecting tall buildings all over the country. The government initiated an urgent programme of checks to identify how many buildings were affected. It quickly became clear that we couldn't afford to wait for the public inquiry to make recommendations on this issue, so in July Sajid Javid set up the Hackitt Review to look at building regulations and fire safety, with a particular focus on high-rise residential buildings.

At the end of her statement on 22 June, the prime minister said:

This is about not just the steps that we take in the first few weeks, but a lasting commitment that we make to supporting the affected families, long after the television cameras have gone.

She appointed Nick Hurd as minister for Grenfell victims. He did an outstanding job, and she herself continued to meet with the various groups that had formed – Grenfell United, the Grenfell Tower Trust, the Grenfell Next of Kin – at Downing Street and in her parliamentary office. She never considered trying to get any publicity for this work. She knew that not meeting publicly with members of the local community on that first day had damaged her reputation, but her priority was winning the trust of survivors and victims' families rather than undoing that damage. She knew from her work with the families of the Hillsborough victims, the families of the victims of the infected blood scandal and child sexual abuse campaigners that when trust in authority has broken down, it can only be rebuilt by hard work, sincerity and determination.

In August 2017, Grenfell United organised a meeting at the Royal

Garden Hotel in Kensington, which was attended by about a hundred residents and survivors. This time there was no disruption and the prime minister spent nearly three hours answering people's questions. It was a big step forward. People felt they had had a chance to air their grievances and that the prime minister had listened.

Days before the first anniversary of the fire, the prime minister visited the site again, attending a vigil at St Clement's Church and an iftar at the Al-Manaar Mosque. She also held a private reception for the families in the garden of Number 10, where two camellia bushes were planted and a plaque was laid in memory of those who lost their lives. She held another reception in 2019, inviting families and members of volunteer groups to mark 'Green for Grenfell', an initiative set up by Grenfell United to celebrate the power of community.

How should we assess the government's response to this crisis? The prime minister kept her word to continue supporting the families after the television cameras had gone. She is driven by a fierce sense of injustice and felt those who died had been let down by institutions that should have protected them. She was determined that they wouldn't have to wait as long as the victims of previous injustices. As I write, the public inquiry is ongoing and uncovering truly shocking evidence. My successor as housing minister, Alok Sharma, held meetings all over the country with tenants and did important work in tackling the stigma attached to social housing. And the government is in the process of implementing the recommendations of the Hackitt Review.

However, it has taken far too long to remove unsafe cladding from some buildings. The Treasury's reluctance for taxpayers to have to pay for the remediation of privately owned buildings is understandable on one level, but nearly four years after the tragedy, there are still tall buildings where remediation work is not yet underway and residents are unable to sell their home and are facing steep bills for additional fire safety measures.

#MeToo

In the autumn of 2017, the bravery of actresses who came forward to tell of the horrific sexual abuse they had suffered at the hands of film producer Harvey Weinstein led to the global #MeToo movement. And anyone who worked in SW1 knew that the same dynamics of middle-aged men in positions of power over young women and men existed there.

On 27 October, *The Sun* ran a story saying that 'cabinet ministers have been named by furious female staff in a secret list of sex-pest MPs to avoid at Westminster'. A couple of days later, MPs on this list began to be named. One had asked his secretary to buy sex toys, while another had sent explicit messages to a nineteen-year-old he had interviewed for a job.

The first cabinet minister to be implicated was the defence secretary Michael Fallon. On 30 October, *The Sun* revealed that the journalist Julia Hartley-Brewer had been referring to him when she talked about a cabinet minister repeatedly putting his hand on her knee during a conference dinner. She had 'calmly and politely explained to him that, if he did it again, I would punch him in the face; he withdrew his hand and that was the end of the matter'. She said she did not feel like a victim of a sexual assault and found the incident 'mildly amusing'.

That might have been the end of the matter, but Fallon's cabinet colleague Andrea Leadsom then alleged that he had made inappropriate comments to her, initiated unwanted physical contact and made similar remarks about female audience members at an event that they were both addressing. On 31 October, chief whip Gavin Williamson and I met with Michael to put these allegations to him. At first, he was emphatic: they had never been raised with him and they were not true. Gavin told him that Andrea had asked to speak to the prime minister and Michael should not seek to discuss the matter with her. But Michael kept talking – and the more he talked, the less emphatic his defence became. At first, he just sounded shocked. He started speculating about her motive for raising this – they were not friends and he didn't rate her. Then he admitted he may have touched her – he was a tactile person – but he had not been trying to make a sexual advance. And then he began to speculate about whether he should stand down as a cabinet minister. He didn't want to go straight away – that would make him look guilty – but maybe he should stand down at Christmas. In a few minutes, he had gone from emphatically denying the allegations to thinking about resigning.

When he saw the prime minister later that day, it was an awkward conversation for both of them. He started by apologising. He admitted squeezing Julia Hartley-Brewer's knee, but he said he was stunned by Andrea's allegation. He accepted that he might have made some derogatory remarks about female audience members and squeezed her hand, but he had not made a sexual advance. The prime minister asked him if there was anything else she should know, and he replied that there was nothing since he had been appointed defence secretary. He asked if the prime minister knew what had brought all this on. Why were incidents from years ago being discussed now? She politely explained that the #MeToo movement was leading to lots of women coming forward to talk about what had happened to them in the past. She would have to consider his position in the light of what Andrea had said and his response. That shook him a bit. He acknowledged that he had engaged in banter that was not acceptable. He had fallen below the standards he set for members of the armed forces, and he accepted that was a problem.

Michael Fallon wasn't the only cabinet minister at risk; Damian Green was being accused of making inappropriate advances towards the journalist and Conservative activist Kate Maltby. Gavin Williamson and I went to see him next. Gavin told him that he suspected Michael Fallon would be leaving the cabinet tomorrow, and warned him that media attention would then switch to him. Was there anything else we needed to know? Damian assured us there was not.

I was increasingly concerned that sexual harassment could be the next expenses scandal, engulfing MPs from all parties. People were now calling me directly to make fresh allegations. If the prime minister had given me a job description in June, I'm pretty sure that fielding such calls would not have been on it. I was conscious that these calls cannot have been easy for the victims to make. They were putting their trust in me to ensure that the appropriate action was taken. Some related to conduct like that Julia Hartley-Brewer had experienced from Michael Fallon; others were more serious. Where I felt a criminal offence might have been committed, I encouraged them to go to the police.

In most cases, they asked me not to reveal their identity to the person they were complaining about. I assured them I would not do so, but despite being convinced of the sincerity of the complainants, I was conscious about the need for natural justice for those accused. How could the prime minister take action if she couldn't tell the ministers concerned what they were being accused of and by who? And where should we draw the line? What conduct was sufficiently serious that any minister guilty of it should be sacked?

At the morning meeting on 1 November, we discussed how to handle the mounting number of allegations. Some related to ministers, but it wasn't clear if the ministerial code covered behaviour prior to their appointment. If a complaint related to a backbench MP, it felt like the Conservative Party, not the government, should be dealing with it, but it turned out not to have a proper complaints procedure. The prime minister asked party chairman Patrick McLoughlin to draw one up as quickly as possible. Some of the complaints were from people who worked in parliament, the most sensitive being from people who worked in an MP's office and were complaining about that MP. Incredibly, parliament didn't have a proper grievance procedure – if you were sexually harassed by the MP you worked for, you were expected to raise a grievance with them. The prime minister asked leader of the house Andrea Leadsom to work with the other parties to get something in place as soon as possible. At Prime Minister's Questions that day, she told the Commons:

> Members on both sides of the House have been deeply concerned about allegations of harassment and mistreatment here in Westminster. I've written to all party leaders to invite them to a meeting early next week so we can discuss a common, transparent and independent grievance procedure for all those working in parliament. We have a duty to ensure that everyone coming here to contribute to public life is treated with respect.

After Prime Minister's Questions, Boris Johnson lobbied me on behalf of Michael Fallon. He was worried about where all this was going to end and was clearly not aware of some of the accusations that had been made against Michael. During the course of that afternoon, we received two further allegations, the first of which was a text from the Conservative MP Anna Soubry. That was the final straw; the prime minister decided that Michael should be offered the chance to resign, and if he didn't he would be sacked. But before she had met with Michael, I received a text from the Labour MP Harriet Harman, saying someone had approached her and would it be OK to give them my mobile number? Although I didn't feel qualified to deal with these calls, there was no one else to take them, so I agreed. I was called by the journalist Jane Merrick (at the time, she asked me to protect her anonymity, but she subsequently decided to tell her story). She described a working lunch she'd had with Michael in 2003. They'd both had a couple of glasses of wine and when they'd got back to parliament, Michael had lunged at her and attempted to kiss her on the lips. She said the experience had been humiliating and degrading. Fourteen years later, she was clearly still very distressed about it. This conversation had a profound impact on me. If you had described that behaviour to me before the call, I would have said that what Michael had done was wrong, but I would not have appreciated the impact it could have. It made me reflect on some of my own behaviour as a young man. I apologised to Jane on behalf of the Conservative Party that one of our MPs had treated her in this way. It probably sounded a bit silly, but she was upset and I felt she deserved an apology. I told her in confidence that I thought Michael would be leaving the government, but I promised to let the prime minister know what she had told me. When Michael saw the prime minister he recognised that he needed to resign, accepting in his resignation letter that 'in the past, I have fallen below the high standards that we require of the armed forces I have the honour to represent'.

As Gavin Williamson had predicted, media attention now turned to Damian Green. Kate Maltby had written an article in *The Times* alleging that Damian had abused his position of power: 'He offered me career advice and in the same breath made it clear he was sexually interested.' The prime minister asked the civil service to investigate whether there had been a breach of the ministerial code; the Guido Fawkes website soon published anonymous allegations from two other women who described similar experiences. The chief whip also alerted the prime minister to very serious allegations against Charlie Elphicke MP and she agreed to suspend the whip, meaning that he would no longer be a Conservative MP.

On 4 November, the story took a bizarre turn when Bob Quick, a former assistant commissioner at the Metropolitan Police, claimed that pornographic material had been discovered on Damian's parliamentary computer back in 2008. The police had, very controversially, raided his office back then as part of an inquiry into government leaks. Damian denied that he had either downloaded or viewed pornography on his parliamentary computers, and said the police had 'never suggested to me that improper material was found'. The prime minister asked the civil service to add this issue to their investigation.

On 11 November, the former Metropolitan Police commissioner Paul Stephenson said he had been aware of allegations concerning pornography being found on Damian's office computer. Damian issued a further statement, saying, 'I reiterate that no allegations about the presence of improper material on my parliamentary computers have ever been put to me or to the parliamentary authorities by the police. I can only assume that they are being made now, nine years later, for ulterior motives.'

Some friends of Damian decided to speak to the *Daily Mail* journalist Andrew Pierce and get him to put the boot into Kate Maltby. Pierce duly obliged, alleging that her parents would be aghast at what she had done and suggesting that her claims were motivated by a desire for personal publicity. Whoever's idea that was, it was a very bad one.

Damian came to see me on 18 December. He was frustrated at the time it was taking civil servants to complete their investigation. I understood his frustration but explained that I couldn't interfere in an investigation like this. 'You're the chief of staff, make it happen,' he replied.

As it turned out, even if I had been willing to intervene, no intervention was required. The next morning, Sue Gray, the director general for propriety and ethics, presented her report. It concluded that Damian's conduct as a minister had generally been both professional and proper; that it was not possible to reach a definitive conclusion on the appropriateness of his behaviour with Kate Maltby given that the two people present gave contradictory accounts, but 'the investigation found Ms Maltby's account to be plausible'; and, crucially, that Damian's statements of 4 and 11 November in which he claimed that he was not aware of indecent material being found on his parliamentary computers, were inaccurate and misleading, as the Metropolitan Police had previously informed him of the existence of this material. These statements therefore fell short of the honesty requirement of the seven principles of public life and constituted a breach of the ministerial code.

We all felt deeply uncomfortable at these conclusions. The prime minister asked the new chief whip, Julian Smith (who had replaced

Gavin Williamson when Gavin was appointed defence secretary), to suggest to Damian that he stand down. Damian refused, so the prime minister referred the matter to Alex Allan, her independent adviser on ministerial standards. Alex agreed with Sue Gray's conclusions and in particular that Damian's misleading statements represented a breach of the ministerial code. On 20 December, the prime minister asked Damian to resign from the government.

Had Damian's initial response been to apologise profusely for any offence caused, that would have been the end of the matter. As in many scandals, it was his denial that led to the further allegations and the inaccurate statements that cost him his job, not the original offence.

This crisis had a coda. David Davis came to see the prime minister, unhappy about Damian's treatment. He had been Damian's boss in 2008 when his office was searched as part of the leak inquiry, so he felt partially responsible. He was also angry about the conduct of the police. The prime minister explained that Damian had been sacked not because of Bob Quick's allegation, but because he had breached the code by issuing two misleading statements. David said he would go away and think about it, and ultimately chose not to resign.

How, then, to view the #MeToo crisis? In political terms, it led to the resignation of two senior members of the government, loyalists who the prime minister would badly miss in the months ahead. More importantly, it also led to long overdue changes in the culture of SW1, both in terms of how the political parties handled complaints and how parliament ensured it was a safe place to work.

Windrush

Some crises break suddenly, while others creep up on a government. As an MP representing a diverse part of south London between 2010 and 2017, I dealt with several cases where the Home Office disputed the immigration status of one of my constituents who had come to the UK from the Caribbean years before. I put these cases down to bureaucratic mistakes, and when my office intervened on the constituent's behalf, we were able to resolve the issue. But in early 2018, campaigners, including Labour MP David Lammy, exposed that these were not individual bureaucratic errors but part of a systemic problem.

On 16 April, home secretary Amber Rudd came to see the prime minister to explain the problem. The Immigration Act of 1971 gave those Commonwealth citizens who arrived in the UK before it came into force in 1973 indefinite leave to remain. This cohort was generally referred to as 'the Windrush generation' after the *Empire Windrush*, a ship that brought some of the first migrants from the Caribbean to the UK, although the act applied to all Commonwealth migrants. They were not given documents to prove their status or asked to apply for any. Most had subsequently acquired some, but some hadn't, and the Home Office was now disputing their status. Some of them had left the UK for a period and found they were unable to get back in. Some had lost access to benefits or their jobs. Some had been threatened with deportation and some had even been detained.

This was a major scandal; it was shameful that after years of contributing to this country, the right of the Windrush generation to live here was being questioned. It was clear from the outset that the prime minister, who had introduced tougher measures to tackle illegal immigration during her six years as home secretary, was going to be implicated. The Windrush generation had inadvertently been caught in those policies, and she was mortified. She was very proud of her record on race relations. She had taken action to reform the way stop and search was disproportionately used on young black men. She had established the Race Disparity Audit to identify where public services were letting down people from certain communities. This scandal threatened to overshadow all that good work.

Once she had briefed the prime minister, Amber answered

questions in the House of Commons. She told MPs that she was 'deeply concerned about the recent experiences of people from the Windrush generation' and was establishing 'a new dedicated team to help them evidence their right to be in this country and access services'. She was unable to say whether anyone had been deported – the Home Office didn't know. This is the nightmare scenario for any minister. Something has gone wrong and you go to the House of Commons to apologise, but your officials can't give you answers to the most basic questions.

The next morning, the prime minister met with a number of Caribbean leaders, who by coincidence were in London for a meeting of Commonwealth heads of government. They were understandably very concerned. Many knew of examples of people who had left the UK and found that they were unable to return to visit family. The Jamaican prime minister Andrew Holness was particularly forceful on the need for a presumption of legal residence, for those who had been detained to be released and for those who had been deported to be helped to return.

18 April was a Wednesday. It was inevitable that Jeremy Corbyn would raise the issue at Prime Minister's Questions. Theresa began with an apology and a strong statement that not only did the Windrush generation have a legal right to be here, they were British:

People in the Windrush generation who came here from Commonwealth countries have built a life here; they have made a massive contribution to the country. These people are British. They are part of us. I want to be absolutely clear that we have no intention of asking anyone to leave who has the right to remain here . . . I want to say sorry to anyone who has felt confusion or anxiety as a result of this.

She then had a major let-off. It had become apparent that in 2010, the Home Office had destroyed the original landing cards that would have helped people prove when they came to this country. Theresa had been home secretary then, and Jeremy Corbyn asked her if she had signed off that decision. No, she replied – although the cards had been destroyed in 2010, the decision had been taken in 2009 by a Labour minister. That took the wind out of his sails.

He then moved on to criticising the 'hostile environment' for illegal immigrants that Theresa had sought to create when home secretary, making it harder for people who had no right to be in the country to rent a home or open a bank account. She replied that it was right to make it difficult for people to live here illegally, but unforgiveable that people who were British had been caught by this policy. Immigration was one of the few areas where I had quite different views to Theresa, but I strongly agreed with her on this point. If we want to make the case for immigration to the British people, it is vital that they have confidence in the system and don't believe that lots of people are able to come here illegally, in addition to those who we allow to settle here.

On 19 April, Amber came to see the prime minister to agree how we were going to deal with this crisis. They decided that we should grant citizenship to anyone who had arrived before 1973, indefinite leave to remain to anyone who had arrived before 1988 (on the grounds that they had been here for over twenty years) and deal with other people on a case-by-case basis. Amber announced the policy on 23 April, adding that Home Office staff would not need to see definitive documentary proof of date of entry or continuous residence. Instead, they would make a judgement based on circumstances and the balance of probabilities. She also announced that those who had suffered loss – for example, people who had lost jobs or homes – would be compensated.

Despite the government having moved quickly to apologise, offer people citizenship and set up a compensation scheme, the prime minister had a harder time at Prime Minister's Questions on 25 April. This time, Jeremy Corbyn focused on where the prime minister was most vulnerable: whether there had been warnings that innocent people might get caught up in measures to tackle illegal immigration. The prime minister countered that when Labour had been in government, ministers had spoken about creating 'a much more hostile environment in this country if you are here illegally'. It was a fair point, but it was one of her most uncomfortable PMQs.

On 29 April, Amber came to see the prime minister for a third time and told her that she needed to resign. She had discovered that she had inadvertently misled parliament when asked by the Home Affairs Committee if there were had been targets for deportations. She had been advised that there were not, but she had now discovered that submissions had come to her office discussing progress against targets. The prime minister didn't want her to go, but Amber was adamant that she had no choice.

It was clear that dealing with this scandal would be a key issue for whoever replaced Amber. After some agonising, the prime minister chose Sajid Javid. He gave a statement to the House of Commons the next day, powerfully evoking his own background to demonstrate the government's determination to resolve the issue:

> When I heard that people who were long-standing pillars of their communities were being impacted for simply not having the right documents to prove their legal status in the UK, I thought that that could be my mum, my brother, my uncle or even me.

A few days later, the prime minister announced that there would be a full review of the lessons learned. It wasn't published until March 2020, eight months after Theresa had stood down as prime minister, and it didn't make for comfortable reading:

> When successive governments wanted to demonstrate that they were being tough on immigration by tightening immigration

control and passing laws creating – and then expanding – the hostile environment, this was done with a complete disregard for the Windrush generation . . . Ministers set the policy and the direction of travel and did not sufficiently question unintended consequences. Officials could and should have done more to examine, consider and explain the impacts of decisions . . . These failings demonstrate an institutional ignorance and thoughtless-ness towards the issue of race and the history of the Windrush generation within the department.

If anything, this was the most difficult of the three crises. We had made Grenfell even more difficult that it would otherwise have been by not overruling advice and having the prime minister meet with local residents on that first day, but she was not responsible for the failures that led to the tragedy. Likewise on #MeToo, she was not responsible for the culture at Westminster and seized the opportunity to change it. But the Windrush scandal had happened, at least in part, on her watch. She was mortified and acted quickly to put it right, but the damage could not be wholly undone. Commonwealth migrants suffered significant racism when they came to this country after the war, and the way in which some of them were caught up in policies to tackle illegal immigration years later added injury to insult.

CHAPTER 6

STRATEGY

Once the government had achieved a measure of stability by securing a confidence and supply agreement with the DUP and passing a Queen's Speech, my thoughts turned to developing a longer-term strategy. The government has hundreds, possibly thousands, of things it is trying to do at the same time, from conserving fish stocks to reducing deaths on our roads and improving girls' access to education around the world. Prime ministers can't hope to be on top of everything. They have to decide what they want to prioritise in terms of their own time, government spending and parliamentary time, and they need to weave these priorities into a narrative about their government's mission. Their priorities and that narrative must be informed by an assessment of the challenges facing the country, the prime minister's personal passions and public opinion – how the government has to position itself in order to maximise its chances of re-election.

Understanding what had gone wrong

The starting point was understanding what had happened at the election. The almost universal perception within the Conservative Party was that it had been an unmitigated disaster. Given that we had done far worse than we were expecting and lost our House of Commons majority, I understood why people felt that way, but it missed the point that we had won more votes than in 2015 and secured our highest share of the vote since 1983. To this day, people are surprised when I point this out. How could we have lost seats if we had got a much higher share of the vote? I remember discussing this with the prime minister after the German federal election in September 2017. Theresa had increased the Conservative vote share by five and a half percentage points and got 42.4 per cent of the vote, whereas Angela Merkel had seen her vote share fall by eight and a half percentage points and got just 33 per cent of the vote – but she was still seen as a winner. The difference was that Merkel's main opponent, the SPD, had also seen its share fall. In the UK, on the other hand, Labour's vote share had increased by even more than ours. They were now just two and a half percentage points behind us, compared to six and a half percentage points in 2015. And in our basically two-party system with its first-past-the-post electoral system, what matters in terms of whether you gain or lose seats is not whether you get more or fewer votes, but whether the gap between you and your main opponent grows or shrinks. In 2019, Boris only got about 330,000 more votes than Theresa got in 2017, but it was regarded as a triumph, whereas 2017 was a disaster, because the Labour vote fell by about 2.6 million votes from 2017 to 2019.

In June 2017, the key question was how different the result would have been if we had run a better campaign. In other words, how much of Labour's success was down to our mistakes and how much of it was down to Jeremy Corbyn doing better than we anticipated? If it was all our own doing, we wouldn't have too much to worry about at the next election. My fear, however, was that the Conservative Party was in danger of underestimating how much of it was down to Jeremy Corbyn. I thought that with a better campaign, we might have got about 45 per cent to Labour's 37.5 per cent instead of 42.4 per cent to their 40 per cent. That would have been enough for a comfortable majority, but it would still have meant a seven percentage point increase in the Labour vote share. We needed to understand how Corbyn had done so well, and how to respond.

The other obvious takeaway from the result was that the geography of British politics was being reshaped by a combination of Brexit, the capture of the Labour Party by the far left and the overreach of the SNP on the question of Scottish independence. We had gained a few traditionally Labour seats in the Midlands and the North and some from the SNP in Scotland, while doing badly in big cities and university towns. What odds would you have got in 2015 on us winning Mansfield but losing Kensington? The key question was, should we try to win back seats like Kensington or focus on trying to win more Mansfields? Should we resist or embrace the realignment of British politics that was taking place?

Put simply, the Conservative vote was becoming increasingly aligned with the Leave vote and the Labour vote with the Remain vote. This was a British manifestation of a wider phenomenon. Across the democratic world, politics is increasingly defined by cultural issues rather than economics, with the result that age, education, ethnicity and whether you live in a city are better predictors of how you vote than class. Centre-right parties are finding it easier to win support among working-class voters in towns and rural areas, but harder to win support among younger, highly educated voters living in cities. This realignment started back in the early 2000s, was accelerated by Brexit and continues to this day, as the 2019 general election and the local elections in May 2021 have demonstrated. Labour convinced itself that its defeat at the 2019 election was all down to Jeremy Corbyn – and he was certainly a significant factor – but his unpopularity obscured the underlying challenge that Labour faces.

Back in June 2017, it was clear that there was a strong strategic case that we should embrace this realignment. First, it would be very difficult for Labour to do so – they would need to stop thinking of themselves as the party of the working class, a huge psychological step for a party whose founding purpose was to represent organised labour. Second, we would have a near monopoly on the Leave vote, but the Remain vote would be split between Labour, the Liberal Democrats, the Green Party and nationalists in Scotland and Wales. And third, the UK's first-past-the-post voting system would favour our new coalition – although the referendum result was close at a national level, the Remain vote was heavily concentrated in London, Scotland and Northern Ireland, so Leave won far more constituencies.

But embracing this realignment would also have downsides. First, it would mean abandoning certain colleagues. It would make it much tougher to win in Scotland, in big cities and in some of the seats we had won back from the Liberal Democrats. When Boris Johnson embraced this strategy in 2019, he avoided most of the downside – apart from in Scotland, where we lost half our seats – because of Jeremy Corbyn's unpopularity, but that may only be a temporary reprieve. Second, it would entail becoming quite a different Conservative Party. If we were increasingly drawing more of our support from working-class voters, it would mean a higher-spending, bigger-government, less-free-market Conservative Party. That's what we're seeing now. I am not sure all the MPs who championed this strategy as a means of 'getting Brexit done' fully considered its implications for other policy areas. And third, there would be a risk that, in the long term, it would prove a dead end. If we allowed Labour to dominate among younger, university-educated voters, what would happen as those voters aged and a higher proportion of the electorate were university educated? Would demography be Labour's long-term friend?

We had commissioned a major review of the campaign that would help to answer these two key questions, but before the summer recess I offered political cabinet some provisional thoughts on what I felt we should do.

First and foremost, despite having been in government for over seven years, we had to be a party of change. Every election comes down to a choice between 'more of the same' or 'time for a change', and the longer you're in government, the more tempting the second message becomes. If you're not careful, you can accelerate this natural pendulum effect by defending your record rather than being honest about things that aren't right. The most successful governments find a way of constantly reinventing themselves. When Theresa became prime minister, she recognised that the Brexit referendum was not just a vote to leave the EU but a vote for change, and in her first speech outside the front door of Number 10, she talked about making Britain a country that works for everyone, tackling burning injustices. But in the recent election, that message had been missing, allowing Labour to paint us as the party of the status quo. We needed to get back to the message of that first speech.

Given the increasing alignment of the Conservative vote with the Leave vote, it was clear that getting Brexit done had to be core to any successful strategy. But nearly 30 per cent of the people who voted Conservative in June had voted Remain in the referendum, so if we were going to keep our coalition together, we needed to deliver a Brexit that brought the country back together.

We also needed to show that we had listened to what the country had told us. It was clear from the latest British Social Attitudes data, from the response on the doorstep during the election and from our post-election research that the electorate felt increasingly strongly that public services needed more money. Labour and the teaching unions had run an effective campaign on school funding that had cost us seats and unnerved many Conservative MPs. We were in danger of falling into the trap of every previous Conservative government, clearing up the mess Labour had made but not recognising when the public wanted the spending taps turned back on. We were never going to beat Jeremy Corbyn in a bidding war, but that didn't mean we shouldn't listen to what people were telling us.

Despite the difficult parliamentary arithmetic, we needed to be in power and not just in office. Gavin Williamson had avoided holding any high-profile votes in the Commons since the election, but there was a danger that people would tire of a government that gave the appearance of clinging on to office without doing much to tackle the country's problems. We needed to think creatively about what could we do without primary legislation. If we did need to legislate, could we get some opposition MPs onside? And could we get better at consulting Conservative MPs, so that we knew everyone was onside before we brought proposals to parliament?

We also needed a better critique of Labour. This is what most of the party was focused on – it's easier to conclude that the reason you did badly was because you didn't convince voters how awful your opponent was than because people were not very keen on what you were offering. Getting our house in order was the most important thing, but it was true that we needed to rethink what we were saying about Jeremy Corbyn. Attacking him for things he had said in the 1980s hadn't worked. We needed to focus on what he would do if he was prime minister, not what he'd said in the past. And although the election result had temporarily united Labour MPs behind him, over time their divisions were bound to reappear – we needed to expose them.

We needed a plan to increase our appeal to key sections of the electorate that weren't voting for us. The media were focused on young voters, but of more concern was how badly we were now doing among people in their late twenties, thirties and forties. The average age of a Conservative voter had increased from fifty at the 2015 election to fifty-five.

When it came to communicating our message, we needed to talk about our values as well as our policies. We were comfortable telling people what we had done, but poor at explaining why we were doing it. I was also keen that we cut out the spin. In my experience, voters often don't have an in-depth knowledge of each party's policies, but they are a better judge of whether a politician means what they are saying. They can tell authenticity a mile off, and they like it. We shouldn't defend things in public that we wouldn't defend in private. And while we needed to be clear about the story we were collectively trying to tell, we shouldn't try to make every minister endlessly repeat the same soundbites – people communicate more effectively when they speak with their own voice.

Finally, we needed to stop discussing strategy in public. We were conducting a public autopsy of the campaign in the way parties do after an election defeat, but we were still in government. If we were going to shift position on an issue, we should discuss it in private and try to catch Labour and the media by surprise, not spend several months signalling what was coming and fall short of expectations.

Looking back, it is striking how these initial thoughts provide an accurate summary of what we tried to do over the next two years: get back to the 'country that works for everyone' message, pursue a compromise on Brexit, increase funding for public services and address the sense of inter-generational unfairness that was costing us support among younger voters, while drawing a distinction between Jeremy Corbyn and previous Labour leaders.

We started to execute this strategy straight away. Just before the summer recess, Justine Greening announced an extra £1.3 billion for schools over the next two years, meaning that per pupil funding would be maintained in real terms. It wasn't easy to convince the Treasury to accept the per pupil funding metric (they rightly point out that no one argues that the schools budget should go down if there are fewer pupils to educate), but Philip Hammond acknowledged that this was how we were being judged. The announcement both neutralised an issue that had hurt us at the election and sent MPs away for the summer in better spirits.

The formal review of the election campaign, which was presented to political cabinet in October 2017, confirmed many of these insights. Perceptions around our values were a major problem. Concerns about the funding of public services had definitely hurt us. The result had not just been due to things we got wrong, but to things Labour got right – in the seats we lost, our share of the vote didn't go down but Labour's surged by nearly eleven percentage points. And to win a working majority, we needed to both win back some of the voters we had lost and win over some of the voters who considered voting for us at the start of the campaign but ultimately stuck with Labour.

The review identified three key audiences: urban, middle-class voters who had switched from us to Labour, 'Conservative considerers' (people who had considered voting for us in 2017 but didn't) and new Conservative supporters (people who had just switched to us, but whose votes would be up for grabs next time).

Priorities and barnacles

As time went on and I got sucked into the detail of Brexit, responsibility for shaping our strategy fell on Alex Dawson and James Johnson. In September 2017, they presented something called a 'political values architecture' to the senior political team. This sought to identify the practical and emotional consequences of a political party having a particular attribute and what values were associated with those emotional consequences. We had healthy leads on attributes relating to Brexit, tackling crime and the economy (but not, to my surprise, on jobs or cost of living), while Labour had healthy leads on attributes relating to the NHS, affordable housing and public transport. The purpose of the research was to determine attributes that we were behind on, but not by much, and which had a significant impact on voters' perceptions of a party's values. Based on this work, we identified three issues that we would prioritise in terms of communications: the environment, housing and school standards.

The environment and housing remained key priorities for the rest of Theresa's premiership, the former being driven very effectively by Michael Gove and the latter being driven by the Number 10 policy unit, with a little help from me. School standards never achieved the same prominence. We wanted to shift the debate from school funding, where we were never going to be able to outbid Labour, to how good an education is your child getting, where we had a better chance – the two things are linked, but there is less correlation than you would think. Most of the policy heavy lifting had been done by Michael Gove between 2010 and 2014. The job now was to embed those reforms and communicate the difference they were making, but the absence of major announcements made it hard to get headlines.

As we went into the autumn, then, we had identified seven issues that we wanted to focus on: Brexit (unavoidably); the economy, sub-divided into cleaning up the mess Labour had made of public finances and helping people with the cost of living; housing; school stand-ards; the environment; and tackling burning injustices. We also drew up a list of what the great Australian campaign guru Lynton Crosby called 'barnacles', issues that we didn't want to talk about all the time, because they were never going to be issues we could win on, but that would continue to be vulnerabilities if unaddressed. We asked our-selves what we would campaign on if we were Labour, and drew up a top ten: NHS spending, school spending, police funding, public sec-tor pay, adult social care, disability benefits, the performance of some of the rail franchises, fox hunting, rough sleeping and student debt. We had already done something on the school funding issue. Over the next two years, we tried to address some of the others.

At the 2017 party conference, we decided to focus on our appeal to people in their late twenties, thirties and forties. Pitched right, this might also resonate with their parents' and grandparents' generations, who worry that young people today have it tougher than they did. We decided to make the need to restore what the prime minister called 'the British dream' – the idea that every generation should have things a little easier than the previous generation – the motif of the prime minister's speech. When it came to policy announcements, we focused on one of our priorities (housing) and addressed one of our barnacles (student debt). We announced a review of post-eighteen education that, as well as addressing the issue of student debt, was intended to give greater prominence to further education. The UK has long had some of the best universities in the world, but our tech-nical education system has never received the funding and attention it deserves. As a signal of intent, we announced that fees would be frozen while the review did its work, and the earnings threshold at which graduates had to start repaying their loans would be increased. It was hard work getting this policy past the education secretary Justine Greening and her deputy, the universities minister Jo Johnson, who seemed to be in denial about how worried parents and grandparents were about the debt their children and grandchildren were getting into. When I spoke to them, Jo insisted that tuition fees were a popular policy. It may have been popular with universities, but I could only conclude that he hadn't knocked on many doors during the election campaign.

On housing, Philip Hammond announced an extension of the popular Help to Buy scheme that was helping so many people get on the housing ladder, but Theresa didn't just want to focus on home ownership. In her view, a country that worked for everyone was one in which everybody, not just those who could afford to buy, had an affordable, secure, decent place to live. So, to supplement Philip's announcement, she announced an extra £2 billion for social housing, with some of this money available for a new generation of council homes. We returned to housing at the budget, with Philip announcing that most first-time buyers would no longer pay stamp duty.

At the start of 2018, we took another step in showing that we had listened to what the country had been trying to tell us at the election. As part of our post-election research, we had asked voters who had switched from the Conservatives to another party what issues they could remember us talking about during the campaign. Brexit was, predictably, the most common answer, but the second most common, remarkably, was fox hunting. This was a good example of how, while most of what politicians say makes little impression on the electorate, a few things cut through. We had barely mentioned fox hunting during the campaign, but our manifesto did include the promise of a free vote on whether to repeal the ban on hunting with dogs. Labour's effective social media campaign made sure lots of people knew about that, as I could testify from my experiences on the doorsteps of Croydon Central. Whatever you think about the issue, it was lousy politics. A poll by ComRes showed that keeping the ban was the most popular policy in the Labour manifesto – 78 per cent of all voters and 64 per cent of Conservative supporters were in favour. So in an interview with Andrew Marr in January 2018, the prime minister confirmed that the ban would stay. Boris Johnson has very sensibly stuck to that line.

A long-term plan for the NHS

The one significant change to the strategy we had put together over the summer of 2017 was driven by Alex Dawson, with enthusiastic support from the health secretary Jeremy Hunt. Alex made the case that the NHS should be one of the issues we prioritised in terms of airtime, rather than an issue we tried to solve but avoided talking about. Though that might seem obvious, it was almost heretical within the Conservative Party, so deeply ingrained was Lynton Crosby's mantra that you shouldn't talk about issues that your opponent was more trusted on.

Alex's argument was that the NHS was too big an issue not to talk about. Our polling since the election had shown that people thought it was the second most important issue facing the country, and in January 2018 it overtook Brexit as the most important issue. And when people were asked about the most important issue facing them personally, it came second to the cost of living.

But if we were going to talk more about the NHS, we had to have a convincing story. Demand for healthcare was increasing. Despite the financial mess we had inherited, we had increased the NHS budget each year – but not by as much as it was used to or as much as it needed. The annual 'winter crisis', when the demand for care during the flu season put the service under pressure, was getting worse each year. When we asked in January 2018 whether people supported increasing funding for the NHS, 64 per cent said they strongly supported it and 26 per cent said they somewhat supported it, with

70 per cent saying the NHS should be the top priority for any extra government spending. However, the electorate didn't buy Labour's argument that the problems in the NHS were *all* down to under-funding. When asked to apportion blame to various factors on a scale of one to ten, they ranked funding as 7.69, but misuse of the NHS at 7.34, an ageing population at 7.00, waste at 6.96 and immigration at 6.38. They understood it was a complex problem. And although Labour had a strong lead on which party voters thought would be best at providing increased funding, we were neck and neck when it came to reducing waste and had a lead when it came to tackling misuse and reducing the pressure of immigration on the service.

Alex's argument was that rather than offering a bit more money each winter, we needed to give the NHS a long-term financial set-tlement so it could plan effectively. And alongside this extra money, we needed to tackle waste and improve public health, in order to re-duce demand on the service. The NHS's seventieth birthday in June provided the perfect hook, and the idea of a long-term plan for the NHS was born. From the moment we announced this, it trans-formed the political debate. When asked at PMQs about lengthening waiting lists, Theresa could acknowledge there was a problem and de-scribe what she doing to address it, rather than having to defend the status quo.

Perceptions of the prime minister

In March 2018, James conducted focus groups to test what voters thought about the prime minister and how they responded to video clips and images of her in different settings. We wanted to use this research to identify what kinds of events presented her in the best light and inform how she spent her time on tour days.

The good news was there were still positive memories of her first speech outside the door of Number 10. There was also respect for her determination and resilience and her ability to take big decisions.

And despite her being prime minister for nearly two years, there was surprisingly little awareness of her background, but when people were told about it, they were much more positive. On the downside, people felt she had been weakened by the election result, that she was too heavily scripted and that she lacked empathy. If her first speech as prime minister had cut through, so had her failure to visit Grenfell on the day after the fire.

Of all the video clips and images, two elicited a particularly positive response. The first was a photo of the prime minister enveloping Tessa Jowell, who had been diagnosed with a terminal brain tumour, in a hug. The participants hadn't seen the compassionate side of her before, and wanted to see more of it. The second was footage of her visiting Salisbury in the aftermath of the chemical weapons attack there, interacting warmly with local people. People liked seeing her 'out and about' – it contrasted positively with their memory of her not visiting Grenfell. The thing that both the photo and the video clip had in common is that they felt authentic – they were Theresa behaving naturally, and they changed people's perceptions of her for the better.

There were three main takeaways from these focus groups. First, they reinforced our thinking about how to prep the prime minister for key media interviews. We needed to get her to focus less on remembering key soundbites – these often didn't sound very natural – and more on our overall argument. Second, we needed to tell people more about her background. We had tried to do that in her 2017 party conference speech but it, quite literally, hadn't been heard. And third, we decided to do fewer stage-managed events. There was a risk in getting the prime minister 'out and about' because you have no control over what's going to happen – in one of the clips the groups reacted negatively to, she had been challenged by a member of the public about cuts to disability benefits. But we were prepared to take that risk. We wanted the electorate to see more of the Theresa May we saw every day.

Progress

Over time, our strategy began to work. Labour had taken a lead in the polls after the election, but we regained the lead in early 2018. The prime minister's response to the chemical weapon attack in Salisbury and to the Assad regime's use of chemical weapons against its own people in Syria reminded voters of her qualities. At the same time, Jeremy Corbyn's response to these two incidents raised questions about his suitability to be prime minister, as did the mounting tide of anti-Semitism within the Labour Party. We lost our lead again briefly in the immediate aftermath of the divisive Chequers cabinet meeting (the problem was not the Chequers proposals themselves, but the perception that the Conservative Party was divided), then regained and held it over the summer and early autumn, until division re-emerged as we tried to agree a Brexit deal. Despite the difficulties the government endured, we continued to poll reasonably well until the decision to extend the Article 50 period.

With the exception of our pursuit of a Brexit compromise, the strategic judgements we made – the 'country that works for everyone' narrative (which has been rebranded as 'levelling up'); the ending of austerity, with more funding for key public services; the focus on tackling the housing crisis and on the environment – have been built on by the Johnson government. There is every reason to believe that if Theresa had been able to secure support for her Brexit deal, she would have been well on the way to restoring her standing as prime minister. But that's a very big if . . .

CHAPTER 7

THE BREXIT CHALLENGE

Some prime ministers have the luxury of choosing what to focus on, but others inherit or are confronted with an issue that defines their premiership. For Theresa, that issue was clearly Brexit. She became prime minister as a result of the referendum, taking office just twenty days after the vote. Failure to implement the will of the British people would inevitably mean the end of her premiership, either at the next election or more likely at the hands of her own MPs. As her chief of staff, it was pretty obvious what my priority should be.

When it comes to Brexit, Theresa's premiership can be divided into three phases. The first, which ended with the 2017 election, was spent preparing for the negotiations. The second – from June 2017 until November 2018 – was spent conducting those negotiations, but the job of agreeing what kind of future relationship the UK wanted hadn't been completed, so we spent the first year of this phase simultaneously doing that. The third phase – from November 2018 until May 2019 – was spent trying to get parliament to approve the deal, or some variant of it.

Later, I will describe the negotiations and the efforts to get parliament to ratify the deal, but I first want to answer one of the questions I get asked most frequently: why did it take so long to get Brexit done? It's a fair question. MPs asked the British people to decide; the British people gave their answer. The result was close, but it was clear. Why did it take three and a half years of parliamentary gridlock, two leadership elections, a confidence vote and two general elections before it began to be resolved? The answer is both complicated and unsatisfactory. I'll start with the reasons it was inherently difficult, and will then look at whether some of the decisions Theresa took made it harder.

Leaving the EU was one of the most complex things this country has ever done

The referendum was a binary question: Leave or Remain? But the consequences of that decision were profound. The UK had been in the EU for over forty years and it had developed over time so that it touched on nearly every aspect of our lives. Towards the end of my time as chief of staff, I met the BBC journalist Nick Robinson, who was making a programme about the Brexit negotiations. He described a conversation he'd had with a telecoms engineer, who had asked him why it was taking so long. Nick replied with an analogy: 'I often see one of your colleagues working on one of those green cabinets with thousands of wires inside. Well, imagine that cabinet is Britain's relationship with Europe – not just the government's relationship with the EU, but the supply chains of businesses, the relationships between our universities, our judicial systems, our law enforcement agencies. Brexit means disconnecting pretty much every wire and reconnecting it somewhere else.' Nick never told me how the guy responded, but I can imagine him saying, 'Ok, that's a big job – but it wouldn't take me three and a half years!'

The referendum didn't specify what our future relationship with the EU should be

The Leave campaign didn't ever define what our relationship with the EU should be after we had left, because those running it judged that doing so would reduce their chances of winning. There was no consensus even among Leave activists, and why give the Remain campaign a specific manifesto to pick holes in?

This decision had two profound consequences. First, it muddied the debate during the referendum campaign. The British people were offered a choice: to remain in the EU on the terms that David Cameron had negotiated, or to leave the EU, but with no clarity about what would follow. We were asking people to make a huge decision about the future of our country, without any precision about what one of the choices might mean. The Remain side said leaving the EU would mean leaving the single market; some prominent figures on the Leave campaign agreed, but others pointed out that some countries are not in the EU but are in the single market.

Who knows whether clarity about our future relationship would have changed the result, but the lack of clarity was undeniably key in the chaos that followed. Some MPs claimed that the British people hadn't voted to leave the single market, quoting Leave campaigners who had denied that Brexit meant doing so. Others – Theresa among them – claimed that the British people had voted to end free movement, which must mean leaving the single market. Some MPs claimed that the British people had voted for an independent trade policy, which must mean leaving the customs union. Some even claimed that the British people had voted for a 'clean break' – not just leaving the single market and the customs union, but trading on World Trade Organisation terms, without even a basic free trade agreement. When those who wanted to maintain a close trading relationship argued that would be better for the economy, those who wanted a more distant relationship claimed that Leave voters were aware that there would be an economic price for Brexit and voted Leave because sovereignty was more important to them than economic wellbeing. I have more sympathy for some of these arguments than others, but you can't prove any of them. Polling can tell us a bit about people's motivations, but no one knows what every one of the 17,410,742 people who voted Leave thought they were voting for, other than that they were voting to leave the EU. It was up to MPs to define our relationship with the EU after we left, and that is where the trouble started. Imagine the

Leave campaign had said, 'If you vote Leave, we will leave the EU, leave the single market, leave the customs union and seek to negotiate a free trade agreement like Canada's.' The Remain campaign would have had an easier time during the referendum campaign, but if Leave had still won, it would have been harder for MPs to vote against a deal that was consistent with that vision.

The government hadn't prepared for a Leave victory

Partly because virtually no one on either side expected Leave to win and partly because the government was campaigning for Remain, very little work was done to prepare for a Leave victory. Combined with the Leave campaign's refusal to define what our future relationship with the EU would be, this meant Theresa inherited a blank sheet of paper.

The EU couldn't allow Brexit to be seen as a success

Throughout the negotiations, many MPs and commentators overestimated the strength of the UK's hand. The European Commission might be difficult, they said, but the member states would ride to our rescue. After all, we were a key security partner for many member states and many of them have a trade surplus with us.

The truth was rather different: the EU couldn't allow Brexit to be seen to be a success. It was a question of self-preservation, not malice. No one had ever left the EU before and if the process was too easy, if Britain got too good a deal, there was a danger that others might follow our example and the whole edifice could come crashing down. This is what the EU meant when it referred to 'protecting the integrity of the single market' – it was Brussels-speak for 'making sure the Brits don't get such a good deal that others are tempted to leave'. As Donald Tusk, the president of the European Council, told the prime minister in March 2018, for the EU, it was a question of 'to be or not to be'. They would have worried about this anyway, but their anxiety was heightened by the fact that the US president was keen to encourage other countries to follow our example. Also, we tend to underestimate just how important the EU is to European politicians. Many Brits think of it as a trading block, but to most continential Europeans it is, at heart, a political project that is about making another European war unthinkable. NATO may have kept Europe safe from the Soviet threat, but it is the European project that has bound France and Germany so closely together that a repeat of the horrors of the twentieth century is unthinkable. In the same way that many Brexiteers would say people voted Leave because they prioritised sovereignty over economics, the EU prioritised 'the integrity of its single market' over economics. They wanted a deal, but not at any price.

'But what about that trade surplus?' I hear you cry. The EU has a trade surplus with Andorra; that doesn't mean Andorra could call the shots in trade negotiations between the two. If you want to assess which party in a trade negotiation has the stronger hand, you should look at what percentage of each party's exports are affected. EU exports to us account for over 2 per cent of EU GDP, but our exports to the EU account for about 8 per cent of our GDP. Of course, it wasn't just about trade, and those who claimed we were in a very weak position were just as wrong as those who believed we held all the cards. We are not Andorra, but far too many people both overestimated the strength of our hand and misunderstood the other side's motivations.

Far from the commission taking the most hardline position, it was the closest thing we had to a friend, particularly towards the end of the negotiations. This was probably for the simple reason that, having devoted a huge amount of time to trying to hammer out a deal, commission officials didn't want that work to be wasted. The British tabloid media regularly lampooned commission president Jean-Claude Juncker and Martin Selmayr, its secretary general, when they were the two people who did most to help behind the scenes.

Juncker in particular was an anglophile, despite the UK having tried to block his appointment as president. I have fond memories of a meeting where Michel Barnier was talking through one of his famous slides that sought to prove that, as a result of our decisions, we would have a similar relationship to the EU as South Korea; Jean-Claude banged the table and said, 'Michel, the United Kingdom will *never* be just another third country.'

The problem was the leaders of the member states. They felt just as strongly as the commission did about protecting the integrity of the EU, but many of them had another motive for not wanting Brexit to be seen as a success: they were facing Eurosceptic parties in their domestic politics. A successful Brexit would be bad for them domestically, as well as damaging to the European project.

French president Emmanuel Macron was most blunt about this. When he visited the UK in January 2018, he waxed lyrical about how keen he was to deepen the bilateral relationship between the UK and France. But at the end of their lunch, he politely told a somewhat startled prime minister that Brexit could not be a success. When he ran for re-election, he expected to end up in another run-off against Marine Le Pen and would need to be able to demonstrate that leaving the European Union was a mistake.

German chancellor Angela Merkel was more diplomatic, but the message was the same. At a EU–Western Balkans summit in Sofia, she was keen to hear what future relationship we wanted, but her first question to Theresa was 'What's the price?' In other words, in what way would we be worse off as a result of leaving? Even Danish prime minister Lars Løkke Rasmussen, one of the more sympathetic members of the European Council, was not immune. When the prime minister met him on 24 November 2017, he noted that it would cause him problems if the UK got too good a deal. On multiple occasions, the heads of government, far from shifting the draft conclusions drawn up by officials in a more helpful direction, toughened them up.

I think there are two reasons why the perception that the member states would come to our rescue persisted for so long. First, we were so wrapped up in *our* domestic politics that too many people didn't stop to think that European leaders might have their own. Some Conservative and DUP MPs grew increasingly exasperated with the Irish taoiseach Leo Varadkar – didn't he understand that Ireland had more to lose from no deal than anyone? Yes he did, but he led a minority government that was dependent on a confidence and supply agreement with his main opponent Fianna Fáil. Our ambassador to Ireland, Robin Barnett, told the prime minister in November 2018 that if Varadkar agreed to a unilateral exit mechanism from the backstop or a time limit on it, Fianna Fáil would pull the plug on the confidence and supply agreement. His politics wouldn't allow him to compromise, even had he wanted to. And as he explained to the prime minister on 9 December 2018, he didn't want to because, for him too, politics trumped economics – 'there are worse things than recessions. I couldn't as taoiseach acquiesce in a return to a hard border.'

Second, while ministers would often lobby their equivalents from the twenty-seven member states on Brexit, the truth was the Croatian transport minister, the Spanish defence minister or the Swedish agriculture minister probably weren't briefed on the detail of the negotiations and when they replied sympathetically were just being polite. In any case, it never made any difference to the position their countries subsequently took in Brussels.

The unique circumstances of Northern Ireland were very hard to address

The potential implications of Brexit for Northern Ireland were barely mentioned during the referendum campaign outside of Northern Ireland itself, but its unique circumstances proved to be the single biggest obstacle to securing and ratifying a Brexit deal. To understand the obstacle, you need to start with the Good Friday Agreement that brought the Troubles to an end. At the heart of that agreement was a key compromise: the Irish state and republicans would recognise that Northern Ireland was part of the United Kingdom, unless a majority of people in both Northern Ireland and Ireland wanted a united Ireland. In return, the UK would dismantle security infrastructure at the border so that it would feel as if there were no border. In essence, the genius of the agreement was that it allowed unionists to feel British and nationalists to feel Irish.

The illusion of no border was only possible because both the UK and Ireland were members of the EU's single market and customs union, but the logical consequence of Brexit (or at least a Brexit in which the UK didn't stay in both the single market and a customs union) was to shatter that illusion, because it would mean the introduction of checks when goods moved between Northern Ireland and Ireland. This wouldn't be against the letter of the Good Friday Agreement – no one ever envisaged it would happen, so the agreement was silent about it – but it would clearly be contrary to its spirit.

Some Conservatives chose to believe that this obstacle was invented by the EU to stop the UK achieving its independence. They argued that both sides could waive the checks or that we could waive the checks and, as Bernard Jenkin told the prime minister in February 2018, 'if they put infrastructure at the border, it's their problem'. These were both fantasies. There was no chance of the EU agreeing to waive checks – it would allow British businesses to continue to have full access to the single market if they moved their goods via Northern Ireland. As for the suggestion that we should waive checks and dare the EU to introduce them, we would be in breach of our World Trade Organisation commitments. The idea that, having caused the issue by deciding to leave the EU, we should take no responsibility for solving it also spoke volumes about the character of those suggesting it. My suspicion is that if the UK had pursued this grossly irresponsible policy, the Irish government would have told the EU to conduct checks when goods moved across the English Channel, removing themselves from the single market and customs union to avoid a border in Ireland. It's not hard to imagine the fury the Irish government and Irish people would have felt at being forced to do that.

Other Conservatives and some Northern Irish unionists acknowledged that there was a problem, but maintained that border checks weren't necessary – they could be done elsewhere. This entirely missed the point. It wasn't just about infrastructure at the border – nationalists were opposed to checks when goods moved from North to South or South to North *wherever they took place*. Some unionists scoffed at this, having apparently forgotten that the Union they care about will only persist if moderate nationalists feel that it respects their identity. Maybe they should have asked themselves how they would feel if goods had to undergo checks – away from the border – when moving from Great Britain to Northern Ireland?

When the fantasies were stripped away, there were four possible solutions:

1. Checks when goods move between Ireland and Northern Ireland.
2. Northern Ireland staying aligned with certain EU rules in order to avoid checks at the Irish border, and checks when goods move from Great Britain to Northern Ireland instead.
3. The UK staying in the single market and the customs union, which would ensure that goods could continue to move freely between Ireland and Northern Ireland, within the UK and between Great Britain and the EU.
4. A new model, where the UK stays aligned with those single market rules that are checked when goods cross a border and is in some form of customs union with the

EU. This would also ensure that goods could continue to move freely between Ireland and Northern Ireland, within the UK and between Great Britain and the EU.

All four options have drawbacks. The first is contrary to the spirit of the Good Friday Agreement, and the EU was adamant that it would only agree a withdrawal agreement if it included commitments to prevent this solution – so adopting this policy would have meant leaving without a deal. It was also clear that if Brexit led to the reintroduction of a border, we could kiss goodbye to any prospect of a trade deal with the US.

Although the second option is also contrary to the spirit of the Good Friday Agreement – creating a partial border within the UK doesn't respect Unionist identity – this was the EU's original proposal. Theresa's view was that a partial border within the UK was unacceptable, but it is what Boris ended up accepting.

The third option, while the most beneficial economically, would make us a rule-taker across our whole economy and prevent us from having an independent trade policy.

The fourth is a compromise. The second best option economically, it would make us a rule-taker in some areas and put some constraints on our independent trade policy. It would, however, be difficult to negotiate because the EU saw it as cherry-picking from the single market. This was Theresa's solution, but Boris rejected it because he thought any rule-taking and constraint on our trade policy was unacceptable.

Because so many people chose to believe fantasies rather than face up to these four options, there was never an honest debate about which of them was the least bad.

The absence of devolved government in Northern Ireland made things even harder

The policy challenge presented by the unique circumstances of Northern Ireland was compounded by the collapse of devolved government in January 2017. Sinn Féin withdrew from their coalition with the DUP, angry that DUP first minister Arlene Foster wouldn't stand aside while a scandal involving a policy she had been responsible for was investigated. Under the terms of the Good Friday Agreement, power had to be shared between unionists and nationalists, so if one of the two largest parties withdrew from government, the executive and the assembly were suspended. For the entire period of the Brexit negotiations, Northern Ireland had no government.

This had profound implications. First, had the executive not collapsed, it would have had to adopt a policy on what relationship Northern Ireland should have with the EU – not easy, given that Sinn Féin had campaigned for Remain and the DUP for Brexit, but they would have had to compromise. And once they had done so, it would have been hard for the UK and the EU not to adopt that position. In such a scenario, the Brexit deal would have had DUP support, making it easier for Theresa to gain parliamentary approval. Out of government, however, the DUP were free to back a harder Brexit. Second, because she was no longer first minister, Arlene Foster didn't have the same status in the negotiations. The European Commission regarded the Irish government as speaking for the people of Northern Ireland, which alienated the DUP and led to the proposal of a backstop which introduced an east–west border that was either ignorant of, or indifferent to, unionist identity.

The EU's legal framework meant that we couldn't
finalise our future relationship until we had left

Article 50 of the Treaty on European Union requires the negotiated
arrangements for the withdrawal of a member state to take account
of the framework for the future relationship that state will have with
the EU, but Article 218 of the Treaty on the Functioning of the European Union says that the EU can only finalise and ratify an agreement
on the future relationship once the member state has left. This meant
two sets of negotiations: one before we left, to agree a legal treaty
on the arrangements for withdrawal and a political agreement on the
future relationship; and another after we had left, to turn that political agreement into another legal treaty.

This was the source of three big problems. First, it meant that
any Brexit deal would involve the UK making binding legal commitments about issues like the financial settlement while relying on
political commitments about the nature of the future trading and
security relationship. This allowed opponents to brand it a 'blind
Brexit'. Second, it meant that any withdrawal agreement would need
to contain transitional arrangements to bridge the period from when
we left the EU to when the future relationship agreement had been
ratified. Unless you were prepared to put businesses and citizens
through two sets of changes, those transitional arrangements needed
to be the status quo. That meant continuing to follow EU rules for
a period after we had left, which was democratically uncomfortable.
Finally, this two-stage process was the genesis of the backstop, which
proved the key stumbling block to Theresa getting her deal through
parliament. There was a risk that the two sides would be unable to
translate the political agreement on their future relationship into a
legal treaty, which would mean a hard border between Ireland and
Northern Ireland at the end of the transition period. The only way
to eliminate that risk was to include an insurance plan in any withdrawal agreement.

If we had been able to negotiate the withdrawal agreement and the future relationship at the same time, it still would have required either a soft Brexit or a separate arrangement for Northern Ireland to avoid a hard border. However, the interaction between these two EU treaties made it even more painful.

> The coalition government removed the ultimate
> threat governments previously used to get key
> policies through the House of Commons

Back in 1993, John Major's government struggled to get parliament to approve the Maastricht Treaty he had negotiated. When he lost a key vote, he tabled a confidence motion, essentially telling rebel Conservative MPs that if they didn't support the government, they would lose the whip and he would call a general election. But the Fixed-term Parliaments Act passed by the coalition government in 2011 ('another genius Oliver Letwin idea', as Liam Fox exasperatedly once called it) had taken away the prime minister's ability to call an election at a time of their choosing, removing the ultimate threat with which a government could get rebel MPs to back its key policies. While the act had made sense in terms of reassuring the Liberal Democrats that the coalition was a five-year project, it made Brexit even harder.

> The collapsed leadership election robbed
> Theresa of the authority a victory over a
> leading Brexiteer would have given her

When David Cameron resigned in June 2016, the expectation was that he would be succeeded by Boris Johnson. Boris had just played a leading role in the Leave campaign and had shown as mayor of London that he could appeal beyond the core Conservative vote. Theresa May was expected to beat him among MPs – those who had campaigned for Remain were angry at his recent conversion to the

Leave cause, while some Leave campaigners questioned whether he was a true believer – but the view was that he would make the final two and probably beat Theresa among the more Eurosceptic party membership.

What followed was the most bizarre leadership election in modern British political history. Shortly before the close of nominations, Michael Gove announced that he was withdrawing his support for Boris and standing himself, having 'come, reluctantly, to the conclusion that Boris cannot provide the leadership or build the team for the task ahead'. Then, at what was supposed to be the launch of his campaign, Boris announced that he agreed he was not the right person for the job. Many MPs were angry at Michael's behaviour and he came a poor third – the two leading Brexiteers had knocked themselves out, leaving Theresa to face Andrea Leadsom in a ballot of party members. A few days later, Andrea withdrew from the race, upset by hostile media coverage of an interview in which she said that Theresa 'possibly has nieces, nephews, but I have children . . . I feel that being a mum means you have a very real stake in the future of our country.'

The collapse of the leadership election meant that Theresa became prime minister on 13 July, nearly two months earlier than she would have anticipated. More importantly, she never received the mandate that would have come from beating a Brexiteer among the party membership. If the election had proceeded as expected, Boris may well have beaten her to the crown. But if she had beaten either him or Andrea in a ballot of party members, she would have been in a stronger position to insist on her vision of Brexit.

* * *

There were lots of reasons, then, why Brexit was always going to be fiendishly difficult. But over the first ten months of her premiership, Theresa made six key decisions that, some have argued, made it even harder.

Not seeking a cross-party consensus at the outset

One of the most common criticisms of Theresa is that, having become prime minister, she should have sought to broker a cross-party consensus about how the referendum result should be implemented. I am sceptical about whether this would have worked. For better or worse, our politics is more tribal than that of many European countries, with our first-past-the-post electoral system making coalition governments rare. Apart from on national security issues, there is no culture of parties working together – the job of the opposition is to oppose.

In fact, it would have been damaging to Theresa's position as leader of the Conservative Party had she sought a deal with opposition parties, and it might even have split the party. She felt the responsibility of both her jobs, prime minister and party leader, very heavily. She was determined to get Brexit done *and* keep the Conservative Party together – in contrast to her successor, who was happy to purge opponents from the party as the price for getting Brexit done. Some people will read this and say, 'See – even her chief of staff admits that she put keeping the Conservative Party together before the national interest!' If you're not a Conservative voter, you might not lose much sleep about the party splitting, but you can hardly expect Theresa to see it like that – she had devoted much of her life to working for it. From her perspective, the party splitting would not be in the national interest because it would almost certainly mean a Labour government.

The situation was made even more difficult by Jeremy Corbyn's leadership of the Labour Party. On the Conservative side, he made co-operation with Labour unthinkable. How could we work with someone we believed was a Marxist, who consistently sided with our country's enemies and who had presided over a rising tide of anti-Semitism in the Labour Party? When Theresa finally tried a cross-party approach, having sought three times to pass a deal on the back of Conservative and DUP support with a few Labour Leavers,

Conservative MPs were livid. That should indicate how they would have reacted if she had tried it in 2016.

If she had tried, it would have been unlikely to receive a positive response. Why would Jeremy Corbyn have helped her? She might have appealed to opposition backbenchers, but many of them represented Remain constituencies that would have been angry to see their MP enabling a Tory Brexit, while those in Leave-voting seats would have been nervous about supporting a Tory Brexit in defiance of their party leadership, given the takeover of many of their local parties by Jeremy Corbyn's supporters. While a cross-party consensus would have avoided the agonies of the next three and a half years, it was never a realistic possibility.

I have more sympathy for the argument that the government should have encouraged a debate about what kind of relationship we wanted with the EU before the negotiations got under way. I can remember being interviewed on *The Daily Politics* by Andrew Neil when I was housing minister. He started by asking me to explain the difference between the single market and the customs union. Luckily I had been discussing the choices available with my brother, who is an economist, so I just about managed the right answer. When Andrew asked the Labour MP next to me whether I was right, he assumed that he wouldn't be asking him if I was, so proceeded to give a different answer. Back then, very few politicians had the understanding of different possible trading relationships that they have today. The government could have published a white paper explaining the challenges and setting out the various options. It could have scheduled votes in parliament. Should we end free movement, or did we want to stay in the single market? Should we stay in a customs union, or did we want to set our own tariffs and accept friction at the border? The government could even have asked parliament to approve a mandate for the UK negotiating team, which would have put opposition MPs on the spot and found out what kind of Brexit there was a majority for. If there turned out not to be a majority for the type of Brexit the government wanted to pursue, it would have given Theresa a stronger rationale for calling a snap election. And if parliament *had* endorsed a mandate, it would have strengthened the UK's hand in the negotiations.

In the event, Theresa decided to try to deliver Brexit through Tory and DUP votes plus a handful of Labour Leavers. She appointed a cabinet that reflected the full spectrum of opinion on Brexit within the parliamentary Conservative Party, from passionate Remainers like Philip Hammond and Amber Rudd, to pragmatists like Sajid Javid and Liz Truss and passionate Leavers like Liam Fox and Boris Johnson (who, remarkably, was less prepared to compromise than those who had believed in Brexit for their whole political careers). That meant that a group of people who had disagreed about whether Brexit was a good thing had to reach a consensus on how to do it. To say they found it difficult would be an understatement.

Drawing red lines

Another regular criticism of Theresa is that she drew too many red lines at the outset, closing off possible compromises and encouraging hardcore Brexiteers to think they were going to get everything they wanted. This critique has probably been most succinctly set out by Philip Hammond, in a quote that speaks volumes about their relationship:

> I was completely stunned by the speech that she made at the Conservative Party conference in October 2016 . . . My assessment of Theresa May's prime ministership, in terms of Brexit, is that she dug a twenty-foot-deep hole in October 2016 in making that speech and, from that moment onwards, cupful by cupful of earth at a time, was trying to fill it in a bit so that she wasn't in such a deep mess.

If you read her October 2016 conference speech, the January 2017 Lancaster House speech, the September 2017 Florence speech and the March 2018 Mansion House speech, it is certainly true that the message becomes more nuanced. However, even the 2016 conference speech acknowledged that 'as ever with international talks, it will be a negotiation, it will require some give and take'. And Philip himself acknowledges the context: the prime minister had campaigned for Remain and been elected leader of the Conservative Party without defeating a Brexiteer in a ballot of party members, so it was understandable that she felt the need to reassure Brexiteers that she could be trusted.

But which of her red lines was such a mistake? The most common answer is that it was her declaration that we would end free movement and take back control of our borders, which ruled out staying in the single market. However, polling shows that ending free movement was one of the key reasons why people had voted to Leave – and that was certainly my anecdotal experience from speaking to people in Croydon during the referendum campaign. I understand why many Remainers wanted to stay in the single market, but it is absurd to think that a Brexit that didn't end free movement and meant continuing to follow all single market rules while also making a significant financial contribution to the EU would have been an acceptable compromise.

The critique that it was a mistake to rule out staying in the customs union is a bit more plausible. I said earlier that no one can be sure what motivated every Leave voter, but I'm confident that more of them cared about ending free movement than about trade policy. This red line wasn't as crucial as some people make out, however. First, although the prime minister wanted to leave the customs union, she wanted to negotiate a new one, albeit a novel one that allowed us to develop an independent trade policy while avoiding customs checks at the EU border. Second, staying in the customs union would not, on its own, have ensured frictionless trade or solved the problem of the Irish border. Staying in the customs union would have been easier to negotiate than the novel customs union the prime minister favoured, but this red line was not a game changer.

There are two arguments I have more sympathy for. The first is that Theresa's conference speech in 2016 went much further than ruling out single market membership. It didn't just rule out free movement, for example, but any negotiation over mobility. The second is that it encouraged hardcore Brexiteers to think they were going to get everything they wanted. As a result, when Theresa compromised – as she was always going to – they felt let down. I remember a briefing for Conservative MPs on the Chequers proposals. John Redwood, Bill Cash and Bernard Jenkin stayed on at the end and I spent over an hour discussing the detail with them. Eventually, exasperated, I said, 'If David Cameron had come back with this from his negotiation, you would have been over the moon.' They denied it, but it's true.

Triggering Article 50 before we knew what we wanted

The prime minister came under immediate pressure from Jeremy Corbyn and some of her own supporters to trigger Article 50, which set out the process for a member state to leave. Once it was triggered, we would leave either after an agreement setting out the terms of our departure had been ratified or after two years. She initially resisted the pressure, but as she explained to the Conservative Party conference in 2016, she couldn't do so indefinitely:

> I said immediately after the referendum that we should not invoke Article 50 before the end of this year. That decision means we have the time to develop our negotiating strategy and avoid setting the clock ticking until our objectives are clear and agreed . . . But it is also right that we should not let things drag on too long. Having voted to leave, I know that the public will soon expect to see, on the horizon, the point at which Britain

does formally leave the European Union. So let me be absolutely clear . . . We will invoke Article 50 no later than the end of March next year.

Critics have argued that her initial instinct to wait until the government had agreed what we were seeking was right, and they have a point. The government made some progress in the months between Theresa becoming prime minister and Article 50 being triggered on 29 March 2017, but it wasn't able to agree a detailed prospectus for the future relationship until June 2018. By that point, it had used up fifteen of the twenty-four months of the Article 50 process, and although good progress had been made on the Withdrawal Agreement, there had been no discussion of the future relationship. Extending the process was always going to be more politically painful for the UK than for the EU – we'd put ourselves in a position where there was a hard deadline and we were under far more pressure to meet it.

The snap election that made things harder

On 18 April 2017, Theresa announced that she would be seeking parliamentary support for a snap election, having concluded that it was 'the only way to guarantee certainty and security for the years ahead'. Many people have identified this decision as another crucial mistake, but I think Theresa was right that it would be very difficult to get a Brexit deal through parliament with the narrow majority she had inherited. Given the range of views within the Conservative Party, it was inevitable than any compromise would be too hard for some and too soft for others. She was right to be nervous about the prospect of relying on opposition votes, and she was right to believe that she had a good chance of significantly increasing her majority, given her healthy lead in the polls. She was also right to be worried about the interaction between the electoral timetable and the Brexit timetable.

The Article 50 process was due to end on 29 March 2019, just over a year before the next election was due. If – as she anticipated – there was some kind of implementation period, we might not be out it by then. Or, if the implementation period was shorter, it might just have ended, in which case any disruption would occur in the run-up to the election. Neither of these was an attractive prospect.

The mistake wasn't her decision to call an election but the campaign she ran, and I know this is her biggest regret. There were a number of problems. First, it was difficult for her to explain why she was calling the election. She could hardly acknowledge that some of her MPs were so far on either side of the argument that she couldn't rely on their support. Nor could she acknowledge the need to shift the electoral timetable to avoid the next election happening during or just after the implementation period. Instead, she had to say that the country needed strong and stable leadership and that the opposition parties were trying to frustrate Brexit. The problems with the former was that she was uncomfortable with the campaign being all about her and voters weren't sure if they wanted a Conservative government with a big majority; the problem with the latter was that the public hadn't seen much evidence of the opposition doing so. Then came the manifesto launch, which confirmed voters' fears about what a landslide Conservative government might mean.

The election result was critical to everything that followed. Some of the consequences were obvious. The new parliamentary arithmetic would make it harder to get any Brexit deal through parliament. Theresa's position was weakened and cabinet ministers who saw themselves as potential successors had at least half an eye on how to position themselves for a future contest rather than helping her sell a compromise. Other consequences took longer to become apparent. The result weakened the prime minister's negotiating position. The EU was sceptical about whether she would be able to get any deal through parliament, so held a few compromises up their sleeve in case they found themselves negotiating with her successor. It also blunted the threat of no deal, which some Brexiteers wanted to use as negotiating leverage. With Speaker Bercow in the chair and a clear majority of MPs opposed to it, the EU no longer saw that as a credible threat. The confidence and supply arrangement with the DUP made the EU – wrongly – doubt the government's sincerity on Northern Ireland and regard the Irish government as speaking for the people of Northern Ireland. And most importantly, their uncertainty about how long Theresa would be in place made them toughen their stance on the backstop. I recall Theresa pressing Jean-Claude Juncker and Michel Barnier on why the EU was insisting on including the full details of the backstop in the Withdrawal Agreement. That was the only thing stopping her passing her deal. Surely, she asked, a legal commitment by the British government to avoid a hard border could be trusted? Michel looked slightly embarrassed and inadvertently let slip their underlying motivation. 'We trust you, Theresa,' he said, 'but we are not sure how long you will be prime minister, and we don't trust what we think is coming next.' Sadly, his mistrust proved well-founded, but here is another of the paradoxes of Brexit: to protect themselves against what they feared was coming next, the EU insisted on nailing down the details of the backstop, which stopped Theresa getting her deal through and led to the future they feared.

Agreeing to sequencing

On 29 April 2017, the European Council adopted its guidelines for the Brexit negotiations. These set out the EU's view that the negotiations should 'proceed according to a phased approach giving priority to an orderly withdrawal'. This included agreeing reciprocal guarantees to safeguard the rights of EU citizens in the UK and UK citizens in the EU; a financial settlement that respected the obligations resulting from the UK's membership; and solutions for the island of Ireland that reflected its unique circumstances, with the aim of avoiding a hard border. Only once 'sufficient progress' had been achieved on these issues should the negotiations discuss the framework for the future relationship and any transitional arrangements.

If we accepted this, we would have to agree on the financial settlement and the plan for avoiding a hard border in Ireland before we could even begin talking about the future relationship. Nonetheless, Theresa agreed to it, somewhat reluctantly, at some point during the 2017 election campaign. Why did she do so? She took some comfort from another element of the guidelines – that the result of the two phases would constitute a single package, with nothing agreed until everything was agreed. But more importantly, the clock had started running and nearly three months had elapsed. The UK couldn't afford a prolonged stand-off about what to talk about first.

Some have argued that this was a serious mistake that led to the backstop. I certainly agree that the artificial hurdle of 'sufficient progress' made things even more difficult, but the backstop was the result of the EU's inability to agree a legal treaty on our future relationship until after we had left rather than the sequencing of the negotiations.

Pursuing a bespoke deal made the negotiations harder

The EU offered the UK a choice. If we wanted a close relationship, we could stay in the single market and the customs union. If we wanted a more distant relationship, we could negotiate a free trade agreement, but with separate arrangements for Northern Ireland. Theresa rejected both options. In her opinion, the first was inconsistent with what people had voted for, while the second would mean a partial border between Great Britain and Northern Ireland. Instead, she sought to create a new model, closer than an FTA but less close than membership of the single market and customs union – something that would maintain a frictionless border with the EU, while ending free movement and allowing the UK to pursue an independent trade policy, but with constraints on regulatory autonomy. It won't surprise you to know that I think a compromise of this kind was in the national interest, but it made the negotiations *much* harder – the EU was *very* resistant to creating a new model.

The irony is that what Boris Johnson wanted was more closely aligned with what the EU was offering. He was happy with a fairly distant, FTA-style relationship. The only major points of difference concerned the arrangements for Northern Ireland, where he gave in, and on level playing field provisions to ensure fair competition, where a compromise was reached.

* * *

On the final reason why it took so long to get Brexit done, you can argue whether the blame lay with Theresa or the MPs who refused to compromise.

Parliament and the country remained deadlocked and became increasingly polarised

MPs sometimes vote against their constituents' wishes, either because they are voting in line with their party or because they feel strongly about a particular issue. But political parties exist to win elections, and if they find themselves out of tune with the electorate, they change their position. That's what Labour has eventually had to do on Brexit. Had public opinion shifted between 2016 and 2019 – if enough Remainers had accepted the result and stopped voting for parties who were blocking Brexit or enough Leavers had concluded that they'd made a mistake and stopped voting for parties who supported Brexit – some MPs would have changed their minds and the gridlock would have been broken. But that didn't happen, so MPs stayed in their trenches.

Not only did they refuse to compromise, they actually hardened their positions. In 2017, the debate was between a soft Brexit and a free trade agreement, but as the impasse dragged on, some MPs began to support leaving without a deal and others a second referendum, in the hope of stopping Brexit altogether. I remember a fierce argument breaking out at one of my weekly lunches with Conservative MPs, between two MPs who opposed the government's deal because they wanted a second referendum and three or four who opposed it because they wanted a more distant relationship. I pointed out that they if they refused to compromise, two things would happen. First, the government would not be able to get its deal through, and second, one group would eventually get what they wanted and the other would lose everything. They agreed, but they both thought it was the other side that had made a massive miscalculation.

* * *

So there are lots of reasons why it was so hard to get Brexit done, but if I was going to single out a few key ones, I would say the challenge posed by Northern Ireland, the fact that the EU was never going to make it easy, the failure to have a cross-party debate at the outset and the impact of the 2017 election on the parliamentary arithmetic and therefore the strength of the prime minister's negotiating position were most crucial.

CHAPTER 8

A PLACE WITH
NO GOVERNMENT

Like many British politicians, I had only a basic understanding of Northern Irish politics when I was appointed chief of staff. I had been the Conservative Party's director of campaigning before I was an MP, so I knew the politics of every constituency in England, Scotland and Wales in detail, but Northern Ireland has its own parties, so I knew much less about it.

The devolved institutions established by the Good Friday Agreement – the Northern Ireland executive and the Northern Ireland assembly, to which the executive is accountable – had collapsed shortly before my appointment. Sinn Féin's Martin McGuinness had resigned as deputy first minister in protest at Arlene Foster's refusal to stand aside during an inquiry into significant overspends on a policy she had been responsible for. The Good Friday Agreement required power-sharing between unionists and nationalists, so when Sinn Féin refused to nominate a replacement for McGuinness, the executive collapsed and the assembly was dissolved on 26 January 2017. Elections were held on 2 March, but they didn't change anything. The law required that if no executive could be formed within a few weeks of the election, another vote should be held, but Northern Ireland secretary James Brokenshire extended the deadline to give the parties more time.

The result of the UK general election complicated matters further. The confidence and supply agreement between the Conservatives and the DUP caused concern in Northern Ireland about whether the UK government could act with impartiality – as it was required to do under the Good Friday Agreement – if its survival depended on the DUP.

But that wasn't all. The SDLP had lost all its seats and because Sinn Féin refuses to take its seats at Westminster, that meant there would be no Irish nationalist voice in the House of Commons. In the absence of the devolved institutions, the UK parliament might at some point have to pass legislation relating to Northern Ireland. Any return to 'direct rule' would be controversial, but doubly so now that the only Northern Irish voices at Westminster were those of the DUP and the independent unionist Sylvia Hermon.

On top of that, the Ulster Unionist Party had also lost all its seats. Northern Ireland had voted Remain in the EU referendum and four of its five main parties (the UUP, Sinn Féin, the SDLP and the cross-community Alliance Party) had campaigned for Remain, but none of them would be present for the crucial debates about how to implement the referendum result.

Finally, the absence of devolved government and the confidence and supply agreement combined to alter the balance of power within the DUP. Previously, their leadership at Stormont had all the power. Now, with no executive and the party key to the UK government's survival, the tables were turned. And because Nigel Dodds, the DUP's leader at Westminster, was determined to keep his group united, hardliners like Sammy Wilson had undue influence.

When I was appointed, Northern Ireland had been without a government for over three months. The Northern Ireland civil service could continue to implement the decisions of previous ministers, but there was no one with the authority to take new ones. The best solution was clearly to restore the devolved institutions, but neither the DUP nor Sinn Féin were in a hurry to get back into government. Neither had been punished by the electorate for their actions – they had increased their shares of the vote in both the assembly and general elections. The suspicion was that Sinn Féin didn't want to be in government until Brexit had been resolved and that the DUP weren't averse to some direct rule – aside from Sylvia Hermon, it was the only Northern Irish voice at Westminster and the confidence and supply agreement gave it leverage. However, as it would discover, direct rule would mean legislation it didn't like on same-sex marriage and abortion, issues on which its views were out of kilter with the prevailing view at Westminster. This wasn't the only issue on which it miscalculated during this period.

If the two parties didn't want to get back into government, there were two other options. We could call another election and hope that the public punished them for not working together, but that seemed unlikely – indeed, it might polarise things further by forcing the parties to rule out certain compromises in their manifestos. Or we could return to direct rule, but that would clearly be a backwards step.

My first exposure to the reality of Northern Ireland's politics was when the prime minister met four leading members of Sinn Féin on 21 November: their president Gerry Adams, a former MP and now a TD (a member of the lower house of the Oireachtas, the Irish parliament); their vice-president Mary Lou McDonald, also a TD and soon to take over from Adams; their leader in the North, Michelle O'Neill, a member of the assembly; and Conor Murphy, an assembly member and a former MP. I'd never met any of them before, but I had obviously known of Adams since I was a teenager. How should you regard someone who has supported political violence in the past, but has also taken significant personal risks to bring about the peace Northern Ireland now enjoyed?

The prime minister began by asking them what it would take to get the devolved institutions back. Adams replied that previous agreements needed to be implemented. Sinn Féin were concerned that the idea of an amnesty for members of the British armed forces, which would be a breach of those agreements, had appeared in a government document. Nor was he convinced that either the British government or the DUP wanted the devolved institutions back. The prime minister forcefully refuted that and he said he believed her, but she needed to understand that Sinn Féin had to take its supporters with it. They had suffered from British terrorism. There were rights available in London that were not available in Belfast, and the British government needed to address that by legislating for marriage equality in Northern Ireland and the protection of the Irish language. The prime minister agreed that those issues needed resolving, but said she was surprised to hear him advocating direct rule. Adams replied that Sinn Féin and the DUP were 'quarrelsome children' and the British government 'carried the white man's burden' of resolving their quarrel. He didn't want the British government to have any role in the North, but the DUP were radicalising people on these issues, so it needed addressing. History has taught us that unionism will only move when it has no other option, he said.

Early in the new year, the DUP met with the prime minister and give her their take on the situation. They had recently met with David Sterling, the interim head of the Northern Ireland civil service, who they said had painted a depressing picture. In the year since the executive had collapsed, a backlog of decisions had built up. A budget needed to be in place by early February. Furthermore, the Sinn Féin MP Barry McElduff had posted a video of himself balancing a loaf of Kingsmill bread on his head on the forty-second anniversary of the Kingsmill massacre, where ten Protestant civilians were shot dead by IRA gunmen; his actions had made it impossible for the DUP to re-enter talks with Sinn Féin. The prime minister understood their anger, but urged them to see the bigger picture: the best way to address the backlog of decisions was to get devolution back.

On 12 February, Theresa and the taoiseach Leo Varadkar went to Stormont, following advice that their presence might give the parties a final push to get things over the line. However, it was clear as soon as she sat down with Arlene Foster and Nigel Dodds that the trip had been a mistake. They were worried about it looking like they'd been pushed into a deal and warned Theresa that if she hoped a deal was going to be done that day, she would leave disappointed. Sinn Féin were more optimistic. Mary Lou McDonald said that while there were a few gaps, they were by no means insurmountable. However, she warned that if they didn't make that final step, things might unravel. The prime minister also met with the other three main parties, the UUP, SDLP and the Alliance Party, who were frustrated to have been excluded from the talks. They were also concerned about sustainability – how to ensure that if the institutions were restored, they stayed in place. Naomi Long, the leader of Alliance, said she hoped the prime minister had brought some magic with her; sadly we hadn't, and the talks collapsed a couple of days later. Our sense was that Arlene had been ready to do a deal, but backed off when she couldn't take her party with her.

When the prime minister met with both parties a week later, Arlene was adamant that she had not agreed to any text. She said the unionist community didn't see why Sinn Féin should be rewarded, given that they had collapsed the institutions in the first place. Mary Lou's insistence on the need for a free-standing Irish Language Act was particularly unhelpful. Sinn Féin said they no longer believed that Arlene could deliver a deal and that, although they weren't comfortable asking a British government to legislate for the North, we needed to sort out the issues relating to the Irish language and marriage equality.

The prime minister had a better meeting with the DUP on 7 March. She told them that the government would be announcing the details of a budget for Northern Ireland the next day, but ran through why she was so reluctant to move any further towards direct rule. They were reassured that action was being taken on the budget and assured her that they didn't want full direct rule – it didn't work for them if nationalism was 'agitated and looking south'. They agreed that the objective had to be to restore devolution, but complained that by leaking the text of the draft agreement, Sinn Féin had damaged trust. Unionist attitudes had hardened, so talks were not going to happen anytime soon.

In May, the government published a consultation paper on how to implement the Stormont House Agreement, in which the British government had committed to establish new institutions to address the legacy of Northern Ireland's past. This was a highly emotive issue on all sides. Over 250,000 people served in Northern Ireland between 1969 and 2007, and over a thousand gave their lives. The defence secretary Gavin Williamson was concerned that the proposed Historical Investigations Unit would come under pressure to reopen old cases. His solution was that the consultation paper should propose a statute of limitations for members of the armed forces in respect of criminal offences relating to the Troubles – in effect, an amnesty. Indeed, he felt so strongly about this that he wrote an extraordinary letter to the prime minister, saying that 'if this means a wider amnesty [i.e. for those who had committed acts of terrorism], so be it'. But our Northern Ireland manifesto had been clear that we would not introduce amnesties. The prime minister overruled him and issued the paper in line with what we had committed to in the Stormont House Agreement.

Theresa wanted to increase the pressure on the DUP to get back into government, so on 8 June she agreed to arrange a meeting of the British Irish Inter-Governmental Conference, a body created by the Good Friday Agreement and one that the DUP were not keen on. On 19 July, she travelled to Northern Ireland in the aftermath of the publication of the Chequers proposals, visiting a pottery business on the border, meeting the parties and giving a speech about what the Chequers plan meant for Northern Ireland. She sought to reassure the UUP, SDLP and the Alliance Party, who were worried about what she would do if the EU didn't accept the Chequers proposals and about the attitude of some Conservative MPs towards the Irish border. She and I had dinner with Arlene and Nigel in the beautiful setting of Crom Castle. This was probably her best meeting with the DUP – the change of setting and format made for a more relaxed conversation. In contrast, her meeting the next morning with Sinn Féin was the most absurd of all of her meetings I witnessed over those two and a bit years. Mary Lou had obviously decided what she was going to say to the cameras and thought, for the sake of consistency, she ought to say the same thing to the prime minister's face. To my astonishment, she accused the prime minister of giving in to the European Research Group and failing to recognise the exceptionality of Ireland. 'You do realise that's the exact opposite of what the prime minister has done?' I said. 'Did you notice David Davis, Boris Johnson and various other ministers resigning? She has put her job on the line to pursue a compromise that protects the unique circumstances of Northern Ireland.'

In the speech, the prime minister was upfront about her unionism, but distinguished her personal views from her responsibilities as prime minister:

> A government I lead will never be neutral in our support for the Union . . . but I also respect the fact that a substantial section of the population here identify as Irish and aspire to a future within a united Ireland. I will always govern in the interests of the whole community in Northern Ireland and not just one part of it.

When it came to Brexit, checks away from the border would be just as unacceptable as any physical infrastructure at the border:

> The seamless border is a foundation stone on which the Belfast Agreement rests, allowing for the 'just and equal treatment for the identity, ethos and aspirations of both communities'. Anything that undermines that is a breach of the spirit of the Belfast Agreement . . . Any agreement we reach with the EU will have to provide for the frictionless movement of goods across the border.

But the same argument applied east–west:

We could never accept that the way to prevent a hard border with Ireland is to create a new border within the United Kingdom. To do so would also be a breach of the spirit of the Belfast Agreement, and for exactly the same reason that a [north–south] border would be. It would not be showing 'parity of esteem' and 'just and equal treatment for the identity, ethos and aspirations' of the unionist community in Northern Ireland to cut their part of the United Kingdom off from the rest of the UK.

On 6 September, the government sought to increase the pressure on the parties. Karen Bradley, who had taken over from James Brokenshire as secretary of state for Northern Ireland, announced that she would legislate to extend the deadline by which an executive had to be formed or elections called, but also announced that she would reduce assembly members' pay, given that they were not performing their full range of legislative functions. A legal case had questioned how much the Northern Ireland civil service could do in the absence of ministers, so Karen announced that the legislation would confirm their powers.

When the prime minister met the DUP a few days later, they were concerned about the cut in assembly members' pay being described as an 'incentive' to restore devolution and about whether the bill went far enough in allowing civil servants to take decisions. The prime minister questioned whether an independent facilitator could help restart talks, but they were strongly against that.

Theresa returned to Northern Ireland on 5 February 2019. This visit profoundly affected her and was key to her decision a few weeks later to ask for an extension to the Article 50 period rather than try to leave without a deal. Nigel Dodds had told her he didn't believe there was anything about Brexit that threatened the Good Friday Agreement, but this was in sharp contrast to what she would hear from the people of Northern Ireland over the next thirty-six hours.

She had a simple message to those people who were concerned

about parliament's rejection of her deal and the fact that she was now seeking changes to the backstop:

> Northern Ireland does not have to rely on the Irish government or the European Union to prevent a return to borders of the past. The UK government will not let that happen. I will not let that happen.

She then met privately with a group of business leaders, many of whom had campaigned in favour of her deal. They were frustrated by the DUP's opposition to it and the collective failure to restore devolved government. They felt that while businesses in Northern Ireland had moved on from the Troubles, its politics hadn't.

But it was a private meeting with five community leaders that really made an impression on the prime minister. They had all been involved in the peace process, and they each shared their concerns about the combined effect of Brexit and the absence of devolved government: 'So much of what we've worked for is in danger of evaporating,' 'Things are starting to unravel,' 'I'm deeply concerned that young people are retrenching,' 'The Good Friday Agreement respected my identity. I felt like a proper citizen in my own country. Now my identity is in danger again.' They warned her of the risk not just to the peace process, but to the Union itself: 'Moderate nationalists are increasing looking to Coveney and Varadkar – they want a border poll, not a restoration of the institutions.' One of them had the perfect response to Nigel Dodds: 'The text of the Good Friday Agreement is not that important – what was important is that it broke down barriers. Now they are retrenching. And the borders in people's minds are more important than the physical one.'

If that wasn't enough to convince the prime minister that she was doing the right thing in trying to find a compromise that worked for Northern Ireland, one of them had this parting shot: 'We're in a dire situation. You are in a dire situation, but you're strong – near as strong as my mother. People in your party are holding you back. They're holding us back, too.' At the bottom of my notes, I've written, 'If only every MP had accompanied us today.' It's an indication of the impact the meeting had on me, but it now feels naïve. The sad truth is that ultra-Brexiteers would have dismissed the concerns as unwarranted or, if they were prepared to acknowledge that the Brexit they wanted would mean checks, they would point out that they were the unavoidable consequence of the democratic decision of the British people. And for those who wanted a second referendum, it would simply have confirmed in their minds that they were right to try to stop Brexit altogether.

The next morning, the prime minister met with each of the parties. The UUP were supportive of leaving with a deal, though raised some concerns about the backstop. They were frustrated about the failure to restore devolution, and concerned about the institutions to address the legacy of Northern Ireland's past. The Alliance Party's Naomi Long said she was 'not just cross with you, but cross with Labour, too – you're trying to preserve the coherence of the Conservative Party, and Corbyn is trying to get an election.' Having said her bit, she asked if there was anything she could do to help. Colum Eastwood, the articulate leader of the SDLP, said that people had lost faith in parliament's ability to do the right thing for Northern Ireland. He was also cross with Labour, the SDLP's sister party. Mary Lou McDonald accused the prime minister of bad faith, Conservatives who opposed the backstop of hostility to Ireland, the DUP of mindless recklessness and predicted the UK wouldn't get any concessions because 'Leo will not be let blink.' Last but not least was Arlene, who was in a softer mood than Nigel Dodds had been the previous day. She reassured the prime minister that the DUP didn't want a hard border, but said they needed some change to the backstop. She was also keen to get devolved government back, though even if it succeeded, it would now be too late for her to play a significant role in the Brexit negotiations.

A last attempt

Towards the end of Theresa's premiership, a reminder of Northern Ireland's past nearly persuaded its politicians to work together again. On 18 April 2019, the journalist Lyra McKee was fatally shot by a member of the dissident republican group the New IRA while reporting on rioting in the Creggan area of Derry. The prime minister attended her funeral at St Anne's Cathedral in Belfast on 24 April. During the service, Father Martin Magill said that he 'commended our political leaders for standing together in Creggan on Friday'. He continued, 'I am, however, left with a question. Why in God's name does it take the death of a twenty-nine-year old woman with her whole life in front of her to get to this point?' His words were greeted by a standing ovation from the congregation. Why indeed?

On 26 April, the prime minister and the taoiseach issued a joint statement, saying that they had 'heard the unmistakable message to all political leaders that people across Northern Ireland want to see a new momentum for political progress'. They agreed 'that what is now needed is actions and not just words from all of us who are in positions of leadership' and were therefore establishing 'a new process of political talks, involving all the main political parties in Northern Ireland, together with the UK and Irish governments . . . to re-establish the democratic institutions of the Good Friday Agreement.' Sadly, this last effort was no more successful than previous ones. As we suspected all along, the parties wouldn't go back into devolved government until Brexit had been resolved.

On a personal level, I left Number 10 knowing this beautiful part of our country a little more and understanding its politics a lot better. If I could understand why nationalists sometimes found the DUP infuriating, I also had a better sense of what we ask of them when we require them to share power with Sinn Féin. Ultimately, however, the Union will only endure if nationalists feel that it respects their identity, language and history. Writing this paragraph, I recalled a dinner with Gavin Williamson, Nigel Dodds and Jeffrey Donaldson early in my time as chief of staff. At the end of the evening, Jeffrey was reflecting on how he was a proud Irishman as well as a proud Brit. He saw no contradiction between the two, but observed that politically speaking, unionists tended to focus on their Britishness. Maybe, he wondered, they should talk more about their Irishness. I think he might have been on to something. Unionism needs to focus on what people in Northern Ireland have in common, not what divides them, as Arlene Foster recognised in her moving resignation statement in April 2021. Politicians on both sides have taken personal risks to get Northern Ireland to where it is today. The question now is whether they can take the final step and leave the past behind them.

CHAPTER 9

DEALING WITH
THE CABINET

Judged by the number of people who work there or the budget it controls, Number 10 is less powerful than the big departments of state like the Treasury, the Foreign Office or the Home Office. If a prime minister is arguing with their chancellor about some aspect of economic policy, they don't have access to anything like the same level of support. Number 10's power depends on the political power of the prime minister, which waxes and wanes.

Before the 2017 election, Theresa had been recently elected as party leader and was riding high in the polls. It would have been a brave cabinet minister who refused to do something she wanted. After the election, that dynamic had changed. Not only was she constrained by the parliamentary arithmetic, she was in a weaker position with her cabinet.

That was, understandably, a source of frustration to her. One of my main roles became brokering deals between her and her ministers, finding compromises that got her most of what she wanted. The key to brokering these deals was credibility. I didn't have any political power of my own; I was only worth talking to if cabinet ministers believed that I was speaking for the prime minister. If I'd ever done a deal that the prime minister refused to sign off, my credibility would have been shot. To be an effective chief of staff, you have to know or be able to predict what the prime minister is thinking on any issue or, if you're not sure, be honest about it and check.

My closest relationship was probably with David Lidington, the prime minister's de facto deputy for the last eighteen months of her premiership. We had a weekly meeting and, as I became more embroiled in Brexit, he increasingly took on the role of brokering deals where the dispute was between two cabinet ministers. He also did a first-class job of managing the relationship between the government and the Scottish and Welsh governments. Another key relationship was with the chief whip Julian Smith. Julian was – and, I'm pleased to say, remains – a personal friend, but our working relationship wasn't always easy. A chief whip has to be a two-way conduit, both persuading backbench MPs to support the government's policy and telling the prime minister when those MPs are not happy with what the government is proposing. In Julian's case, that tension was accentuated by the fact that he personally supported a Brexit compromise of the kind the prime minister was trying to negotiate, but his whips' office wanted a harder Brexit. As a result, he was at times one of the most powerful advocates of reaching out to the opposition and one of the strongest critics of people's various fantasy solutions, but at other times he was insistent that we should go back to Brussels for the umpteenth time or not whip against a backbench amendment that was clearly inconsistent with our policy. There were numerous occasions on which he stormed out of a meeting or I put the phone down on him, but we always made up. No one worked harder to try to get the prime minister's deal over the line, so he was a popular figure in Number 10. People worried about the stress he was under and the impact it was having on him.

If David and Julian were in the prime minister's innermost circle, her three other key relationships were with Philip Hammond, Boris Johnson and David Davis – and it is to these that I will devote the majority of this chapter.

Ambassador to Number 11

The relationship between the prime minister and their chancellor is the most important in any government. And when that goes wrong – think Thatcher and Lawson or Blair and Brown – it has consequences for the whole government.

When I was appointed chief of staff, the prime minister's relationship with Philip Hammond was not in a good place. He felt he had been sidelined during the election campaign and that if the prime minister had won with a large majority, he would have been sacked. Together with the prime minister's deputy principal private secretary Will Macfarlane, who was responsible for the relationship between Number 10 and the Treasury at the official level, I worked hard to improve the relationship, with fluctuating success. Indeed, I spent so much time in the leather armchairs of the chancellor's study that I sometimes felt I was the prime minister's ambassador to Number 11 rather than her chief of staff. I came to consider Philip a friend and was touched when, after we had both left Downing Street, he asked me to introduce him to the House of Lords. But his stubbornness and reluctance to think party politically sometimes drove me to distraction.

To understand Theresa and Philip's relationship, you need to know five things. First, there is an inevitable tension between Number 10 and Number 11: prime ministers often want to do things that involve spending money, and chancellors sometimes have to say 'No' (or 'Yes, but only if you're prepared to raise taxes or cut spending elsewhere'). That tension was more pronounced than usual in this particular case because Philip had decided that sorting out the public finances – finishing the job George Osborne had started – was to be his personal legacy. Given the subsequent damage done to the public finances by the COVID-19 pandemic, it's a good job the Cameron and May governments took action to get the deficit under control, but Philip prioritised this above all else. The prime minister didn't want to go on a huge spending spree, but she did want to address some of the pressures on public services after years of austerity. She eventually persuaded him, but by God, it was a struggle.

Second, Theresa thought the Treasury was too powerful. She wanted to strengthen the Department for Business and give it lead responsibility for the government's industrial strategy. Unsurprisingly, the Treasury didn't like that at all, and nor did Philip – initially, it was a struggle to get him to even say the words 'industrial strategy'. It is noticeable that Rishi Sunak has succeeded in mothballing the industrial strategy and ensuring that its replacement – the Plan for Growth – is Treasury-led.

Third, Philip was intellectually brilliant but not very political. A good example was the need to replace dangerous cladding on high-rise residential buildings after the Grenfell Tower fire. The government had a clear responsibility to help local councils fund the remediation of buildings they owned, but the Treasury's view was that, when it came to privately owned buildings, it wasn't fair to ask taxpayers to pick up the cost for something that wasn't their responsibility, and it would set a bad precedent. Intellectually, this was a perfectly valid argument, but it was politically indefensible. Nearly two years after Grenfell, people were still living in dangerous buildings because the freeholders hadn't taken action. Many could not sell their homes and were facing significant additional bills to cover the cost of twenty-four-hour fire safety patrols.

Fourth, Philip may have been right to worry about the consequences of a hard Brexit and the need for fiscal conservatism, but he could be a bit of a reactionary on some issues. I remember being completely flabbergasted when, during a discussion about tackling the burning injustices Theresa had referred to in her first speech as prime minister, he told me there were no burning injustices in Britain today.

And the fifth thing was Brexit, of course. Prior to the referendum, I'd always thought of Philip as a Eurosceptic. But when I attended an event during the referendum campaign at which he was the key speaker, I was surprised by how passionate he was about the Remain cause. Had he been prime minister, he would have pursued a slightly softer Brexit than Theresa (he would have been happy for the UK to stay in the customs union and to give EU nationals preference in our immigration system, for example), but he could live with her compromise. His biggest concern was that we might end up leaving the EU without a deal, with all the economic harm that would do. That fed into his views on fiscal policy – one of the reasons he was so cautious about spending was that until we had agreed a Brexit deal, he wanted to keep a fiscal reserve in case of no deal. Theresa didn't want to leave without a deal, either; the differences between them on Brexit were about tactics and temperament rather than policy. First, Philip wanted to rule out no deal; Theresa didn't feel she could do that – the logical consequence was that you would revoke Article 50 and stay in the EU if you couldn't negotiate an acceptable deal. Second, Theresa wanted to agree what future relationship we wanted, see how the EU responded and then, if we needed to compromise to get a deal, cross that bridge when we came to it. Philip, worried that we were running out of time, wanted to war-game the whole negotiation. When the EU said no to plan A, what was plan B? She found that infuriating. Could we not just concentrate on selling plan A for a while, rather than assuming it was doomed and trying to agree plan B? Finally, Philip viewed Brexit as an exercise in damage limitation and was determined to tell the unvarnished truth as he saw it about what the different options would mean economically. The benefits of trade deals with other countries were an order of magnitude less than what we would lose by leaving the single market. As a result, any version of Brexit was worse than staying in the EU and the more distant our future relationship, the bigger the economic hit. Leaving the EU without a deal would be economically catastrophic. To Brexiteers, this was 'Project Fear' all over again, and talking down no deal weakened our negotiating position. Rather than persuading them to back the government's compromise, it made them angry. Theresa was more optimistic about our future outside the EU: yes, there were costs to leaving, but there were opportunities, too, and we could make a success of it.

The practical consequence in terms of my relationship with Philip was that Brexit dominated everything. I would go to see him to agree a package of measures we could announce at party conference and it might be forty or fifty minutes before we even started talking about what the meeting was meant to be about. I sometimes felt like Jerry Maguire, the eponymous sports agent played in the film by Tom Cruise, who has one client who doesn't see the need to please the crowd in order to get the improved contract he wants. Maguire, desperate to keep his business afloat, begs him to 'Help me help you.' Philip wanted to bring down the deficit? So did I, and so did the prime minister. Philip didn't want us to leave without a deal? Neither did I, and nor did the prime minister. But if he wanted a deal, he had to help us rather than antagonising the people we needed to vote for it. And opening the spending taps just a little to allow us to address some of the government's domestic policy vulnerabilities would strengthen the prime minister, making it easier to make progress on Brexit. Help me help you, Philip.

Initially, my efforts to build a better relationship paid off. Philip agreed to Justine Greening announcing an increase in the schools budget that protected per pupil funding in real terms in July 2017. Although this didn't cost the Treasury anything (money was reallocated from within the Department for Education's budget), it created an expectation for the future. Philip's initial priority on Brexit was to secure an implementation period, so that businesses unsure about our future trading relationship wouldn't take any precipitate decisions in late 2017 and early 2018. He was therefore delighted when the prime minister argued for such a period in her speech in Florence in September 2017. His November 2017 budget dovetailed well with our emerging strategy, the key announcement being the exemption of most first-time buyers from stamp duty. And he was relieved when we achieved the 'sufficient progress' milestone in the Brexit negotiations just before Christmas. When he saw the prime minister on the day of the January 2018 cabinet reshuffle, he told her that he felt the period leading up to the budget should be a model for how they should work together.

At around this time, the prime minister decided that she wanted to agree a multi-year funding settlement for the NHS that allowed it to plan for the long term and cope with rising demand while improving performance. It was clear that there was broad support for increasing NHS funding, but what the prime minister wanted involved settling the budget for the Department of Health outside of the spending review process. The Treasury didn't like that, preferring to look at all spending pressures in the round.

The health secretary Jeremy Hunt, on the other hand, was enthusiastic about the idea. Jeremy was soon to become the longest-serving health secretary in British political history, but he hadn't had an easy time in the job. Although the NHS budget had risen each year, the increases had been smaller than the NHS had been used to and his imposition of a new junior doctors' contract had proved controversial. He was, however, incredibly passionate about the role – and in particular about improving patient safety in the wake of the Francis Inquiry into failings at Mid Staffordshire NHS Foundation Trust – as I saw when I accompanied him on a visit to Great Ormond Street Hospital in March 2018. If it hadn't been for Brexit, I would have tried to do more visits with cabinet ministers. Spending time with them outside the confines of bilateral meetings with the prime minister allowed me to build personal relationships with them and get a feel for their priorities.

To deliver what the prime minister wanted, I needed to get Philip and Jeremy on the same page. We needed a package that was big enough for the prime minister and Jeremy – and more importantly, NHS chief executive Simon Stevens – to sell, enough to cope with rising demand and get performance to where we wanted it to be. But the package also had to be one that Philip and the Treasury considered affordable and which had something in it to tackle waste and drive up financial underperformance in parts of the NHS. The question was, how to get him and the Treasury to engage?

A combination of four things did the trick. First, we needed an independent piece of work that demonstrated how much money was required to cope with the predicted demand and improve performance, something the Treasury couldn't dismiss as a Department of Health wish list. As a former Treasury civil servant, Jeremy Heywood understand exactly what was required. He commissioned one of his officials in the Cabinet Office to produce the necessary analysis. Second, the prime minister needed to meet Philip halfway. She told him she accepted that we couldn't increase NHS spending by as much as she wanted to while meeting our fiscal rules in terms of reducing the deficit and overall debt, so she was prepared to advocate a tax increase to help fund the package. That showed him she was serious. Third, we worked with Simon Stevens to ensure the package had a significant reform element. The plan had to give NHS leaders the resources they needed, but they had to be responsible for getting Trust finances back into balance and tackling variation in performance. We made it clear that we were prepared to act on requests from NHS leaders to reform its structures, undoing the Lansley reforms if that was helpful, and to introduce public health measures to reduce demand on the service. Finally, the chief whip took soundings of the parliamentary party. Of the 255 MPs who responded, 239 agreed that the NHS should be the top priority for any additional government spending and there was significant support for asking everyone to contribute a bit more to pay for it.

It was a long and gruelling process, but we finally got there on 13 June. Philip was content to proceed, subject to two conditions and a question. First, he wanted to agree what the prime minister would say about how the plan was going to be paid for (to put it bluntly, he wanted her to own the tax rise). The words we agreed on were:

Some of the extra funding I am promising today will come from using the money we will no longer spend on our annual membership subscription to the EU after we have left. But the commitment I am making goes beyond the Brexit dividend . . . So, across the nation, taxpayers will have to contribute a bit more in a fair and balanced way to support the NHS we all use . . . We will stick to our fiscal rules, reduce our debt but prioritise our NHS within public spending.

Philip wasn't very keen on the 'Brexit dividend' language because it didn't actually exist – the impact of the spike in inflation caused by the devaluation of the pound immediately after the referendum and the lower projected economic growth far outweighed our annual contribution to Brussels. However, the impact on our economy was already factored into the forecasts, whereas we hadn't yet reallocated our annual financial contribution – in this sense there was a dividend and he could see that it was helpful in party management terms to use the language, even if it grated with him.

The second condition was that he wanted the prime minister to meet with the secretaries of state for the other major spending departments, in order to make it clear that this decision to settle the Department of Health budget before the spending review and make it our top priority would have consequences for how much was available for their departments. She duly met with the education secretary Damian Hinds the next day and the defence secretary Gavin Williamson before the key cabinet meeting on 18 June.

The question was, who would agree the final figures with Simon Stevens? It wasn't enough for the prime minister or Jeremy to say the package was what the NHS needed; we needed Simon and other NHS leaders to say it. To put it bluntly, Philip didn't trust Jeremy to do it – in his mind, Jeremy was after every extra penny he could get. Equally bluntly, it didn't feel like a bilateral between Philip and Simon Stevens would be a meeting of like minds. My diary doesn't record whose idea it was, but someone suggested I should lead a three-person negotiating team with Philip and Jeremy. They both agreed, which suggested that they both thought I was on their side.

We spent 15 June negotiating with Simon, who drove a hard bargain – as NHS staff would have expected. He wanted to frontload some of the money; we wanted a more flat profile, because we feared that if we agreed to frontloading, we would ultimately be forced to agree to extra money in the latter years. After arguments about what was a realistic productivity target, how to deal with the uncertainty around the NHS drugs bill and whether some extra funding for pay was a one-off or should be built into the budget, we eventually agreed that the NHS budget would grow by an average of 3.4 per cent in real terms each year for the next five years, not including funding to cover a pension pressure. By 2023–24, we would be spending £20.5 billion more on our NHS after inflation – about £394 million extra a week, or slightly more than the figure Vote Leave had put on the side of their bus.

At the cabinet meeting where the plan was signed off, Jeremy generously paid tribute to my work in getting him, Simon Stevens and Philip on the same page, saying that if the government ever needed someone to negotiate the Middle East peace process, he knew who to ask. Philip observed, 'it's an extraordinary thing the Treasury are doing,' and he was right. He may have been reluctant initially, but he deserves a share of plaudits for putting the NHS's finances back on a stable footing.

If the long-term plan was an example of successful brokering, I took a different approach in the run-up to the 2018 Conservative Party conference. Towards the end of the summer recess, Will Macfarlane and I attended a meeting at the Treasury to review the state of the public finances. It became clear that officials were expecting the next economic forecast by the independent Office for Budget Responsibility to significantly upgrade the public finances, and I spotted that this would provide the opportunity to end the austerity the country had been enduring since the global financial crisis at the next spending review. This felt like an announcement the prime minister could make in her conference speech.

A few weeks later, Will confirmed to the prime minister that the OBR were projecting a massive £70 billion improvement. Having worked hard to improve relations between the prime minister and her chancellor, my usual instinct was to keep him in the loop, but on this occasion I agreed that we should not tell him until we were in Birmingham. I warned the prime minister that it would damage our relationship with him, but said that telling him weeks in advance would mean endless arguments over the text, with the addition of so many caveats that it lost its political impact. At this point we were fighting for our political lives, trying to sell the Chequers proposals to a hostile EU and Conservative Party, and we needed a bold speech that lifted the prime minister's standing.

In the end, we shared the speech with Philip at the last minute. He was predictably furious, not just about the 'end of austerity' line, but about two policy announcements that hadn't been cleared, one confirming that fuel duty would be frozen in this year's budget and the other abolishing the cap on how much local councils could borrow to build new homes. He asked how I could possibly have included the line about the end of austerity without being briefed by his team, at which point I unwisely mentioned that I had met with some of them. That just made things worse – he was now furious both with me and with his officials, for meeting with me without telling him. He told Theresa he could live with removing the cap on council borrowing, but not the fuel duty announcement – she would be taking one of the good news announcements from the Budget, which would make his job even harder. He was entitled to be angry, both about not being shown the text earlier and the two policy announcements, but signalling an end to austerity was good politics and we'd had enough of him blocking announcements. Once he had calmed down, he suggested some changes to the language that we could accept, the key one being that ending austerity would be conditional on securing a Brexit deal.

When we got back to London, I was definitely on the naughty step, along with the rest of the Number 10 political team. Philip was still just about talking to me, but he wouldn't let Robbie see the budget in advance – I had to leak him the papers so he could do his job. I felt guilty about how we had behaved, but not about our political judgement. Philip could see from the very positive coverage that the speech received that it was the right message, and it was one that he adopted in his budget a month later.

The prime minister had a pre-meeting with Philip about the budget on 9 October and went out of her way to thank him 'for his forbearance at conference'. The main issue we lobbied him on was an increase of work allowances in universal credit, effectively a tax cut for the low-paid – after we'd included most of what we wanted in the prime minister's conference speech, it would have felt like adding insult to injury if we'd asked for much more.

This budget was Philip Hammond's finest hour. The OBR windfall allowed him to meet his fiscal rules three years early while signalling that austerity was coming to an end, increasing the personal allowance and higher rate income tax threshold and making our requested increase to work allowances in universal credit. He even said, 'sound public finances are essential, but they are not an end in themselves'. He made a start on important long-term tax reforms, announcing a digital sales tax and a tax on plastic packaging. And he struck the right tone on Brexit, pleasing Brexiteers by providing more funding to prepare for no deal, while reminding them that a deal would both boost economic growth and allow him to release his fiscal reserve. And there was a gentle telling off for me:

Every chancellor likes to have a rabbit or two in his hat as he approaches a budget, but this year, some of my star bunnies appear to have escaped just a little bit early.

The negotiations concerning the NHS long-term plan had a post-script. On 26 October, Simon Stevens called me to say that the scale of the planned budget announcements had made the OBR adjust their prediction of inflation, which meant the NHS needed more money for our average annual increase of 3.4 per cent after inflation to be true. The Treasury were furious, but the deal we had done was based on real-terms increases rather than cash figures, so they had no choice but to give in.

Sadly, the final phase of Theresa's relationship with her chancellor was not a happy one. Once she had announced that she was going to stand down as party leader, she was determined to get as much as possible done in her last two months. Philip, however, was more interested in leaving the public finances in the best possible state and blocked a key announcement on education funding. That said, for most of my two and a bit years, this relationship was in a better state than it had been when I arrived, and I like to think I played a small role in that.

A frustrated foreign secretary

If Theresa's most important working relationship was with the chancellor, the next most important was with her foreign secretary, Boris Johnson.

At the time of my appointment, I was closer to Boris than I was to Philip. As mayor of London, he had regularly come to Croydon to campaign for me (we produced an election poster with him posing, Lord Kitchener-style, with the slogan 'Croydon needs Barwell'). I knew him well, liked him and owed him for his support.

But when I was appointed chief of staff, things became much more difficult. His relationship with the prime minister wasn't good, and whereas I was able to improve things with Philip, this relationship got steadily worse. There were a number of reasons. The prime minister was frustrated with him because he was gaffe-prone and not on top of his brief. He was frustrated with her because he felt excluded from decision-making on Brexit and was worried that it was taking too long to reach a collective view about what we wanted. While I had some sympathy with the latter view, he was one of the main barriers to a consensus. He was less flexible than long-term Brexiteers like Liam Fox and Chris Grayling; they were prepared to compromise in order to get Brexit done, but he had concluded that it wasn't worth doing at all unless you broke all ties and achieved complete autonomy. I found this absolutism very hard to square with the mayor of London I'd known.

The problem was compounded by Boris's refusal to grapple with the policy detail. It was obvious that the kind of future relationship he wanted – a free trade agreement with the EU similar to the one Canada had recently negotiated – suffered from two fatal flaws. First, it wasn't on the table. The EU would be happy to have that kind of relationship with Great Britain – indeed, they would prefer it to Theresa's more ambitious ask – but they were insistent on special arrangements for Northern Ireland that would create a partial border within our own country. And if by some chance they backed down and agreed to a Canada-style agreement for the whole of the UK, it would mean a border between Ireland and Northern Ireland – with all the potential implications for the peace process – just as there is a customs and regulatory border between Canada and the EU.

Boris had no answer to either of these points, so simply refused to acknowledge the problem. The prime minister and I were being defeatist. If Canada could have that kind of relationship with the EU, why couldn't we? All this talk of Northern Ireland was a smokescreen, an attempt to keep us aligned with the EU – modern technology would avoid the need for checks when goods crossed the border. This latter point was a common canard. It may be that in the future, technology will obviate the need for border checks, but Boris couldn't produce a single example of where it was currently happening. Furthermore, suggesting that technology was the answer showed a misunderstanding of the problem. Even if it were possible to avoid the need for physical infrastructure at the border, nationalists would object to having to complete customs declarations and get regulatory approval to move goods within the island of Ireland, just as unionists would object to having to do so to move goods within the United Kingdom. When you pointed out these facts to him, he would become exasperated. It didn't surprise me when, in June 2018, he was reported to have said 'fuck business' in response to business leaders' concerns that a hard Brexit would damage the economy. At the time of writing, the Westminster village is engrossed in a row about whether, in the autumn of 2020, he said, 'No more fucking lockdowns – let the bodies pile up in their thousands.' My experience of Boris is that this is exactly the kind of thing he would say if he was exasperated by the advice he was being given. It doesn't mean that he is anti-business or that he wouldn't order another lockdown – it's merely a sign of his frustration at what he is being told.

Some of these discussions with Boris got quite heated. On one occasion, he blurted out, 'You don't like Brexit because you blame it and me for losing your seat.' I was taken aback. It was true that I hadn't wanted the UK to leave the EU, but whatever my personal views, I accepted our obligation to implement the will of the people. Brexit had been a factor in me losing Croydon Central, but it had been less important than the disastrous national campaign, Labour's success in aligning the anti-Conservative vote behind them and underlying demographic change. And while I was disappointed that Boris had chosen to back Leave, I certainly didn't blame him for me losing. During my seven years as an MP, he had done more than any other prominent member of the Conservative Party to support me, and I remain grateful for his help. I made these points to him. I was angry, but it wasn't to do with what he had done in the referendum; it was about him trying to pretend the thorny issues it had thrown up in Northern Ireland didn't exist.

A few weeks later, a letter from Boris to the prime minister, in which he said it would be 'wrong to see the government's task as maintaining no border' and that we should focus on making sure the border did not become 'significantly harder', leaked. On 4 March, a 'key ally' of Boris accused me of having leaked it (I hadn't – revealing that the foreign secretary didn't want us to abide by what we had agreed with the EU a few months before would hardly help the prime minister's cause). I was more concerned that Boris had clearly told other people his story about me blaming him and Brexit for the loss of my seat, because the 'key ally' told journalists that was my motivation for leaking the letter.

The final cause of friction in my relationship with Boris was his repeated habit of briefing the press in ways that were contrary to government policy. On 29 September 2017, just before Conservative Party conference, he gave an interview to *The Sun* in which he set his own four red lines over Brexit. On 15 January 2018, he gave an interview to the *Guardian* in which he said he had sympathy with the case for a royal commission on NHS funding and social care. A week later, he informed the media that he was going to tell his cabinet colleagues that the experts were agreed on the need for an urgent financial boost for the NHS. This story exemplifies what was so frustrating about him. The case he was making was a good one. He didn't know it, but we had already decided to give the NHS a big increase in funding. But the way in which he was doing it was discourteous to his colleagues (who were furious and said so to his face) and ill-disciplined – if we were going to make a strategic change, we should agree it privately and try to catch the media and opposition by surprise, not tell everyone in advance. Government couldn't function if everyone behaved like that, but he didn't appear to believe that the rules should apply to him.

A man of deep contradictions

The prime minister's third key relationship was with her secretary of state for exiting the European Union, David Davis. On a personal level, I would say that in the first half of her premiership, she was closer to David than to any of her senior ministers. As time went on, differences emerged between them over what kind of future relationship they wanted with the EU, but the prime minister wanted to keep David on board – and I think he had a strong loyalty to her.

The main source of friction between them was institutional. The prime minister had decided to set up a Department for Exiting the European Union rather than running the negotiations from the Cabinet Office, as David Cameron had with his renegotiation of the terms of the UK's membership, but the reality was that she was responsible for Brexit. David was Michel Barnier's opposite number in the negotiations, but the discussions at key moments were between the prime minister, the heads of government of the member states and the presidents of the European Commission and Council. And even outside this context, Brexit was too big an issue to delegate to a secretary of state. This tension was compounded by the fact that Olly Robbins, the permanent secretary of David's department, was also the prime minister's EU sherpa. Olly saw the prime minister as his boss, which frustrated David. Things got a little easier when we separated his roles and appointed a new permanent secretary at DExEU, but it didn't solve the problem completely. In January 2018, he had to be talked out of resigning when he discovered that he had inadvertently misled parliament by saying there had been no economic analysis of different possible future relationships – he hadn't been copied in on analysis that was sent to the prime minister.

I have a soft spot for David for a number of reasons. He lived in Croydon for a while, so we have something in common. He wasn't born with a silver spoon in his mouth and had worked hard to get to the top. And although he had a reputation as a hardman – in part because of his service in the SAS reserve – he's actually a very emotional man, as anyone who has heard him talk about his grand-daughter, who suffers from an incurable genetic condition, will know. I thought he had a legitimate complaint about the way the civil service tended to bypass him, and I should have tried harder to address it. But most of all, whereas Boris wasn't prepared to acknowledge the policy detail, David was – at least privately.

Some of the officials he worked with would probably be surprised to hear me say that. He was certainly capable of asserting that it was all very simple, but I think he was privately wrestling with the fact that he knew what kind of Brexit he wanted but couldn't see a way to get it – he once told me that the job was stretching him to his limits. He was a man of deep contradictions – he resigned from the cabinet over the Chequers proposals, but was one of the first senior Brexiteer backbenchers to support the prime minister's deal.

Thawing a deep freeze

It wasn't just with cabinet ministers that I acted as a go between. Relations between the prime minister and George Osborne had been in the deep freeze (almost literally – he was said to have told colleagues at the *Evening Standard* that he would not rest until she was 'chopped up in bags in my freezer') since she had sacked him as chancellor.

It was clearly unhelpful to have George using his platform as *Evening Standard* editor to knock lumps out of the prime minister, but it also felt wrong that relations between two people who had worked together at the top of government for over six years were in such a poor state. Without being told to do so by the prime minister, I took it on myself to reach out to George. He was keen for a rapprochement, so we met for lunch away from Westminster on 19 February 2018.

During this lunch, three things rapidly became clear. First, he regretted his freezer comment, which had crossed the line between an expression of legitimate differences on policy into personal unpleas-antness. Second, he had a higher regard for the prime minister than his recent public comments implied – he said that after David Cam-eron and William Hague, he had considered her his most formidable cabinet colleague during the Cameron government. But third, he was *very* angry with her. It wasn't just that he had been sacked – he understood that as the strongest cheerleader for Remain during the referendum campaign, it was impossible for him to continue as chancellor when Leave won – but the way it had been done. He said Theresa had told him to go away and get to know the Conservative Party better. Having spent his life working for the party, he hadn't taken this well, but her aides had then briefed the media on this con-versation, which he felt was intended to humiliate him. Although he had criticisms of how she had handled Brexit, behind his attacks was a deep anger concerning her treatment of him.

It was a classic example of how politics is at least as much to do with personal relationships as policies or strategy. Theresa and George are not poles apart ideologically, but they are very different in terms of background and temperament. They were never going to be soul-mates, but cordial respect was not too much to ask for. I don't believe for one minute that Theresa meant to humiliate George. I think she correctly judged that he couldn't stay as chancellor and happened to phrase her explanation in a way that riled him. Had I been chief of staff at the time, I would have smoothed it out – and what she'd told him would not have been briefed to the media, which is what really caused the offence.

After I arranged for Theresa and George to have a clear-the-air chat, relations went from very bad to cool – significant progress. When she announced that she was standing down as leader of the Conservative Party, she listed some of the achievements she was most proud of. One of them – 'the deficit is almost eliminated, our national debt is falling and we are bringing an end to austerity' – included a hat tip to David Cameron and George. It was my suggestion that she refer to George as well as David, but she didn't take any persuading. Before I had got back to my desk, George had texted, asking me to thank her.

* * *

These four examples illustrate the importance of relationships in politics. When the chips are down, politicians depend on the support of their colleagues – they need to spend more time cultivating those relationships and less time with their ever-growing coterie of advisers.

CHAPTER 10

SHUFFLING THE PACK

If most prime ministers enjoy the perks of the job – weekends at Chequers and hosting receptions at Number 10 for causes they care about – reshuffling their government is something that nearly all of them come to hate.

No one enjoys sacking people, but it's not just that. Prime ministers know they can't win – it's a golden rule of reshuffles that they upset more people than they please. For starters, there are the people you sack. It's not like being sacked from a normal job – you can't go and get another job because you're still an MP, so you're in the same working environment as the person who has sacked you and the person who now has your job. Some people take it gracefully – in my time, Robert Goodwill was the classiest, telling the prime minister, 'I'll be with you in the [voting] lobby every time.' Others never forgive the prime minister. Then there are the backbenchers who think they should be running the country and are outraged that their talents have once again been ignored. And finally, some of the people you promote may be grumpy with you if they didn't get the job they wanted – while they might be happy to be a minister, they might not be interested in farming and now have to spend the next year or two pretending otherwise. Every time a prime minister reshuffles their government, the pool of people who have a grudge against them grows, bringing the end of their time in Downing Street closer.

When I was housing minister, everybody in the sector bemoaned the constant ministerial merry-go-round. A new minister would be appointed, they'd spend six months getting to know people and the subject area, they'd start to make a few changes and then they'd be promoted, moved sideways or sacked, and the cycle would start all over again. The result was constant tinkering when what people wanted was policy stability, and ministers never being given the time to develop subject expertise. So why do prime ministers reshuffle the pack so often? Do they really believe that changing one group of ministers most people have never heard of for another is going to transform their government's electoral prospects?

No, of course they don't. They reshuffle for two reasons. Sometimes, they are forced into it when a minister has a health problem, does something wrong or resigns on an issue of principle. If that minister is relatively senior, the prime minister may bring a former minister back into government to replace them, but it is more likely that they will promote or move an existing minister sideways, who then also has to be replaced. As a result, one departure can lead to a number of changes.

Every now and then, prime ministers will do a premeditated reshuffle. They do this partly to freshen up their government – some of the people they appointed will have turned out to be unsuited to their roles – and partly to keep the parliamentary party happy. A significant proportion of politicians become MPs because they want to be ministers. Most will deny it, but look how many MPs leave parliament once they have got as far as they think they are going to get in terms of a ministerial career. In my thirty years in politics, the time new MPs are prepared to wait before they begin to expect promotion has got shorter and shorter. So prime ministers can't win: when they do reshuffle, they upset more people than they please, and when they go too long without a reshuffle, backbenchers get grumpy.

Who to promote and who to sack?

In an ideal world, the most able people would be appointed to high office – all governments would resemble Abraham Lincoln's 'Team of Rivals', his cabinet that included several of his opponents for the Republican nomination, because he believed picking the most capable people was what mattered in a time of crisis. However, it's not that simple. For starters, British prime ministers are at a disadvantage compared to American presidents. President Biden can appoint who he wants to his cabinet, subject to confirmation by the Senate; although Boris Johnson can theoretically appoint anyone as a minister, in practice there is a convention that ministers must be members of the House of Commons or the House of Lords so that they can be accountable to parliament. And although Boris can appoint someone to the House of Lords and then make them a minister, there is a widespread view that cabinet ministers should be accountable to the democratically elected chamber of parliament; in practice, a prime minister has to find nearly all their cabinet from among their colleagues in the House of Commons. And as politics has become less attractive as a career, that talent pool has shrunk.

Even then, talent is not the only criteria. A prime minister has to reward at least some of the people who helped them get the top job, and they need some key allies around the cabinet table. On the other hand, cabinet needs to reflect the range of views within the parliamentary party – if it is drawn too narrowly from a particular wing of the party, the government may find that it is unable to get its legislation through parliament. You need to give thought to the mix of people you are appointing. What's the gender balance? Are there sufficient numbers from black and minority ethnic backgrounds? What's the geographical spread in terms of the constituencies represented? A Conservative prime minister needs to be wary of appointing too many MPs who were privately educated, particularly at the country's most prestigious schools, for fear of reinforcing some of the negative perceptions of the party. And on top of all that, Theresa also had to think about the Remain/Leave balance of her government. This became particularly tricky towards the end of her premiership, when a number of senior Leave MPs resigned from their ministerial positions.

The process

I was familiar with how reshuffles work from my time as a whip. A prime minister gets advice from three main sources: the chief whip, who will give their view of how effective ministers are in the chamber and whether they engage with backbench MPs; the Cabinet Secretary and the Number 10 political team. Robbie would say which ministers and backbenchers were good advocates for the government and willing to help out on a difficult news day; James would say which ministers the policy unit was impressed with and which backbench MPs were coming to them with policy ideas; Parky would indicate who Conservative Campaign Headquarters were impressed with. I was in a good position to give the prime minister advice – as a former MP and whip, I knew the parliamentary party well, and particularly the 2010 and 2015 intakes from which new members of the government were likely to be drawn (I had been a member of the 2010 intake and as a whip had overseen the induction of the 2015 intake).

The hardest part of a premeditated reshuffle is identifying who you are going to sack – if you want to bring people into government, you need some vacancies first. Sometimes a minister might indicate that they want to stand down for personal reasons, but most of the time you have to create vacancies. The starting point was a list of ministers who everyone agreed were not particularly strong. Occasionally, ministers might avoid the chop if the prime minister felt very loyal to them or if they were important to the government in terms of balance. In order to create enough vacancies, that list was normally supplemented by a few people who were doing a perfectly good job but who had been in government for a long time and were not likely to be promoted any higher.

At this point, Sue Gray or her successor Helen MacNamara from the propriety and ethics team in the Cabinet Office would produce a whiteboard that breaks the government down by department, with a magnetic name tag for each minister. You start by removing the people who are going to be sacked, so you can see where the vacancies are. You might have a list of people you are considering for promotion, but it's now a question of finding the right people for the vacancies. Some jobs require a lot of policy development work, some require mastery of a complex technical brief and some principally require good inter-personal and communication skills. Theresa would give us some initial steers and we would go back to her with a worked-up plan for her sign-off. However, just as the Prussian field marshal Helmuth von Moltke said 'No military plan survives contact with the enemy,' very few reshuffle plans survive contact with the people you are trying to shuffle.

On the day itself, the prime minister starts by seeing those ministers who are getting sacked. In recent years, prime ministers have held these meetings in their parliamentary office, so those losing their jobs don't have to walk up Downing Street to hear their fate in full view of the cameras. The soon-to-be ex-ministers know what's coming. Some of them try to make it easy for the prime minister, some try to bargain for something by way of compensation and a few try to change the prime minister's mind.

Once these awkward conversations are over, the prime minister heads back to Downing Street for what will hopefully be the easier part of the day. If all goes smoothly, it works rather like a conveyor belt. The Number 10 switchboard calls those the prime minister wants to promote or move and they begin to assemble in various waiting rooms. When the prime minister was ready to see someone, I liked to collect them from wherever they were waiting and take them to the Cabinet Room. It gave me a chance to get a sense of their frame of mind, temper their expectation if what was coming was a sideways move rather than a big promotion or, if they were new to government, begin to build a personal relationship with them. I would then sit in on the conversation. Assuming they accepted the job on offer, they would then have a brief conversation with the director general for propriety and ethics about the ministerial code if they were joining the government for the first time, before heading off to their new department with a smile and a few words for the assembled media outside Number 10.

A full reshuffle takes more than twenty-four hours, with the cabinet generally being done on the first day and junior ministers on the second. When we finally emerged at the end, the civil servants would present JoJo and I with one last task: agreeing the cabinet order of precedence (if two cabinet members meet, the junior one goes to the office of the senior one) and seating plan (the most senior cabinet minister sits opposite the prime minister, the next most senior sits to the prime minister's left and so on, with those sitting in the prime positions finding it easier to catch the prime minister's eye during cabinet meetings). This may sound trivial, but get it wrong and you have a major diplomatic incident on your hands. There are no hard and fast rules about the order of precedence, but it is based on some combination of length of service and seniority of position – which gave rise to questions about the seniority of a new department like DExEU compared to some of the established departments.

Replacing Michael Fallon

If the changes the prime minister made to her cabinet in June 2017 – creating a de facto deputy, bringing Michael Gove back into government and making Andrea Leadsom leader of the house – served her well, the next change she made did not.

Michael Fallon resigned on 1 November 2017, having accepted that some of his conduct before he was appointed secretary of state for defence had fallen below the high standards that he expected of the armed forces. He was right to resign, but his departure was a big blow to the government – both David Cameron and Theresa had found him a competent minister and a powerful advocate for the government on broadcast media.

Having played a key role – alongside me – in persuading Michael to resign, the chief whip Gavin Williamson made it clear to the prime minister that he wanted to replace Michael – and that he would quit as chief whip if he wasn't given the job. He claimed to be burned out from years as David Cameron's parliamentary private secretary and then chief whip and wanted a policy role. I tried to convince Gavin that he was making a mistake – I wasn't sure secretary of state for defence was the right role for him, and it would look to his colleagues like he had given Michael the push in order to advance his own career. Wasn't there another cabinet role to which he was better suited? However, his heart was set on defence.

This put the prime minister in a difficult position. On the one hand, she could understand Gavin's desire to move to a policy role and he had run her leadership campaign and played a crucial role in securing her position after the 2017 election, so she owed him. On the other hand, she wasn't sure he had the experience to be secretary of state for defence, nor, given his organisational skills, did she want him to resign and cause trouble on the backbenches. In the end, pragmatism won out and she gave him the job – only to spend most of the next eighteen months regretting it. As chief whip, he had been a key ally in cabinet; as defence secretary, he quickly became one of the hardest voices on Brexit. If that was frustrating, more serious was his refusal to find savings in the MoD budget (he preferred to publicly berate Philip Hammond for not giving him more funding); the suspicion that he was a leaker (evidence of which ultimately led to his sacking in May 2019); his relationship with MoD officials; and, above all, his lack of gravitas, epitomised by his telling Russia to 'go away and shut up' after the Salisbury attack. Boris Johnson chose to bring him back as education secretary, and he has struggled in that role, too.

If Gavin's promotion was a mistake, Theresa's decision to replace him as chief whip with his deputy, Julian Smith, proved a better decision. Other than the prime minister, Julian had the hardest job in government over the next eighteen months. He went on to serve with distinction as Northern Ireland secretary in Boris Johnson's first government, helping to restore devolved government. I was very disappointed to see him sacked after achieving so much, and I hope he will be brought back at some point.

Replacing Priti Patel

A week later, the prime minister was forced to make another change to her cabinet, when Priti Patel resigned as international development secretary following revelations that she had met with Israeli politicians and officials without her own officials, and had not been open when the revelations came to light. Theresa replaced Priti with Penny Mordaunt, a talented middle-ranking minister who was in line for promotion and who was also a conviction Leaver, maintaining balance in cabinet. This proved a good appointment – Penny proved an effective international development secretary and later defence secretary. Much like Andrea Leadsom, though she was uncomfortable with elements of Theresa's Brexit deal, she was personally supportive.

The reshuffle that went wrong

The prime minister had to ask Damian Green to resign from the government on 20 December 2017, after an investigation found that he had breached the ministerial code. In addition, James Brokenshire had informed her that he had been diagnosed with lung cancer and needed to stand down as Northern Ireland secretary. These were two big losses – Damian was her deputy in all but name and James was one of the few cabinet ministers she was personally close to.

Having secured 'sufficient progress' in the Brexit negotiations, the prime minister was in a slightly stronger political position, so she decided to make other changes to her cabinet rather than simply filling these gaps. Some people in Number 10 would have loved her to replace Philip Hammond with a chancellor who was less fiscally conservative, more supportive of the industrial strategy and less prone to winding up the ERG, and others would have loved her to replace Boris Johnson with a foreign secretary who was more loyal and less gaffe-prone, but she judged that it would be impossible to sack one without sacking the other – and sacking both of them would be too destabilising. The aims of the reshuffle were therefore more modest: to move people in middle-ranking cabinet roles to jobs where they would be a better fit, to bring some fresh blood into cabinet and to bring some of the talented women from the 2015 intake into the junior ranks of the government, in order that the government looked more like the country it aspired to serve.

Chief among the problems Theresa wanted to solve were Jeremy Hunt at Health and Justine Greening at Education. Jeremy was a talented minister and passionate about improving patient safety, but the long-running dispute about junior doctors' pay had damaged his standing: in this crucial policy area, he was no longer the right person to make our case. He had told the prime minister after the 2017 election that he wanted a change, although he had more recently expressed nervousness about moving during the winter crisis. We needed to replace him with someone who could rebuild relations with NHS staff, and the prime minister settled on Greg Clark. He had shown an ability to win over key stakeholder groups as secretary of state for communities and local government and then as secretary of state for business. He would move to Health, with Jeremy taking his role as business secretary.

Justine had many admirable qualities. She represented a marginal seat and had a clearer sense than most of how the Conservative Party needed to change if it wanted to hold on to seats like hers, and she was a passionate advocate for social mobility and equality. However, she and the prime minister didn't see eye to eye on education policy. The prime minister wanted lower university fees and a school system with more free schools, more faith schools and more grammar schools. Justine wasn't keen on any of these things. Contrary to some media briefing, there was no question of sacking her, but we needed to move her to a department where she was better aligned with the prime minister. We knew that she didn't want to move, so thought hard about how we could make the offer as attractive as possible. Her passion was social mobility, so we settled on the Department for Work and Pensions. It was a similarly ranked job and would enable her to retain responsibility for the issue she cared most about.

Damian and James's departures provided two vacancies. The prime minister reluctantly decided to create a third by asking Patrick McLoughlin to stand down as party chairman. He had served in shadow cabinet and then cabinet for over twelve years under both David Cameron and Theresa, first as chief whip, then as secretary of state for transport and then as party chairman. He hadn't really wanted to leave Transport, but he had loyally done what he was asked and as party chairman shouldered some of the blame for the 2017 campaign, although he was not in any way responsible. It was the right decision to ask him to make way, but Theresa took no pleasure in doing it.

In terms of new blood, we settled on Damian Hinds, Matt Hancock and Esther McVey, and also invited Claire Perry, the minister for energy, to attend cabinet, squeezing one more chair around an already crowded table. I advocated strongly for Damian – I knew education was his passion, so he was an obvious replacement for Justine. Matt's career is a lesson on how to deal with adversity in politics. During the Cameron government, he was the golden boy of our intake, George

Osborne's protégé and mercilessly ribbed as such (in an after-dinner speech, the blunt-speaking MP Philip Davies joked that he dreamed of becoming part of David Cameron's Chipping Norton set and 'getting so far up George Osborne's arse that he could see Matt Hancock's feet'). When Theresa became prime minister, he was one of a number of cabinet ministers who were only offered junior ministerial jobs. Whereas some chose to return to the backbenches rather than be demoted and remain there to this day, Matt took the demotion, demonstrated his talent to his new boss and was now being rewarded for his perseverance. You could see how much it meant to him when he came out of the Cabinet Room after being appointed, as he clenched his fist and mouthed 'Yes!' Esther was an authentic northern voice, a good communicator and her presence gave the cabinet a better Remain/Leave balance. And Claire was a Duracell bunny of a politician – a bit abrasive sometimes, but full of energy and passion.

The only remaining question was who should get which jobs, starting with who should replace Damian as Theresa's deputy. We wanted someone who was not a future leadership contender (so it didn't look as if she was anointing a successor), whose loyalty we could rely on and who was respected by their colleagues. David Lidington was the obvious choice. The only downside was moving him from Justice, where he had begun to rebuild bridges with the legal profession, after just six months. David Gauke was a replacement of similar temperament, who would hopefully continue that work. Justine would hopefully take over from him, and Damian would come in at Education. Karen would take over from James at Northern Ireland and Matt would take over from her at Culture. Chris Grayling, who was struggling as transport secretary but was loyal and the ultimate party man, would become party chairman, Brandon Lewis would replace him at Transport and Esther would become minister for immigration. It felt like a solid plan: while not spectacular, it would freshen up cabinet and get round pegs in round holes.

The next morning, things started to go wrong almost straight away. I briefed the morning pre-meeting on what the prime minister was planning, but then, at the prime minister's morning meeting, JoJo argued for a rethink on who should be party chairman: she thought it would be better to leave Chris Grayling at Transport and make Brandon chairman. The prime minister accepted her advice, but unfortunately Iain Carter from CCHQ had heard the original plan and didn't wait for official confirmation before tweeting that Chris Grayling had been appointed party chairman as he saw him leaving Number 10. If the rest of the day had gone smoothly, this would have been quickly forgotten, but it was to be the first in a series of foul-ups.

The prime minister started by offering David Lidington the position of chancellor of the duchy of Lancaster. This was not quite as prestigious a title as first secretary of state, and I'm not sure whether David initially understood that he was being offered a big promotion. He asked if this would be a full cabinet role. The prime minister, sensing his confusion, confirmed that it would be the second most senior position in cabinet – he would sit opposite her in cabinet meetings. He left the Cabinet Room a happy man.

Next up was Jeremy Hunt, who said he would be happy to change in a few months' time, but could not leave Health at the height of the winter crisis. The prime minister responded that she hadn't chosen the timing of this reshuffle – it had been forced on her by Damian and James's resignations. She asked him to go away and reflect, but when he returned he was adamant that he would not accept any other role. As well as his concern about leaving during a crisis, I think his heart was set on being the longest-serving health secretary and the NHS's seventieth birthday later that year. She reluctantly gave in.

David Gauke seemed pleased with his move to Justice, and then the prime minister saw Justine. She was highly agitated following media speculation that she was going to be sacked, and was surprised to be offered DWP. She questioned why she was being moved and the prime minister was honest with her – she valued her contribution in cabinet, but they had different views on school reform. Justine replied that if she couldn't carry on at Education, she would rather leave the government. As with Jeremy, the prime minister asked her to go and have a chat with the chief whip.

At this point, Julian and I made a massive mistake. We spent a couple of hours trying to talk Justine round, when we should have advised the prime minister to press her for a decision. In the end, she choose to go anyway, but by then the day had descended into chaos. Justine's refusal to move to DWP meant we needed to change the plan. The prime minister decided to offer Esther that job because she had previous experience and to appoint Caroline Nokes as minister for immigration.

The next day we reshuffled the junior ministerial team, bringing, among others, Rishi Sunak, Oliver Dowden, Robert Jenrick, Suella Fernandes and Amanda Milling into government. Looking back, that was probably the most significant thing about this reshuffle. Presentationally, it had been a disaster, though the longer-term picture was more nuanced. David Lidington's appointment was a great decision – Theresa could not have asked for a more loyal and supportive deputy. Matt and Damian also proved to be effective and loyal secretaries of state. On the other side of the coin, Karen found Northern Ireland harder than Culture and Esther struggled at DWP. She had clearly been unsure when she was offered it, telling the prime minister she would be 'up for the challenge if that's what you think I'll be best at'. We had thought her previous experience in the department would make this a good first cabinet role for her, but she clearly hadn't enjoyed it first time around. The reshuffle may have solved some problems, but it didn't solve the issue with Jeremy at Health and it also created some new ones. Not our finest hour.

When I came to write this chapter, my diaries reminded me of something I'd forgotten: on the day of the reshuffle, the prime minister met not just with the cabinet ministers she was moving and the junior ministers she was appointing to the cabinet, but also with the ministers she was not moving. These conversations provide a fascinating insight into her relationships with her cabinet at the start of 2018.

Her relationship with Philip Hammond was at a high point, following her advocacy of an implementation period at Florence, a successful budget and the achievement of sufficient progress in the Brexit negotiations. He told her he believed that he would be comfortable with where she was trying to get to on Brexit, but he was worried that Boris felt the same way – and they couldn't both be right. The prime minister said she hoped there would be less blocking of things by the Treasury going forward, to which he replied that often the official advice he received was to block everything.

David Davis told her he had been hoping she would retire him. Boris Johnson was keen for more one-to-one time with her and lobbied for the NHS to get a Brexit dividend; the prime minister gently reminded him that this was a Vote Leave, not a government, pledge and that there were other pressures we had to consider alongside NHS spending. Sajid Javid asked for the name of his department to be changed from the Department of Communities and Local Government to the Ministry for Housing, Communities and Local Government and for the prime minister's personal mobile number. Both requests were granted, a sign that this was another relationship that was now in a better place. The prime minister told Gavin Williamson that he couldn't continue to make his case for more funding for the MoD through the newspapers. Gavin accepted that he wasn't completely blameless, but stressed that the leaks didn't all come from him – the MoD was a leaky colander. And finally, the prime minister lavished praise on Michael Gove for the work he was doing on the environment, farming and fishing, but encouraged him to work more through civil service channels.

Replacing Amber Rudd

The next change Theresa made to her cabinet was another enforced one: on 29 April, Amber Rudd came to see the prime minister at the height of the Windrush scandal, to tell her that she felt she had no choice but to resign as home secretary because she'd become aware that she'd misled parliament over whether there were targets for deportations. This was another huge blow: the prime minister trusted and rated Amber. Alongside Philip Hammond, she was the leading proponent in cabinet of a soft Brexit, so her departure risked upsetting the delicate balance that the prime minister had sought to maintain.

We drew up a long list of potential successors to discuss with the PM. Top of the list was Sajid Javid. He had already spoken out on Windrush and was clearly the person who would have the most credibility dealing with this issue. He was also a potential future leader of the Conservative Party and deserved to be tested in one of the three great offices of state, but appointing him would tilt the balance on EUXT(SN), the cabinet committee responsible for agreeing our strategy for the Brexit negotiations. When we spoke to the prime minister, she was nervous about appointing him – she cared deeply about the Home Office and wasn't sure they would see eye to eye on some of the key policies. She whittled the list down to him and three other possibilities: James Brokenshire (who had by now recovered from his operation), David Lidington and David Gauke.

It's fair to say that neither I, nor the chief whip nor any of the prime minister's other advisers were keen on these other options. As a former minister for immigration, it would be difficult for James to have responsibility for Windrush. David Lidington was doing an outstanding job, so we didn't want to move him. And David Gauke was facing criticism for the government's decision not to oppose a Parole Board decision to release the 'black cab rapist' John Worboys.

In the end, the prime minister bowed to these arguments. And while it soon became clear that we had been right about the pros of appointing Sajid, she had been right about the cons. His appointment was widely welcomed and over time he was able to diffuse the Windrush scandal, but his appointment upset the balance on the crucial EUXT(SN) committee. He also proceeded to try to undo some of the key reforms that she had made during her time as home secretary, in particular to stop and search. To her credit, I think she only said 'I told you so' once.

Sajid's appointment left a vacancy at the Ministry for Housing, Communities and Local Government, which allowed the prime minister to bring James Brokenshire back into government, albeit in a less senior position than she would have liked.

Replacing David Davis and Boris Johnson

The next resignations came after the crucial Chequers cabinet meeting that agreed what kind of relationship we wanted with the EU after we had left, with David Davis resigning on Sunday 8 July and Boris Johnson following the next day.

When it came to how to replace David at DExEU, the same arguments played out as after Amber's resignation – our unanimous advice to the prime minister was that she needed to appoint a prominent Leaver, with Dom Raab the leading candidate; the prime minister, however, was nervous about whether he really backed the compromise she was trying to land. Once again, she was persuaded to go with our advice, and on this occasion she was proved 100 per cent right. With the benefit of hindsight, I don't think Dom ever intended to see the job through. He took the promotion and resigned a few months later, having boosted his prospects in any future leadership election.

The prime minister decided to ask Jeremy Hunt to replace Boris

Johnson as foreign secretary, and this time Jeremy was happy to move. Matt Hancock replaced him at the Department of Health and Social Care, with the prime minister telling him that his twin priorities were to deliver the NHS long-term plan and produce a social care green paper. Matt observed that the latter was a tricky political challenge, and the prime minister acknowledged that she hadn't made it any easier with the 2017 manifesto. Matt has continued as health secretary in Boris Johnson's government, where he has been on the right side of the argument on the need for COVID-19 lockdowns and helped to oversee the successful vaccine rollout.

Jeremy Wright welcomed a move from attorney general to a political role as secretary of state for culture, media and sport, which allowed the prime minister to appoint Geoffrey Cox as attorney general. Geoffrey was one of the MPs I was responsible for as a whip. The whips' office had a negative view of him because he continued to practise as a barrister and sometimes missed votes as a result. I tried to give him more than the usual two weeks' notice of when key votes were likely to take place and we struck up a friendship. Most lawyers who become MPs are keener to concentrate on politics than on being pigeonholed as a law officer, but I knew that being attorney general was Geoffrey's ambition. He had auditioned for the job at a meeting of the parliamentary party that afternoon, speaking in support of the compromise the prime minister was trying to achieve, and when he heard that the prime minister wanted to see him, he literally ran to Downing Street. After she had offered him the job of his dreams, he told her she should lean on him in any way that she wished and could be assured of his total loyalty. He would play a crucial role in the remainder of this story.

Replacing Dom Raab
and Esther McVey

The next resignations came on 14 and 15 November, when Dom Raab and Esther McVey resigned after the cabinet meeting that agreed the Withdrawal Agreement. The decision on who should replace Esther was a simple one. Two weeks previously, a report by Alex Allan had concluded that Amber Rudd 'was not supported as she should have been' before, during and after her appearance before the home affairs select committee during which she had misled parliament. This opened the way for her to return to cabinet as secretary of state for work and pensions.

The decision about who to appoint as DExEU secretary was more difficult. Everyone was agreed that we couldn't afford to repeat the Dom Raab mistake – we had to be confident that whoever we appointed would last the course. The prime minister wanted Michael Gove to do it, but he was only willing to do so if she was prepared to reopen the backstop. Theresa knew from the hundreds of conversations she'd had with Juncker and Tusk and her fellow heads of government that this was a blind alley – aside from a Northern Ireland-only backstop that the government had already rejected, there was no other alternative. Some of the Number 10 team argued for Brandon Lewis, but appointing someone who had campaigned for Remain felt like an admission that we couldn't find a Leaver who was prepared to take the job. Some argued for Steve Barclay, a Leaver who was Matt's number two at the Department of Health, while others argued that the prime minister should be her own DExEU secretary to reflect the fact that she was leading the negotiations. Steve was a close friend, so I called him up and was honest about the situation: we wanted him to do the job, but we had to be sure he would back the deal through the difficult months ahead. He appreciated my candour and replied that although bits of the deal were clearly uncomfortable, he was prepared to do it. And over the remaining months of

Theresa's premiership, he was as good as his word, giving her candid advice in private and loyal support in public.

Replacing Gavin Williamson

Remarkably, the next six months saw one of the longest periods of cabinet stability of the May government, but this period of calm came to an end on 1 May 2019.

Details of a National Security Council meeting on 23 April that discussed Chinese telecom giant Huawei's involvement in the UK's 5G network were leaked to Steven Swinford, the deputy political editor of the *Daily Telegraph*. We had all become dulled to the regular leaking of cabinet meetings, but the NSC had been the one meeting which had not leaked – if the heads of the intelligence agencies couldn't speak with candour at these meetings, there was little point having them. The prime minister was livid and ordered an immediate inquiry. I was clear with special advisers that if the inquiry uncovered the source of the leak, the culprit would be sacked, however senior they were. It was an indication of how endemic the problem had become that this comment itself leaked.

The inquiry spoke to all the people who had either attended the NSC or had been told about the discussion before the story appeared online, and had accessed the phones of thirty-five of them. It concluded that there was 'compelling circumstantial evidence' that Gavin Williamson was responsible. First, Gavin admitted speaking to Steve after the meeting, though he denied being the source of the leak. Second, immediately after he had spoken to Gavin, Steve called James Slack, the prime minister's official spokesman, and the advisers of other ministers who had attended the meeting, asking them to confirm a detailed account of what had happened. Third, Gavin spoke to others after the meeting, who reported that he was highly agitated about the outcome of the meeting and that his account of it was very similar to the account in Steve's story. In addition, I had to speak to one of his special advisers, who also admitted to talking to Steve and was refusing to co-operate with the inquiry.

Gavin came to see me later that day. The gist of his defence was that Mark Sedwill had it in for him – he had warned Gavin when they'd clashed over another issue that he had 'a vindictive personality'. Gavin alleged that Mark had told an official-level NSC meeting that he was responsible, pre-judging the inquiry. Journalists were phoning him to tell him that Mark had it in for him. He had sent Mark an abusive text message the day after the leak because he had assumed it was a deliberate leak by officials, but when he sent a further text to apologise, the fact that he had apologised had been leaked to the *Daily Mail*.

Having set out why he felt he was being badly treated, Gavin moved on to threats. If we thought he was the kind of person who would take the blame for something he hadn't done, we were mis-judging his personality. And if the prime minister tried to get rid of him, there would be the world's biggest shitshow. The conversation ended with him attempting to blame someone else – he'd heard that Amber thought Sajid was responsible. I promised to pass all of this on to the prime minister; it didn't help his case.

After reflecting on the report of the leak inquiry overnight, she decided that she no longer had full confidence in him and had no choice but to ask him to leave the government. It had been a mis-take to appoint him secretary of state for defence but he had been an effective chief whip and was in large part responsible for hold-ing the government together after the 2017 election, so I suggested that she end her letter to him with some acknowledgement of those contributions.

The prime minister promoted Penny Mordaunt, a Royal Navy reservist, to be the first female secretary of state for defence, deserved recognition of her work at International Development, with Rory Stewart replacing her. For the few remaining weeks of the May gov-ernment, Rory proved to be an absolute star, as he would later be in the Conservative leadership election – we should have promoted him far sooner. He was the first politician to recognise the need for a COVID-19 lockdown in March 2020, and the Conservative Party is far poorer without him.

Covering for Claire Perry

In early May, Claire Perry came to tell the prime minister that she wanted to stand down as energy minister to care for a family member who was unwell. The prime minister offered her a leave of absence, with Chris Skidmore, the capable minister for universities, science, research and innovation, covering her role.

Replacing Andrea Leadsom

The final change to Theresa's cabinet came a few weeks later, when Andrea Leadsom finally reached her breaking point on Brexit. The prime minister appointed Mel Stride to serve as leader of the house for the last two months of her government, another good addition who, in hindsight, should have got his chance much earlier.

Postscript

Of the twenty-seven ministers who attended the first cabinet meeting after the 2017 election, just seventeen served continuously for the next two and a bit years, with eight leaving the government and two resigning but then returning. However, even this statistic gives too rosy an impression of the stability at the top of the government: of the six most important jobs, only Philip Hammond was an ever-present, and there were two changes at DExEU and Defence. This turbulence was unprecedented – George Osborne, Theresa and Oliver Letwin served as chancellor, home secretary and chancellor of the duchy of Lancaster for the whole of David Cameron's premiership.

It was partly down to Brexit, but the majority of the changes were the result of ministers making mistakes that led to them resigning or having to be sacked, examples of the bad luck of which Theresa had more than her fair share.

CHAPTER 11

MEDIA RELATIONS

Theresa wasn't very interested in communications. She understood that at significant moments – when we discovered a chemical weapon had been used on the streets of Salisbury or when she had agreed a Brexit deal with the EU, for example – the public expected to hear directly from her. But aside from those moments, she didn't think she should be spending much time talking to the media. Her job, as she saw it, was to make sure the government had the right priorities and the right policies to achieve them. She took the view that if she got these things right, the message would sell itself. Prime ministers shouldn't be wining and dining editors or giving interviews every other day – the job was about being on top of the detail and making the right decisions.

She was particularly sceptical about social media. She didn't use it herself, so she wasn't aware of its power. And if she didn't think prime ministers should be giving interviews every other day, she certainly didn't think they should be tweeting about the latest England football match.

Part of me admired her for this. I would certainly prefer a prime minister who was focused on getting the decisions right to one who was more interested in photo opportunities, who was on social media all the time or so thin-skinned they would phone up the editor every time a newspaper said something uncomplimentary about them. But it wasn't an either/or choice. Yes, having the right priorities and getting the decisions right were the most important things, but she also needed to communicate what the government was doing, both via traditional media and directly to voters via social media. Like it or not, it was part of the job. There was also a political imperative. During the election campaign, she had been uncomfortable with what she was being asked to do, and it showed in her media performances, plus Labour had completely out-campaigned us on social media. If she wanted to lead the Conservative Party into the next election, she had to demonstrate to the parliamentary party that she could lead a national campaign, online and in traditional media.

We hired Mario Creatura, who had worked on my communications when I was an MP, to work with the civil servants who managed the Number 10 social media accounts. At first, the prime minister was hesitant. To win her over, we set some ground rules: no commenting on trivia, and focus on causes with which she was already associated. We also agreed that any tweet had to be approved by JoJo. Mario and the team found that a bit frustrating, but I think this was the right approach. It meant there wasn't any sudden transformation, going from not tweeting at all to suddenly commenting on everything, and it ensured that her accounts were authentic. We had a breakthrough when the prime minister agreed to a light-hearted, self-deprecating tweet after her disastrous conference speech in October 2017 and it got a warm reception. It is testament to the work of Mario and the team that she has continued to use social media since leaving Number 10.

When it came to broadcast interviews, my role was to support Robbie when he sought to persuade the prime minister to do them, and to help brief her. There are three interviews that stand out in my memory. One is her first major interview after the election, with Emma Barnett on BBC 5 Live in July 2017. Emma had interviewed me during the election campaign about housing policy and I had been very impressed. She had started off with some soft questions about my kids and then, when she had lulled me into a false sense of security, she hit me with the zinger: 'And how old do you think they'll be before they have any chance of owning their own home in the area where they've grown up?' But if the interview had been challenging, I also came away thinking it had been very fair. The longer format had allowed her to cover a lot of ground and me to set out my case. So when we were discussing who the prime minister's first post-election interview should be with, I suggested her name. I think Robbie felt that the prime minister might be more comfortable doing this than the usual *Andrew Marr Show* or *Today* programme.

It was obvious that this first interview would focus on the election campaign – how the prime minister had felt when she heard the results and what lessons she had learned from it. This wouldn't be easy territory for her because the wounds were still raw, but we encouraged her to open up and talk about how she had felt.

For reasons I can't remember, we did the interview in the prime minister's office. To allow Emma and her team time to set up, we moved the prime minister's morning meeting to another room and then she came down to join Emma. Just before they were due to start recording, Emma attempted some small talk, saying that it was good of the prime minister to let them use her office for the interview. 'Yes it was,' the prime minister replied. So much for small talk!

At the start of the interview, Emma said she was delighted to be hosting the prime minister's first interview since the election, to which Theresa replied that she was very pleased to be joining her. While I don't think that was altogether true, the interview was a success. We'd wanted the prime minister to show a bit more of herself, and the main headline from it was the story she told of Philip watching the exit poll for her, telling her the devastating numbers and giving her a hug. Emma asked her if she'd shed a little tear. Watching it back, you can tell that the prime minister didn't really want to answer that question, but yes, she said, she had.

The other two interviews that stand out in my mind were with Andrew Marr. The first one was at the 2017 conference and he pressed her on an announcement we were making that week on student finance. When she was initially reluctant to describe it as a U-turn, he played footage of the 'nothing has changed' moment from the election campaign that I'd discussed with her on the day she appointed me. 'Again, you're saying nothing has changed,' he claimed. 'On student fees we have made a change, I've said that,' she quickly replied, avoiding the trap he had set for her and showing that she'd learned from the election campaign. The second interview was in June 2018. We had agreed to do it because we wanted to talk about the long-term financial settlement for the NHS. However, on the morning of the interview, the Treasury were still wrangling over the figures. We only got the key figure – how much extra money the NHS would get per week above inflation – to her a few minutes before the interview started, but she somehow delivered her best performance in the time I worked for her.

Although she got better at doing these set-piece interviews, I suspect that if you asked her, Theresa would say she never really enjoyed doing them. They are gladiatorial in nature, with the interviewer trying to get a 'gotcha' moment where their guest is unable to give a convincing answer. They do this either by focusing in detail on an issue that their guest might not be expecting; by quoting one of their guest's colleagues who has said something they don't agree with but don't want to publicly disagree with, either; or by asking their guest to speculate on what the government might do if, for example, it loses a key vote (questions that are often impossible to answer, because the government hasn't decided yet what it will do).

Journalists are entitled to ask politicians whatever they like, but now that I'm just an ordinary viewer, I hope they won't mind me observing that I'm not sure these attempts at a 'gotcha' moment are in the best interests of their audience. The person who I thought was best at interviewing Theresa May – and by that I mean the most successful at getting her engaged in a conversation – was Nick Ferrari. He didn't ask these 'gotcha' questions, didn't interrupt her all the time and, as a result, I suspect his audience learned a lot more about what Theresa was trying to do, and why.

One of Theresa's biggest frustrations with the media was the interviews during foreign trips. She would fly halfway around the world for an important meeting, and the communications team would always ask her to do a series of interviews. However, they would inevitably ignore the purpose of her visit and just ask about the latest Brexit goings-on back home.

Spin doctoring

I generally left the job of briefing the media to Robbie, the prime minister's press secretary Paul Harrison, her official spokesman James Slack and their team. There were three occasions when James invited me to join him for a 'huddle' where he would answer questions from 'the lobby', and all three were Brexit-related. The first was in Florence immediately after the prime minister's speech in September 2017. It was one of the most terrifying twenty minutes of my life and left me with a much higher regard for what James and Paul had to do every day. We were completely surrounded and everyone started asking questions at once. They had immediately identified the key sections of the speech that we'd carefully drafted to hint at things we were not yet ready to say explicitly. 'What does that phrase mean?' I didn't think James would appreciate me giving the honest answer: 'It could be taken to mean different things to different people, which is why we chose it.' I managed to avoid any major faux pas and was relieved when James announced that we had to go. The second occasion was after the Mansion House speech in March 2018. I was better prepared for what was to come, and it was an easier speech to brief on because its message was more explicit. The final occasion was after we agreed the Withdrawal Agreement. That was another tough one, because the lobby zeroed in on the one thing that was still up in the air – how long the implementation period would last. The government hadn't yet decided, so the question was impossible to answer – if I ruled out a long extension, Philip Hammond and co would be upset, and if I failed to do so, the Brexiteers would be.

As well as these three occasions with James, Robbie occasionally asked me to do background briefings for journalists. These were generally more sedate affairs, with Robbie in the chair and questions being asked one at a time. And very occasionally, I would call particular journalists if there was a message I wanted to get across. I tried to do it as little as possible, because the more you do it, the more journalists will come to you. Without realising, you will undermine the authority of those in Number 10 whose job it is to speak for the PM.

Front of house

The White House chief of staff is a public figure, who regularly gives broadcast interviews. In the UK, political advisers are prevented from doing this under the terms of their contract. However, in the last few days of her premiership, the prime minister allowed me to record an interview with Nick Robinson for a documentary he was producing about Brexit and to be interviewed on the *Today* programme on the morning of her last day in Number 10. Having previously served as a minister, I would have been happy to do more of this, but there is a risk in an adviser becoming a public figure. It is noteworthy that the Johnson government flirted with the idea of the prime minister's official spokesman giving on-camera briefings, before backing away from the idea.

Leaking like a sieve

All governments leak. If you are making a big announcement – not in terms of its newsworthiness, but in terms of its scale – lots of people within government will know at least some of the details. SW1 is a bubble containing a few thousand politicians, spin doctors, senior civil servants, lobbyists and journalists all working within a few hundred metres of each other, eating in the same restaurants and drinking in the same bars. If more than a handful of people know something, it will leak.

Sometimes, leaks happen by accident. Someone might send an email to the wrong address, be overheard saying something on the phone, leave their papers somewhere or say more than they should when talking to a journalist. I was always nervous about doing the latter because I found it hard to keep track of which of the 101 things that had recently crossed my desk were still with the prime minister, which she had signed off but had not yet been agreed by other ministers, which had been collectively agreed but not announced and which were in the public domain. Then there are leaks that are deliberate, but not malicious. The leaker isn't trying to use the media to fight a battle within government – they're just feeding scraps to a journalist in the hope that they will think better of them. Finally, there are leaks that are both deliberate and malicious. They're intended to portray the leaker – or the leaker's boss – in a good light, to denigrate a colleague or to kill off a particular policy that is being considered by provoking a strong public reaction against it.

Although some leaks are inevitable, leaking became endemic in the May government. As the Brexit debate became more polarised, ministers and their advisers stopped thinking of themselves as a team and instead started trying to win the argument by waging it in the media rather than around the cabinet table.

If you work in government, leaks are extremely irritating at best and incredibly damaging at worst. Some are relatively harmless – they might, for example, release information that was going to be announced a few days later – but even those are infuriating if you're trying to organise the government's communications. However, some are politically damaging to the government and a few are damaging to the national interest. The leak of draft economic analysis of potential future relationships with the EU, which showed that they were all worse than remaining a member, nearly caused the resignation of David Davis at the end of January 2018. A month later, the leak of a letter from Boris Johnson to the prime minister suggesting that we row back on the commitments we had made in the joint report regarding Northern Ireland enraged the EU, and the Irish government in particular. I had to phone Brian Murphy, my opposite number in Dublin, to reassure him that the prime minister had no intention of doing any such thing. Although he was grateful for the reassurance, the leak reinforced the EU's fear that there were people in the Conservative Party who couldn't be trusted to abide by general political commitments to avoid a hard border and that they should include detailed legal commitments in any withdrawal agreement. And the leak of a number of diptels from our ambassador in Washington, Kim Darroch, which – to put it mildly – were unflattering about President Trump and his administration, led to the president ordering that no one in the administration have anything to do with Kim, forcing him to resign and damaging UK–US relations.

Having been a whip and then housing minister, I knew that junior ministers rarely have any contact with the prime minister and don't get a chance to take part in collective discussion of policy, yet they are expected to toe the line and have to do most of the grunt work. So whenever we had a major announcement – a budget or a big Brexit speech – I tried to give them a briefing either just beforehand or immediately afterwards. Sadly, as things became more polarised, even these meetings started to leak.

But the worst aspect was the routine leaking of cabinet meetings. In July 2018, someone leaked the minutes of the crucial Chequers cabinet meeting to *The Times*. In October, *The Times* got hold of a detailed account of a key cabinet meeting and a copy of a paper that had been presented to cabinet. In February 2019, a submission to the prime minister that was only copied to four other ministers and fifteen civil servants and political advisers, all of them members of the prime minister's inner circle, nonetheless leaked to the *Telegraph*. Things got so bad that we confiscated ministers' mobile phones before they went into meetings.

This behaviour had three negative consequences. First, it meant that cabinet ministers couldn't speak freely in meetings. Second, the prime minister increasingly only consulted full cabinet on sensitive matters when she absolutely had to, relying instead on a smaller inner cabinet that didn't leak. And third, I started to further restrict who could attend meetings and receive submissions. All three things made for worse government.

It may surprise you to learn that there are often quite significant differences of view on policy within a government. Everybody has to defend a decision once it is made, but it's important that there is a robust debate prior to that. The endemic leaking obstructed those debates, and it was demoralising for those people who had not been responsible for the leaks but found themselves excluded from key meetings.

Things reached a nadir when a meeting of the National Security Council leaked. How could intelligence and security officials present highly sensitive information to ministers if they could not be confident that it would remain private? The prime minister ordered a leak inquiry; this was the one occasion on which we were able to find compelling evidence suggesting who was responsible, leading to the sacking of Gavin Williamson. There was one other occasion when we found out who was responsible for a leak. A whistleblower told me they had seen the name of a journalist on a minister's mobile phone screen before the minister took a call and then overheard them briefing the journalist on what had been said in cabinet. The prime minister would have fired them, but the whistleblower got cold feet and without a witness who would testify to what the minister had done, Theresa didn't feel she could take action.

Don't believe the hype

I'll end this chapter with a depressing lesson I learned during my time in Number 10. When you're in meetings where big decisions are made and have access to secret intelligence briefings, you have a privileged insight into what is happening in the world. And you quickly realise how much of what passes for 'news', particularly in the print media, isn't entirely true. Most of the time it's broadly right, but with some errors on points of detail. Sometimes there's a grain of truth, but the overall presentation is misleading. And sometimes it's plain wrong. Now that I'm on the outside, it has left me pretty sceptical about what I read. And if this is how political journalism works, why would sports or business journalism be any different?

Before I give some examples from my time in Number 10, let me give a more recent one. I now run my own business, advising clients on trends in politics, and over the last year, much of my focus has been on the COVID-19 pandemic. How would it develop over time? How long would we stay in lockdown? How long would the government maintain support for businesses that were unable to trade normally? In January, the prime minister said that on 22 February he would publish a roadmap setting out the route out of lockdown. In the weeks leading up to that date, the media was full of contradictory stories of what it was going to say. A few turned out to be spot on, some were partially right and some were miles off. My point is, a lot of what you read in the papers is informed speculation rather than news, and this culture of informed speculation has serious consequences. Because major announcements have usually been partially leaked beforehand, either unintentionally or deliberately to secure positive press coverage, there's often not much coverage of the detail the next day – by then it's old news. Call me old-fashioned, but that doesn't strike me as the best way to debate complex issues.

I don't blame journalists for this state of affairs. They have an important job to do, one that is becoming increasingly difficult, as politicians seek to avoid difficult questions and newspapers' budgets are squeezed due to falling circulations. In an increasingly tough market, the competition to be first with a scoop is fierce.

The errors occur in a number of ways. It's often not the people who are in a meeting who talk to a journalist – although Jeremy Heywood did once tell me a story about a leak investigation ordered by an angry prime minister that concluded that the source of the leak had been the prime minister himself. Rather, someone who was in the room will go back to their department and give their team a partial account of what was said. Then one of their team might speak to a journalist or mention it in passing to a friend over a few drinks, who then speaks to a journalist. As the story gets passed along, key details get missed or misremembered, and the result is a story that is basically true but with some inaccurate details. Sometimes the person who briefs the journalist is out of date. They were in the room for the original discussion, but there was a further meeting that they weren't in and the decision was changed. Sometimes the government deliberately leaks a bit of a document and you get a story that is true, but an inaccurate representation of the announcement as a whole. And sometimes you get a malicious briefing.

As the Brexit debate became more polarised, I was on the end of a fair bit of the latter. Sometimes, someone would take something with a grain of truth and give it a malicious spin; occasionally they would just make something up. The most common briefing against me was that I was in favour of the UK staying in the customs union. I thought there was probably a majority in the House of Commons in favour of that, but I didn't want it to happen – it would probably mean the end of the government.

Another common criticism was that I was in favour of a second referendum. On 17 December 2018, the MP Chris Green at least had the integrity to openly brief the papers to this effect, rather than doing so anonymously. I had certainly told the prime minister that the only surefire way I could see of getting her deal through would be to put it to a second referendum, but I didn't want one myself. The first one had been deeply divisive and I feared a second one would be much worse, while also undermining our argument against a second independence referendum in Scotland.

The worst example of a malicious briefing against me came in the *Sunday Times* on 27 January 2019. It reported:

Theresa May's husband has been dragged into a Downing Street civil war after urging the prime minister to keep fighting for her Brexit deal . . . Gavin Barwell, the Number 10 chief of staff, has accused him of thwarting a plan to get a cross-party deal for a customs union with the EU. Barwell said, in front of witnesses, that Philip May helped to 'scupper' attempts to reach out to Labour MPs. Accounts of his comments came from two reliable sources. One said: 'Philip May was flamed by Barwell for scuppering the outreach to Labour.' Another said he 'took a pop at Philip May'.

To this day, I don't know who these 'reliable sources' were, but the story was a complete fabrication, a deliberate attempt to undermine my relationship with the prime minister. Not only did I never criticise Philip, to this day I have no idea what his views were. Contrary to some recent nonsense in the media, Philip never attended policy meetings, and nor did the prime minister ever cite his views. I have no idea what private advice he gave to Theresa, only that – unlike the advice she got from many others – it would have had her best interests at heart.

CHAPTER 12

A TALE OF TWO
CONFERENCE SPEECHES

Each October, the Conservative Party gathers in Birmingham or Manchester for its annual conference. When I started going in the early 1990s, the main conference hall was the forum for debate about what direction the party should take. Today, the main sessions are increasingly stage-managed and the interesting discussion takes place in the fringe events, but the leader's speech on the Wednesday morning is still A Big Thing. And the two conference speeches I had a hand in were the cause of one of my most painful memories as chief of staff and one of my happiest.

We would start working on Theresa's speech in August. A lot of staff time went into it – in truth, a disproportionate amount, because conference speeches rarely shift public opinion. As I've written this chapter, I've tried to think of how many conference speeches from the period before I started working in politics I could remember, and only three came to mind: Margaret Thatcher's 'You turn if you want to. The lady's not for turning'; Neil Kinnock's attack on Militant – 'You end in the grotesque chaos of a Labour council, a *Labour council*, hiring taxis to scuttle round the city handing out redundancy notices to its own workers'; and another Kinnock line, probably the best exposition of the left's case I've ever heard: 'Why am I the first Kinnock in a thousand generations to be able to get to university? Why is my wife Glenys the first woman in her family in a thousand generations to be able to get to university? Was it because all our predecessors were thick? . . . Does anybody really think that they didn't get what we had because they didn't have the talent, or the strength, or the endurance, or the commitment?' I'm a political nerd, and if I can only recall three conference speeches, it's hardly surprising that they don't register with most voters.

Why, then, do party leaders put so much effort into them? The answer is that although they rarely shift public opinion, they influence how a leader is perceived by their MPs and activists and by the media. In a world that is increasingly dominated by soundbites and social media clips, they are the one time each year when a leader makes a detailed argument not just about a particular policy issue but about the country as a whole, as well as a critique of their opponents. They are, of course, a test of a leader's oratorical skills, but the real test is whether they have a compelling story to tell about who they are and what they stand for.

Manchester 2017: If anything can go wrong, it will . . .

Theresa needed to tell such a story in 2017. Her standing had been damaged by the disastrous election campaign, and conference was a chance for a reset. She wanted her speech to focus on her domestic agenda, which she was worried might be squeezed out by Brexit. We decided to give a major speech on Brexit shortly before conference, so that we could justify not covering it in such detail in Manchester.

The rationale was sound, but this meant she would be giving five major speeches in less than three weeks. And with an EU digital summit in Tallinn on 28 and 29 September and a visit to Canada and the United States also in her schedule, there was going to be a lot of foreign travel during this period, too.

This workload had two consequences. First, it meant we needed some help. My initial focus had to be on the Brexit speech she was giving in Florence, so we asked Chris Wilkins, who had left Number

10 in July, whether he would do some consultancy work for us and hold the pen for the conference speech. The second consequence was that the prime minister turned up at conference with a cold and a strained voice.

At this point, I should have insisted that she cancel most of her engagements and focus on the speech and a couple of key media interviews. However, she didn't want to rest and I understood why – conference was her chance to meet activists, councillors, staff and donors and rebuild her standing in the party. She went to nearly all the main receptions, events that are always rammed full of people, most of whom are enjoying a drink. Even with a sound system, the guest speaker usually has to shout to make themselves heard. When she wasn't doing that, she was doing media interviews or rehearsing her speech, and she was up late every night having drinks with journalists, senior members of the party and key donors. She couldn't have put more strain on her voice if she'd tried, but by some miracle it was a bit better on the Wednesday morning, and the speech was in a good state.

When we started thinking about it back in the summer, the first question was how to deal with the election result. One school of thought was that apologising would start the speech on a defensive note – besides, the election was four months ago and everyone would have read about her apology to the 1922 Committee. On the other hand, the activists at conference had worked so hard during the campaign, and she'd never apologised to them. Ultimately, the prime minister felt she owed them an apology:

> I called that election. And I know all of you in this hall worked day and night to secure the right result . . . But we did not get the victory we wanted because our national campaign fell short . . . I hold my hands up for that. I take responsibility. I led the campaign. And I am sorry.

The second question was what the central theme of the speech should be. Here, too, the election was fresh in our minds. We had done particularly badly among younger voters, and the challenges they faced – student debt, the difficulty they were having getting on the housing ladder, saving for retirement – were not just costing us their votes, they were undermining our appeal to their parents and grandparents. Each generation has had life a little bit easier than the one before, but for the first time it felt like that might not be the case.

We decided to make this idea of generational progress the speech's central theme. Chris branded it 'the British dream', with the prime minister arguing, 'what the general election earlier this year showed is that . . . for too many people in our country that dream feels distant, [and] our party's ability to deliver it is in question'.

Before setting out some solutions, we wanted to address a third issue from the election campaign. The prime minister had been widely criticised – ridiculed, even – during the campaign as 'the Maybot', a robot incapable of showing any emotion. I didn't recognise this caricature of the person I worked for. Theresa is shy and not easy to get to know, and as a woman at the top of politics, she had learned that showing emotion led to her being treated differently to the men around her. However, when you do get to know her, she's a warm, caring person with a dry sense of humour. We wanted to show a bit more of Theresa May in this speech.

There are three sections that stand out. In describing the British dream, she revealed a bit about her background. Her grandmother 'was a domestic servant, who worked as a lady's maid below stairs. She worked hard and made sacrifices, because she believed in a better future for her family. And that servant, that lady's maid, among her grandchildren boasts three professors and a prime minister. That is why the British dream inspires me'.

She addressed why she carried on after all the flak she had taken during and after the election, an authentic insight into her motivations:

When people ask me why I put myself through it – the long hours, the pressure, the criticism and insults that inevitably go with the job – I tell them this: I do it to root out injustice and to give everyone in our country a voice. That's why, when I reflect on my time in politics, the things that make me proud are not the positions I have held, the world leaders I have met, the great global gatherings to which I have been, but knowing that I made a difference. That I helped those who couldn't be heard. Like the families of the ninety-six men, women and children who tragically lost their lives at Hillsborough . . . Like the victims and survivors of child sexual abuse, ignored for years by people in positions of power, now on the long road to the truth . . . Like Alexander Paul, a young man who came to this conference three years ago to tell his story. The story of a young black boy growing up in modern Britain who without causing any trouble – without doing anything wrong – found himself being stopped and searched by people in authority, time and time and time again . . . That's what I'm in this for.

But my favourite section is a bit of the speech I had a hand in writing. I can remember scribbling a first draft of it longhand on the flight back from the Tallinn digital summit the previous month. It is deeply personal and it also addresses the critique Andrea Leadsom was interpreted to have made of Theresa that because she didn't have children, she didn't have the same personal stake as those of us who do in the future of the country:

> It has always been a great sadness for me and Philip that we were never blessed with children. It seems some things in life are just never meant to be. But I believe in the dream that life should be better for the next generation as much as any mother. Any father. Any grandparent. The only difference is that I have the privileged position of being able to do more than most to bring

that dream to life. So I will dedicate my premiership to fixing this problem – to restoring hope. To renewing the British dream for a new generation of people.

There was one other lesson from the election that she reflected on. Jeremy Corbyn had seemed the ideal leader of the opposition from a Conservative perspective, but he had done much better than expected – and not just because of our poor campaign. It was clear that we needed to refight some ideological battles we had thought won:

> The free market – and the values of freedom, equality, rights, responsibilities and the rule of law that lie at its heart – remains the greatest agent of collective human progress ever created. So let us win this argument for a new generation and defend free and open markets with all our might.

The remainder of the speech sketched out some policy solutions for how we might revive the British dream. We had announced that we would undertake a major review of university funding and student financing and, in the meantime, scrap the planned increases in fees and increase the amount graduates could earn before they had to repay their debt. Earlier in the week, Philip Hammond had announced that we would invest a further £10 billion in the government's Help to Buy scheme. And now the prime minister announced that we would invest an additional £2 billion in affordable housing and allow homes to be built for social rent well below the market level in those parts of the country where rents were highest, ushering in a new generation of council homes:

> Whether you're trying to buy your own home, renting privately and looking for more security, or have been waiting for years on a council list, help is on the way. It won't be quick or easy, but as prime minister I am going to make it my mission to

solve this problem. I will take personal charge of the government's response.

Lots of people assume that as a former housing minister, I was the driving force behind this announcement. I certainly encouraged the prime minister to do more in this area, but she had been clear with me in 2016 about her determination to tackle the housing crisis. The credit for pushing housing up the political agenda belongs to her.

Looking back on it now, while it isn't a great speech, it is a solid one that correctly analysed the 2017 election and how the Conservative Party needed to respond to it. Sadly, the content proved irrelevant, as the prime minister experienced the full force of Murphy's Law: 'If anything can go wrong, it will.'

Things started to go off the rails when a comedian who had managed to acquire a press pass and position himself just below the stage with the photographers, somehow got up on to the stage and handed the prime minister a fake P45, telling her, 'Boris asked me to give you this.' The shock brought on her cough and caused her to start losing her voice. That made her more anxious, which made her voice even worse. Then, just to cap things off, the letters of the slogan on the set behind her began to fall down, a fitting metaphor.

I was sitting next to her husband Philip and it was agonising to watch. There were a couple of moments where it got so bad that I wondered if I should do something to draw things to a close. Amber Rudd led standing ovations to give Theresa a chance to have some water and a bit of a break, while Philip Hammond sourced some cough sweets from somewhere. Somehow, displaying the resilience that is one of her hallmarks, she got through it. At the end, Philip went up on the stage and gave her a hug.

Afterwards, the cabinet and her political team gathered in the green room behind the stage. She was apologetic that everyone's hard work had been wasted, even though the blame lay with those who had allowed the prankster to get up on stage, those responsible for the set design and me, for not enforcing more rest earlier in the week. Her cabinet was full of praise for her resilience, and as a result, when she left to be driven back to Sonning, I don't think she appreciated how much of a disaster it had been. It was not just a once-in-a-year opportunity foregone. The fact that it was not her fault was irrelevant; she was beginning to get a reputation for being unlucky in a profession where the prevailing view is that you make your own luck.

Once the cabinet had left, Theresa's political team sat in the green room and ate the leftover sandwiches while trying to think of ways to salvage the situation. In reality, there was little we could do, but Kirsty Buchanan from Robbie's team came up with an idea that might help a little. At the time, we were trying to persuade the prime minister to start using social media, and Kirsty suggested a photo of an array of cough sweets, a prime ministerial red box and the message '*coughs*', which would at least show some self-deprecating humour in adversity. Though we were slightly clutching at straws, everyone agreed this was a great idea, but to execute this plan, someone would have to call the prime minister at the end of a bad day to persuade her to tweet – something she had repeatedly made clear she didn't really like doing – about the nightmare she had just endured. It turned out that everyone else thought that someone should be me. She took a little bit of persuading, but in the end said, 'Go on then, I don't suppose it's going to make it any worse.' And, in fact, it made things slightly better and helped persuade her to do more on social media.

When I got back to Euston, I took the rare step of calling BBC political editor Laura Kuenssberg and ITV political editor Robert Peston, in a vain attempt to persuade them to report the significant things the prime minister had said as well as what had gone wrong. They were both very polite, but left me in no doubt that the story would be 'prime minister has utter nightmare'.

So ended one of my worst days in the job. When you fall off your bike, the best thing to do is get straight back on. But when a conference speech goes wrong, you have to wait an entire year for the chance to do it again. And the nearer the chance for redemption gets, the more the anxiety builds that it might happen all over again . . .

Birmingham 2018: 'Dancing Queen'

If anything, the context for the 2018 conference was even more challenging. The prime minister's position had been strengthened by her response to the treatment she had received from EU leaders at Salzburg in mid-September, but a section of the party was in open revolt over the Chequers plan. The Conservative Home website organised a fringe meeting for Boris Johnson two days before the prime minister's speech, at which he declared before a packed crowd:

> The Chequers proposal . . . is not a compromise. It is dangerous and unstable, politically and economically. This is not democracy. This is not what we voted for . . . This is the moment – and there is time – to chuck Chequers . . . If we get it wrong – if we bottle Brexit now – believe me, the people of this country will find it hard to forgive . . . And so, for one last time, I urge our friends in government to deliver what the people voted for, to back Theresa May in the best way possible – by softly, quietly and sensibly backing her original plan. And in so doing to believe in conservatism and to believe in Britain.

Ignore the sophistry of his call to back Theresa May in the penultimate sentence: he was accusing the prime minister of not being a Conservative, not believing in Britain and bottling Brexit, betraying those who voted Leave. It was a naked attempt to provoke a confidence vote in her leadership. The stakes when the prime minister came onto the stage to deliver her response could not have been higher.

This time round, Keelan Carr, an urbane member of Alex Dawson's team with a beautiful turn of phrase, held the pen. The process of producing a major prime ministerial speech can be incredibly frustrating for all concerned. Whoever holds the pen labours for hours to produce a first draft, sends it to a large cast list and is then deluged with comments requesting changes to passages they've lovingly slaved over. And because many of these comments are contradictory, those who submitted them are often frustrated when the second draft hasn't taken on board all their suggestions.

On this occasion, we took a different approach. Keelan did the initial draft, but once we got to Birmingham we formed a team of four to refine it: Keelan, JoJo, Alex and myself. Nothing was changed unless we were all happy with it. And instead of JoJo, Alex and I marking Keelan's homework, if there were sections of the speech we weren't happy with, each of us took one. It was a genuine collaborative effort, and one of the happiest memories of my time as Chief of Staff.

Such an approach wouldn't have been possible for any other speech – if we'd been at Number 10, JoJo, Alex and I would all have had numerous other things to do – but for those three days, we had nothing to do but prep the prime minister for media interviews and work on her speech. We'd meet after breakfast in a lounge on one of the top floors of the Hyatt Regency and review the text, before going back to our rooms to work on particular sections, meeting with the prime minister to get her comments, ordering some food and repeating the cycle. I don't think I left the hotel and conference centre for the whole five days.

If the 2017 speech was solid but not spectacular, I'm proud of the 2018 speech. It's a very good exposition of Theresa's politics. There are five sections that felt particularly important at the time, several of which are still relevant.

The first was something I was initially keen to make the main theme: the state of our politics. Each time the prime minister made a statement to the House of Commons on Brexit, I would listen from the box for civil servants in the corner of the chamber and notice that the mood felt a bit more polarised. But this wasn't limited to Brexit – there was a growing populism on both the left and the right, a new generation of media commentators whose modus operandi was to foster division. And people in elected office were suffering an increasing amount of abuse on social media. To paraphrase Vice-Admiral Beatty's famous remark at the Battle of Jutland, it felt like there was something wrong with our politics. The prime minister didn't want to make this the core theme of the speech, but it was retained as the introductory argument:

> We understood when we got involved [in politics] that sometimes it's adversarial. But in the last few years, something's changed for the worse. I feel it. I am sure you do too. Rigorous debate between political opponents is becoming more like a confrontation between enemies.

She ended this section with a call for her party to 'stand up for a politics that unites us rather than divides us', which linked neatly into the next section: her assessment of the Labour Party under Jeremy Corbyn's leadership:

> That used to be Labour's position too. But when I look at its leadership today, I worry that's no longer the case. We all remember what the Labour Party used to be. We passionately disagreed with many of their policies . . . but at least they had some basic qualities that everyone could respect. They were proud of our institutions. They were proud of our armed forces. They were proud of Britain. Today, when I look across at the opposition benches, I can still see that Labour Party. The heirs of Hugh Gaitskell and Barbara Castle, Dennis Healy and John Smith. But not on the front bench. Instead, their faces stare blankly out from the rows behind, while another party occupies prime position: the Jeremy Corbyn Party. Compare Jeremy Corbyn's

behaviour to that of his predecessors. Would Neil Kinnock, who stood up to the hard left, have stood by while his own MPs faced deselection and needed police protection at their party conference? Would Jim Callaghan, who served in the Royal Navy, have asked the Russian government to confirm the findings of our own intelligence agencies? Would Clement Attlee, Churchill's trusted deputy during the Second World War, have told British Jews they didn't know the meaning of anti-Semitism? What has befallen Labour is a national tragedy.

This was powerful because it was an honest assessment of the position rather than the usual tribal rhetoric, and many Labour MPs agreed with it – as some told me afterwards. The prime minister was speaking for the national interest. There were some Conservatives who thought Jeremy Corbyn's leadership was good news because it increased the Conservative Party's chances of winning the next election, but the prime minister was describing it as 'a national tragedy'. Why? Because Labour is one of our two great parties. Sooner or later, the Conservative Party was bound to lose an election, and if the hard left was still in control of Labour when they won, they would do profound damage to our country. Their control of Labour was nothing to celebrate.

This critique was also strategically smart because it drove a wedge between Corbyn and much of his party. In the aftermath of the conference, we tried to get ministers and Conservative MPs to distinguish between the Jeremy Corbyn Party and the Labour Party, but many found this hard to do – tribalism is deeply ingrained on both sides.

This section led to the third section I want to highlight: if we wanted to make sure that Jeremy Corbyn didn't become prime minister, the Conservative Party had to be a party for the whole country:

Because today, millions of people, who have never supported our party in the past, are appalled by what Jeremy Corbyn has done to Labour. They want to support a party that is decent, moderate and patriotic. One that puts the national interest first. Delivers on the issues they care about. And is comfortable with modern Britain in all its diversity. We must show everyone in this country that we are that party.

Theresa went on to define the characteristics of a decent, modern and patriotic Conservative Party, including a neat rebuttal to Corbyn's divisive 'For the many, not the few' slogan:

A party that conserves the best of our inheritance, but is not afraid of change. A party of patriotism, but not nationalism. A party that believes in business, but is not afraid to hold businesses to account. A party that believes in the good that government can do, but knows government will never have all the answers. A party that believes your success in life should not be defined by who you love, your faith, the colour of your skin, who your parents were or where you were raised, but by your talent and your hard work. Above all, a party of Unionism, not just of four proud nations, but of all our people. A party not for the few, not even for the many, but for everyone who is willing to work hard and do their best.

The fourth key section was on Brexit. From the moment Keelan started writing the speech, it was clear that we couldn't duck talking about it this year – the question was how we should do so. Should the prime minister mount a passionate defence of the Chequers proposals and a response to her critics, who were promising things that would never be on the table? Or was a presentation that recognised that opinions differed but argued that unless the Conservative Party came together, it risked losing Brexit altogether, more likely to work?

In the end, the prime minister opted for something between the two. She told the audience the truth about no deal ('Britain isn't

200

afraid to leave with no deal if we have to . . . but [it] would be a bad outcome for the UK and the EU') and defended her pursuit of frictionless trade on the grounds that it would protect jobs and a seamless border in Northern Ireland, which a free trade agreement could not do. However, she acknowledged that she wasn't going to convince everyone ('We have had disagreements in this party about Britain's membership of the EU for a long time, so it is no surprise that we have had a range of different views expressed this week'). Her job as prime minister was 'to do what I believe to be in the national interest', and even if people didn't agree with every part of the Chequers proposals, the party needed to come together because 'if we all go off in different directions in pursuit of our own visions of the perfect Brexit, we risk ending up with no Brexit at all'.

The most important moment in the speech came towards the end. A couple of months earlier, I'd spotted that if the Office for Budget Responsibility improved its economic forecasts as expected, we could announce an end to the austerity the country had been enduring since the global financial crisis. This was the headline we were looking for:

After a decade of austerity, people need to know that their hard work has paid off. Because of that hard work, and the decisions taken by the chancellor, our national debt is starting to fall for the first time in a generation. This is a historic achievement. But getting to this turning point wasn't easy. Public sector workers had their wages frozen. Local services had to do more with less. And families felt the squeeze. Fixing our finances was necessary. There must be no return to the uncontrolled borrowing of the past. No undoing all the progress of the last eight years. No taking Britain back to square one. But the British people need to know that the end is in sight. And our message to them must be this: we get it. We are not just a party to clean up a mess, we are the party to steer a course to a better future. Sound finances are essential, but they are not the limit of our ambition. Because you made sacrifices, there are better days ahead. So, when we've secured a good Brexit deal for Britain, at the spending review next year we will set out our approach for the future. Debt as a share of the economy will continue to go down, support for public services will go up. Because, a decade after the financial crash, people need to know that the austerity it led to is over and that their hard work has paid off.

The key message – that we understood the need for more investment in our public services – is one that Boris Johnson and Rishi Sunak have embraced, both before and in the wake of the COVID-19 pandemic.

With the text finally agreed, the moment I'd been both looking forward to and dreading was at hand. I knew we had a good speech, but although we had been more sensible about her diary at conference this year, the prime minister had another cough and was bound to be nervous after what had happened the year before. In a surreal moment, I received a call during the final rehearsal of the speech to say that a commercial aircraft was not responding to instructions – the military needed the prime minister on the phone in case she had to give the order to shoot it down. Thankfully, contact with the plane was re-established and we could go back to worrying about the speech. We went over to the conference hall and I waited nervously by her side backstage.

Parky had come up with the inspired idea of asking Geoffrey Cox to be her warm-up act. A natural performer, Geoffrey soon had the audience in the right mood and even brought a smile to the prime minister's face. A couple of minutes before she was due on, I wished her luck and went to my seat. I'd chickened out of sitting in the main body of the hall with Philip and the cabinet this time, instead watching from a balcony that overlooked the stage.

The prime minister had chosen ABBA's 'Dancing Queen' as her walk-on music and came on stage dancing. I'd spent the last fifteen months telling her to relax and be herself, so I could hardly complain – and the audience loved it. From the moment she started, it was obviously going to go well – everyone in the hall was desperate for her to succeed and she visibly relaxed. At the end, when she and Philip came to leave the stage, I got a smile from her and a thumbs-up from Philip. I was, I confess, quite emotional. I slipped out of my seat and waited for her in the corridor to the green room and, for the first and only time, gave her a hug. The atmosphere in the green room was a complete contrast with a year earlier.

To return to where I started this chapter, did it really matter? Within a few weeks, Dom Raab and Esther McVey had resigned from the cabinet and Theresa's leadership was under threat again. How many of you reading this book remember the speech at all? But the 'end of austerity' line garnered good headlines and the commentariat regarded this as her best speech. Nothing she said on domestic policy could change the situation on Brexit, but the speech suggested that she was a politician who, if she could secure and pass a Brexit deal, still had much to give.

CHAPTER 13

DEALING WITH THE DONALD

Those who make it to the very top of British politics enter Number 10 with plans to strengthen our economy, improve public services, protect the environment, tackle injustice and make Britain a safer place to live. But once they become prime minister, they find themselves spending much of their time dealing with the intricacies of foreign policy rather than the issues that got them to Number 10 and will determine how long they will stay there. Their diary fills up with G7 summits, G20 summits, NATO summits, Commonwealth heads of government meetings, annual meetings of the UN General Assembly, visits of other heads of government to the UK, visits to other countries and, until recently, meetings of the European Council.

Over time, most prime ministers find that spending time with people who are grappling with similar challenges to them is a welcome respite from domestic politics. Relations with other heads of government depend on a combination of how well the two countries get on and personal chemistry. But in Theresa's case, the relationship that for most British prime ministers is one of the easiest – with the President of the United States, our closest ally – was one of the most difficult.

The dilemma

Domestically, association with President Trump was politically toxic. Theresa had visited Washington shortly after his election, and a photo

of the president taking her hand as they walked down a ramp outside the White House had been used by her opponents to suggest
she was literally hand in hand with someone who, in reality, was a
very different kind of politician. If you looked at the polls, it was
easy to see why her opponents tried to associate her with him. A poll
just before the 2016 US presidential election showed that, of those
who had a preference, just 19 per cent of British voters – and just 20
per cent of Conservative supporters – wanted Donald Trump to win.
Those figures didn't change much during his presidency. A poll just
before the 2020 presidential election found that, of those who had
a preference, 24 per cent of voters – and 35 per cent of Conservative
supporters – wanted to see him re-elected. The reason the latter figure had increased was not because people had changed their mind
about him but because the Conservative Party had largely absorbed
the UKIP vote, 74 per cent of whom had backed Trump in 2016.

The toxicity around Trump was driven by some of his policies,
such as the ban on people entering the United States from certain
Muslim countries and the decision to withdraw from the Paris Agreement on tackling climate change, as well as by the language he used
and in particular some of the things he tweeted. The prime minister
was regularly asked for her views on what he had done or said, and
on each occasion had to balance the diplomatic imperative not to
fall out with the leader of our most important ally with the moral
imperative to stand up for what was right and the political imperative
to differentiate herself from him. In November 2017, the president
retweeted a number of anti-Muslim videos posted by Jayda Fransen,
the deputy leader of a far-right group called Britain First. The prime
minister agreed that her spokesman should give the following robust
response:

Britain First seeks to divide communities by their use of hate-
ful narratives that peddle lies and stoke tensions. British people
overwhelmingly reject the prejudiced rhetoric of the far right,

which is the antithesis of the values this country represents: decency, tolerance and respect.

That provoked a presidential tweet (with the incorrect Twitter handle): '@TheresaMay, don't focus on me, focus on the destructive Radical Islamic Terrorism that is taking place within the United Kingdom.' He hadn't forgotten about it when they met in Davos in January 2018, although this time there was no anger. As we made our way into the room, he said to our delegation, 'Don't we love the prime minister? Mind you, every now and then she hits me about Muslims.' She shot back 'Only when you've said something first' and he dropped the subject.

In June, shortly before he was due to visit the UK, distressing pictures emerged from the US–Mexico border of children being detained separately from their parents. The president had also made remarks about illegal immigrants pouring into and 'infesting' the country. The prime minister was challenged about it at Prime Minister's Questions and once again, was robust:

> The pictures of children being held in what appear to be cages are deeply disturbing. This is wrong. This is not something that we agree with. This is not the United Kingdom's approach; indeed, when I was home secretary, I ended the routine detention of families with children . . . When we disagree with the United States, we tell them so.

Just after Trump's state visit in June 2019, he was at it again, this time retweeting a tweet by Katie Hopkins that referred to London as 'stab city' and 'Khan's Londonistan'. In a statement of the obvious, the prime minister's spokesman said that she would never retweet Katie Hopkins or use such language.

The critique from the left was that such episodes showed that she should have nothing to do with the president. She had been wrong to rush over to Washington shortly after his election, they said, and wrong to offer him the honour of a state visit to the UK. This smacked of double standards – they never complained if she met the president of Russia or China, but the president of our closest ally was some-how beyond the pale. For all our differences with President Trump, it seemed a bizarre worldview.

These criticisms also ignored three key points in favour of close engagement. First, President Trump was shifting US policy in ways that were damaging to UK interests. He was, at best, lukewarm towards NATO. He didn't believe in the multilateral institutions that formed the international rules-based order, support for which had long been a cornerstone of UK foreign policy – he withdrew the US from the United Nations Educational, Scientific and Cultural Organisation in October 2017 and from the UN Human Rights Council in June 2018, and he was constantly threatening to leave the World Trade Organisation. He wanted to end the deal with Iran which, though imperfect, was the only thing stopping them from acquiring nuclear weapons. And he was keen to remove US forces from Afghanistan and the Middle East, which would endanger our counter-terrorist operations.

Second, only through talking to him was there a chance of pre-venting some of these decisions. As our ambassador to Washington Kim Darroch advised, 'there is no substitute for this highest-level channel'. After the initial shock of his victory, lots of people convinced themselves that the US system – the State Department, the Pentagon and the national security infrastructure – would stop him from radically shifting US policy. Few, if any, countries in the world have closer ties with the US than us – surely we would be able to use our channels into these organisations to protect our interests? But this proved to be a pipe dream. President Trump would some-times listen to what the US system told him, but there were no guarantees. In December 2018, he overruled his military and civilian advisers and announced in a video that he posted on Twitter, 'We have won against ISIS. Our boys, our young women, our men – they're all coming back, and they're coming back now.' Neither we, nor the French nor the Kurds were given any warning, even though the security of our personnel would be compromised by a rapid US withdrawal. Eventually, a combination of lobbying from allies and the efforts of people within the US system got this decision partially rowed back, but it is a good example of why relying on traditional links didn't work. I once asked Fiona Hill, a British-born US national security official, who President Trump listened to, in the hope that we could use them as a conduit. She thought for a moment and replied, 'I really think the only people are the Queen and the Pope.' If you wanted to influence US policy, you had to talk to the person in charge.

And third, engaging with him did sometimes work. His initial response to the request to expel Russian intelligence officers following the use of a chemical weapon in Salisbury was lukewarm, but sustained lobbying of him resulted in sixty expulsions, far and away the largest of any country.

The prime minister's visit to Washington shortly after Trump's election was another case in point, as well as an illustration of the dilemma. Her decision to go was vindicated by her success in getting him to make a stronger commitment to NATO, but it came at the cost of the image of them hand in hand and the promise of a state visit, both of which were used against her. Opposition politicians, and particularly those who don't expect to be in government, can focus on what will play well politically, but prime ministers have to focus on the national interest, which is often served by working with those whose views you don't share.

'What's President Trump like?'

During my time as chief of staff, I met President Trump six times and listened in on numerous phone calls between him and the prime minister. One of the most frequent questions people ask me is 'What's Donald Trump like?'

The answer is pretty much what you would expect. He has an opinion on everything. He can say outrageous things, leaving you unsure if he believes them or is just saying them for effect (on a call in April 2018, he asserted that London would soon be a majority-Muslim city). It is difficult to have a normal meeting with him, partly because he tends to dominate any conversation, but mostly because he talks in a stream of consciousness, jumping from one issue to another. His mood is quite unpredictable. Sometimes he can be surly and aggressive. Sometimes he can be mellow – on a call in December 2017, just after the UK had voted with every other member of the UN Security Council to call for the withdrawal of his unilateral recognition of Jerusalem as the capital of Israel, he said, 'I see you voted against us on Jerusalem, but that's OK.' And sometimes he can be charming. The first time I met him in New York in September 2017, he was in his element. Rather than meet at the UN Headquarters, he invited the prime minister to meet him at one of his hotels and took the time to introduce himself to each member of the prime minister's team. At the end of the meeting, he said he was looking forward to visiting the UK and was planning to go to one of his golf courses in Scotland once the official part of the visit was over. 'Do you play golf?' he asked the prime minister. She didn't. He turned to me as the next most senior member of the delegation: 'How about you?' 'Well, yes, a bit.' 'You should come and play me with me at my course.'

He is quite insecure, and he would regularly criticise his predecessors in a way I can't recall any other head of government doing. During a call in December 2017, he spent a long time telling the prime minister what a terrible deal President Obama had done in moving the US embassy to Battersea. He was constantly looking for praise. In a call in March 2018, the prime minister had three things to thank him for: the expulsion of Russian intelligence officers after the attack in Salisbury, UK exemptions for some tariffs he had imposed on the EU and an agreement to allow for the exchange of data in law enforcement cases. The president asked the prime minister to 'let the people of the UK know I've done a lot for them, more than anyone else', suggesting that he cared more about what people in other countries thought of him than he let on.

He was also far more averse to using military force than most people would assume. Though he was happy to threaten military action publicly, he had more in common with the anti-war movement than either would like to admit. During his visit in June 2018, he mused about what would have happened if George Bush, 'our great genius president', had never attacked the Middle East. 'It's been a disaster. We're in for $7 trillion, 2 million lives. Every time we kick someone out, it's always a disaster next.' During the state visit, his fear of nuclear weapons was clear. 'That's why we're working so hard with Iran and North Korea,' he said.

If you want to understand Donald Trump's approach to foreign affairs, there are three things you need to know.

Everything's a zero-sum game

The starting point is that everything is a deal, and deals are zero-sum games – he was only getting a better deal if the other side was getting a worse one. In his view, America was getting a raw deal from many of the agreements his predecessors had negotiated. And it is important to recognise that – in some cases, at least – he had a point. At a NATO summit in July 2018, he told his fellow leaders that for too many years, the US had born a disproportionate share of protecting the alliance. It accounted for 90 per cent of NATO defence spending, and that was no longer acceptable. While you might take issue with how he pressured others to raise their game – essentially implying that the US would leave NATO if they didn't – it's hard to argue with his underlying case. The fact that a number of allies increased their defence spending was one of his key foreign policy successes, but his approach has led many European countries to question whether the US is a reliable long-term partner because they fear there is significant support for his brand of politics in the US, and they will therefore see other presidents like him.

Traditional alliances don't count for much

It often felt like the president had more time for some of the world's authoritarian leaders than for the leaders of the liberal democracies who were America's traditional allies. At Davos in January 2018, he told the prime minister that President Xi Jinping of China was 'a great guy'. He had just released some American college basketball players who had been arrested for shoplifting, and there seemed a hint of envy when he reflected that Xi 'doesn't have to go through the system like we do'. In a discussion on Syria at Chequers in July 2018, he said, 'You've got to hand it to Assad', before moving on to Russia: 'Putin asked for a meeting. We have good chemistry. I'm going to find out what he wants.' Addressing the UN Security Council in September, he was said he was proud of recent progress on the Korean peninsula. There had been no missile tests recently, hostages had been released and the remains of US servicemen killed in the Korean War returned. He was entitled to feel proud about these achievements, but he raised some eyebrows when he referred to Kim Jong-un, the supreme leader of North Korea, as 'a man I have gotten to know and like'.

In contrast, he rarely had a good word to say about America's traditional allies. At Davos in January 2018, he said to the prime minister, 'Canada is a tough player – I may have to terminate NAFTA.' He had a particular problem with Germany. At the meeting of the UN General Assembly in September 2018, he mused that 'in theory, people who trade with Iran can't trade with us. We can't do that with the UK. Germany, I wouldn't mind.' When criticising Germany, he would often refer to the fact that his father was German, but it was never clear whether this was to demonstrate that he couldn't possibly be prejudiced against Germany, or whether his hostility to Germany was in some way revealing about his relationship with his father.

Brexit good, EU bad

The president was a big fan of Brexit. At Davos in January 2018, he told the prime minister, 'You're a great country, you shouldn't be in a group.' The EU hadn't been treating the UK well in the negotiations – was there any way he could help? The prime minister asked if he could impress on them the need for a close security relationship after we had left. The president suggested he could help with the DUP, perhaps by inviting them to the Oval Office. And he reassured her, 'We're going to have a great trade relationship. We're pulling back from people that haven't treated us properly, but we're there for you more than for anybody.'

On the face of it, this was hugely helpful – the president wanted to help, and the fact that we had other options would give us leverage in the negotiations with the EU. However, he wasn't just supportive of the UK; he was actively hostile to the EU and keen to see other countries follow our example. At Davos, he told the prime minister that he had never liked the EU: 'We have a horrible relationship with them – they're worse than China.' At the UN General Assembly in September 2018, he told her that when it came to trade, 'the potential with you is fantastic; it may go the other way with them' and he was keen to know if other countries would leave. During the state visit in June 2019, he suggested that commission vice-president Margrethe Vestager 'hates the US more than anyone else alive'.

These weren't just private views. The EU knew how he felt and there was an escalating trade war between the two sides. Trump's desire to see other member states follow the UK's example made Brexit more dangerous from the EU's perspective. If the UK got too good a deal, there was a danger that the institutions they had spent sixty years building might collapse. And not only did Trump's position harden the EU's position, it also deprived us of a go-between. A president who enjoyed good relations with both sides might have acted as a bridge, but President Trump was neither inclined to play that role nor suited to it.

If Trump's public support for leaving was music to Brexiteer ears, they would have found his private assessment of the situation less to their liking. The problem, he told the prime minister in September 2018, was that the EU didn't have any downside and 'you don't have any cards'. So what should the UK do? His advice, which he first gave to her in September 2017, was to use his tactics and stop being reasonable. 'Sue them for $1 trillion, $5 trillion.'

The June 2018 visit

Ever since the prime minister had made the offer, the US embassy had been pushing for a date for the state visit. We eventually agreed to a non-state visit in July 2018 (after the May elections, given the potential political impact), with a formal state visit to follow the next year. In the event, the first visit ended up being just after the crucial Chequers cabinet meeting and the resulting resignations of David Davis and Boris Johnson.

The itinerary avoided central London and other major cities, to keep the president away from the inevitable mass protests. The first event was a formal dinner at Blenheim Palace. Just before we arrived, *The Sun* started publishing extracts of an interview with the president that was political dynamite. Commenting on the Chequers proposals, he said:

> If they do a deal like that, we would be dealing with the European Union instead of dealing with the UK, so it will probably kill the deal [a trade deal with the US] . . . I would have done it much differently. I actually told Theresa May how to do it, but she didn't agree, she didn't listen to me . . . The deal she is

striking is a much different deal than the one the people voted on.

Just in case anyone hadn't got the message, he added that Boris Johnson 'would be a great prime minister'. I wasn't in the best mood when I sat down for dinner, only to discover I was seated next to Stephen Miller, a senior adviser to the president and the architect of his immigration and refugee policies. I was polite, but it was not a meeting of minds.

The next morning, we went to Sandhurst for a demonstration by a combined team of US and UK special forces. The president arrived on Marine One, accompanied by two Osprey helicopters. The prime minister had sensibly retreated inside a shelter, but the rest of the UK delegation waited under two oak trees, keen to see the Ospreys close up. Their downforce brought a significant proportion of the trees down on us, leaving us looking like we'd been dragged through a hedge. Once we had dusted ourselves down, the demonstration got under way. The aim was to show the president that while we couldn't come close to matching the scale of the US military, we had world-class capability in certain areas. And it worked – he commented later, 'I was very impressed with your people this morning, and I'm not easily impressed.' It also gave me the chance to meet my opposite number, General John Kelly. If I thought my job was hard, imagine trying to staff Donald Trump.

We then went on to Chequers for discussions between the leaders that began with a briefing on the situation in Yemen from senior security and intelligence officials. Our aim was to persuade the president to use his influence with the Saudis to convince them to end the war and seek a political solution. He agreed, though it felt like his main focus was on getting them to pay more for the support they received from US forces.

We then moved on to Iran. In May, the president had withdrawn from the Joint Comprehensive Plan of Action, which Iran, the US, the UK, France, Russia, China and the EU had agreed in 2015. The prime minister had issued a joint statement with President Macron and Chancellor Merkel, saying that Trump's decision was a matter of 'regret and concern'. Our view was that while the JCPOA didn't address all the issues we had with the Iranian regime, it was preventing them from developing a nuclear weapon. The president sought to reassure us that sanctions were working and would force the Iranians to the table. In what felt like a throwaway remark, he asked whether we should 'take out Soleimani' (Qasem Soleimani, the commander of the Quds Force, a branch of Iran's Islamic Revolutionary Guards Corps, who would be killed in a US airstrike in January 2020).

Towards the end of the meeting, attention turned to Brexit. Trump was obviously embarrassed by the way *The Sun* had written up his interview. 'I said such good things about the prime minister, but they didn't write them,' he complained. It felt as though he had been encouraged to do the interview by Nigel Farage or one of our party's own ultra-Brexiteers, some of whom his national security adviser John Bolton was close to. When the prime minister patiently took him through the detail of the Chequers proposals, she was very clear that any deal had to ensure there would be no checks between Ireland and Northern Ireland, and that point seemed to hit home.

Once the meeting was over, the president and the prime minister held a joint press conference in the Chequers sunshine, following some more hand-holding as they came down some steps. It was a remarkable affair, which mainly consisted of the president sparring with US media. From my point of view, the key thing was his tone concerning the prime minister and the prospects of a UK–US trade deal, which was very different from his interview with *The Sun*. Responding to a question from the BBC's political editor Laura Kuenssberg on the subject, he said he had apologised to the prime minister for the story, that he had 'said very good things about her – they just didn't put it in the headlines' and that he had 'a lot of respect' for her. Given the narrative of eighteen hours earlier, that was about as much as I could have hoped for.

The state visit

In the build-up to the state visit in June 2019, Kim Darroch wrote a diptel outlining the ways in which US policy was diverging from ours, warning that this was likely to accelerate and arguing that 'at the moment, the US isn't behaving as our best friend – on the contrary, some of what the US is doing is damaging our national security'.

The latest difference of opinion was over the role of the Chinese technology company Huawei in our 5G telephone network. We had decided to let them have a role in parts of the network, but not to let them have access to the core – our security officials were confident that this would address the security concerns, and a team from the US had pored over the technical details and gone away satisfied. The alternative – banning them from the network altogether – would slow down the rollout of 5G, which would put us at a competitive disadvantage. On 5 May, US Secretary of State Mike Pompeo came to London and met the prime minister. He didn't push too hard, limiting himself to saying, 'We have great confidence you will make a good decision.' However, he later gave a speech to the CPS in which he said:

> Would the Iron Lady . . . allow China to control the internet of the future? Insufficient security will impede the United States' ability to share certain information within trusted networks. This is just what China wants – to divide Western alliances through bits and bytes, not bullets and bombs.

At the same time, the US national security adviser John Bolton wrote to his UK equivalent Mark Sedwill, acknowledging that we had addressed their concerns about security, but arguing that 'the decision has broader implications beyond the question of technical security'. He went on to say:

> In light of the importance of this matter to the integrity and functionality of the long-standing US–UK alliance, we ask that your government postpone any affirmative decision that would allow Huawei to build any element of the UK's 5G network, issue a public announcement to that effect and that consultations with Five Eyes partners will inform the ultimate decision.

This was not just ignorant of the current position – Huawei was already involved in the UK's 5G network – but a thinly veiled threat. Bolton was effectively saying, 'We intend to block this company from the global market – and if you want our current security co-operation to continue, you need to toe the line.'

Trump's state visit played out much like his visit of the previous year. Shortly before his arrival, he gave an interview with the *Sunday Times*, in which he said we should leave without a deal, refuse to pay the money we had agreed to pay and involve Nigel Farage in the negotiations. However, once he got to the UK, he was sweetness and light.

In the main discussions, the prime minister, Philip Hammond and Jeremy Hunt made our case on Huawei. They told Trump that we took the threat seriously but had come up with a different solution because our network was configured differently. And, they said, there was a danger that this row was deflecting us from the real issue, which was how we could work together to ensure that we retained scientific and technological leadership – that when it came to 6G, for example, we did not find ourselves dependent on a Chinese company.

For the president and his family, the highlight of the visit was the state banquet at Buckingham Palace. They also enjoyed a tour of the Cabinet War Rooms, where I found myself acting as an impromptu tour guide to his four children – another duty that wouldn't have been in my job description.

As in 2018, Trump's visit ended with a press conference where he contradicted what he had said in the *Sunday Times* interview. On Huawei, 'we are going to be able to work out any differences', while the prime minister had brought Brexit 'to a very good point' and overall had 'done a very good job'.

An angry ending

That press conference would have made a decent end to their relationship, but it was not to be. On 7 July, the *Mail on Sunday* published extracts from a number of diptels from Kim Darroch that were critical of the president and his administration. It was Kim's job to give people in London a candid account of what was going on in DC, but I'd received a number of the diptels and had been surprised at some of the language, given how widely they were circulated.

To say the president took it badly would be an understatement. He vented his rage on Kim, the prime minister and her government, tweeting:

> I have been very critical about the way the UK and prime minister Theresa May handled Brexit. What a mess she and her representatives have created. I told her how it should be done, but she decided to go another way. I do not know the ambassador, but he is not liked or well thought of within the US. We will no longer deal with him. The good news for the wonderful United Kingdom is that they will soon have a new prime minister.

Theresa expressed her full faith in Kim, while adding that she did not necessarily agree with everything he had said. Boris Johnson, on the other hand, who was by this point the strong favourite to take over from her two weeks later, refused to do so. That and the fact the president instructed his administration not to deal with Kim, making it impossible for him to do his job, led to his resignation.

Postscript

It's tempting to think that Joe Biden's victory in the 2020 presidential election has restored normality to the White House and we should view Donald Trump's presidency as an aberration. However, I think that would be a mistake – after all, Trump received the second highest number of votes of any presidential candidate in US history. Although Biden won fairly comfortably in the end, his margins in the states that switched from 2016 were quite narrow, and it is likely that without the COVID-19 pandemic, Trump would have been re-elected. He could be back in four years' time, and in any case, we are not going to see a return to the Republican Party of George H. W. Bush and John McCain. We are likely to see more presidents like him, in terms of policy, if not style. Liberal democracies around the world need to think about what that means, rather than deluding ourselves and pretending that the last four years were a one-off.

CHAPTER 14

NATIONAL SECURITY

Before she became prime minister, Theresa May served as home secretary for over six years, longer than anyone in the modern era. She had a deep understanding of the threats from both domestic and international terrorism and the work of various government agencies to counter them. And she wasn't just knowledgeable about this area of the government's work; she was passionate about it. Most prime ministers leave the detailed oversight of the security services to their home secretaries, but she had a weekly meeting with her home secretary and senior officials to review the latest operational matters.

When I was appointed chief of staff, the UK terror threat level was severe, following a number of attacks in the first six months of 2017. On 22 March, five people were killed and nearly fifty were injured when an Islamist drove a car into pedestrians on Westminster Bridge and ran into the grounds of the Houses of Parliament, where he fatally stabbed PC Keith Palmer. On 22 May, the election campaign was brought to a halt when an Islamist suicide bomber blew himself up at Manchester Arena as people were leaving a concert, killing twenty-two and injuring 139, many of them children. Less than two weeks later, three Islamists drove a van into pedestrians on London Bridge before stabbing people in and around Borough Market, killing eight people and injuring forty-eight others.

The police and security services were concerned that these attacks were increasingly home-grown, committed by people radicalised in their bedrooms by extremist material on the internet. This made attacks much more difficult to disrupt. If individuals were travelling to Syria for training or were part of a network, it was easier for the security services to find out what was being planned. At the UN General Assembly in September 2017, the prime minister joined President Macron and Italian prime minister Paolo Gentiloni in convening the first-ever UN summit of government and industry, to try to reduce the time it took to remove terrorist content from the internet and, ideally, to stop it being uploaded in the first place. At Davos a few months later, she said:

> These companies have some of the best brains in the world. They must focus their brightest and best on meeting these fundamental social responsibilities. And just as these big companies need to step up, we also need cross-industry responses, because smaller platforms can quickly become home to criminals and terrorists . . . As governments, it is also right that we look at the legal liability that social media companies have for the content shared on their sites.

This work ultimately led to the 'Online Harms White Paper', which the government published in April 2019.

I was new to this area of policy, so it was a steep learning curve. There's a limit to what I can disclose about those meetings, but I was shocked by the number of individuals the security services were monitoring, the ease with which people could access material and the leniency of some of the sentences received by people who had clearly been planning attacks.

Dealing with emergencies

The first attack during my time as chief of staff happened on 19 June 2017. I was woken by a phone call from the Downing Street switchboard in the middle of the night. They told me they were about to wake the prime minister to inform her of a suspected terrorist attack outside a mosque in Finsbury Park in London. Would I like to join the call?

When a terrorist attack or some other emergency takes place, the prime minister chairs what is known as a COBR meeting – the acronym stands for Cabinet Office Briefing Room, where such meetings take place. The key ministers, officials from the relevant agencies and sometimes local political leaders are brought together to co-ordinate the response and agree what information should be put in the public domain. The prime minister chaired one such meeting that morning. It appeared that a British man had driven a van into worshippers gathered outside the mosque and an elderly man, who had collapsed before the attack, had subsequently died. In a statement after the meeting, the prime minister said it was a reminder that 'terrorism, extremism and hatred take many forms, and our determination to tackle them must be the same, whoever is responsible'.

Salisbury

Theresa's biggest test on national security came in March 2018. On 5 March – a day that was otherwise dominated, as was increasingly the case, by Brexit – she was informed that a man and a woman had been found having seizures on a park bench in the centre of Salisbury the previous day. The initial assumption was that they had overdosed on drugs, but their symptoms and profile didn't quite fit. Once the man was identified as Sergei Skripal – a former Russian intelligence officer who had been accused of acting as a double agent for the British intelligence services – and the woman as his daughter Yulia, the intelligence services were contacted.

On 6 March, the prime minister was told that experts at the Defence Science and Technology Laboratory at Porton Down had confirmed that the Skripals had been poisoned with a nerve agent.

That day, in response to an urgent question in the House of Commons, Boris Johnson said that it was 'too early to speculate' about what had happened, 'but members will have their suspicions. If those suspicions prove to be well-founded, this government will take whatever measures we deem necessary to protect the lives of the people in this country, our values and our freedoms.'

The next day, the national security adviser Mark Sedwill confirmed that the poisonings were almost certainly the work of the Russian government. The Skripals had been poisoned with one of a group of military-grade nerve agents known as Novichok that were developed in Russia. It was difficult to overstate the enormity of the situation. It appeared that not only had the Russian state attempted an assassination on British soil, with echoes of the murder of Alexander Litvinenko in 2006, but that it wanted everyone to know about it – using Novichok was like leaving a calling card. And it had done it in a way that had put the lives of hundreds of innocent people at risk – traces of the nerve agent were found in a Zizzi restaurant and a local pub. On 8 March, the home secretary Amber Rudd informed the House of Commons that a police officer who had been one of the first responders, later named as Detective Sergeant Nick Bailey, had also fallen ill. Far from being a covert assassination, this was both brazen and reckless.

I had two concerns. If – as looked almost certain – Russia was responsible, how could we mount a more effective response than we had to the murder of Alexander Litvinenko and deter Putin from doing this again? And when could the prime minister say something? Boris Johnson had responded to the urgent question on 6 March and Amber Rudd had made a statement on 8 March. There was already criticism in the press that the prime minister looked 'weak' in the face of aggression.

Theresa had wanted to wait until she had the formal assessment before commenting. On the morning of 12 March, the National Security Council met to hear that assessment and discuss how the

UK should respond. I'm unable to repeat everything that was said at that meeting, but I can recount those things that have subsequently been made public. Based on the positive identification of a Novichok nerve agent, our knowledge that Russia had previously produced this agent and would still be capable of doing so, that it had investigated ways to deliver nerve agents during the 2000s its record of conducting state-sponsored assassinations and our assessment that it viewed some defectors as legitimate targets for assassinations, the assessment was that it was 'highly likely' that Russia was responsible.

There were only two plausible explanations: either this was a deliberate act by the Russian state, or it had allowed its supply of a military-grade nerve agent to get into the hands of others. It was agreed that we should make this assessment public and give the Russian government the opportunity to respond before deciding what action to take. The foreign secretary summoned the Russian ambassador to the Foreign Office for what is known as a 'démarche' – a formal government-to-government request. He set out what we knew, demanded that Russia immediately provide full and complete disclosure of their Novichok programme to the Organisation for the Prohibition of Chemical Weapons and asked for a formal response from the Russian government by the end of the following day.

The prime minister then made a statement to the House of Commons. At this point, there was a growing impatience with what was perceived to be the slow pace of the government's response. The prime minister told the House that while she understood that impatience, 'as a nation that believes in the rule of law, it is essential that we proceed in the right way – led not by speculation but by the evidence. That is why we have given the police the space and time to carry out their investigation properly.' She set out the government's assessment that there were only two possibilities and the clear message the foreign secretary had communicated to the Russian ambassador. She ended by saying:

On Wednesday, we will consider the response from the Russian state. Should there be no credible response, we will conclude that this action amounts to an unlawful use of force by the Russian state against the United Kingdom, and I will come back to this House to set out the full range of measures that we will take in response.

What followed was one of the most remarkable interventions I've ever seen in the House of Commons. In his response to the prime minister's statement, Jeremy Corbyn focused on Russian oligarchs' donations to the Conservative Party and said that whatever action the government took 'once the facts are clear' – despite it already being clear that a Russian military nerve agent had been used on British soil – needed to be 'proportionate and focused on reducing conflict and tensions, rather than increasing them'. The contrast with Ian Blackford, the Westminster leader of the SNP – who said that 'firm and strong action must be taken to send a clear message to the Kremlin' could not have been more stark.

The reaction on the Labour benches as Corbyn spoke was one of incredulity, and they rose one by one to state that they agreed with the prime minister. Yvette Cooper said it was 'hard to see any alternative' to the prime minister's 'grave conclusion' and that she hoped 'the whole House will be able to come together behind a firm response from the government'. Chris Leslie said 'there should be unity across the House on what I feel is the proportionate and sensible approach that she has taken'. John Woodcock said the prime minister's statement was 'hugely welcome' and pointedly observed that 'it would put our national security at significant risk if we were led by anyone who did not understand the gravity of the threat that Russia poses to this nation'. And Liam Byrne said that 'the prime minister should know that if, by Wednesday, she concludes that we are indeed embattled, she will find both unity and resolve across the House as we face down a common threat'. It was moving to hear such strong support for the prime minister from her political opponents. I made sure that key privy councillors, including the SNP leader in Westminster Ian Blackford, had access to official-level briefing. It was clear that his party's position was in complete contrast to that of their former leader Alex Salmond, who was happy to take the Russian government's shilling as a presenter on RT.

The Russian government failed to provide any credible explanation by 13 March, so the National Security Council met again to agree what action we should take. There was unanimity among ministers that those elements of our response that could be made public should convey how seriously we were taking this, but that the number of diplomats expelled should not be so high that when the Russians inevitably responded in kind, we would no longer be able to run an effective embassy in Moscow. The focus should be on having the maximum impact on Russian hostile state activity rather than the highest possible number of expulsions.

That afternoon, the prime minister presented those elements of the response that the NSC had agreed that could be made public in the House of Commons. We would expel twenty-three Russian diplomats who we knew were undeclared GRU (Russian military intelligence) officers – the entire GRU capability in the UK, demonstrating that we knew precisely which of their diplomats were spies. We would harden our defences against hostile state activity by introducing a power to detain those suspected of it at the border. We would increase checks on private flights, customs and freight, freeze Russian state assets where we had evidence that they might be used to threaten the life or property of UK nationals or residents and bring the capabilities of UK law enforcement to bear against serious criminals and corrupt elites. And we would suspend all high-level bilateral contacts between the UK and Russia – no government ministers or members of the royal family would attend that summer's World Cup. There were other elements of the response that the prime minister couldn't announce publicly for reasons of national security, and nor can I set them out here.

Jeremy Corbyn couldn't bring himself to admit that Russia was culpable, but every other opposition leader and pretty much every backbench Labour MP who spoke expressed strong support for the prime minister's response. Corbyn's official spokesman then briefed journalists that Corbyn didn't believe there was proof that Russia was responsible and suggested that the intelligence services might be wrong, saying, 'there is a history between weapons of mass destruction and intelligence which is problematic, to put it mildly'. It is remarkable that while the Skripals and Detective Sergeant Bailey were fighting for their lives in hospital, the instinct of the leader of one of our two main political parties was to believe Russia rather than our own intelligence agencies. We are lucky that our country's safety was never in Jeremy Corbyn's hands.

Immediately after her return from the Commons, the prime minister had a meeting of what is known as JMC(P), a committee that comprises ministers from the UK and the devolved governments. This gave her the chance to discuss the matter with Nicola Sturgeon and Carwyn Jones, first ministers of Scotland and Wales, both of whom expressed their support.

Her attention then turned to securing a co-ordinated international response. She spoke to Justin Trudeau that evening, who expressed Canada's 'unflinching' support, and over the next few days to Emmanuel Macron, who said there was 'no doubt over attribution' and expressed his 'full solidarity with the UK'; to Italian prime minister Paolo Gentiloni and Australian prime minister Malcolm Turnbull, both of whom also expressed their solidarity; to European Council president Donald Tusk, who said that he wanted to strengthen the conclusions of the forthcoming European Council on the issue; and to the Polish prime minister Mateusz Morawiecki, who said that Poland would probably also expel some Russian diplomats, but didn't want to act alone.

On 21 March, the prime minister spoke to President Trump. In such circumstances, the UK would expect the United States to be its more steadfast ally, but not this time. The president said he would only take action if there was a unified European response. We subsequently learned that he had been presented with three possible responses of increasing severity and rejected all of them.

The next day, we headed to Brussels for the European Council, taking the deputy national security adviser Christian Turner with us. Before the formal meeting got under way, the prime minister met with the heads of government of the Nordic and Baltic member states. Christian gave them a short briefing, setting out the evidence that had led us to conclude it was highly likely that Russia was responsible. The prime minister said she would be asking all member states to take co-ordinated action, not just out of solidarity with the UK but in their own interest. Their response was in direct contrast with her conversation with President Trump: they were all prepared to expel Russian intelligence officers and thought the draft council conclusions needed to be tougher.

She then met with President Macron and Chancellor Merkel. Macron said that as the first offensive use of a nerve agent on European soil since the foundation of NATO and the EU, this was an extremely serious incident. The UK was being tested, but so was France and every other country. It would be a serious mistake not to respond – France would expel a number of Russian intelligence officers. Speaking to President Trump had strengthened his view that a unified European response was essential – it might persuade the president that he too should act. He was prepared to wait a few days, but thought it was important to respond quickly. Merkel was in a trickier position. She wanted Germany to be part of any response, but she led a coalition and 'we have a strange debate about Russia'. She asked for time to consult her coalition partner.

The prime minister then went into the formal council meeting to make her case to all twenty-seven member states. The council strengthened its conclusions, stating that it 'agrees with the United

Kingdom government's assessment that it is highly likely that the Russian Federation is responsible and that there is no alternative plausible explanation'. It continued:

> We stand in unqualified solidarity with the United Kingdom in the face of this grave challenge to our shared security. The use of chemical weapons . . . is completely unacceptable, must be systematically and rigorously condemned and constitutes a security threat to us all. Member states will coordinate on the consequences to be drawn in the light of the answers provided by the Russian authorities.

This was the response we'd been looking for. As we flew back to Brussels, I observed to the prime minister that it would have been harder to galvanise such a response had we not been a member of the EU. Not only had she been able to lobby twenty-seven countries in one go, but those countries most sympathetic to our case had put pressure on others to act. It reinforced in our minds the need for a strong security partnership after we had left the EU.

The unified European response had a knock-on effect: as the prime minister and President Macron had hoped, it helped US national security officials change President Trump's mind. On Monday, the prime minister gave a statement to the House of Commons, updating MPs on what had been agreed at the council. She was able to announce that eighteen countries were ever expelling more than a hundred Russian intelligence officers, the largest ever collective expulsion of Russian intelligence officers. To President Trump's credit, once he decided to act, the package he approved was significant, expelling sixty Russian intelligence officers and closing the Russian consulate in Seattle. The list eventually grew to twenty-seven countries (eighteen EU member states and six other European countries, plus the US, Canada and Australia), with some smaller countries that didn't have any Russian intelligence officers to expel finding other ways to express their solidarity. Israel was a notable exception from the list, and the prime minister expressed her disappointment to Prime Minister Netanyahu.

On 12 April, the Organisation for the Prohibition of Chemical Weapons published its analyses of the environmental and biomedical samples its team had collected, which 'confirm the findings of the United Kingdom relating to the identity of the toxic chemical that was used in Salisbury and severely injured three people'.

About ten weeks later, the prime minister met with Alex Younger, chief of MI6 (or 'C', for James Bond aficionados), who informed her that we had been able to identify the two individuals responsible, who were both GRU officers. We knew when they had entered the country, where they had stayed, the route they took to Salisbury and when they left. It was evidence of how data analytics is making espionage much more transparent. Mark Sedwill suggested to the prime minister that he communicate this information to his opposite number in Russia. There was some risk in this – if the Russians made it public, would we look weak for making first contact? However, the prime minister judged that the potential benefits outweighed the risks. We had already demonstrated that we were able to muster a more co-ordinated international response than Putin would have anticipated and that we knew which Russian 'diplomats' were GRU officers, but it would be helpful to demonstrate to him how poor the GRU's tradecraft had been.

On 30 June, a forty-five-year-old man and a forty-four-year-old woman, later named as Charlie Rowley and Dawn Sturgess, were found unwell at a property in Amesbury. Having been admitted to the accident and emergency department at Salisbury District Hospital, they were treated for exposure to an unknown substance. Doctors initially believed they had taken contaminated illegal drugs, but they grew concerned about some of their symptoms and on 2 July sent samples to Porton Down. On 4 July, it was confirmed that Rowley and Sturgess had been poisoned with the same nerve agent that had been used against the Skripals. When the home secretary Sajid Javid informed the House of Commons on 5 July, both were in a critical condition.

Dawn Sturgess died three days later, so this was now a murder investigation. The question was, how had she and Charlie Rowley come into contact with a Novichok? There was nothing in either of their backgrounds to suggest they might have been targeted. All the sites that the Skripals and the GRU officers had visited had been decontaminated and, in any case, there was no evidence that Rowley or Sturgess had visited any of them. The working assumption was that the couple had come into contact with the Novichok somewhere else.

On 4 September, the OPCW published the analysis of its samples, which 'confirm the findings of the United Kingdom relating to the identity of the toxic chemical that intoxicated two individuals in Amesbury and resulted in one fatality. It is the same toxic chemical that was found in the biomedical and environmental samples relating to the poisoning of Mr Sergei Skripal, Ms Yulia Skripal and Mr Nicholas Bailey on 4 March 2018 in Salisbury.'

The next day, the prime minister updated the House of Commons. The police investigation had found sufficient evidence for charges to be brought against two Russian nationals for the conspiracy to murder Sergei Skripal; the attempted murder of Sergei and Yulia Skripal and Detective Sergeant Nick Bailey; the use and possession of Novichok; and causing grievous bodily harm with intent to Yulia Skripal and Nick Bailey. These Russian nationals had travelled under the names Alexander Petrov and Ruslan Boshirov, which the police believed to be aliases. Traces of Novichok were found in the hotel room in London where they stayed, and CCTV footage placed them in the immediate vicinity of the Skripals' house shortly before the Skripals were poisoned via Novichok applied to their front door. The same two men, the prime minister said, were the prime suspects for the murder of Dawn Sturgess. The police had found a small glass counterfeit perfume bottle containing Novichok in Charlie Rowley's house, which it appeared they had recklessly disposed of. Finally, the prime minister confirmed that the government had concluded that the two individuals were GRU officers. She did not say that we knew their real names, because the police had asked us not to reveal them at this stage.

On 12 September, Vladimir Putin said that Russia had identified the two individuals and they were civilians. The next day they gave a comical interview on Russia's state-controlled TV channel, RT. Looking deeply uncomfortable, 'Boshirov' said that they had gone to Salisbury to visit its cathedral, 'famous not just in Europe but in the whole world for its 123-metre spire'. Social media had fun with that, but it was just the latest in a Russian disinformation campaign that had, at various stages, claimed that they never produced Novichoks, that they produced them but then destroyed them, that Slovakia was to blame, that Sweden was to blame, that the Czech Republic was to blame, that terrorists were to blame, that the future mother-in-law of Yulia Skripal was to blame and that the UK was to blame. These risible claims were part of a deliberate strategy of flooding social media with a mass of stories rather than sticking to one, which we could then disprove.

Two weeks later, the Bellingcat website revealed Borishov's real name: Colonel Anatoliy Chepiga. A few days later, they revealed Petrov's real name: Dr Aleksander Mishkin. Both men were in the GRU. To any objective observer, the UK had been vindicated, but the government's response to Salisbury cannot be judged a complete success: we have not been able to secure justice for the family of Dawn Sturgess by prosecuting those responsible for her death. However, we had been far more successful than we were after the murder of Alexander Litvinenko at proving what happened, mobilising international support for our claim and ensuring Putin paid a price for his actions. That success was down to the tradecraft of our intelligence agencies and the efforts of the prime minister, her senior national security advisers and foreign secretary Boris Johnson in assembling an international coalition.

The work to shine a light on the activities of the GRU continues. Just a few weeks after the prime minister's statement in September 2017, the UK helped the Dutch security services foil a GRU plot to hack the headquarters of the OPCW. It is easy to go about our everyday lives blissfully unaware of the threat we face from hostile states like Russia – the cyber attacks on our businesses, the attempts to interfere in our elections and the recent attempts to spread disinformation about the safety of COVID-19 vaccines. We are defended from these threats by the extraordinary men and women of our intelligence agencies. When he was briefed on how the agencies had identified who tried to murder the Skripals, foreign secretary Jeremy Hunt said, 'I'm a very proud taxpayer.' And that's exactly how I felt, too.

I find our relationship with Russia one of the most depressing things about our increasingly dangerous world. As someone who grew up during the 1980s, I had hoped that the collapse of the Soviet Union would herald closer ties between our countries. We owe the Russian people a far greater debt for their heroism in the Second World War than we generally acknowledge. It is tragic that Putin has chosen this course.

CHAPTER 15

AUTHORISING THE USE OF FORCE

The decision to use military force is the most difficult that any prime minister has to make. To be a good prime minister, you must be willing to put the brave men and women of our armed forces in harm's way when the national interest demands it. And though the advent of precision weapons has reduced the risk of civilian casualties, you must also be prepared for the possibility that your decision may lead to the deaths of innocent people. Anyone who can take such decisions easily is not someone I would want to be my prime minister – but nor would I want anyone who is unable to take such decisions to keep our country safe.

Syria

Theresa was only confronted with this decision once during her premiership. In the early hours of 8 April 2018, reports began to emerge of a suspected chemical weapons attack in Douma, the last rebel-held city in Syria's Eastern Ghouta. A number of medical, monitoring and activist groups reported that Syrian Air Force helicopters had dropped barrel bombs on the area. Haunting video footage from the scene showed the bodies of men, women and children with foam bubbling from their mouths and survivors gasping for breath. Witnesses reported a strong smell of chlorine. The Union of Medical Relief Organizations, a charity working in Syrian hospitals, said that seventy people had been killed and many others were being treated for symptoms consistent with nerve or mixed nerve and chlorine gas exposure.

By this point, the Syrian civil war was in its eighth year. About half the civilian population had been displaced, with refugees fleeing into Jordan, Lebanon and Turkey. The Assad regime had used chemical weapons before and been largely allowed to get away with it – the most shameful moment of my seven years as an MP was the vote on 29 August 2013 when parliament, presented with evidence of a chemical weapons attack in Damascus that had led to the deaths of over 800 people, rejected the use of military force. A clear red line had been crossed, and we ducked out of enforcing it. Our failure to act was compounded by President Obama's decision not to do so, leaving innocent Syrian civilians to their fate. The message to Assad and his Russian and Iranian backers was clear: Western governments will wring their hands, but after mistakes in Afghanistan, Iraq and Libya, they have lost the will to act. Diplomatic efforts by the Obama administration did get the Assad regime to commit to dismantling its chemical weapons programme, but the regime never fully complied and attacks continued. In April 2017, a sarin attack killed around a hundred people at Khan Shaykhun. This finally led to some response. President Trump authorised a one-off strike on the Syrian Air Force base from which the attack had been launched, but there continued to be reports of the use of chlorine, and now it looked like there had been another major attack.

On 8 April, a Foreign Office spokesman said: 'These are very concerning reports . . . which, if correct, are further proof of Assad's brutality against innocent civilians and his backers' callous disregard for international norms. An urgent investigation is needed and the international community must respond.' The next day, while the prime minister was travelling to Copenhagen and Stockholm to talk to the Danish and Swedish prime ministers about Brexit, I took a call from Boris Johnson, who was keen for the prime minister to talk to President Trump as soon as possible. His officials were telling him that the US and the French were thinking about taking action, and he thought we should join them. The prime minister spoke to Mark Sedwill, who told her that it was highly likely that the Assad regime was responsible for the attack and that the US and French systems shared that assessment. President Macron was pushing for a military response, but the US was more cautious. The prime minister asked what the attorney general's advice was on the legal position. Mark said that we didn't yet have enough detail for the attorney to provide advice, but given that it was highly unlikely that the UN Security Council would authorise military action (Russia would almost certainly veto any resolution), the only available legal basis was humanitarian. Mark recommended that the prime minister speak to Trump and Macron the next day, and she then let Boris Johnson know what they had agreed.

Theresa was appalled by the footage emerging from Douma. She would later tell the House of Commons that 'the fact that such an atrocity can take place in our world today is a stain on our humanity'. She was equally clear, however, that any military action must be legal and make a positive difference in terms of preventing or deterring the regime from carrying out further attacks.

Early on 10 April, I spoke to Ed Llewellyn, our ambassador to France, who emphasised that the prime minister's decision would have a significant impact on our relationships with France and the US and our wider standing in the world. It was an issue close to his heart – he had been doing my job back in 2013, when parliament voted against military action.

The prime minister then spoke to President Macron, who said France had no doubt regarding the responsibility of the Assad regime. We had collectively defined a clear red line over the use of chemical weapons, so it was vital that we acted. He had taken the decision in principle to use military force and had in mind striking three to four targets. President Trump was in agreement, and they were looking to act in the next seventy-two hours. He very much hoped that the UK would be willing to join them. The prime minister replied that any military action had to be effective in protecting innocent lives. The US cruise missile strike in response to the attack on Khan Shaykhun in 2017 hadn't deterred the regime from further use of chemical weapons. Macron agreed – the aim should be the drastic reduction of the regime's capability to launch these attacks, and he wanted a renewed diplomatic effort alongside the use of military force. It was extremely important to him that the UK be part of this. The prime minister said the government would take a decision later that day.

The conversation with President Trump was, as you might expect, tonally quite different. He started by saying 'we have some mess over in the Middle East' and asked how the PM felt about it in terms of 'retribution'. The PM replied that this couldn't be about retribution – it had to be about stopping the Assad regime from doing this again and part of a wider plan to address Syria's humanitarian crisis. She asked what timeframe the president had in mind. He replied that the Syrians knew a response was coming and we should 'let them get a little tired waiting', but he wanted to act by Saturday and the response should be 'bigger this time'. 'Emmanuel is very enthusiastic and I'm with him. Hopefully you'll be a part of it.'

The prime minister then chaired a meeting of the National Security Council. I can't include everything that was said, but I can mention those things that the prime minister made public at her press conference on 14 April and in her statement to the House of Commons two days later. On the question of whether chemical weapons had been used, the government's assessment was it was likely. On the question of whether the regime was responsible, regime forces had reportedly been searching evacuees from Douma to ensure that samples of gas were not being smuggled from the area. A wider operation to conceal the facts of the attack, supported by the Russians, was also under way. Open-source accounts stated that barrel bombs had been used to deliver the chemicals. Barrel bombs are usually delivered by helicopters, and both intelligence and open-source reports indicated that regime helicopters had operated over Douma on the evening of 7 April and that Syrian military officials co-ordinated what appeared to be the use of chlorine weapons. The opposition did not operate helicopters or use barrel bombs and Daesh did not have a presence in Douma, so this was the only plausible explanation. Finally, the regime had a track record of using chemical weapons, and the reports of this attack were consistent with its previous attacks.

The chief of the defence staff set out the capabilities we possessed that could be deployed should the prime minister decide to authorise the use of military force and the attorney general advised on the legal position. I can summarise his advice, based on what the government subsequently published. In the absence of UN authorisation, he said that the only legal basis for action was the alleviation of humanitarian suffering. The UK had relied on this basis before – for example, for the NATO intervention in Kosovo. It required three conditions to be met. First, there must be convincing evidence of extreme humanitarian distress on a large scale and requiring urgent relief. Secondly, it must be objectively clear that there was no practicable alternative to the use of force if lives were to be saved. Thirdly, the proposed use of force must be necessary and proportionate to the aim of the relief of humanitarian suffering and limited in time and scope to this aim.

There was unanimous agreement that it was in the national interest for us to participate, in order that the use of chemical weapons did not become normalised. There was discussion about the risk to our aircraft, given that Syrian air defences included the latest Russian equipment; about the potential impact on our ability to conduct counter-terrorist operations against Daesh in eastern Syria; and about the risk of escalation if Russian personnel were injured or killed. Mark Sedwill subsequently reassured the prime minister that we would notify the Russians of the targets to be hit in advance – enough time for them to move any personnel, but not enough for the regime to move the stockpiles and equipment we sought to destroy.

There was also a discussion about whether parliament should be recalled. The chief whip's advice was that there was no need to do so. This was also the prime minister's view, for reasons she set out in a statement to parliament after it had returned from the Easter recess on 16 April:

> The speed with which we acted was essential . . . to alleviate further humanitarian suffering and to maintain the vital security of our operations. This was a limited, targeted strike on a legal basis that has been used before. And it was a decision that required the evaluation of intelligence and information, much of which was of a nature that could not be shared with parliament. We have always been clear that the government have the right to act quickly in the national interest. I am absolutely clear that it is parliament's responsibility to hold me to account for such decisions – and parliament will do so. But it is my responsibility as prime minister to make these decisions, and I will make them.

That evening, we received confirmation that the Russians had vetoed a UN resolution to establish an independent investigation to attribute responsibility for what had happened. I managed to speak to nearly all the members of the cabinet who were not members of the NSC to check whether they were supportive of taking action and of not recalling parliament. With the exception of David Lidington, who was supportive of taking action but thought a vote in parliament was desirable, and Chris Grayling, who was not opposed to action but was concerned what the end point would be, there was unanimous support on both fronts.

At the morning meeting on 11 April, Jeremy Heywood argued that there ought to be a formal cabinet meeting to give an opportunity for collective discussion of the issue. James Slack agreed that the media would expect this, so a meeting was called for the next day. There was then a smaller meeting to review the targets: in order to pass the legal test, we needed to hit enough targets for the action to be likely to be effective in preventing further attacks, but not so many as to be disproportionate and escalatory. Officials reported that President Trump wanted to target some of Assad's personal property, which clearly had nothing to do with the regime's capacity to use chemical weapons. And the president didn't help matters by implying the decision had already been taken, tweeting, 'Russia vows to shoot down any and all missiles fired at Syria. Get ready Russia, because they will be coming, nice and new and "smart!"'

When the cabinet met on the morning of 12 April and considered the assessment of the evidence and the legal position, there was very strong support both for the use of force and for the decision not to recall parliament. Ministers were clear that this was not about taking sides in a civil war or regime change; it was about sending a clear message that the use of chemical weapons was unacceptable. The prime minister said that the final decision would be for her, the attorney general and the secretary of state for defence, and it was likely to be made over the next forty-eight hours. She implored the cabinet not to leak what had been discussed – the lives of our personnel were at risk – and on this occasion there was none of the usual anonymous briefing to favoured journalists.

Later that day, the prime minister had another brief conversation with President Trump, who was content with the target set that had been selected. On 13 April, she signed off the final target set in consultation with the secretary of state for defence and the attorney general and had a brief conversation with President Macron, which he ended 'Fingers crossed and let's speak tomorrow.' That evening, she spoke to John Major and David Cameron, and to opposition leaders to give them a few hours' notice of what was coming. I called Michael Howard, Iain Duncan Smith and Graham Brady, the chairman of the 1922 Committee, on her behalf. In the early hours of 14 April,

US, French and British forces – including four RAF Tornado GR4s from Akrotiri in Cyprus – attacked three sites in Syria: the Barzeh branch of the Scientific Studies and Research Centre in northern Damascus, a centre for the development of Syria's chemical and bio-logical programme; the Him Shinsar chemical weapons bunkers, fifteen miles west of Homs, which contained a chemical weapons equipment and storage facility and an important command post; and the Him Shinsar chemical weapons storage site and former missile base, which was assessed to be a location of sarin and precursor pro-duction equipment. While a full assessment of the attacks would take time, the initial assessment was that they had been successful, and neither we nor our allies had suffered any casualties.

As her chief of staff, I thought the prime minister had done the right thing: other regimes around the world would be watching to see if Assad got away with breaking the international prohibition on the use of chemical weapons; if they concluded that he had, the world would be less safe. But as her most senior political adviser, I was nerv-ous about what MPs and the public would think. The long conflicts we had been sucked into in Afghanistan and Iraq had left their mark on British politics. There had always been those who believed that the use of force was only legitimate if authorised by the United Nations, a position I found bizarre, since it amounted to saying, 'We're OK with anything that Vladimir Putin and Xi Jinping think is OK.' But those who insisted on UN authorisation had been joined by those who were sceptical about whether military intervention made things any better. Their argument boiled down to, 'Yes, the pictures from Syria are horrific, but remember what happened in Afghanistan, Iraq and Libya.' I had some sympathy with these arguments, but we were not proposing to invade Syria or bring down the Assad regime; this was a one-off strike to degrade the regime's ability to use chemical weapons against its own people and deter it and others from doing so in the future.

More problematically, what has become known as the 'dodgy

dossier' in the run-up to the Iraq War had made people less trust-
ing when the government said, 'We have intelligence that convinces
us the Assad regime was responsible, but we can't share it all with
you.' This was an understandable reaction, but now I was working
at the heart of the government and knew that there *were* things that
increased our confidence that the regime was responsible for what
happened in Douma, but which we couldn't say, because making
public what we knew might allow the Assad regime to work out how
we knew it. I pushed for as much evidence as possible to be put into
the public domain and had an ally in Mark Sedwill, but the challenge
remained: how could we convince MPs and the public that what we
were saying hadn't been 'sexed up' and that they should trust us when
we said there was more evidence we couldn't make public?

I was also concerned about MPs' reaction to the decision not to
recall parliament. Again, I thought the prime minister was doing the
right thing – this was a one-off strike, not a declaration of war, and
a vote in parliament would have delayed the operation and given the
Syrians warning. But my years as a whip had taught me that MPs
often prefer to have a row about process rather than grapple with a
difficult policy choice, and we were giving them an excuse to do just
that.

I discussed these concerns with the prime minister, but her focus
was on what was the right thing to do – only once she had taken
that decision would she think about how to persuade others. On the
Saturday morning, she returned to Downing Street to hold a press
conference at which she set out her case. She acknowledged the
seriousness of the decision to use force and explained why she had
concluded it was necessary:

> There is no graver decision for a prime minister than to commit
> our forces to combat – and this is the first time that I have had to
> do so . . . We would have preferred an alternative path. But on
> this occasion there is none. We cannot allow the use of chemical

weapons to become normalised . . . This action is absolutely in Britain's national interest. The lesson of history is that when the global rules and standards that keep us safe come under threat, we must take a stand and defend them.

She then proceeded to answer over twenty questions. It was quite a contrast to the Theresa May who was reluctant to do set-piece political interviews. She understood the need to explain why she had taken this decision, she was confident that she had done the right thing and she was in complete command of the detail. It was a very impressive performance, and further evidence that she was most comfortable when dealing with issues of national security.

She and I spent most of the next thirty-six hours on the phone, in her case speaking to a succession of world leaders. Chancellor Merkel welcomed the US, France and the UK taking responsibility on behalf of the international community. Prime Minister Turnbull of Australia thought the response was well calibrated. President Erdogan of Turkey thought the action was helpful, though warned that it was important to avoid escalation with Russia. Prime Minister Anastasiades of Cyprus was fully supportive and grateful for the measures taken to avoid retaliatory action against Cyprus. Prime Minister Gentiloni of Italy thought the response was justified, but hoped it would be limited. Crown Prince Mohammed bin Salman said that Saudi Arabia always supported her allies in steps such as these. Prime Minister Trudeau of Canada agreed with the action and thought it was good that it had been multilateral. Prime Minister Netanyahu of Israel also thought the multilateral nature of the strikes important; the prime minister asked him to reinforce our resolve with Putin, with whom Netanyahu had a good relationship. Jean-Claude Juncker, president of the European Commission, thought it had been the right thing to do. António Guterres, the secretary general of the United Nations, stressed that compliance with the UN Charter was important, but his main concern was avoiding escalation.

I called senior Conservative and Labour MPs and a few grandees. On the Conservative side, I spoke to four former members of Theresa's cabinet – Damian Green, Justine Greening, James Brokenshire and Priti Patel – and to Ken Clarke, George Osborne and Ruth Davidson. All were supportive. Ken felt she should have recalled parliament, but he was avoiding doing media interviews because he was conscious they would focus on that and not his support for the action.

Both the prime minister and I had been deeply moved by the support she had received from the Labour benches over Salisbury. We recognised that this would be more difficult – Salisbury had been an attack on Britain; this was us using military force, albeit in defence of our national interests – but if we could secure some opposition support, it would make things much easier. I had already had an opaque conversation with John Woodcock the day before; he had been supportive of the prime minister's right to take this decision and suggested some other names for me to call. Chris Leslie thought the PM had got it about right and expected twenty to thirty Labour MPs to support the government if there was a vote. Phil Wilson said he would support the government, but that it was vital to keep repeating that this was about chemical weapons and not regime change. Kevan Jones said he supported military action, but the key question was what came next. Ben Bradshaw had already tweeted his support by the time I called, but thought the prime minister should seek retrospective approval from parliament. Alison McGovern and Stephen Doughty were interested in the wider strategy to address the refugee crisis. And Yvette Cooper thought parliament should have been consulted, but agreed that there was a moral justification for action. All appreciated the invitation to a cross-party briefing for MPs and peers by Charles Farr, Mark Sedwill and Air Vice-Marshal Andrew Turner on Monday morning.

On Monday afternoon, the prime minister gave a statement to parliament. She set out why the government believed military action was not just morally right, but legal. This was 'a limited, targeted and effective strike that sought to alleviate the humanitarian suffering of the Syrian people by degrading the Syrian regime's chemical weapons capability and deterring their use'. It met the three tests for humanitarian intervention. First, there was clear evidence of extreme humanitarian distress and an urgent need to act; based on the regime's persistent pattern of behaviour and the cumulative analysis of specific incidents, we judged it highly likely that it would have continued to use chemical weapons. Second, there was no alternative to the use of force if lives were to be saved. We had tried to resolve this issue diplomatically for nearly five years, and we had been repeatedly thwarted. The Assad regime had promised to dismantle its chemical weapons programme back in 2013, but it had not done so – and Russia was increasingly blocking any attempts to hold the regime to account. It had just vetoed a UN resolution that would have established an independent investigation to determine responsibility for what happened in Douma. Finally, the use of force had been proportionate. We had 'expressly sought to avoid escalation and did everything possible to prevent civilian casualties' but these strikes 'were significantly larger than the US action a year ago after the attack at Khan Shaykhun' in order that they had 'a greater impact on the regime's capability and willingness to use chemical weapons'.

In his response, Jeremy Corbyn accepted that chemical weapons had been used against civilians in Douma, but argued that 'while much suspicion rightly points to the Assad regime', it could have been someone else. And even if it *was* the Assad regime, he certainly didn't support taking military action to stop it happening again – he disputed whether alleviating humanitarian suffering could ever provide a legal basis for military action and argued that, despite the repeated Russian vetoes, we should keep trying with the diplomacy. It was a shameful argument for letting Assad get away with it.

Fortunately, plenty of Labour MPs disagreed with him. Liz Kendall, Chris Leslie, Ben Bradshaw, Barry Sheerman, Mike Gapes, Emma Reynolds, Kevan Jones, Chris Bryant, Mary Creagh, Jess

Phillips, John Woodcock, Peter Kyle, Steve McCabe and Anna Turley all rose from the Labour benches to support the prime minister's decision to take action, although some of them made it clear that they thought she should have recalled parliament first. Mike Gapes reminded everyone just how different Jeremy Corbyn was from previous Labour leaders:

> It was a Labour government, with Robin Cook as foreign secretary, that carried out airstrikes in Iraq under Operation Desert Fox in 1998, without a UN resolution. It was a Labour government that restored President Kabbah in Sierra Leone, without a UN resolution. It was a Labour government that stopped the ethnic cleansing in Kosovo, without a UN resolution. There is a long-standing and noble tradition on these benches of supporting humanitarian intervention.

The prime minister answered questions from 140 backbench MPs and then spoke in the ensuing emergency debate. She was back in the Commons the next day for another emergency debate, this time on a motion proposed by Jeremy Corbyn on parliament's rights in relation to the approval of military action. It had been clear the previous day that there was widespread support for taking action against the Assad regime, but also that opinion was divided on whether the prime minister should have come to parliament first. In her speech, she tried to correct a widespread misperception:

> Let me begin by being absolutely clear about the government's policy in relation to the convention that has developed, because there is a fundamental difference between the policy and the perception of it that is conveyed in today's motion. The cabinet manual states, 'In 2011, the government acknowledged that a convention had developed in parliament that before troops were committed, the House of Commons should have an opportunity

to debate the matter and said that it proposed to observe that convention except where there was an emergency and such action would not be appropriate.' More detail on the government's position was then set out in 2016, in a written ministerial statement from then defence secretary, my right honourable friend the member for Sevenoaks [Sir Michael Fallon], who wrote: '[. . .] In observing the convention, we must ensure that the ability of our armed forces to act quickly and decisively, and to maintain the security of their operations, is not compromised.'

There were, she argued, situations like the Iraq War, when the scale of the military build-up required the movement of assets over weeks and it was appropriate for parliament to debate military action in advance, but 'that does not mean that is always appropriate – this, therefore, cannot and should not be codified into a parliamentary right to debate every overseas mission in advance'. This was a controversial view, but it was something she believed very strongly.

Emergency debates take the form 'That this House has considered . . .' so there isn't anything to vote for or against at the end – the purpose is to give MPs the chance to debate an issue and question the relevant minister. In this case, Jeremy Corbyn invited MPs who agreed with him to vote against this rather bland motion, but it passed by 317 votes to 256.

Several years on, how we should assess the prime minister's decision? First, it clearly had some impact on the Assad regime's capability and willingness to use chemical weapons: there have been no more major attacks. She had also clearly reasserted the right of the government to use military force without first going to parliament in certain circumstances, although she was helped by the fact that the House wasn't sitting during the crucial week. The contrast between her and Jeremy Corbyn over both Salisbury and Syria led to an improvement in her and the government's standing, both among the media and the general public. Her favourability ratings had been worse than

Jeremy Corbyn's since the general election; now she was back ahead. The Conservatives opened up a small lead in the polls, and the local election results in May were better than we expected. It was the closest she came during my two years working for her to regaining the authority she'd had before the election.

CHAPTER 16

NEGOTIATING WITH BRUSSELS

By the time I was appointed chief of staff, many of the pieces on the Brexit chess board were already in place. The Article 50 clock was ticking and the sequencing of the negotiations had been agreed. It would have been very difficult for Theresa to call another election, so the parliamentary arithmetic was set in stone. Devolved government in Northern Ireland had collapsed and there was little incentive for either the DUP or Sinn Féin to restore it.

The key figures we would be dealing with were also in place: Jean-Claude Juncker, the president of the European Commission; Michel Barnier, the EU's chief negotiator; and Donald Tusk, the president of the European Council, and the key heads of government, including French president Emmanuel Macron, German chancellor Angela Merkel and Irish taoiseach Leo Varadkar.

Varadkar was the youngest ever Taoiseach, of mixed Irish/Indian heritage and the first ever Irish minister to come out as gay, in many ways the embodiment of the new, socially liberal Ireland. He and Theresa didn't instantly hit it off, but their relationship improved over time.

Macron and Merkel were contrasting figures. The French president was a fluent English speaker, new on the scene, and liked to think of himself as a big, strategic thinker. Brexit had come before he had been able to formulate and sell his vision of a Europe of concentric rings. He didn't want to agree a bespoke deal for the UK; he wanted to think more generally about what kind of relationship the

EU wanted with countries in the outer ring, outside the single market but on its border. He was an anglophile and wanted a closer bilateral relationship with the UK, but he was also very open with the prime minister that Brexit couldn't be a success and it never seemed to occur to him that his attitude towards Brexit might have consequences for his desire for a much closer relationship with the UK.

Merkel was vastly experienced, a master of the detail, and would sometimes gently school Macron. In a discussion about the JCOPA agreement with Iran at the EU–Western Balkans Summit in Sofia in May 2018, she told him that 'the Americans see us as children that need to be disciplined, so we shouldn't confirm that impression', and when Macron suggested speaking to other European leaders to see if any of them were tempted to support the US position, she said, 'you're close to [Austrian Chancellor Sebastian] Kurz in age – you speak to him.' On Brexit, she was determined to find a landing zone for a deal, though not at any price – Boris Johnson was fortunate that Germany had the rotating presidency of the European Council in the second half of 2020. She would occassionally literally translate German idioms into English to amusing effect. On one occasion, she was enquiring whether it would be helpful for her to make an intervention in British politics to tell people some hard facts, but it came out as 'Would it help if I got the big hammer out?' One of her aides suppressed a laugh and said, 'Chancellor, I'm not sure that's what you intended to say.'

Our own negotiating team was also in place by the time I arrived in Number 10. In July 2016, Theresa had appointed Olly Robbins, who she had worked with at the Home Office, as her EU sherpa. He would lead the negotiations at official level, opposite the commission's Sabine Weyand. Olly is a brilliant man – highly intelligent with an incredible work ethic and a passion for public service. Over the two years I worked with him, he was repeatedly subjected to hostile briefings from some of my former colleagues, who chose to pick on a civil servant who they knew couldn't answer back rather than the ministers whose instructions he was following. When you stand for elected office, you accept that people will say unpleasant things about you, particularly in this age of social media. Civil servants do not expect or deserve such public scrutiny; it was upsetting to Olly and his family, and we should have done more to put a stop to it.

Olly built an incredible team, many of whom have gone on to senior roles in the civil service. Despite the difficulties the government had in reaching collective agreement about what the UK wanted – and the difficulties some ministers then had in sticking to the script – Olly's team was highly respected by their EU counterparts. As I will explain, they succeeded in extracting some significant concessions from the EU, despite having a weaker negotiating hand. They never got much credit for it because the deal they were asked to negotiate was too soft for some MPs and too hard for others, but the Withdrawal Agreement Boris Johnson eventually ratified is 95 per cent their and Theresa's work. And they were ably supported by the senior Foreign Office official in Brussels, our permanent representative to the EU Tim Barrow. If Olly had an incredible eye for policy detail, Tim believed in diplomacy by personal relationships. He knew anyone who was anyone in Brussels, and was a gracious host every time we stayed overnight in Brussels.

Olly saw himself as reporting to the prime minister. This was initially a big problem, because as well as being the prime minister's EU sherpa, he was also the permanent secretary of the Department for Exiting the European Union, in which capacity he reported to David Davis. We separated the two jobs in September 2017, but the problem persisted. This was, at least in part, inevitable: whoever was secretary of state expected to play a leading role in the negotiations, but at the key moments they had to be led by the prime minister. However, this tension was exacerbated by Olly's judgement that interactions between Michel Barnier and the secretary of state were rarely helpful. He was probably right about that, but I struggled to get him to see that while they might not move things forward, it was vital that the parliamentary party saw that a leading Brexiteer was involved in the negotiations.

In terms of what the UK was seeking to negotiate, the prime minister's Lancaster House speech in January 2017 had set out twelve objectives:

1. Guarantee the rights of EU citizens already living in Britain and the rights of British nationals in other member states as quickly as possible.
2. Seek to negotiate a unique arrangement, rather than adopting a model already enjoyed by other countries.
3. Take back control of our laws and bring an end to the jurisdiction of the Court of Justice of the European Union in the UK.
4. Maintain the common travel area with Ireland.
5. Other than that, take back control of the number of people coming to Britain from the EU by ending free movement.
6. Leave the single market, but negotiate the greatest possible access to it through a comprehensive and ambitious free trade agreement, which might take in elements of current single market arrangements.
7. Leave the common commercial policy, so the UK would not be bound by the common external tariff, but have a customs arrangement with the EU, to make trade tariff-free and as frictionless as possible.
8. Potentially continue to participate in some EU programmes, making an appropriate financial contribution.
9. End vast annual financial contributions to the EU.
10. Continue to collaborate on major science, research and technology initiatives.
11. Agree practical arrangements on matters of law enforcement and the sharing of intelligence material.

12. Agree a phased process of implementation, in which Britain, the EU institutions, member states, businesses and citizens could prepare for the new arrangements.

It was clear from comparing these objectives with the EU's negotiating guidelines that there were some areas where the two sides wanted similar things and others where there was a significant gap between our respective positions. Both sides wanted to protect British citizens who had settled in the EU and EU citizens who had settled in the UK, but Theresa's desire to do so in advance of settling other issues was in tension with the EU's 'nothing is agreed until everything is agreed' principle. On trade, her desire for a free trade agreement that might 'include elements of current single market arrangements in certain areas' was potentially in tension with the EU's insistence that there could be no sector-by-sector approach to participation. Her desire that the UK might continue to participate in certain EU programmes was in tension with her desire to end the jurisdiction of the Court of Justice of the European Union. But potentially, the most difficult objective was her desire for a bespoke British model. Although the UK's unique circumstances warranted one, the EU was reluctant to create a new model, preferring to offer us a choice between the single market/customs union and a free trade agreement.

It was immediately clear that customs was going to be the most difficult issue. If the UK didn't stay in some form of customs union with the EU, that would logically mean customs declarations when goods moved between Ireland and Northern Ireland. But if it stayed in some form of customs union, how would it have the freedom to set its own tariffs, a key element of an independent trade policy? The ability to do trade deals with non-EU countries, along with regulatory autonomy, were the key upsides of Brexit. What was the point of leaving in a way that prevented you from enjoying these upsides? The government had to find a way of squaring this circle.

We made a start in August, publishing a paper on future customs arrangements that set out two options. The first, which came to be known as 'maximum facilitations' or 'max fac', involved building on the UK's existing tried-and-tested third country customs processes with additional facilitations, as well as implementing technology-based solutions to make it easier for businesses to comply with them. Though it allowed a fully independent trade policy, the drawback was that it could not remove friction at the border entirely and would not prevent a hard border in Ireland.

The second option, which came to be known as 'hybrid', involved effectively acting as the EU's customs agent for imports coming into the UK that were destined for the EU, but charging our own tariffs on goods that were destined for the UK market. Its advantage was that, if combined with regulatory alignment, it avoided the need for a hard border in Ireland and allowed an independent trade policy, but the drawback was that the technology was unproven. The debate between these two options would consume the government for the next ten months.

Florence

Following the publication of these papers, the prime minister decided to give a major speech on Brexit shortly before party conference. There were four aims: to reassure the EU that the UK would remain a reliable long-term partner after Brexit; to give a helpful push on a couple of the key issues in the first phase of the negotiations; to provide more detail about the future relationship we were seeking; and to allow the prime minister to devote more of her conference speech to domestic policy.

Brexit speeches were difficult to write because they had to cater to a domestic and a European audience, and you found yourself walking a tightrope between trying to advance the negotiations and avoiding causing an eruption at home. Every word was argued over, with Olly sometimes being given permission to explain what the prime minister was hinting at because we didn't feel she could say it bluntly. For this speech, we were more focused on the European audience, so we decided the prime minister should deliver it in a member state. We eventually settled on Florence, the birthplace of the Renaissance.

Because of the timing of the speech – sandwiched between the prime minister's address to the UN General Assembly and her party conference speech – it had to be written while we were in New York. This included a surreal drafting session on the overnight flight back, where I tried to focus despite Boris Johnson snoring just behind me and then had to tiptoe past a sleeping prime minister to take my comments to Alex Dawson and Denzil Davidson in the middle cabin of the RAF Voyager.

The final text offered reassurance that, unlike President Trump, who would clearly have been happy to see the EU fall apart, the UK believed that 'the success of the EU is profoundly in our national interest and that of the wider world'. It also rebutted media speculation that we might withdraw security co-operation if we weren't given sufficient market access, stating clearly that 'the United Kingdom is unconditionally committed to maintaining Europe's security'.

In terms of the issues in the first phase of the negotiations, the prime minister addressed concerns over the financial settlement and the risk that the rights of EU citizens in the UK and UK citizens in the EU would diverge over time:

> I want to incorporate our agreement fully into UK law and make sure the UK courts can refer directly to it. Where there is uncertainty around underlying EU law, I want the UK courts to be able to take into account the judgements of the European Court of Justice with a view to ensuring consistent interpretation. On this basis, I hope our teams can reach firm agreement quickly . . . Some of the claims made on [our financial obligations] are exaggerated and unhelpful and we can only resolve this as part of the settlement of all the issues I have been talking

about today. Still, I do not want our partners to fear that they will need to pay more or receive less over the remainder of the current budget plan as a result of our decision to leave: the UK will honour commitments we have made during the period of our membership.

But the most significant elements of the speech were about the future relationship and implementation arrangements. On the future relationship, the prime minister explained why she thought none of the existing models would work for the UK – or indeed the EU – explicitly rejecting the Canada-style FTA that some Brexiteers wanted:

> European Economic Area [single market] membership would mean the UK having to adopt at home – automatically and in their entirety – new EU rules. Rules over which, in future, we will have little influence and no vote . . . As for a Canadian-style free trade agreement, we should recognise that this is the most advanced free trade agreement the EU has yet concluded. . . but compared with what exists between Britain and the EU today, it would nevertheless represent such a restriction on our mutual market access that it would benefit neither of our economies.

She recognised that any new model would have to strike a new balance between rights and obligations:

> We recognise that the single market is built on a balance of rights and obligations. And we do not pretend that you can have all the benefits of membership of the single market without its obligations. So our task is to find a new framework that allows for a close economic partnership but holds those rights and obligations in a new and different balance.

And she acknowledged that the trade deal we were looking to negotiate would not be about removing barriers to trade, as most trade deals do, but about when and by how much to put them up when regulatory standards diverged. She then tentatively sketched out what this might mean in terms of regulatory policy:

> There will be areas of policy and regulation which are outside the scope of our trade and economic relations where this should be straightforward. There will be areas which do affect our economic relations where we and our European friends may have different goals; or where we share the same goals but want to achieve them through different means. And there will be areas where we want to achieve the same goals in the same ways, because it makes sense for our economies. And because rights and obligations must be held in balance, the decisions we both take will have consequences for the UK's access to European markets and vice versa.

What became known as the 'three buckets' approach gave the EU an insight into her thinking. She was saying there were some areas where we were going to do things differently, and we accepted that we would have to pay a price for that in terms of market access. She was questioning whether, if we were achieving the same thing in a slightly different way – but it didn't give our businesses a competitive advantage – it had to mean less market access. And she was hinting that in some areas, we would be happy to carry on having the same rules as the EU – but crucially, without saying whether we would make a legal commitment to staying aligned. Brexiteers had no problem with having the same laws as the EU if that is what our elected parliament chose to do, but many did have a problem with making a legal commitment that we would continue to do so in certain areas.

The prime minister then turned to implementation arrangements. She had said at Lancaster House in January that such arrangements might be necessary, and Philip Hammond had spent the summer lobbying her to ask for an implementation period. His argument was simple enough. Under EU law, any future relationship treaty could only be negotiated and ratified after we had left, so – unless we were going to trade on WTO terms in the interim, which would mean tariffs, border checks, loss of access for service providers and therefore significant economic disruption – some interim arrangements were required. We needed certainty that there would be such a period as soon as possible. Without it, some UK businesses would start setting up entities in the EU to ensure they could continue to trade in the event of no deal, which would mean jobs moving from the UK to the EU that probably wouldn't come back even if we ultimately got a deal. It didn't make sense to make businesses go through two sets of changes, so the framework for this interim period should be the status quo. But that would mean continuing to follow EU rules after we had legally left and no longer had any say in those rules, which was deeply uncomfortable.

On this, Philip had an unlikely ally in David Davis. David's judgement was that as long as any implementation period ended by the spring of 2021, so that we'd sorted out any disruption and voters could see the benefits of Brexit before the next election, it was a good idea because it would ensure leaving was a smooth process. This alliance between two senior ministers who had been on different sides of the Brexit argument convinced the PM, so her speech included a clear request for such a period – but she stressed that it should be time-limited.

Ruling out a Canada-style FTA and proposing that we should continue to follow EU rules for a period after we had legally left were two big pills for hardcore Brexiteers to swallow. I remember being nervous about their reaction, but when the prime minister made a statement to the House of Commons after the conference recess, Iain Duncan Smith warmly welcomed it, while Anna Soubry, from the opposite side of the argument, described it as 'an excellent speech'.

But the real test was the EU reaction, and it had the desired effect here, too. At the end of the fourth round of negotiations, which took place the week after the speech, Michel Barnier declared that Florence had created 'a new dynamic'. Although we would not achieve 'sufficient progress' at the October European Council, we were heading in the right direction.

Sufficient progress

In the aftermath of the Florence speech, we were confident of achieving 'sufficient progress' at the December council. A team of Treasury civil servants managed to roughly halve the EU's demands in terms of the financial settlement, and on citizens' rights, we reached agreement on reciprocal healthcare and pensions.

Some difficult issues remained, in particular the EU's insistence that the only way to ensure that the rights of EU citizens in the UK and UK citizens in the EU didn't diverge was for the UK to continue to abide by the CJEU's interpretation of those rights. A meeting of the cabinet committee responsible for our negotiation strategy, known as EUXT(SN), was called. David Davis forcefully argued that we had to achieve sufficient progress at the December council. None of the issues would get any easier if we left it to March, and if the implementation period the prime minister had asked for wasn't confirmed until 2018, businesses would already have taken decisions to move jobs to the EU. His biggest concern was citizens' rights – he was happy for our courts to pay due regard to CJEU decisions, but opposed to any referral process from our courts to the CJEU. Boris was less enthusiastic about doing the deal – he felt we were making big concessions, he shared David's concern about the role of the CJEU, and he questioned how we could address the Irish problem until we knew what future relationship we wanted. But everybody else agreed that we had to try to get over the hurdle in December. Damian Green, Philip Hammond, Amber Rudd and Greg Clark were the most positive, arguing that the government needed to demonstrate momentum or business confidence would suffer. Gavin Williamson stressed the importance of agreeing citizens' rights before the forthcoming London local elections and suggested a referral process to the CJEU was acceptable, provided it had a sunset clause. James Brokenshire, Liam Fox and Michael Gove supported making progress, but with caveats. James shared Boris's frustration that we were being asked for a solution to the Irish border problem before we could talk about the future relationship, and he was worried about EU citizens in the UK having more generous family reunion rights than UK citizens. Liam could defend the financial settlement, but shared the concerns about family reunion and the CJEU and wanted to be able to sign trade deals during the implementation period. And Michael Gove was worried about the fishing industry during the implementation period. The prime minister had the agreement of her senior ministers to try to reach a deal.

On 24 November, Theresa was in Brussels for a summit between the EU and some of its eastern neighbours, which gave her a chance to talk to Donald Tusk. He told her there was 'active interest' from member states in achieving sufficient progress, but warned that he was concerned about Ireland. The Irish taoiseach Leo Varadkar was being tougher in private than he was in public, and if he wasn't satisfied, others wouldn't be. Jeppe Tranholm-Mikkelsen, the secretary general of the council, was blunt: our 'imaginative solutions' on customs hadn't convinced the EU or the Irish. They wanted any withdrawal agreement to include something more detailed than a general commitment not to allow a return to a hard border, something that spelt out how we would do that if the overall UK–EU future relationship didn't achieve it or wasn't concluded by the end of any implementation period. The prime minister raised the concerns regarding the referral process to the CJEU on citizens' rights. Here, Tusk said the French were taking the most hardline position and encouraged her to settle the issue in the negotiations rather than leaving it to be settled at the council. The prime minister was due to see the commission president Jean-Claude Juncker and Michel Barnier on 4 December. If Barnier judged after that meeting that sufficient progress had been achieved, Tusk's teams could draft guidelines for the next phase of the negotiations for approval by the European Council on 15 December.

The negotiations continued and it felt like we were nearly there. At the end of November, the prime minister briefed ministers. Again, Boris struck the most negative note, arguing that the referral process to the CJEU was 'wrong in principle and will go down badly'. But Philip Hammond and David Davis reprised their arguments that the government needed some momentum – if we were going to have an implementation period, they said, we needed an agreement as soon as possible. Everyone else agreed that we needed to make progress, with Andrea Leadsom presciently warning that getting any deal through parliament would be as big a challenge as negotiating it.

Then, just a few days before the prime minister was due to meet President Juncker, the EU negotiating team presented our team with revised text on Northern Ireland, which went much further than we were expecting. The key section was what would become paragraph 49 of the joint report that was published a week later. It said that the UK was committed to protecting north–south co-operation and avoiding a hard border, and that we hoped to achieve these objectives through the overall EU–UK future relationship, but should this not be possible, we would propose specific solutions to address the unique circumstances of the island of Ireland; in their absence, we would maintain full alignment with those rules of the internal market and the customs union which supported north–south co-operation, the all-island economy and the protection of the 1998 agreement. Put simply, plan A was that the overall UK–EU future relationship solved the problem, plan B was the future relationship plus a few Ireland-specific measures did and plan C was a backstop in the withdrawal agreement, in case neither plan A nor plan B could be agreed.

The prime minister was hugely frustrated when Olly told her about this text. She was exasperated at being asked to make commitments about what we would do if we couldn't reach an agreement about our future relationship before we'd even had a chance to talk about it. Furthermore, if we were unable to reach agreement, plan C would mean either the UK staying in the customs union and aligned with some single market rules or Northern Ireland doing so, which would mean a partial border within our own country – something she was not prepared to countenance. And the DUP – whose support she depended on – were bound to feel the same way.

Nevertheless, it was clear that if we rejected the text outright, we would not be able to achieve 'sufficient progress'. What, then, should we do? We were the ones under time pressure; the EU could stick to its position, safe in the knowledge that a parliamentary majority was opposed to no deal, so the UK would have to compromise sooner or later. The prime minister began to think about whether we could live with the text and deal with the problems in the next phase of the negotiations. She spoke to David Davis, who was also coming round to the idea that we could sort things out down the line.

Theresa's frustration wasn't helped by the fact that Leo Varadkar studiously avoided taking her calls that weekend, something that I can't remember any other head of government doing. And, as if things weren't difficult enough, on 2 December Donald Tusk visited Dublin for talks with Varadkar and, having explained that if the UK offer was unacceptable to Ireland it would be unacceptable to the EU, added, 'This is why the key to the UK's future lies, in some ways, in Dublin.' It is difficult to think of anything more inflammatory he could have said as far as the DUP were concerned, and it wasn't the only time he made such remarks. Maybe they were slips of the tongue, maybe they were gestures of solidarity to a fellow EU member or maybe, as a Pole, he had a natural sympathy for a country having to deal with a larger neighbour.

On 4 December, the prime minister, despite her misgivings, went to Brussels to meet with President Juncker and agree the joint report. It was one of the very few occasions I didn't accompany her on a visit to Brussels – I stayed in London, to brief MPs on the deal at the request of Julian Smith, who had recently taken over as chief whip. What followed was one of the worst days of my time as chief of staff. Arlene Foster said in an interview that 'any form of regulatory divergence' between Northern Ireland and Great Britain was unacceptable. Julian and I were both contacted by a number of Conservative MPs, who either supported the DUP's position or were worried that we were about to do something that would lead to the collapse of the confidence and supply agreement and therefore the end of the government. Julian called the prime minister to inform her that it was too dangerous to proceed. She called Arlene from Brussels, but she was unable to talk her round and had to return to London without an agreement.

We were now in a deep hole. We needed to quickly repair relations with the DUP, identify changes to the text that would address their concerns and see if they were negotiable. President Juncker had told the prime minister, in confidence, that he had a personal commitment he couldn't move on Friday morning. If we wanted to secure 'sufficient progress' at the December council, Thursday evening would be our last chance.

We formed a small negotiating team made up of me, Northern Ireland secretary James Brokenshire; Jonathan Caine, a special adviser in the Northern Ireland Office; Denzil Davidson; and Simon Case and Brendan Threlfall from Olly's team. We spent most of Tuesday in discussion with the DUP team in the chief whip's office in 9 Downing Street. We started by showing them the text of the entire joint report, despite the fact that member state governments had not yet seen it. Thankfully, they had no concerns with the other sections. Then we began to discuss potential amendments to the section relating to Northern Ireland. On Wednesday, Theresa apologised to Arlene and thanked her for the work of her negotiating team, but also let her know that she felt that the national interest would be best served by achieving sufficient progress at the December council, so we had to resolve the problem quickly. She then had a positive conversation with Leo Varadkar. He explained that he couldn't agree to the key part of the text being watered down – he didn't want to be remembered as the taoiseach who agreed to the reintroduction of a border between north and south – but he understood that she needed to secure some changes. He also promised to be the UK's best friend in the second phase of the negotiations – after all, the east–west trading relationship was economically even more important than the north–south one. Rather cheekily, given his refusal to take her calls over the weekend, he suggested that they should talk more.

At lunchtime on Thursday, Olly called from Brussels to talk the prime minister through eight changes he had secured to the text. Both parties now recognised the need to respect the provisions of the Good Friday Agreement regarding the constitutional status of Northern Ireland and the principle of consent. In the event that we found ourselves in the backstop, the UK would ensure unfettered access for Northern Ireland's businesses to the whole of the UK internal market and also that no new regulatory barriers developed between Northern Ireland and the rest of the United Kingdom, unless the Northern Ireland executive and assembly agreed that distinct arrangements were appropriate. And the text now referred to 'the Good Friday or Belfast Agreement', rather than just the Good Friday Agreement, which was what nationalists called it.

Olly was sent back to try for more and managed to secure one further change. By that point it was early evening and Juncker wanted to know if the prime minister was coming to Brussels. To add a surreal element to proceedings, the Number 10 Christmas party was getting under way. We discovered that the DUP negotiating team had gone back to Belfast without telling us, so we tried to call Arlene. The prime minister spoke to her at 9.45 p.m. and they agreed that Arlene would call back by 11 p.m. after speaking to her team.

While we waited – with 'Come on Eileen' by Dexys Midnight Runners blaring out from upstairs at one point – I had a private chat with the prime minister about what she would do if Arlene didn't give her the all-clear. As her senior political adviser, I had to warn her that she would be taking a massive risk if she called the DUP's bluff, but I was worried about the consequences if we didn't get into the next phase of the negotiations. She said she understood the risk, but felt she had to do what she thought was in the national interest.

For me, that conversation – just the two of us, in her private office – was an important moment in our relationship. If you are going to sacrifice other areas of your life for your job, you have to believe in what you're doing. If that job is working for a senior politician, you'll never agree with them on every issue, but you have to believe their motivation is right – that when the chips are down, they'll do what they believe is right for the country. Every day I worked for her, Theresa May passed that test, but that conversation – in a moment of the greatest possible stress – is one that stands out.

I then had a brief conversation with David Davis, who was supportive of her agreeing the revised text. I passed the phone to the prime minister, aware that his support would reassure her about the risk she was about to take, before putting Philip Hammond and Amber Rudd through, who were equally supportive. Arlene hadn't called back by 11 p.m., so the prime minister called her. Arlene requested some further changes. The prime minister thanked her and her team for their time over the last few days, but told her we had run out of time. She said she knew how much Arlene cared about the Union; as prime minister of that Union, she had to do what was in the national interest. We woke the taoiseach – who, to our surprise, agreed to one final change – and President Juncker, who agreed to meet for an early breakfast meeting before his personal commitment. For the second time that week, the prime minister headed to Brussels without me. There's a lovely photo of her boarding an RAF plane in the middle of the night, aware that she was risking her premiership. It is the image that comes to mind when I think of her, because it somehow captures key elements of her personality: determination, duty and a certain stoicism. While she was on her way to Brussels and the office Christmas party came to a drunken conclusion, a group of us prepared materials for the next morning – lines to take, a 'Dear Colleague' letter for MPs and peers, a list of the areas where the EU had compromised and an analysis of how the deal was consistent with the principles the prime minister had set out in her Lancaster House speech. I left Number 10 at about 1.30 a.m., dropped Denzil home and got to bed at about 2.15 a.m., only to be rudely awakened by my alarm two hours later. The prime minister and President Juncker held a joint press conference at about 6.45 a.m., after which I rang all the members of the cabinet. Their overwhelming reaction was one of relief.

On the following Monday, the prime minister made a statement to the House. She was congratulated by both Ken Clarke and Iain Duncan Smith, while Nigel Dodds offered this praise:

> The prime minister said at her Friday press conference that the deal arrived at represented a significant improvement from Monday, and we on these benches agree wholeheartedly with that. May I thank the prime minister for her personal devotion to working to get the text, as she put it today, 'strengthened' in relation to the 'constitutional and economic integrity' of the whole United Kingdom.

It appeared that the gamble had paid off, but appearances can be deceptive. Our hopes that there might be some flexibility in the language were ultimately dashed, and the DUP were never really reconciled to what we had signed up to. If the EU's legal inability to agree the future relationship until after we had left made a backstop inevitable, paragraph 49 of the joint report was key to its development – and to our eventual failure to secure parliamentary support for the deal Theresa negotiated.

A first defeat in parliament

It felt like we'd taken a giant leap forward, but we were quickly brought back down to earth. The House of Commons had been considering the government's EU Withdrawal Bill, which was intended to do two important things: repeal the European Communities Act 1972 at the point at which we left the EU, thereby removing the competence of the EU institutions to legislate for the UK, and provide legal continuity during Brexit by transposing all the directly applicable existent EU law into UK law. But given the tight parliamentary arithmetic, it was vulnerable to amendments.

On 13 December – the night before the December European Council – eleven Conservative MPs, including the former cabinet ministers Ken Clarke and Nicky Morgan, voted with the opposition to amend the bill to say we couldn't leave without 'the prior enactment of a statute by parliament approving the final terms of withdrawal'. Theresa had already said in her Lancaster House speech that there should be a vote in parliament on the deal she negotiated, but this went further – there would not just be a yes/no vote, but a piece of legislation that MPs might amend, making it inconsistent with what we had agreed and preventing us from ratifying the deal.

After the vote, Nicky Morgan tweeted, 'Tonight parliament took control of the EU withdrawal process.' That proved to be premature, but it was an ominous warning of trouble ahead. Nicky's prediction would ultimately come true, but the trouble was that although parliament knew what it was against, it proved even less able than the government to decide what it was for.

'Project Fear' or an uncomfortable truth?

In January 2018, economic analysis of various possible future relationships was submitted to the prime minister. It showed that although the economy would grow in every scenario, there was no version of Brexit that was as good for the economy as staying in the EU – and the more distant the economic relationship, the bigger the economic hit.

To Brexiteers, this was 'Project Fear' all over again. After all, they said, forecasts were only as good as the assumptions they were based on, and these forecasts were based on pessimistic assumptions about the economic benefits of trade deals and regulatory freedom. They blamed Philip Hammond for putting Treasury civil servants up to it, although it should be noted that the current government's refusal to publish an economic analysis of its deal suggests that a change of chancellor hasn't made the analysis any more rosy. To Remainers, it was an uncomfortable reminder that they were pursuing a policy that would make the country worse off. As usual, the prime minister found herself somewhere between these two extremes: she accepted that a more distant relationship would have an economic cost but questioned some of the assumptions and the way the analysis was presented.

Munich and Mansion House

The December European Council had agreed to negotiate a transition period and called on the negotiating teams to work on those withdrawal issues not covered by the joint report and to turn it into a legal text, the Withdrawal Agreement. The council also said it would adopt additional guidelines in March 2018 on the framework for the future relationship and called on the UK 'to provide further clarity' about what it wanted.

Shortly before Christmas the prime minister called the first of a series of meetings of the committee that winter, with the aim of doing just that. It was clear from this first discussion that there were major differences on both substance and tactics.

On tactics, David Davis and Damian Green favoured an ambitious opening position, leaving room for concessions, whereas Philip Hammond and Liam Fox thought a realistic opening position would be preferable because making concessions would be politically damaging. On substance, Boris Johnson was, as usual, the most hardline: regulatory divergence wasn't just necessary to do trade deals with other countries; it was important that voters could see that we had taken back control. He questioned the underlying assumption that divergence meant less market access and was supported to some extent by David Davis, Gavin Williamson and Michael Gove, who pointed out that existing businesses would favour staying aligned with EU rules, having absorbed the cost of complying with them, but they were a barrier to entry to new competitors. Philip Hammond responded that everyone wanted maximum access with minimum obligations, but said that Boris was wrong – there was a clear trade-off between divergence and market access.

The second meeting, early in the New Year, focused on the implementation period. There was disagreement both on what the terms should be and the desirable length. On length, Philip Hammond thought two years was 'at the optimistic end of the spectrum' – we would probably need longer than that – whereas the Brexiteers thought two years was the maximum that would be acceptable, and the prime minister agreed. On terms, David Davis was happy to accept EU laws that were in place when we left, but was nervous about accepting new ones, Michael Gove was concerned about the EU representing us in international fishing negotiations and Liam Fox wanted to be able to negotiate, ratify and implement trade deals. Philip Hammond, Greg Clark and Amber Rudd agreed that some of the terms were suboptimal, but felt that it was essential to get it agreed as soon as possible. The prime minister wanted to try to address some of the concerns, but agreed on the importance of getting it signed off by the end of March.

The third meeting, towards the end of January, considered security, and here there was more consensus. That enabled the prime minister to give a speech setting out the future security partnership we wanted at the annual Munich Security Conference on 16 February. At the start of the speech, she reflected on the decisions she had taken as home secretary, which she saw as a model of the kind of pragmatism that was required now:

> When justice and home affairs ceased to be intergovernmental and became a shared EU competence, there were some in the UK who would have had us adopt the EU's approach whole-sale, just as there were some who would have had us reject it outright. As home secretary, I was determined to find a practical and pragmatic way in which the UK and EU could continue to co-operate on our common security. That is why I reviewed each provision in turn and successfully made the case for the UK to opt back in to those that were clearly in our national interest.

On internal security, she argued that there was 'no existing security agreement between the EU and a third country that captures the full depth and breadth of our existing relationship'. If the EU concluded that it couldn't continue to co-operate to the same extent once the UK was a third country, that 'would put all our citizens at greater risk'. We clearly couldn't enjoy the same access to the single market after we had left, but there was no reason why we couldn't maintain security co-operation. The UK was therefore seeking a security partnership that preserved operational capabilities. But the prime minister recognised that in order for that co-operation to continue, the UK must make certain commitments:

> So, for example, when participating in EU agencies, the UK will respect the remit of the European Court of Justice . . . We must also recognise the importance of comprehensive and robust data protection arrangements.

On external security, she argued that:

We should have the means to consult each other regularly on the global challenges we face, and coordinate how we use the levers we hold where our interests align . . . Where we can both be most effective by the UK deploying its significant capabilities and resources with and indeed through EU mechanisms, we should both be open to that . . . But if we are to choose to work together in these ways, the UK must be able to play an appropriate role in shaping our collective actions in these areas.

It is a shame that Boris didn't include any institutional arrangements on foreign and defence policy in his deal. This is an area where the UK and EU remain very well aligned; co-operation here might help to smooth the inevitable tension in the trading relationship.

Having made progress on the future security relationship, ministers now turned to the economic relationship. David Davis described the Conservative Party's views on this issue as a 'non-intersecting Venn diagram'. A first meeting focused on labour mobility and customs. On the former, there were differences of opinion on whether it would be acceptable to offer EU citizens preference in our immigration system if that got us better access to the single market, though no one favoured making that offer upfront.

On customs, the prime minister said the government needed to be driven by practicality rather than theology. Boris said that the Irish border was 'the tail wagging the Brexit dog', denied there was a problem and said it was fruitless to continue with the hybrid customs option. He may have thought that, but others who understood the issues better disagreed – when the prime minister met with Chancellor Merkel at the Munich Security Conference, Olly's equivalent, Uwe Corsepius, had observed, 'If you want a close relationship, Ireland will be a small problem, but if you want a Canada-style relationship, it will be a big problem.' Gavin Williamson supported Boris, arguing that we shouldn't 'compromise the benefits of Brexit to satisfy Ireland', while Michael Gove mused on what was meant by a hard border. Was the Swiss–EU border hard, he asked. 'Yes!' replied the doves. Michael accepted that hybrid solved the problems intellectually, but argued that it wasn't practical.

There was a subsequent discussion about other aspects of the economic partnership. What would become the second key argument about the Chequers proposals emerged for the first time – whether the UK should align with EU rules on goods that were checked when they crossed the EU's external border. The argument in favour of doing this was that, in combination with the right answer on customs, it might avoid the introduction of checks at the UK–EU border, solving the Northern Ireland border issue and protecting jobs that would be at risk if businesses' costs increased. Boris wrote to the prime minister in a communication which found its way into the press to put the argument against:

> Aligning ourselves with EU rules is to accept that we continue to abide by rules in our country determined outside our country and over which we have no influence. It is a fundamental question of democracy.

An away day on 22 February was more productive, clearing the way for the prime minister to give a speech on the future economic partnership we were seeking at Mansion House on 2 March. But before that, the EU published a draft Withdrawal Agreement that included a hugely problematic protocol on Ireland and Northern Ireland. The EU had translated the Northern Ireland section of the joint report into a legally operative backstop that essentially kept Northern Ireland in the customs union and parts of the single market. It would create a border within our country, breaking up the UK single market, and it was contrary to the spirit of the Good Friday Agreement – an east–west border was just as offensive to unionist identity as a north–south one was to nationalists. So we found ourselves facing two challenges: what kind of future relationship did we want and what was our counter-proposal to the backstop?

Along with the 2018 conference speech, Mansion House is the speech of Theresa's I'm most proud of. It started by setting five tests for any Brexit deal:

> First, the agreement we reach with the EU must respect the referendum. It was a vote to take control of our borders, laws and money . . . but it was not a vote for a distant relationship with our neighbours. Second, the new agreement we reach with the EU must endure . . . Third, it must protect people's jobs and security . . . Fourth, it must be consistent with the kind of country we want to be as we leave: a modern, open, outward-looking, tolerant, European democracy . . . And fifth, in doing all of these things, it must strengthen our union of nations and our union of people.

The section I'm most proud of is a section entitled 'hard truths'. I wish the government had said these things in the summer of 2016, but better late than never – and if some of them seem obvious now, I can tell you that we were conscious of the risk we were taking in saying them so bluntly. First, 'in certain ways, our access to each other's markets will be less than it is now'. Second, 'even after we have left the jurisdiction of the ECJ, EU law and the decisions of the ECJ will continue to affect us'. Why? Because our courts would continue to look at the ECJ's judgements, and because our companies that exported to the EU would have to continue to follow EU law. Third, 'if we want good access to each other's markets, it has to be on fair terms. As with any trade agreement, we must accept the need for binding commitments.' But most importantly:

> We need to resolve the tensions between some of our key objectives. We want the freedom to negotiate trade agreements with other countries around the world. We want to take back control

of our laws. We also want as frictionless a border as possible between us and the EU, so that we don't damage the integrated supply chains our industries depend on and don't have a hard border between Northern Ireland and Ireland.

The key section of the speech related to trade in goods. Why this emphasis, when the UK economy is services-dominated? First, it was critical to resolving the issues relating to the Ireland–Northern Ireland border; and second, the single market was more developed when it came to goods, so there was more to lose. The prime minister said that 'a fundamental principle in our negotiating strategy should be that trade at the UK–EU border should be as frictionless as possible'. On customs, the speech merely set out the two options we had already published, but on regulation it made a big move:

> Our default is that UK law may not necessarily be identical to EU law, but it should achieve the same outcomes. In some cases parliament might choose to pass an identical law – businesses who export to the EU tell us that it is strongly in their interest to have a single set of regulatory standards that mean they can sell into the UK and EU markets . . . It may make sense for our courts to look at the appropriate ECJ judgements so that we both interpret those laws consistently . . . We recognise this would constrain our ability to lower regulatory standards for industrial goods. But in practice, we are unlikely to want to reduce our standards . . . If the parliament of the day decided not to achieve the same outcomes as EU law, it would be in the knowledge that there may be consequences for our market access.

She also said the UK wanted to explore remaining part of EU regulatory agencies in sectors like chemicals, medicines and aerospace, and accepted that this would mean abiding by their rules. This wasn't dynamic alignment across all goods sectors, but it was in some areas.

The speech ended with a defence of Theresa's negotiating style:

> We will not be buffeted by the demands to talk tough or threaten a walk-out, just as we will not accept the counsels of despair that this simply cannot be done. We will move forward by calm, patient discussion of each other's positions.

As with Florence, I was expecting a strong pushback from hard Brexiteers, but once again, it landed pretty well. We had advanced a bit further while managing to keep our coalition together.

The road to Chequers

Attention now turned to the March European Council. We had two objectives: to agree the legal text on the financial settlement, citizens' rights and the implementation period; and to influence the EU's guidelines for the negotiations on the future relationship. On 20 March, ministers reviewed our position. David Davis gave a punchy defence of the implementation period: not having it would be 'too horrible to mention'. Boris was less enthusiastic – we would be a 'vassal state' while we were in it, he said. The fishing industry was concerned about the delay in regaining control of our waters. Michael Gove summed it up: the implementation period was 'necessary but painful, and we should be honest about that'.

There were no surprises when we got to the March council. It duly signed off the legal text on the financial settlement, citizens' rights and the implementation period and adopted negotiating guidelines on the future relationship that set the tone for what was to follow over the next eight months, and indeed during Boris's negotiation. On the upside, they offered 'zero tariffs and no quantitative restrictions' across all sectors, but linked that to maintaining 'existing reciprocal access to fishing waters and resources' and 'robust guarantees which ensure a level playing field' to 'prevent unfair competitive advantage'.

On the downside, they were well below the prime minister's ambition for a bespoke model somewhere between the single market/customs union and a standard free trade agreement. If we wanted to shift them, we needed to present a compelling alternative vision for our future relationship.

On 12 April, David Davis wrote to the prime minister, stating that we had to 'reach a substantive agreement with the EU on all the important elements of our future relationship, ideally by October, but certainly by the end of this year at the absolute latest'. The prime minister agreed – she wanted to publish a detailed white paper before the June European Council.

Another meeting of senior ministers was arranged for 25 April. Everyone agreed that we needed a collective position on what we were asking for, with Boris arguing that we were 'doing a brilliant impersonation of a country that doesn't know what it wants'. He was spot on – but the reason for that was his and others' refusal to compromise. Philip Hammond argued that we need to evolve our position if we were to get a deal in time. David Davis argued that we needed to 'talk their language' by asking for an association agreement. Liam Fox worried that we were 'seeking to preserve what we have [rather than] taking a long-term view of where the advantages are'. In a comment that revealed his underlying worldview, he said 'we're competitors, not partners'. And Julian Smith reminded them that 'Brussels isn't the only constraint; there is a majority for Brexit in parliament, but only for a pragmatic one'.

The next meeting would return to the most difficult issue: customs. Everyone agreed that we needed to choose between the two models we'd published the previous summer, max fac and hybrid, but we couldn't agree on which. David Davis had warned me that four cabinet ministers could resign if the decision was for the prime minister's preferred hybrid model. On 30 April, she met Liam Fox to try to sell it to him, but his view was that it would make trade deals more difficult – third countries would get access to our market via the EU

– and it would prevent us from having our own trade remedies. At the end of the meeting, he mentioned something that would become a litmus test for the Chequers proposals: in his view, the biggest prize of an independent trade policy was accession to the Comprehensive and Progressive Agreement for Trans-Pacific Partnership; he couldn't support any future relationship that prevented that.

On 1 May, the prime minister met separately with David Davis and Boris Johnson, to try to sell hybrid to them. David said his position had 'not moved one iota'. In addition to Liam's objections, he said it would make us tax collectors for the EU and be unworkable for some businesses. Boris was even more dismissive. David at least acknowledged why the prime minister favoured hybrid, but Boris was contemptuous of that. 'The Northern Ireland issue is a gnat,' he declared. The ERG was also making its opposition known.

At the meeting the next day, the prime minister, David Lidington, Philip Hammond, Greg Clark and Karen Bradley supported the hybrid model, while David Davis, Liam Fox, Boris Johnson, Michael Gove and Gavin Williamson supported max fac. But so did Sajid Javid, who had by now replaced Amber Rudd. 'Six-five!' crowed Boris and he, or one of the other hawks, briefed the result to the media as soon as they'd left the meeting. The truth was, it was a stalemate. And not only that, they were also unable to agree a counter-proposal to the EU's recently published backstop. There was no use proposing something novel – the entire rational for the backstop was to have something in reserve in case it proved impossible to negotiate something novel. The only viable alternative was to propose the whole of the UK being in a customs union with the EU in the backstop. Though far from ideal, it was better than a border within our own country – but the committee couldn't agree on that, either. I was in despair. We had now used up thirteen of the twenty-four months of the Article 50 period and we couldn't agree on the fundamental question of what kind of customs arrangement we wanted.

Once I'd calmed down a bit, I sent the prime minister a memo listing the things she could do that might break the impasse. She could go back to the committee and try again; she could take the issue to full cabinet, where there would be a majority in favour of hybrid; she could allow David Davis to run with max fac and let the EU reject it; she could ask officials to find a new model between the two; she could put both options in the white paper; or she could pass the issue to parliament to decide. In the end, she chose to try to find a new model between the two, setting up two working groups, each containing 'soft Brexit' and 'hard Brexit' cabinet members.

On 15 May, she convened another meeting of senior ministers to try to agree a counter-proposal to the backstop. This time, David Davis supported what officials were proposing, subject to certain conditions. He argued that it was 'hard to imagine any backstop plan that is acceptable', but we had to have a counter-proposal, and the key thing was to design it in a way that didn't incentivise the EU to trap us in a customs union. His support made the difference.

With that hurdle out of the way, I wrote the prime minister another note about how we might get collective agreement to the other decisions we needed to take before we could publish the white paper. First, I was honest with her about the risk: 'We have to face the fact that an attempt to make the necessary changes to our negotiating position could trigger a confidence vote in your leadership.' On timing, we had hoped to publish the white paper early enough that, if it landed well with the EU, they could evolve their guidelines at the June European Council, but it was too late for that. There were three options: publish something after the half-term recess but before the June council; after the June council but before the summer recess; or after the summer recess. I recommended the middle option – we couldn't afford to delay to the autumn, but landing something on them just before the June council risked an immediate negative response. On process, I argued that the idea of a series of further meetings was not appealing and that maybe it would be better to have a cabinet away day and try to sign off the whole package in one go, rather than inching forward step by step? And if she was minded to go down that route, who did she want to take into her confidence, given the risk of it leaking if she shared too widely?

On 6 June, the row about the backstop counter-proposal blew up again. Our proposal had leaked, so we needed to publish it, but one of David's conditions for agreeing to it had been that it wouldn't be published before the white paper. Furthermore, the document didn't include a time limit and had been widened to cover regulation as well as customs (it wouldn't have been credible if it didn't), but David hadn't been consulted about these things. He was understandably angry and there was speculation that he might resign. The prime minister cancelled a trip to the theatre and invited him to meet with her, but he didn't reply. She delayed publication until the next day, but was determined to go ahead.

The next day, she saw Liam, Boris and David. The conversation with Liam was easiest: he could live with the paper, as long as we were out of the backstop by the next election. The conversation with Boris was probably the worst meeting of her premiership. He was so rude that I came close to interrupting and asking him to leave. He said we'd made a massive mistake in signing up to the joint report. Why had we agreed to all this mumbo jumbo about Northern Ireland? He was normally the person telling us to get a move on, but now he was arguing that we shouldn't publish anything. I had more sympathy with David, who was frustrated rather than angry. He wanted to stick with what we had originally agreed, but the prime minister was clear from a recent conversation with Leo Varadkar that publishing a counter-proposal that only dealt with customs and not regulation would make us look ridiculous. She was only prepared to make a small drafting change. To my surprise, David backed down.

We then went straight in to another meeting of the committee where we tried to agree what our stance should be on the remaining areas of the draft Withdrawal Agreement. Everyone was so exhausted from the arguments about the backstop counter-proposal that what

I'd expected to be another difficult meeting was actually plain sailing. When we emerged, we were due to depart for the G7 in Canada, but given the fraught political situation, Julian Smith and Jeremy Heywood convinced the prime minister that I should stay behind.

Once she was back from Canada, the prime minister decided to go ahead with the idea of a cabinet away day at Chequers, to resolve the remaining issues in one go. Olly's team were commissioned to analyse four options: a no-deal Brexit, a Canada-style free trade agreement, the bespoke model the prime minister favoured and membership of the single market and customs union.

Over the next couple of weeks, Olly and his team held meetings with the prime minister, to establish exactly what she wanted to propose. The core of the Chequers proposals was a free trade area for goods between the UK and the EU with no customs and regulatory checks at the UK–EU border, protecting jobs and solving the Irish border issue and allowing for an independent trade policy.

In return for the benefit of frictionless trade in goods with the EU, we were prepared to make four commitments. First, to ongoing harmonisation with some EU rules on industrial goods and agri-food products, removing the need for regulatory checks at the UK–EU border. This was democratically uncomfortable and it would place constraints on the trade deals we could do, but the EU's rules in these areas were stable and we were unlikely to want to change them – so the prime minister judged that being a rule-taker in these specific areas was a price worth paying. Second, to a facilitated customs arrangement – a compromise between max fac and hybrid – that would remove the need for customs checks at the UK–EU border. This was a customs union, albeit a novel one that allowed for an independent trade policy, but we didn't use the term because it was toxic with many Conservative MPs. In hindsight, we should have been upfront about it. Third, to fair trade through ongoing harmonisation with EU state aid rules and non-regression commitments on issues like environmental standards. And finally, to the consistent interpretation of these rules, with UK courts paying due regard to EU case law in those areas where the UK continued to harmonise with EU rules and a dispute resolution mechanism founded on binding independent arbitration, but with an ability to seek an interpretation of EU law from the Court of Justice of the EU.

Once the prime minister had decided on the package, she took David Davis into her confidence. On 25 June, she told him of the plan to hold a cabinet away day on 6 July and made it clear that she was looking at a bespoke option between a Canada-style FTA and single market/customs union membership. He said his officials had been working on a draft white paper – they were on their eighth version and it was 185 pages long. It was a sign of how dysfunctional the government had become that they had been drafting it without any reference to the team who were conducting the negotiations. David suggested that DExEU would work on background papers for the away day, but the prime minister replied that Olly and DExEU permanent secretary Philip Rycroft should work on them together.

At the end of the meeting, I wasn't sure whether David had understood what the prime minister had hinted at or if he was waiting for her to say it more bluntly. The next day I spoke to his excellent special adviser Raoul Ruparel, who told me that the prime minister needed to level with David – he could see what was coming. When she saw him again on 28 June, she didn't soft-soap things: she described each of the four models, said that Olly would hold the pen and promised they would come to him for comment over the weekend. After his resignation, there was some briefing that the prime minister tried to 'bounce' David over the Chequers proposals, but as the above account makes clear, that's not true. She certainly had her own meetings with officials to develop the proposals, but she shared them with David well before any other cabinet minister.

The prime minister also had an initial conversation with Boris on 28 June, but it didn't go well. He claimed that concerns about Northern Ireland and the economic consequences of introducing friction at the border were being 'hugely overstated' and accused her of being 'scared by the Treasury'. It was just about the worst thing he could have said to her. First, there was the suggestion that she had a different view to him because she was scared rather than because she had taken the time to understand the issues better than he had. Second, the implication that, as a woman, she was easily scared. And third, the idea that she might be scared of the Treasury, of all things.

On 2 July, she took Liam Fox into her confidence. As was often the case, he could see both sides of the argument. He accepted that 'the UK is too small to have its own regulatory standards' and would accept a position of alignment 'as long as we preserved the ability to unalign'; what he didn't want was anything that would tie our hands when it came to doing trade deals. She told him that she'd asked officials to assess the proposals against his desire to join CPTPP, and the paper that was eventually presented to cabinet concluded that the Chequers proposals would not prevent us doing so, which proved key. She then saw David Davis again and took him through the plan's key elements. He sighed and was silent for a while. He had concerns about the policy, but his main worry was tactical: if we made a concession at this stage, the EU would just wait for the next one. This concern illustrated the contradiction in David's approach to Brexit: he wanted to have agreed a detailed prospectus of the future relationship by October, but he also wanted to stick to our guns, in the hope that the other side would blink at the last minute. Even if it had worked, that was not consistent with the idea of getting the detail sorted by October.

I spoke to Philip Hammond and David Gauke. Philip was at his empathetic best, telling me the test of whether the proposals were radical enough would be whether they provoked a vote of confidence in Theresa's leadership. David agreed that we needed to develop our position. He wasn't sure whether the prime minister's plan would be negotiable, but said it was 'a big step in the right direction'.

The next day, the prime minister headed to the Hague to test how the proposals were likely to land with the EU. She knew there was a significant chance that they might lead to multiple cabinet resignations; it was only worth taking that risk if they gave us a chance of making progress in the negotiations. We went to the Catshuis, the official residence of the Dutch prime minister, and Theresa went for a stroll around the gardens with Prime Minister Rutte. When they returned, he briefed his officials on what she'd told him and asked them to pick it apart. After half an hour of questioning, he asked them what they thought. 'This could work,' they replied. No one had ever said that to us before.

The next day, David Davis wrote to Theresa, setting out in more detail what he had said to her on 2 July. In a further conversation with her, he warned that she shouldn't be deceived about how strongly he felt and said I was one of 'the villains' responsible for the proposals. She also talked to Michael Gove, who kept his cards close to his chest but said he had concerns about whether the proposals were negotiable.

On 5 July, the prime minister flew to Berlin to test the proposals with Angela Merkel. It was a smaller meeting than with Rutte, with just the prime minister, Chancellor Merkel, Olly, his German equivalent Uwe Corsepius and me. After another grilling, Merkel asked Uwe for his verdict. He was a little more guarded than the Dutch, arguing that the distinction between goods and services wasn't clear-cut and that we were asking the EU to allow a non-member to act as its customs agent, but he also called the plan 'a bone with some meat on it'. Then he gave us some advice: 'Don't let the Brussels system close the door on it before they've read the paper.' As we flew home that evening, we thought we had something that could break the impasse, if we could only get the cabinet to back it.

CHAPTER 17

CHEQUERS AND
DOING THE DEAL

As I made my way to Chequers, I had no idea how the day would pan out. It could be a breakthrough moment when the government finally settled on what it wanted, or it could lead to the end of Theresa's premiership. We had spoken to every member of the cabinet. There was definitely a majority in favour of her proposal, but there was a risk that a number of Leave-supporting ministers might resign. The media that morning quoted an anonymous government source as saying that business cards for a local taxi firm would be available 'for those who decide they can't face making the right decision for the country', the implication being that anyone who resigned wouldn't have their ministerial car to take them home. It was the wrong note on which to start the day.

There was an informal discussion before the actual Cabinet meeting got underway. The prime minister invited Julian Smith to brief ministers on the parliamentary arithmetic. 'Oh God,' said Boris, knowing what was coming. Julian calmly set out the reality of the situation. A number of government bills had been amended to express support for a customs union, and without a policy that would convince those Conservative MPs who wanted a soft Brexit, there was not a majority to overturn those amendments. The cabinet wouldn't be taking its decision in a vacuum; they had to take the parliamentary arithmetic into account. Natalie Evans, the leader of the House of Lords, added that however bad the arithmetic was in the Commons, it was much worse in the Lords.

There was then a chance for ministers to ask questions of Olly and Tim Barrow, which drifted into a discussion of the proposals. As usual, Boris had the most colourful turn of phrase, claiming that 'the coffin lid has pinged off' the hybrid plan and that 'a certain amount of turd-polishing has gone on'. He did, at least, acknowledge that the prime minister had some talented turd-polishers, which I took as a compliment. Liz Truss asked if there was a plan B, but given that we hadn't managed to agree plan A, that seemed premature. The Welsh secretary Alun Cairns asked the most pertinent question: to what extent could this model evolve once we had left? Perhaps we could leave for a relationship some might regard as non-ideal and then adapt it over time.

The formal cabinet meeting then got under way. It was a swel-teringly hot day, with lots of people crammed into the room. First jackets were taken off, then ties. At some point, the Chequers staff brought in jugs of iced water. David Lidington spoke first. He said that he supported the prime minister's proposal because frictionless trade with the EU was good for the economy and it addressed the Northern Ireland border issue, which was crucial for the Union. The prime minister then called David Davis, even though she knew he would speak against the proposals. He rewarded her with a respect-ful and nuanced presentation of the arguments. He acknowledged that there was a complex balance of judgements to be made about negotiability, the parliamentary arithmetic and public opinion, and that the new customs proposal was better than hybrid, but he had a number of policy concerns and feared that we would be pushed into further concessions. Boris was also more nuanced than he had previously been but said he was 'sad' that we would be locked into the EU's regulatory framework. Northern Ireland secretary Karen Bradley spoke powerfully in favour – she could sell these proposals in Northern Ireland and to her constituents. Gavin Williamson was encouragingly neutral – the security section was sensible, but there were some challenges with the economic proposals. Business secretary Greg Clark was supportive, but wished the proposals went further on services. Sajid Javid supported the idea of a new model between a free trade agreement and the single market/customs union, but had some concerns about the common rulebook. Philip Hammond argued that the prime minister's plan was the only practical way forward. Then Michael Gove made what was the crucial intervention. He argued that we should acknowledge that this was a shift in our position. He didn't feel joyous about it, but he understood the reasons for it, and he supported it. Most of the other members of the cabinet who had campaigned for Leave fell in behind him. Liam Fox said it was 'at the limit of being able to be reconciled with our promises'. Chris Grayling said it was clear there was a majority in favour, praised the customs proposal as 'ingenious' and noted that he hadn't campaigned to Leave to change the technical specifications of goods. Andrea Leadsom was the most candid when she said she hated the plan but accepted that we needed to do it. Summing up, the prime minister said there was a clear majority in favour and agreed to minor changes to reflect some of the points made. She acknowledged that it had taken a long time to get to this point, but now that cabinet had an agreed plan, collective responsibility should apply and ministers should speak with one voice to sell it.

There was one other thing that was clear from this mammoth meeting, but it was left unsaid. Some ministers said that if the EU rejected the Chequers proposals, they wanted to go back to a more distant model, while others said they would then support membership of the single market and customs union. It was clear that if plan A didn't work, the May government would never be able to agree a plan B.

The prime minister had invited everyone to stay for dinner. It was an upstairs–downstairs affair, with ministers in one room and civil servants and political advisers in another. The atmosphere in our room was one of weary satisfaction, but the ministers were having a whale of a time, toasting each other and agreeing to write joint editorials promoting the compromise. Frustration had been replaced by euphoria, but I was more nervous. I'd had a brief conversation with David Davis, who was visibly deflated – he'd expected more support for his position. The prime minister had taken a risk in delivering the Florence speech and it had paid off. She'd gambled again with the Mansion House speech and got away with it. Now she'd tested her luck a third time. Despite the noisy celebrations, it wasn't clear whether she was going to get away with it again.

The next day, I called Brian Murphy in Dublin to brief him on what had been agreed. He gave it a cautious welcome, saying that the Irish government would study the white paper and listen to whether ministers stuck to the prime minister's line over the next few days – in the past, when the prime minister had tried to move things forward, others had pushed back. On Sunday, the chief whip warned the prime minister that David Davis was likely to resign, and David called her a few hours later. He said he'd thought long and hard, before coming to the conclusion that he couldn't live with the policy – someone else should 'pick up the baton'. The prime minister said she was very disappointed to hear that – they'd come a long way together. They agreed that we needed to agree the detail of the future relationship by October and so had to move now. He said he didn't want to be a reluctant conscript, but wished her well and said he would support her as much as he could from the backbenches. In his resignation letter, he acknowledged that 'it is possible that you are right and I am wrong', honourable words from an honourable man.

There were three significant knock-on effects. First, one of his junior ministers, Steve Baker, resigned too. He would become a leader of the backbench efforts to block the deal. Second, the chief whip and the political team persuaded a reluctant prime minister to replace David with Dom Raab. Her reticence would be proved right – Dom was more hardline than David and didn't feel the same personal loyalty to her. Third – and most importantly – David's resignation pushed Boris into resigning the next day. I was at parliament briefing

MPs when I received a call to come back to Number 10 as soon as possible. When I got to the prime minister's office, she was on the phone to Boris. It was the most bizarre call – it was unclear from listening to the prime minister's end of the conversation whether he was going or not. Eventually, she said, 'Boris, I need to go now, so I need you to tell me whether you're actually resigning or not.' I'm convinced that if David hadn't resigned, Boris would have stayed in cabinet.

I mentioned earlier that as I was heading to Chequers, I didn't know how things would turn out. It could have been a breakthrough or it could have been the end; it turned out to be neither. The government managed to agree a way forward, but it was weakened by the resignations. David was true to his word and did not try to cause trouble from the backbenches, but Boris became the figurehead for backbench opposition to the government's policy. Nervousness about other resignations led to the white paper, which was published on 12 July, being more nuanced than the summary we had released after the meeting. More importantly, at a time when we should have been straining every sinew to sell the proposals to the EU, we were instead engaged in a desperate effort to sell them to the Conservative Party. And while we were doing that, Uwe Corsepius's warning came true: the commission was busy trying to kill Chequers.

A war on two fronts

Had the EU welcomed the Chequers plan, it would have been easier to convince those MPs who wanted a close relationship that we were on the right track. And had the Conservative Party closed ranks behind the prime minister, it would have been easier to persuade the EU to compromise. Trying to do persuade both at the same time was almost impossible. Those like Boris Johnson who claimed that the proposals would turn the UK into an EU colony might have paused to consider why the EU wasn't welcoming them with open arms.

At the NATO summit on 12 July, the prime minister spoke to the Danish prime minister Lars Løkke Rasmussen. He told her he hoped Chequers would be a turning point, but said it was up to Barnier. When she gently suggested that the heads of government needed to encourage Barnier to take the proposals seriously, he replied that while Denmark would be supportive, the prime minister needed to be realistic – the twenty-seven had to stick together.

On 17 July, James Johnson sent me polling data that showed awareness of the Chequers proposals was low, but that when people were told about them, there was strong support, with just 6 per cent of people saying they were angry about them. The proposals only became contentious because senior Brexiteers started to knock lumps out of them. If they had chosen to support them, they would have been perfectly acceptable to Leave voters.

On 3 August, the prime minister flew to meet President Macron at Fort de Brégançon, his official summer residence. He had a briefing document in front of him on which he had made copious handwritten notes, and asked detailed questions about our alternative to the backstop, our proposed customs arrangement and what the Chequers proposals would mean for our ability to do trade deals. His concern was the usual one – if a deal allowed the UK to pick and mix the bits of EU membership it wanted, others would be tempted to follow suit. The prime minister replied that all trade deals involved a degree of pick and mix – the way to address his concern was to ensure that the rights the UK had in any future relationship were balanced by obligations. It felt like she made most progress on the backstop, pressing him on how he would feel if goods had to be checked between Corsica and mainland France (a similar question to the one Boris Johnson reportedly asked him at the Carbis Bay G7 Summit). Macron said he could see the desirability of finding a solution that preserved the integrity of the UK as well as the single market and the current invisible border between Ireland and Northern Ireland. After the meeting, the prime minister and Philip had a private dinner with

Macron and his wife, while Olly, Ed Llewellyn and I dined with our equivalents. It was a beautiful setting, marred only slightly by the fact that we were eaten alive by mosquitoes while we ate.

On 2 September, three separate interventions illustrated the difficulty of fighting a war on two fronts. Boris wrote an article in the *Telegraph* equating the Chequers proposals with 'waving the white flag', but the person he alleged we were surrendering to, Michel Barnier, said he was 'strongly opposed' to them. And in an internal meeting, Dom Raab said we should think about switching to a plan B if the EU rejected the Chequers proposals at the informal European Council in late September. In truth, he had already switched to a plan B – EU officials told us that Barnier had been flabbergasted when, in a recent meeting, Raab had told him that the UK wanted a distant economic relationship, completely contrary to government policy.

The prime minister spoke to Angela Merkel on 10 September, who said she understood why Barnier was taking the line he was, but this could not be left to him. It would be a 'challenge' to formulate a single market for goods, but she said, 'our people are co-operating very closely'. President Juncker's 'state of the union' speech on 12 September was a mixed bag. He welcomed the prime minister's proposal 'to develop an ambitious new partnership for the future after Brexit,' saying, 'we agree with the statement made in Chequers that the starting point for such a partnership should be a free trade area between the UK and the EU.' But there was also a warning: 'If you leave the Union, you are of course no longer part of our single market, and certainly not only in the parts of it you choose.'

On 16 September, Olly and I flew to Dublin for dinner with our equivalents Brian Murphy and John Callinan. Though the company was good, the message was less encouraging: Chequers might work for Ireland, but we shouldn't expect them to speak up for it.

Salzburg

At Salzburg, the prime minister had another good conversation with Angela Merkel. She was concerned about our customs proposal and about level playing field provisions, but there was nothing to suggest what was about to happen. At the end of the council, the prime minister had a short meeting with Donald Tusk, so that he could brief her on what he was about to say to the media. He told her it was 'realistic to say that the atmosphere was better' and that it was 'even more tangible that everyone wants a deal'. Then he went and told the waiting media that 'everybody shared the view that while there are positive elements in the Chequers proposal, the suggested framework for economic co-operation will not work – not least because it risks undermining the single market'. Watching him on the television in our delegation room, we were dumbstruck. This was political dynamite, and it had been grossly discourteous of him not to tell the prime minister what he was going to say. She had about ten minutes to compose herself and rewrite her statement before her own press conference, and she walked into the room bristling with anger.

The next morning, the prime minister gave a statement from Downing Street in which she acknowledged that we had to 'face up to the fact that, despite the progress we have made, there are two big issues where we remain a long way apart'. On the backstop, she argued that:

> Creating any form of customs border between Northern Ireland and the rest of the UK would not respect that Northern Ireland is an integral part of the United Kingdom, in line with the principle of consent, as set out clearly in the Belfast/Good Friday Agreement. It is something I will never agree to – indeed, in my judgement, it is something no British prime minister would ever agree to.

She would be proved wrong about that. On the future relationship, she was just as blunt:

> Yesterday, Donald Tusk said our proposals would undermine the single market. He didn't explain how or make any counter-proposal, so we are at an impasse. Throughout this process, I have treated the EU with nothing but respect. The UK expects the same . . . Now we need to hear from the EU what the real issues are and what their alternative is so that we can discuss them. Until we do, we cannot make progress.

This statement was received very positively by Conservative MPs and the Conservative-supporting papers. Although it hadn't felt like it at the time, Donald Tusk had done the prime minister a favour. She hadn't wanted a row – that wasn't her style – but it was how the Conservative Party liked to see its leaders negotiate with Europe. And we received a number of messages of support from national capitals, appalled at how the prime minister had been treated.

Breakthrough

In early October, the obstacles to securing a deal continued to mount. On 4 October, the chief whip reported that the DUP were becoming increasingly bellicose about the backstop. A few days later, Dom Raab emailed me insisting on a conditionality clause in the Withdrawal Agreement, requiring the parties to act in good faith to translate the political declaration into a legal treaty. He also said that he could not support the backstop without a time limit. The first ask was a key negotiating priority, but the second was clearly unnegotiable. In terms of his future, the writing was clearly on the wall.

On 9 October, Olly reported good news on several fronts. He had secured the conditionality clause and was making good progress on the political declaration, except on the key issues of goods and customs. But most importantly, the commission was prepared to move away from a Northern Ireland-only backstop. For the moment, however, they were worried that it might not be possible to negotiate our proposed UK-wide customs union in time, so wanted to keep the Northern Ireland-only version as a backstop to the new backstop.

This left us with two remaining issues on the Withdrawal Agreement. First, the Northern Ireland-only arrangement was still unacceptable, even as a backstop to the backstop. Second, we needed to ensure that we couldn't be kept in the backstop indefinitely. At cabinet on 16 October, there were different views about what we should ask for. Some argued that we needed an end date, while others said that wasn't realistic and we needed to make the backstop as uncomfortable for the EU as it was for us, so they had no incentive to keep us in it indefinitely.

There was further positive news from Brussels later that day when the commission secretary general Martin Selmayr intervened, suggesting that the UK-wide customs union could be included in the Withdrawal Agreement, obviating the need for a backstop to the backstop. He had also mooted the idea of allowing the implementation period to be extended, so that if the future relationship wasn't agreed, the UK and EU could choose between that and going into the backstop.

On 17 October, the prime minister travelled to Brussels for the October European Council. Beforehand, she met with President Juncker, Michel Barnier and Martin Selmayr. The discussion was positive on the Withdrawal Agreement, but less so on the future relationship. Barnier and Selmayr were insistent that the only way to have frictionless trade in goods was to be part of the EU. Ever the fixer, Juncker said that we needed to avoid over-dramatising the remaining differences – he didn't want a repeat of Salzburg. She also met with Leo Varadkar, who said he was comfortable with the proposed change to the backstop. The mood music was completely different to Salzburg, as the council called on Barnier to continue his efforts to reach an agreement and declared their readiness to convene a European Council if and when decisive progress had been made.

The next morning, the prime minister had a conversation with Angela Merkel, in which Merkel said that while the Good Friday Agreement was important, with respect to world history it was not the most important thing. I'm confident that she was not suggesting any lack of commitment to the peace process; she meant that geopolitically we couldn't allow the difficulties of finding a solution to the Irish border to derail the UK–EU relationship. We were 'digging more and more into a hole and not finding the solution'. She saw that sequencing had made things harder. Much of the solution lay in the future relationship, she said, which is why it was so hard to agree the backstop, but if we wanted a close relationship, 'the problem of the Irish border becomes smaller'. It would not be possible to have completely frictionless trade outside the EU, but if we could get close, we only needed a few Ireland-specific measures to solve the problem. 'I want your success and not your rivals,' she told the prime minister. I thought long and hard about whether to include this quote, because this is obviously not something she would ever have said publicly – she wouldn't dream of interfering in British politics and indeed worked constructively with Boris Johnson once he became prime minister. I decided to include it because it is evidence that EU leaders wanted a closer relationship with the UK than the one we have ended up with and, as I discuss in the epilogue, they, like Theresa and others in British politics, have to take some responsibility for how things have turned out.

Theresa had a conference call with senior ministers on 20 October and with other cabinet ministers the following day, in which she sounded them out on the attractiveness of an extension of the implementation period. Predictably, opinions differed: some liked the idea because it was economically preferable to the backstop; others disliked it because it would mean spending longer as a rule-taker and a delay in taking back control of our waters. On 22 October, she was able to tell the House that 95 per cent of the Withdrawal Agreement and its protocols were settled. I chiefly remember this statement because the Labour MP George Howarth gave what is my favourite Brexit quote:

> Aren't the hard facts that the European Union will not agree anything that is not in its interests, the cabinet is split three ways, the House is split at least seven ways and in terms of any solution the prime minister comes up with, half the country will think she has gone too far and the other half will think she has not gone far enough?

Ministers met again on 23 October and had one of those discussions where there is a strong disagreement and both sides have a point. Jeremy Hunt, Sajid Javid and Michael Gove said that without a unilateral exit mechanism, we wouldn't get the deal through the House of Commons. Philip Hammond replied that people were worrying about something that wasn't going to happen – the EU wouldn't want to be trapped in the backstop, either. A unilateral mechanism was unnegotiable, so ministers who refused to agree a deal without one were effectively arguing for no deal. He received unexpected support from Geoffrey Cox, who said the cabinet faced a stark choice between this deal or no deal. David Lidington and Greg Clark reminded cabinet that if we didn't reach a deal, parliament would take control.

On 29 October, Olly reported a breakthrough: the EU had dropped the 'backstop to the backstop' idea. Seeing off the idea of customs checks when goods moved within the UK was a huge negotiating win, but the prime minister received little credit because many Conservative MPs didn't like the UK-wide customs union we replaced it with. We never managed to convince them of the key point: while this new backstop would prevent us having an independent trade policy, there was much less chance that we would get trapped in it. A Northern Ireland-only backstop would be very painful for the UK, while posing few concerns for the EU. The new backstop gave the whole of the UK tariff-free access to the single market without any enforceable level playing field provisions or any deal on fisheries. The EU would not want that to continue for long.

No deal: contingency, last resort, negotiating leverage or an acceptable outcome?

While the government struggled to agree what kind of relationship it wanted with the EU after we'd left, it was also struggling to agree how it felt about leaving without a deal.

Some people outside government wanted the government to rule out a no-deal exit altogether, but no one in cabinet thought that was credible. We had triggered Article 50: if parliament refused to accept any of the possible ways forward, a point might come where the EU would refuse to grant an extension and, unless we were prepared to revoke Article 50 and abandon Brexit altogether, we would have no choice but to leave without a deal. While most cabinet ministers saw no deal as undesirable, all agreed it was a contingency that had to be prepared for.

Some ministers thought no deal was so undesirable that we would only do it if the only other choice was to revoke Article 50. A second group agreed that leaving without a deal was undesirable, but could foresee circumstances in which we might choose to do so if the deal on the table wasn't good enough – 'no deal was better than a bad deal', as the prime minister had put it. If the EU had refused to compromise on the original version of the backstop, I think the prime minister would have advocated rejecting the deal and leaving without one – in her view, no prime minister could agree to a customs border within the UK.

A third group privately agreed that a no-deal outcome was undesirable, but thought that threatening to leave without one gave the UK leverage in the negotiations. However, this position suffered from two fatal flaws. First, the parliamentary arithmetic meant that it wasn't a credible threat – the EU never believed we were going to leave without a deal because it didn't believe parliament would let us do it. Second, it also lacked credibility because no deal would hurt us more than it would hurt the EU. The proponents of this strategy got themselves into the tortuous position of arguing that no deal was simultaneously nothing to worry about and so bad that the mere threat of it would force the EU to back down.

A final group argued that no deal would be a perfectly good outcome. This was the position that Boris Johnson appeared to take when he became prime minister, rebranding no deal as an 'Australian-style trading relationship' and apparently wandering around Number 10 whistling *Waltzing Matilda* to demonstrate how relaxed he was about it. I don't think he actually believed that for a minute, though – if he had, he would have adopted it as a policy when he was unable to negotiate the deal he wanted. The Brexiteers who advocated no deal also found themselves in a tortuous position: the reason they opposed a closer relationship with the EU was that any level playing field provisions would limit the UK's ability to do trade deals with other countries. These trade deals were vital. But a trade deal with twenty-seven of our nearest neighbours, who between them accounted for nearly half of our exports? That was apparently totally unnecessary.

The reality of what no deal would mean was brought home by a meeting I had with Dave Lewis, chief executive of Tesco, in August 2018. He told me that between 40 and 50 per cent of our food is imported; trading with the EU on WTO terms would add, on average, 6 per cent to prices due to tariffs. Friction at the border from customs declarations and regulatory checks would add further costs, plus there would be increased wastage due to the inevitable delays.

The philosophical differences within cabinet about whether no deal was a contingency, a last resort, negotiating leverage or a good outcome were compounded by more practical arguments. There were frustrations that those ministers who were sceptical about the merits of no deal were not putting sufficient energy into no-deal preparations.

Philip Hammond was accused – somewhat unfairly – of refusing to provide sufficient funding and – more fairly – of being reluctant to set out what his economic plan would be in the event of no deal. This culminated in one cabinet meeting where a number of ministers filled the gap, in what felt like auditions for the chancellor's job.

Those ministers who were most heavily involved in no-deal preparations quickly discovered that the British government could only do so much. How disruptive it would be would depend not just on our level of preparation, but on what approach the EU and its member states took and how well prepared businesses were. The EU and its member states weren't prepared to negotiate about no-deal preparations and many businesses were reluctant to spend too much preparing because they, like the EU, judged that the parliamentary arithmetic made it unlikely. And the government's attitude to how much it wanted business to prepare was slightly schizophrenic – it wanted firms to take the risk seriously, but it didn't want them to move jobs to the EU, given that they would be unlikely to come back. There were even limits on how much the government could prepare, with the whips questioning whether we would be able to pass the necessary legislation. Finally, some of the decisions the government would have to take in the event of no deal – what we would do at the Ireland–Northern Ireland border and what tariffs would we charge – were very sensitive. Indeed, the row among cabinet ministers over a potential trade deal with Australia in May 2021 illustrates that even among Brexiteers, there is a lack of agreement about whether we should reduce tariffs to secure access to other markets or get rid of them altogether to cut prices for British consumers and disregard the consequences for our producers. We didn't want to have these arguments unless we absolutely had to.

Steve Baker, then a junior minister at DExEU with responsibility for no-deal planning, neatly summarised the problem when he came to see me in May 2018. He argued that the no-deal strategy was becoming increasingly unviable because the start points for various plans were passing without action due to a reluctance to engage with third parties. He conceded this reluctance was entirely reasonable – ministers and officials were afraid that visibly accelerating no-deal plans would spook the markets and scare businesses into moving jobs. But they were labouring under a false hope that the plans could be ramped up at the last minute if needed.

Final details

On 30 October, the prime minister was in Oslo for the Northern Future Forum. She had bilateral meetings with a number of Scandinavian and Baltic heads of government, but it was a comment by the Danish prime minister Lars Løkke Rasmussen that sticks in the mind. He mused, 'If we'd gone further with Cameron, history might have been different.' Yet here they were again, repeating the same mistake of not offering quite enough to help the UK politicians who wanted to maintain a close relationship.

On 1 November, the DUP wrote to the prime minister, setting out their objections to the backstop. It was a mixture of legitimate concerns, misunderstandings of what was being proposed and demands we had no chance of negotiating. Like some cabinet ministers, they were, in effect, arguing for no deal. The prime minister had a conference call with senior ministers to decide whether to continue seeking a unilateral exit mechanism. It was another discussion where everyone had a point. It would, of course, be easier to get a deal through with a unilateral exit mechanism, but there was zero evidence that would be negotiable – Dom Raab had tried with the Irish tánaiste Simon Coveney a few days earlier and got precisely nowhere. The decision was made to have one last try.

A few days later, the Irish government responded to media reports of what we were seeking. Simon Coveney tweeted, 'a backstop that could be ended by the UK unilaterally would never be agreed by Ireland or the EU. These ideas are not backstops at all and don't deliver on previous UK commitments.' The prime minister spoke to Leo Varadkar, who said he was prepared to talk about 'a review mechanism, but anything unilateral I can't get through'.

On 6 November, there was yet another cabinet discussion. This one was nominally focused on whether we should agree a deal in November, given the need to pass a long, complex piece of legislation before 29 March, or hold out to December in the hope of further concessions. All but one of the ministers who spoke agreed that we should aim for November, although some added the caveat 'not at any price'. Greg Clark noted that there was no suggestion that things would be easier if we had more time; indeed, parliamentary pressure was only likely to grow.

A couple of days later, Olly reported that his team had made some progress on a termination clause, but said there was no prospect of something unilateral. When the prime minister spoke to Geoffrey Cox the next morning, his view was that these changes were of 'cosmetic' value. The key change had been getting rid of the Northern Ireland-only backstop – the revised backstop was much less attractive to the EU, which made it much less likely that we would be stuck in it. This feeling was reinforced by a discussion the prime minister had with President Macron, who argued that the UK needed to harmonise with EU rules on things like environmental protections and workers' rights, or it would have a competitive advantage with tariff-free access. We also heard from Brussels that other member states were worried the commission was being too generous.

On 13 November, Olly reported that he had got as far as he could on the Withdrawal Agreement and now also had an agreed outline political declaration. If the government was happy with the former, the latter would be fleshed out before the European Council. The prime minister had individual conversations with a number of cabinet ministers, of whom only Jeremy Hunt was opposed to doing the deal – he thought we should say we were prepared to leave without a deal and see if the EU blinked. Dom Raab was worried about the lack of a unilateral exit mechanism from the backstop, but conceded that we weren't going to get any more. On the basis of that feedback, she decided to take the package to cabinet the next day.

The details of this discussion have been widely leaked by many of the participants. The prime minister said there were many elements to the deal that the government could be proud of, though she acknowledged the backstop was uncomfortable. Nevertheless, the choice was now this deal, leaving without a deal or no Brexit. Dom Raab agreed that there were lots of positives, but said the lack of an exit mechanism from the backstop, its Northern Ireland-only regulatory aspect and the fact the future relationship would 'build on' it meant he could not support it. The latter was an unhelpful phrase added to the political declaration by the EU at their lawyers' insistence, to justify a Uwide arrangement to deal with the unique circumstances of Northern Ireland. At the time, I had some sympathy with Dom's argument that we couldn't break international law, and therefore without an exit mechanism we could be trapped in the backstop. I have less sympathy now, given that he has been happy to serve in a government that has been open about its willingness to break international law.

Most of the other cabinet ministers who had campaigned for Leave reluctantly supported the deal. Geoffrey Cox said the backstop was 'an exquisite balance of risks', but he did not believe it was likely we would be trapped. The deal was 'an inelegant vessel, but it would float us to sea' and he could not see any alternative that would achieve Brexit, so he would support it, but 'with reluctance and a degree of nausea'. 'Who wants to follow that?' asked Philip Hammond. Jeremy Hunt and Sajid Javid both recognised the significant negotiating achievements, but had grave reservations about whether the deal would get through parliament and would have liked to try a bit longer. Liam Fox was concerned about the backstop, but welcomed the ability to extend the implementation period. Michael Gove said he had 'needed a drink after reading the documents' and thought getting it through parliament would be a challenge, but we couldn't sell no deal, so despite disliking it, he would support it. Penny Mordaunt thought we should go back and try for more. Andrea Leadsom was keen to support the prime minister, but feared she would face a leadership challenge. The only other member of the cabinet who couldn't support the deal was Esther McVey. At the end of what had already been a mammoth meeting, she tried to force a vote, to the irritation of most of her colleagues.

The prime minister delivered a brief statement outside Number 10, saying:

> When you strip away the detail, the choice before us is clear. This deal, which delivers on the vote of the referendum, which brings back control of our money, laws and borders; ends free movement; protects jobs, security and our union; or leave with no deal; or no Brexit at all . . . I believe that what I owe to this country is to take decisions that are in the national interest, and I firmly believe with my head and my heart that this is a decision which is in the best interests of our entire United Kingdom.

She then met with the officers of the 1922 Committee, the DUP and Jeremy Corbyn, and spoke to Nicola Sturgeon, Carwyn Jones and Sinn Féin's Michelle O'Neill, while I briefed Ruth Davidson, junior ministers and the media.

It came as no surprise to anyone in Number 10 when Dom Raab resigned that evening – it felt like that had been his plan from the moment he accepted the job – with Esther McVey following the next day. At one point we feared that Michael Gove might go too, which would probably have been terminal for the government. But having reflected for twenty-four hours, he choose to stay, and would be one of the most effective advocates for the deal.

If we were having a hard week, Michel Barnier and his team were having an equally tough time – some member states were concerned that the backstop gave us tariff-free access to the single market, with minimal level playing field provisions and no agreement on fisheries. Spain was also aggrieved that the draft political declaration didn't give them a veto over whether it applied to Gibraltar. Meanwhile, the two negotiating teams were trying to flesh out the outline political declaration.

On 21 November, the prime minister travelled to Brussels for a final negotiation with President Junker. They charged their teams to work overnight and the deal was done the next morning. The key section of the final political declaration was paragraph 28, which stated:

The parties envisage that the extent of the United Kingdom's commitments on customs and regulatory co-operation, including with regard to alignment of rules, would be taken into account in the application of related checks and controls, considering this as a factor in reducing risk. This, combined with the use of all available facilitative arrangements as described above, can lead to a spectrum of different outcomes for administrative processes as well as checks and controls, and the parties note in this context their wish to be as ambitious as possible, while respecting the integrity of their respective markets and legal orders.

This was a partial triumph. The prime minister had succeeded in creating a new model between the single market/customs union and a free trade agreement. The Chequers package of customs co-operation and the alignment of rules would lead to less friction at the border, but the EU would not agree to zero checks – this paragraph deferred the question to the next round of the negotiations. As with the backstop, the prime minister got little credit for this negotiating triumph because many of her MPs wanted a more distant relationship, despite the damage it would do to the economy.

As we were driven away from the commission's headquarters, the prime minister and I were both relieved that the deal was finally done and anxious about what was to come.

CHAPTER 18

A LUCKY BREAK

We now had a deal, but we had to get it ratified by parliament. I'll tell the story of our efforts to do that in the next chapter, but will first jump forward a few weeks. Just after the decision to postpone the vote on the deal, Theresa finally had a lucky break, when her opponents in the party tried to get rid of her. That may not sound lucky, but if she could see off this challenge, there couldn't be a further one for twelve months, which would strengthen her position.

The rules of the 1922 Committee no longer required someone to put their head above the parapet and challenge for the party leadership if MPs had lost confidence in their leader. They now stated that a vote of confidence should be held if 15 per cent of Conservative MPs wrote to the chairman of the 1922 Committee demanding such a vote. The names of those who submitted letters would not be made public, so MPs were not risking their career prospects by submitting a letter. If the leader failed to get a simple majority, they had to resign and would not be able to stand in the subsequent leadership election. If they got a simple majority, they kept their job (although in practice their position might be untenable if the vote was very close). In 2018, 15 per cent of the parliamentary party amounted to forty-eight MPs.

This sword of Damocles had been hanging over us ever since Chequers. The chief whip had first raised the possibility on 28 August, asking the prime minister what she would do if Graham Brady told her he had the requisite number of letters. How quickly would she want a ballot to take place? What would her key messages be? Would she give a timescale for how long she intended to continue as leader? And what would she do if she won narrowly?

On 11 October, Graham Brady suggested to the prime minister that the numbers were getting tight. A week later, the chief whip called me to say that Jacob Rees-Mogg was submitting a letter and Graham Brady had said that the numbers were very close to the threshold. I felt duty-bound to tell the prime minister, who found it infuriating that this was going on while she was battling night and day to get an acceptable Brexit deal. The papers were full of speculation about how many letters had gone in, which was undermining her position in those negotiations – why would EU leaders offer a concession to someone who might not be there in a few weeks' time? And some of the anonymous briefings to the media were beneath contempt: one MP told *The Times*, 'The moment is coming when the knife gets heated, stuck in her front and twisted. She'll be dead soon.' Another said that she should 'bring her own noose' to a meeting of the 1922 Committee on 24 October. There are lots of good people in politics, but there are also those who think using such language is appropriate. One of the upsides of not being chief of staff is I no longer have to work with such people.

The 1922 Committee meeting on 24 October was less hostile than the anonymous briefers had predicted. Indeed, there was real anger across the party about the language being used in these briefings. Philip Davies, who I had always got on well with, despite us being on different wings of the party, put it best when he suggested that if people didn't have the courage to put their names to quotes, they should keep their thoughts to themselves.

That meeting calmed things down for a few weeks, but after the resignations of Dom Raab and Esther McVey, it was clear that pressure was building again. Philip Hammond thought some loyalists should put in letters to provoke a vote, buying the prime minister twelve months' breathing space if – as he expected – she won; the prime minister was understandably not keen on that idea. On 19 November, *The Sun* reported that forty-two MPs had submitted letters to Graham Brady, just six short of the threshold.

The prime minister secured her deal on 21 November, but it rapidly became apparent that it was heading for a heavy defeat in the House of Commons. On 10 December, she announced she was pulling the vote and would instead seek further reassurances on the question of the backstop from the EU.

We left for the Hague that night and met with the Dutch prime minister Mark Rutte the next morning, before going on to Berlin to see Chancellor Merkel and to Brussels to see Donald Tusk and Jean-Claude Juncker. While we were in the meeting with Tusk, I received word that Graham Brady wanted to see the prime minister when she got back to London; Westminster was alive with rumours that he had forty-eight letters. It was late in the evening when we landed at RAF Northolt. Almost as soon as we'd got in the car to take us back to Downing Street, another call confirmed that Graham had received the necessary number of letters. I was sitting next to the prime minister and she could tell that it was bad news. After a long and difficult day, we were both tired and despondent.

When we got back to Number 10, most of the senior political team and some senior officials were waiting. With Robbie Gibb taking the lead, they set about convincing the prime minister that she should call Graham Brady to tell him she wanted the vote tomorrow. We had prepared for a confidence vote and the prime minister's opponents had got their timing wrong, launching their coup when the prime minister was in Brussels seeking further assurances rather than waiting until after the vote, which – assuming the government lost badly – would be the time when she was most vulnerable. If they got their way, it was impossible that a new leader would be in place by the 21 January deadline parliament had set for reaching a deal, so the party would be handing control of the Brexit negotiations to parliament. And a leader elected in February couldn't possibly negotiate and ratify a deal by 29 March, so the Article 50 deadline would have to be extended.

Robbie's infectious energy transformed the prime minister's mood. We got Graham on the phone and she told him she didn't want a long campaign – everyone knew the issue at stake, and the last thing the country needed was a delay in the negotiations while the Conservative Party engaged in some navel-gazing. Graham sounded surprised that the prime minister wanted such a short timetable, but he nevertheless agreed.

At 7 a.m. the next morning, we met to finalise the prime minister's initial statement and to agree who would speak to which MPs. The whips were in charge of the canvassing operation, but a number of the Number 10 political team had close friends among the parliamentary party and were keen to help. Given that MPs might be reluctant to confess that they were not supporting the prime minister, it made sense for several different people to talk to each MP. I spoke to James Cartlidge, Stephen Crabb, Glyn Davies, Phillip Lee, Alan Mak, Huw Merriman, Stephen Metcalfe, Chris Philp, Rebecca Pow, Victoria Prentis and Sarah Wollaston, all of whom were supportive. Damian Collins and Mark Field didn't return my calls, which wasn't a good sign.

The prime minister gave a short statement at 9 a.m., in which she vowed to contest the vote 'with everything I've got'. She set out why a change of leader wasn't in the interests of the Conservative Party, or the country:

A new leader wouldn't be in place by the 21 January legal deadline, so a leadership election risks handing control of the Brexit negotiations to opposition MPs in parliament. The new leader wouldn't have time to renegotiate a withdrawal agreement and get the legislation through parliament by 29 March, so one of their first acts would have to be extending or rescinding Article 50 . . . And a leadership election would not change

the fundamentals of the negotiation, or the parliamentary arithmetic. Weeks spent tearing ourselves apart will only create more
division, just as we should be standing together to serve our
country.

At midday, she was in the House of Commons for PMQs. When she
was asked the traditional first question about her engagements for the
day, she drily replied, 'Today, I will have meetings – possibly many
meetings – with ministerial colleagues and others.' There were supportive questions from Mark Pawsey, Maggie Throup, Neil O'Brien,
Kevin Hollinrake and the Father of the House Ken Clarke, who
kindly gave her this softball question:

> At a time of grave national crisis on an issue that we all agree is of
> huge importance to future generations, can my right honourable
> friend think of anything more unhelpful, irrelevant and irre-
> sponsible than for the Conservative Party to embark on weeks
> of a Conservative leadership election?

After PMQs, Theresa's closest advisers gathered in her parliamentary
office. It had been clear ever since we first discussed the possibility of
a confidence vote that, if it happened, she would be asked how long
she intended to serve as prime minister should she win the vote. The
chief whip felt it was his duty to let her know that a sizeable chunk of
the parliamentary party wanted her to get Brexit done but didn't want
her to lead the party into the next election – and that she'd improve
her chances of winning if she made it clear that she understood that.
She had clearly been thinking about it and now told us that she
intended to state at the 1922 Committee meeting that afternoon that
she did not intend to lead the party into the next election.

As the meeting broke up, Theresa asked me and JoJo to stay
behind. She wanted to check we were OK – if she stood down as
prime minister, we would lose our jobs. This was typical of her: on

the day when she would give up on her dream of leading the party into the next election and laying to rest the ghosts of 2017, she was thinking about what her decision meant for her staff. I told her that all I wanted was to help her get her deal through, and I thought she was doing the right thing to maximise her chances of doing that.

In the middle of this critical day, Theresa then spent an hour with Arlene Foster and Nigel Dodds, briefing them on how she was addressing their concerns about the backstop. Then it was back to canvassing MPs. I spoke to David Cameron, who was talking to those MPs he remained close to, and then had a chat with Mike Penning that encapsulated the increasing challenges prime ministers face the longer they are in office. Mike had served as a minister under David Cameron and then Theresa, until she had sacked him to bring fresh faces into government. The longer you are in office, the larger the pool of backbenchers who are either angry because they were sacked or because they were never promoted. And when you add them to the people who ideologically would prefer a different leader, you have a problem.

At 5 p.m., when the prime minister addressed the 1922 Committee, the mood was less good than in PMQs. Ross Thomson and Richard Bacon were concerned that the DUP might walk away from the confidence and supply agreement, Steve Double said he held the prime minister responsible for the mess the government was in and Lee Rowley said stamina wasn't a strategy for delivering Brexit. But there was a good question from Robert Halfon, who reminded everyone about Theresa's commitment to tackling injustices, before the prime minister stated that she would not seek to lead the party into the next election.

The result was declared by Graham Brady at 9 p.m.: the prime minister had won by 200 votes to 117. When she got back to Number 10, a group of political advisers and civil servants had gathered outside the Cabinet Room. Our celebrations went on for a good few hours, and it was great to see her relaxing with her team.

The instinct to celebrate was a natural one. After all, she had secured more votes than in the final round of the leadership election in 2016 and the victory gave her a measure of security. But as she acknowledged in her statement, a significant number of her colleagues had voted against her, and she had been pressured into ruling out leading the party into the next election. We'd had a lucky escape because her opponents had got their timing wrong, but it was clear there was very significant opposition to her Brexit compromise.

CHAPTER 19

PARLIAMENTARY SHENANIGANS

Now that we had a deal, we had to get it ratified by parliament, and that was a two-stage process. First, because of a defeat we had suffered during the passage of the EU Withdrawal Act, we had to win a so-called 'meaningful vote'. Then we had to take the Withdrawal Agreement Bill, a large, complex piece of legislation, through both Houses of Parliament without it being amended in a way that was inconsistent with the deal we had agreed.

False start

The morning after agreeing the deal, the prime minister held a conference call with senior ministers, who were in good spirits. Sajid Javid and Michael Gove welcomed her 'very good progress', Liam Fox called it 'a good deal that was now more saleable' and Geoffrey Cox said it provided the government with 'the marching song we need'. The prime minister then gave a brief statement outside Number 10, in which she said the deal 'delivers on the vote of the referendum: it brings back control of our borders, our money and our laws, and it does so while protecting jobs, protecting our security and protecting the integrity of the United Kingdom.'

If the cabinet liked what it saw, parliament did not. Responding to a statement from the prime minister, Jeremy Corbyn echoed ultra-Brexiteers' concern about the backstop and portrayed the political declaration as a 'blindfold Brexit' that provided no certainty about the future relationship. Other Labour MPs repeated the attack that the political declaration was not legally binding. This was setting the prime minister an impossible test, because the EU was insistent that it could not agree a legal treaty on our future relationship until after we'd left. Corbyn's claim that the political declaration was 'twenty-six pages of waffle' was belied by the fact that the EU had argued over every single dot and comma. The leaders of his socialist sister parties around Europe, and particularly the Irish government, were horrified by his attacks on the backstop (the latter reported back to us that, when they challenged Labour on this, they were honest that they were taking this position purely for partisan advantage).

But Jeremy Corbyn's response was far from the only problem. Jeffrey Donaldson said that if the prime minister wanted the DUP's support, 'we need to see an end of the backstop', and Boris Johnson made the same demand. This was another impossible test. There was no deal available without special arrangements for Northern Ireland, as Boris would later find out. The Labour MP Luciana Berger asked for 'a guarantee that our UK services sector will enjoy the same access to the single market that it enjoys today'. Unless we stayed in the single market, this was also impossible – the EU was not going to give us the benefits of being in the single market without the obligations. I was frustrated that so many MPs were living in cloud cuckoo land about the choices available, but the government had to take some responsibility for that. If it had spelt out clearly what the choices were at the outset, we might have had a more constructive debate.

The prime minister went on tour around the country, selling the deal to the public, in the hope that they would put pressure on MPs to back it. Northern Ireland was the one part of the country where that worked. The DUP were so embarrassed by the strong support for the deal from business that they came to see the prime minister and asked her to stop Northern Ireland secretary Karen Bradley and her team promoting it. While the prime minister was on tour, many of us moved out of Number 10 into a large open-plan office in the Cabinet Office. Despite our struggle to sell the deal, we enjoyed the experience of working closely together rather than being segregated into different offices.

On 23 November, the chief whip warned the prime minister that, as things stood, ninety-one colleagues were on course to oppose the deal, with concerns about a further forty. If anyone in Number 10 was under the illusion that negotiating a deal with the EU was the hard part of getting Brexit done, this thought had been quickly shattered. On 27 November, President Trump added fuel to the fire, saying that the package sounded 'like a good deal for the EU' and that 'as the deal stands, [the UK] may not be able to trade with the US'.

A poll in the *Daily Mail* on 28 November offered some encouragement, showing that voters were more positive about the deal than MPs. 52 per cent said it was the best deal on offer, with 19 per cent disagreeing. This mirrored our own polling, which showed that Conservative voters supported the deal. Some Brexiteers have conceded to me privately that Theresa's deal may have been the best available, but they argue that it would never have worked politically because so many Leave voters opposed it. However, the truth is that the deal was perfectly acceptable to Leave voters until Brexiteer MPs started attacking it. If the Conservative Party had got behind it, it would have worked politically, as well as being better for our economy and the Union.

A *Financial Times* editorial the next day neatly illustrated the problem. The deal, it argued, was 'imperfect but ultimately pragmatic, which is why the *Financial Times*, reluctantly, offers conditional support'. Opponents of the deal, whether they wanted the hardest of Brexits or to stop Brexit altogether, were passionate in their opposition. The people who supported it, meanwhile, saw it as an inelegant but necessary compromise and couldn't summon the same passion for it. The Dutch prime minister Mark Rutte told the prime minister that the UK and the EU had a joint red line of no hard border in

Ireland, while she had three additional red lines – no partial border between Great Britain and Northern Ireland, no free movement and no membership of the customs union. As a result, he conceded, the deal was 'not a beautiful thing'.

There was now a widespread view that we were going to lose the meaningful vote badly, and that made the numbers even worse. First, no Labour politician was going to take the flak they'd get for supporting a Tory Brexit if the deal wasn't going to pass (Andy Burnham, the mayor of Greater Manchester, told Greg Clark that he'd come out in favour of the deal 'when the time is right'). Second, if wavering Conservative MPs thought the government was going to lose anyway, it made sense for them to rebel and boost their credentials with ultra-Brexiteer members of their local party, before supporting the government second time around. And third, some of those who supported the government's position stopped fighting for it and started discussing plan B. On 1 December, I sent the prime minister a note, giving her advance warning that the chief whip Julian Smith wanted to talk to her on Monday morning about pulling the vote. He was very concerned about what might follow a defeat – in particular, that Labour might table a motion of no confidence, and the DUP might then say to Conservative MPs 'Unless you change leader, we're voting with Labour.'

I argued that there were three possible coalitions we could build: Conservative and DUP MPs plus a few Leave-supporting Labour MPs; most, but not all, Conservative and DUP MPs, coupled with a larger number of opposition MPs; or a cross-party consensus. The first was obviously the usual way of doing things, but was almost certainly not viable – while we should be able to significantly reduce the number of Conservative MPs saying they wouldn't back the deal, there was a hard core who were adamantly opposed to a close relationship after we had left, and a few who were determined to reverse Brexit. Moreover, it was not just a question of winning the meaningful vote – we then had to get the Withdrawal Agreement Bill through on a very tight timescale and it would be difficult to do that if we were relying on a very narrow majority including some MPs who were reluctant supporters. The second option was therefore a better prospect, but backbench Labour MPs were currently reluctant to back the deal because it looked like there was no chance of it passing. I noted that the Chief Whip was attracted to the third option – he thought the prime minister should say she was not going to proceed with a vote until there was sufficient support and invite the opposition to cross-party talks. I said I was concerned about what such an approach would mean for the future of the Conservative Party.

I ended by pointing out that there were two other options. We could try to sequence a series of votes to test support for various options, in the hope that this would kill off the alternatives. Or we could reluctantly adopt a second referendum. I knew the prime minister didn't like this idea and told her I hated it too – both because I thought it would entrench rather than heal divisions and because it must mean extending the Article 50 period – but we needed to think about it because it might be the only way to get enough votes for the deal.

The one part of the week I tried to keep work-free was Sunday mornings, when I played football – I found that physical exercise helped me deal with the stress I was under. On the morning of 2 December, I got a call from Alastair Campbell just as my game was about to start. He shared the chief whip's view that we were heading for a big defeat and thought the prime minister should pivot to a second referendum. I explained why I thought the prime minister was unlikely to do that, but promised to pass his views on. Sure enough, the prime minister wasn't ready to give up yet. On 4 December, she opened what was scheduled to be a mammoth five-day debate. But before it even started, the House amended the business motion to ensure that any motion the government moved if it was unable to secure a deal by 21 January would be amendable. It was the first signal that there was a majority in the House that was prepared to wrest control from the government to prevent no deal.

On 6 December, the prime minister met with senior ministers to get their advice on whether to pull the vote. A majority were in favour of going ahead if we were heading for a reasonably narrow defeat, but not if we were going to get hammered. The next day, she reluctantly decided to pull it, but to delay an announcement until Monday, when the House was sitting.

The prime minister informed the wider cabinet of her decision on the Monday morning. There was unanimous support but predictable differences of opinion over what to do next, with some ministers wanting to reopen the deal and others wanting to test what the House would support. She had a much tougher time in the House of Commons that afternoon, where she acknowledged that 'if we went ahead and held the vote tomorrow, the deal would be rejected by a significant margin'. Vince Cable of the Liberal Democrats and Liz Saville Roberts of Plaid Cymru pledged to support a vote of no confidence in the government if Jeremy Corbyn tabled one, while Ken Clarke presciently observed that 'there is no predictable majority for any single course of action'. After a torrid few hours, the prime minister left for the Hague, to see if European leaders were prepared to offer anything to help her get the deal through parliament.

Can we have some more?

Based on his conversations with his opposite numbers, Olly Robbins reported that there was 'blanket resistance to the idea of reopening the withdrawal agreement' and that if we sought to do so on the issue of the backstop, others would seek to reopen issues like fishing or the status of Gibraltar and we could end up with a worse deal. It might, he said, be possible to secure some council conclusions on the timetable for agreeing the future relationship that reduced the perceived risk of the backstop coming into force and some kind of interpretative legal instrument on the backstop. The latter would take time to negotiate, however, and the difficulty was that such an instrument would have to say something new in order to be helpful, but if it did, wasn't that reopening the withdrawal agreement? Although we were running out of time to get any deal through before 29 March, the prime minister's judgement was that political assurances wouldn't be enough – she needed something legal, and she also needed to be seen to be fighting for the best possible assurances so taking a few weeks was probably necessary.

The Dutch prime minister Mark Rutte drily observed that Theresa was 'entering a fascinating phase' of her premiership and offered to come to parliament to tell MPs that this was the best deal on offer. Olly's Dutch equivalent Michael Stibbe made the point that leaders were more likely to offer something if they thought it would make the difference. On one level, this was understandable, but it meant we were stuck in a chicken-and-egg situation – we needed something to change the arithmetic, but the EU needed to see evidence of better arithmetic before they would offer something. Angela Merkel was less positive, warning that it would be tough to achieve anything that felt like reopening the withdrawal agreement. Donald Tusk tried to lower the prime minister's expectations of what the December European Council would agree, while Jean-Claude Juncker was more positive: renegotiation was out of the question, but something interpretative was possible – though the Irish would have to be onside.

It was at this point that the prime minister's opponents in the Conservative Party got their timing wrong and triggered the vote of confidence in her leadership. Having won the vote, she was secure for another twelve months and on 13 December she was back in Brussels for the December European Council. She was looking for a combination of council conclusions and a legal instrument that expressed a determination to get the future relationship in place by December 2021; agreement to start the future relationship negotiations as soon as the meaningful vote had passed and agreement that the future relationship could be provisionally applied before it was ratified, all of which reduce the likelihood of the backstop being needed; and agreement for the political declaration to be attached to the With-drawal Agreement, thereby reducing concerns about a blind Brexit.

Conscious of Jean-Claude Juncker's advice, the prime minister met with the Irish taoiseach Leo Varadkar before the council got under way, but it didn't go well. There was no point her trying to get the DUP onside, he said – they would only be happy if the Irish government was unhappy. The EU needed the guarantee of the backstop because British politics was so uncertain. Olly's Irish equivalent John Callinan spelled it out even more clearly – they were concerned that if there was a time limit on the backstop, a future UK government would try to use the border issue as leverage in the future relationship negotiations. The next meeting with Donald Tusk wasn't much better, with him warning her that most leaders were unlikely to agree to a further legal instrument.

When the council announced its conclusions, there was good and bad news. They sent a clear message to parliament that the deal was 'not open for renegotiation' and said they would 'ensure that negotiations can start as soon as possible after the UK's withdrawal'. They emphasised that 'it is the Union's firm determination to work speedily on a subsequent agreement that establishes by 31 December 2020 alternative arrangements, so that the backstop will not need to be triggered' and that 'if the backstop were nevertheless to be triggered, it would apply temporarily . . . [and] would only be in place for as long as strictly necessary'. This was all helpful, but they also removed a sentence from the published draft conclusions about a forward process that might deliver the legal instrument we were looking for. The prime minister was understandably very angry. In my two years working with her, it was the closest she came to thinking we would have to leave without a deal.

Why did they do this? They were, I think, increasingly exasperated with British politics. Brexit had taken up too much of their time and they didn't want another round of negotiations, but there were also other factors at play. Their judgement was that there was no risk of no deal and that the longer the impasse went on, the greater the chance of a majority either for a closer relationship or a second referendum and the tantalising prospect of reversing Brexit. Why not wait and see how things played out?

Trying to kill off the alternatives

President Juncker hinted in his press conference that there may still be some way to provide legal clarification, and the prime minister was caught on camera the next morning having a fairly robust conversation with him to try to keep that possibility alive. However, back in Westminster, she was under pressure to say when the meaningful vote would be held – there was a misplaced fear that the government was trying to drag things out in an attempt to leave without a deal. In her statement about the European Council, the prime minister announced that the debate would resume in the week commencing 7 January, with the vote taking place the following week. She also hinted that as well as seeking legal assurances from the EU, we were looking at 'new ways of empowering the House of Commons to ensure that any provision for a backstop has democratic legitimacy, and to place its own obligations on the government to ensure that the backstop cannot be in place indefinitely'. After her statement, Labour tabled a motion of no confidence in the prime minister and said that if we didn't make time to debate it, they would table a motion of no confidence in the government as a whole. We made it clear that while we would not make time for their motion, we would, of course, make time for a formal no-confidence motion. Bizarrely, they backed off.

At around this time, it became clear to most people that while we had to continue to prepare for no deal, it was not a policy the government could ever adopt. Shortly before Christmas, Philip Hammond, Amber Rudd, David Gauke and Greg Clark had told the prime minister they couldn't support it, and Scottish secretary David

Mundell had told the prime minister we should extend the Article 50 period to avoid it. Nick Boles, Anna Soubry and Sarah Wollaston had made it clear that they would leave the Conservative Party if it adopted no deal as a policy. On 8 January, the House of Commons amended the Finance Bill to prevent the Treasury implementing no deal measures unless parliament had sanctioned a no-deal exit. On 9 January, the Speaker selected an amendment from Dominic Grieve to a motion that was meant to be unamendable, a powerful demonstration that he wasn't neutral and was prepared to turn convention on its head. And over the weekend of 19 and 20 January, I was subjected to a concerted lobbying campaign by junior ministers and parliamentary private secretaries, who made it clear that they could not support no deal.

We worked hard to explain what the alternatives to the prime minister's deal would mean. A second referendum would mean extending the Article 50 period and holding European elections. The 'Norway-plus' option – remaining in the single market and customs union – would mean rule-taking across the whole economy and no independent trade policy. Staying in the customs union meant no independent trade policy and didn't avoid a hard border in Ireland or provide frictionless trade at the Great Britain–EU border because it only dealt with customs checks, not regulatory checks. We also tried to kill off a few 'unicorns' – fantasy solutions that were utterly unnegotiable. One was the idea of a 'managed no deal' – leaving without a deal, but with a deal that made not having a deal less painful, a ludicrous contradiction in terms. The EU was not going to agree any deal unless it included a financial settlement, the protection of citizens' rights and the Northern Ireland protocol. Another unicorn was the idea of a standard free trade agreement for the whole of the UK. If we wanted one, it would be for Great Britain only, with arrangements for Northern Ireland that would mean a partial border down the Irish Sea, which is where we've ended up. And despite the name, such an agreement would mean less free trade, as we have discovered.

The build-up to the first vote

The prime minister returned from her Christmas break to a note from the chief whip setting out the latest parliamentary arithmetic. He thought that about twenty opposition MPs would support a deal if there was a chance of it passing but that approximately 120 Conservative MPs would oppose it, eight of them because they wanted a second referendum and the remainder because they didn't like the backstop or wanted a more distant relationship. The DUP were also opposed, and they were key to unlocking Conservative votes – many MPs were worried that if we passed a deal which the DUP didn't support, the confidence and supply agreement would unravel and we would be facing an election. But the DUP were saying that, as a minimum, they wanted an exit clause or time limit on the backstop, neither of which was negotiable. The chief whip's advice was that we should draft a conditional amendment approving the deal, subject to certain conditions, which a backbencher could table but that we could accept. This wouldn't ratify the deal – the EU would say we were unilaterally changing its terms and refuse to compromise, confident that parliament would take control after 21 January. However, it would unite the party and might get us out of the chicken-and-egg trap, demonstrating that a concession could unlock the arithmetic. He also suggested that the prime minister should commit to 'more cross-party involvement in the next phase', and to the protection of workers' rights and environmental standards, in order to build support among opposition MPs, and to 'a different negotiating model', to mollify Conservative MPs who were unfairly blaming Olly Robbins.

On 3 January, the prime minister met with the DExEU secretary Steve Barclay, who shared the chief whip's view that a different negotiating model for the next phase would help bring over Conservative rebels. He was concerned about how little time was left to get the Withdrawal Agreement Bill through both Houses of Parliament. The prime minister replied that she wanted to get the bill through without extending the Article 50 period, but she conceded for the first time that it 'might not be possible'.

On 7 January, disturbing footage of Anna Soubry being abused as she made her way to parliament was a powerful reminder of the need to resolve this issue. The debate resumed on 9 January, and it was clear that we were heading for a significant defeat. I sent the prime minister a memo with suggestions of how she should respond. The legal position was that a minister would have to make a written statement setting out how the government proposed to proceed within twenty-one days and move an amendable motion within seven days of that statement. The Grieve amendment, while not legally binding, meant that we needed to table a motion by 17 January, but I thought the prime minister needed to say something immediately from the despatch box, to ensure we remained in control of events. What she should say would depend on what the House had voted for. The most likely scenario seemed to be that the House would vote down the government's motion rather than amend it in some way, in which case I suggested:

> The right response would be to say that the government respects the will of the House, but the House has not given any indication of what it would support. You will therefore be inviting party leaders and/or other senior parliamentarians, e.g. members of the liaison committee, to urgent talks supported by the civil service. As well as offering cross-party talks, you could also say that the government will be scheduling a series of indicative votes on a range of options, to test if there is an option that enjoys sufficient support across the House.

She decided to go with talks with party leaders but not indicative votes, which had led to confusion when used for other issues. She also decided that we should try to force Labour into calling a confidence vote, the logic being that if we suffered a heavy defeat, we would need to restore the government's authority by winning such a vote. I started to work on the form of words the prime minister could use.

On 14 January, we published an exchange of letters between the prime minister and President Tusk and President Juncker. The prime minister's letter walked a fine tightrope between not asking for the Withdrawal Agreement to be reopened and at the same time pointing out that MPs' concerns 'could be mitigated by changes to the backstop'. She asked for undertakings on the timing of negotiations on the future relationship and provisional application of any agreement, as well as a clearer legal connection between the Withdrawal Agreement and the political declaration to address concerns about a blind Brexit. In response, they confirmed that the December council conclusions 'constitute part of the context in which an international agreement, such as the Withdrawal Agreement, will be interpreted', agreed to provisional application and 'to engage with you on a work programme as soon as the United Kingdom parliament has signalled its agreement in principle to the Withdrawal Agreement and the European Parliament has approved it'.

None of that made any difference to the result of the meaningful vote. The Speaker didn't select the amendment the whips' office had cooked up for the party to unite around and Labour and the SNP withdrew their amendments, so it was a straight vote on the deal. The government lost by 432 votes to 202, an unprecedented margin on a flagship policy.

What next?

The prime minister immediately rose to set out how the government would proceed:

> Mr Speaker, the House has spoken and the government will listen. It is clear that the House does not support this deal, but tonight's vote tells us nothing about what it does support;

nothing about how, or even if, it intends to honour the decision the British people took in a referendum that parliament decided to hold . . . So with your permission, Mr Speaker, I would like to set out briefly how the government intends to proceed.

First, we need to confirm whether the government still enjoys the confidence of the House. I believe that it does, but given the scale and importance of tonight's vote, it is right that others have the chance to test that question if they wish to do so. I can therefore confirm that if the official opposition table a confidence motion this evening in the form required by the Fixed-term Parliaments Act, the government will make time to debate that motion tomorrow. And if – as happened before Christmas – the official opposition declines to do so, we will on this occasion consider making time tomorrow to debate any motion in the form required from the other opposition parties, should they put one forward.

Second, if the House confirms its confidence in this government, I will then hold meetings with my colleagues, our confidence and supply partner the Democratic Unionist Party and senior parliamentarians from across the House, to identify what would be required to secure the backing of the House. The government will approach those meetings in a constructive spirit, but given the urgent need to make progress, we must focus on ideas that are genuinely negotiable and have sufficient support in this House.

Third, if those meetings yield such ideas, the government will then explore them with the European Union.

She ended by confirming that the government would comply with the Grieve amendment and table an amendable motion by Monday.

The next day, Labour went ahead with a confidence motion. The prime minister met with Graham Brady and then with Arlene Foster and Nigel Dodds. Graham was keen to find a motion that brought the party together. His message was that although there was a hard core of thirty to thirty-five rebels, most Conservative MPs wanted to find a way forward. He was worried about the prime minister reaching out to other parties – the only way to get Brexit done while keeping the party together was to pass it mainly on Conservative and DUP votes, he argued. Although Arlene and Nigel's objections to the deal remained, they vowed to vote with the government in the confidence motion and said they wanted to help pass a deal for the UK to leave on 29 March.

With the Conservative Party back together and the DUP onside, we won the confidence vote by 325 votes to 306. For the second night running, the prime minister rose to make a point of order immediately after the result, announcing, 'I should like to invite the leaders of parliamentary parties to meet me individually, and I should like to start those meetings tonight.' However, Jeremy Corbyn refused to meet unless the prime minister ruled out no deal. The prime minister had been clear that she didn't want to leave without a deal, but the only way to guarantee we didn't do so was to say that the government would revoke Article 50 if the EU wouldn't grant an extension, and she wasn't prepared to do that. She did, however, have discussions that evening with Ian Blackford from the SNP, Liz Saville Roberts from Plaid Cymru and Vince Cable from the Liberal Democrats. All three favoured a second referendum and, failing that, membership of the customs union and single market, but they were nonetheless keen to talk. The prime minister told them she had asked David Lidington, Michael Gove and myself to lead the negotiations on behalf of the government.

The next day we had discussions with the Liberal Democrat and Plaid Cymru teams. While they were civil, they were too far away from our position for any obvious compromise. Jeremy Corbyn may have declined to take part, but we had good discussions with a number of Labour MPs. We started with Hilary Benn and Yvette Cooper, whose implicit position was that it was the political declaration rather than the Withdrawal Agreement that was the problem. Hilary was in favour of indicative votes and a second referendum on whatever emerged. Yvette talked vaguely about the need for some process by which the House might identify a way forward and the need for any deal to have public consent. Next up were Stephen Kinnock, Lucy Powell and a third Labour MP who asked me to keep their participation private. They said that the political declaration was the problem and they wanted a closer relationship, staying in the customs union and the single market.

Then we met a group of Labour MPs who favoured a second referendum. As with the Liberal Democrats and Plaid, the discussion was civil, despite the lack of common ground. If anything, some of them were more hardline than the other opposition parties – when asked what their fallback was if there wasn't a majority for a second referendum, they said 'Revoke Article 50'. On 21 January, we met with Harriet Harman and Margaret Beckett, two of Labour's most experienced MPs. They both favoured membership of the customs union. Margaret wanted a second referendum, but Harriett was worried that it wouldn't deliver the result its supporters expected. They both wanted the government to lead a process to help the House come to a decision. And the next day, we met Lisa Nandy, Stella Creasy and Liz Kendall. Lisa said she was looking for reasons to vote for the Withdrawal Agreement, whereas Stella was one of the few MPs who had opposed invoking Article 50 – but all three favoured some kind of citizens' jury as a way of breaking the impasse.

On 21 January, the prime minister made another statement to the House. She explained why she couldn't rule out no deal and wouldn't support a second referendum, but offered movement elsewhere. In a hat tip to Conservative rebels, she said that the negotiating team for the next phase would draw 'on the widest expertise available, from trade negotiators to security experts and specialists in data and financial services' and that we needed to find a way to deliver our commitment to no hard border in Ireland that both the House and the EU could support. And in a hat tip to opposition MPs, she said that parliament would have 'a proper say' on the mandate for the next phase, that the devolved administrations would have 'an enhanced role' and that the government would engage with business, civil society and trade unions. The government would also provide a guarantee that workers' rights and environmental protections would not be eroded after Brexit. Conscious that she needed to announce something that would get a warm response in the chamber, I suggested that she commit to waiving the application fee for EU citizens wanting to stay in the UK.

On the morning of 24 January, I met with Nicky Morgan, one of the Conservative MPs arguing for a softer Brexit. The prime minister had invited her, Damian Green and the Brexiteers Steve Baker and Jacob Rees-Mogg to lunch at Chequers and asked them if they could come up with a way to break the impasse. The junior minister Kit Malthouse had somehow got involved, and they'd come up with what would become known as the 'Malthouse compromise'. The idea was that the government would seek to negotiate a new version of the backstop, using as-yet-unproven technology. If this was impossible, we would seek to agree a managed no deal – to agree citizens' rights and the financial settlement and have a transition period to WTO terms at the end of 2021. I was flabbergasted. I liked Kit, but it was jaw-dropping that a government minister with no responsibility for Brexit policy had got involved without informing the prime minister. And I couldn't understand why Nicky was supporting it – neither the technology-based backstop nor a managed no deal were negotiable, so, far from being a compromise, it would give the hardliners what they wanted: a no deal Brexit. It was depressing that sensible people were prepared to entertain such nonsense.

Later the same day, the prime minister had a fascinating meeting with Len McCluskey, the general secretary of the Unite trade union. He welcomed the chance to have a chat – 'better late than never' – and said he was worried about growing support for a second referendum but even more concerned about no deal. He understood that the only way to avoid it was to agree a deal. So the question was, how did the deal need to change? To his mind, the key things were legislation on workers' rights and something on customs. He understood the sensitivity around the term 'customs union' – he didn't care 'what it's called'; what was important was that manufacturing businesses could continue to export goods without customs checks. He advised that Labour were 'concerned about being branded co-authors of Brexit' so were never going to whip for a deal, but it might be possible to get to the point where their MPs had a free vote. He 'carried some influence in the Labour Party'. If he was going to help, he'd need to believe the prime minister was willing to talk about issues other than Brexit. People had voted to leave because they felt left behind and because of concerns about migrant labour undercutting their pay and conditions. What was the government doing about that? I think of all the meetings the prime minister had on Brexit, this was my favourite: Len was the one person who showed some understanding of where the prime minister was coming from and was honest about what he was looking for.

The Brady amendment

Another key vote was approaching on 29 January. The government had put down a motion setting out how it intended to proceed and a number of amendments had gone down, two of which – from Dominic Grieve and Labour's Yvette Cooper – would enable the House to take control of business away from the government, in order that it could legislate to prevent the UK leaving without a deal on 29 March. To give an idea of how polarised opinions were becoming, Jacob Rees-Mogg suggested that if the House tried to do that, the government should suspend parliament.

On 28 January, the prime minister met with the Malthouse group. She was more polite than I would have been, telling them there were 'some problems' with their proposal. Steve Baker became emotional, saying he was sick of being told his idea wasn't negotiable. They were desperate for the government to put down an amendment to its own motion that the party could unite around, preventing soft-Brexit Conservative MPs from voting for the Grieve or Cooper amendments. However, that would mean saying we wanted to reopen the Withdrawal Agreement, and the prime minister feared that if we did that, the deal would get worse. She then met with a group of junior ministers and parliamentary private secretaries who, worried about the UK leaving without a deal, were tempted to vote for an amendment tabled by the Conservative MP Caroline Spelman that added 'and rejects the United Kingdom leaving the European Union without a withdrawal agreement and a framework for the future relationship' to the government's motion.

We then had an internal meeting, in which the prime minister agreed that the government should signal a willingness to accept an amendment tabled by Graham Brady that added to the motion 'and requires the Northern Ireland backstop to be replaced with alternative arrangements to avoid a hard border; supports leaving the European Union with a deal and would therefore support the Withdrawal Agreement subject to this change'. We could just about justify doing so because Graham had written in an article for the *Sunday Telegraph*, 'We don't need the agreement reopened, just a legally binding codicil.' The chief whip then stretched the elastic a little further, stage-managing a meeting of the parliamentary party to pressure the prime minister into not just accepting the Brady amendment, but actively whipping for it. There was a strong desire in the room that the party should come together, most earthily expressed by the Brigg and Goole MP Andrew Percy, who told his colleagues that his constituents currently thought the Conservative Party was 'a shower of shite'.

There was a testy ministerial meeting on the day of the debate. The soft Brexit faction was prepared to vote for Brady, but stressed that there were flaws with the Malthouse compromise and that it was important to reassure people that there would be an opportunity to block no deal. Andrea Leadsom said that if ministers couldn't support the government's position, they should resign. The prime minister then called President Juncker to inform him of what she was doing, stressing that her commitment to no hard border remained. Juncker replied that he had a clear instruction from the twenty-seven member states not to reopen the Withdrawal Agreement and didn't see that changing.

For all its flaws, the plan worked, at least in terms of preventing Conservative MPs voting for the Cooper and Grieve amendments. The Brady amendment passed by sixteen votes, with the DUP, all but eight Conservative MPs and a few Labour and independent MPs voting for it. The Spelman amendment also passed, making 29 January a high-water mark in terms of parliament indicating what kind of Brexit it would support: it was opposed to leaving without a deal, and there would have been a majority for Theresa's deal were it not for the backstop. In response, Donald Tusk released a statement saying that 'the backstop is part of the Withdrawal Agreement, and the Withdrawal Agreement is not open for renegotiation'. Brady hadn't solved the problem, but it had clarified what it was and temporarily unified the party.

The road to the second meaningful vote

We now had a plan: we needed to secure changes to the backstop and to develop proposals on workers' rights and on how we would involve parliament in the next phase. Together, these three things might give us the coalition we needed.

On 30 January, the prime minister met with Geoffrey Cox. He was clear that the Malthouse ideas might only be of use when the technology was proven. He judged that the only possibility was some modest modification of the deal, perhaps via a legal instrument. He didn't know if that would be enough for colleagues, but he was prepared to put his 'not inconsiderable weight' behind it.

She also had a curious conversation with Jeremy Corbyn – now that the Commons had ruled out no deal, he was prepared to talk. He seemed to share the concerns of many Conservative MPs about the backstop. This was potentially useful in demonstrating to the EU that concerns went wider than the ERG and the DUP, but a bit odd – the reason Conservative MPs didn't like it was that it was a customs union, but Labour were meant to be in favour of a customs union. His spokesman Seamus Milne made it clear that Labour wanted an end to free movement and freedom from EU rules on state aid and competition policy, but supported dynamic alignment with EU rules in some areas. Despite the rhetoric at the despatch box, the two sides were not too far apart.

On 2 February, senior ministers had a conference call to agree what modifications to the deal we should ask for. They considered three options: a new backstop, an end date or an exit mechanism. On the face of it, all three were unnegotiable, but the latter felt like the best prospect. The attorney general said that the key test for whatever we achieved would be whether it allowed him to change his legal advice that there was no unilateral exit mechanism. They also agreed that we should raise the Malthouse group's 'alternative arrangements' idea, while being realistic that it was a long-term solution and not a replacement for the backstop. The plan was for the prime minister to go to Northern Ireland to reassure people that we remained committed to avoiding a hard border, to Dublin to see if we could persuade the Irish government to move a little, and finally to Brussels.

On 4 February, I travelled to Brussels to meet with key officials from the commission, council and parliament. Some people were concerned that opening up this new channel would undermine Olly's position as the prime minister's sherpa, but the prime minister wanted to use political and official channels to get our message across.

Accompanied by Tim Barrow, I met with the commission secretary general Martin Selmayr, who was in an uncompromising mood. He was, he said, 'a far outlier'. Most people's patience was 'exhausted'. It was 'disingenuous' of the UK to keep negotiating after we'd agreed something. A time limit or unilateral exit mechanism was 'not going to happen', and the margin for manoeuvre on the Withdrawal Agreement was 'practically zero'. President Juncker would listen to what the prime minister had to say, but I should manage her expectations. I replied that the prime minister was frustrated, too. She wanted to get the deal through, but there wasn't a majority for it in parliament – what choice did she have but to see if the EU was prepared to look again at the one issue that threatened the whole deal? As our conversation drew to a close, Selmayr acknowledged that it might be possible to agree something 'complementary to the Withdrawal Agreement' with 'enough substance to go into a final controlled process'. This was short of what the DUP and some Conservative MPs were looking for, but it was progress.

We then went to see Jeppe Tranholm-Mikkelsen, the secretary general of the European Council. The message was the same: patience was in short supply. The position that the Withdrawal Agreement should not be reopened was 'widespread and firm'. That 'didn't mean nothing was possible', but time limits and unilateral exit mechanisms had been discussed before and ruled out 'for good reasons'. It was up to us to come up with something new. They had already dragged the heads of government to Brussels for one special European Council. They were not going to do it again, so if they did agree anything additional, it would be at the scheduled council in March. This was not good news – even if they did agree on something that was enough for us to win a meaningful vote, we wouldn't have time to get the Withdrawal Agreement Bill through by 29 March.

We met Irish EU trade commissioner Phil Hogan the next morning, and he was a little warmer. There was a nervousness about reopening the Withdrawal Agreement ('at the moment, we've got all the hens in the pen'), so the more technical we made whatever we were asking for, the better. I rushed back to London and joined the prime minister on her visit to Northern Ireland. I've written about that trip at length in an earlier chapter, but it is worth mentioning the huge impression that a meeting with community leaders who warned about the risk Brexit was posing to the Union and the peace process made on her. It was a key factor in her eventual decision not to try to leave without a deal on 29 March, despite her awareness of the political damage an extension would cause.

When the prime minister headed back to London, I got the train to Dublin to meet with my Irish opposite number, Brian Murphy. The contrast between travelling with the prime minister and on my own was always stark: one moment I was being flown around in an RAF plane and driven in an armoured Jaguar with a police escort; the next I was stood on my own at Belfast Central Station. Brian and I had both been concerned that some of the prime minister and the taoiseach's meetings had been a bit scratchy. We had come up with the idea that the two of them, plus a small number of officials, should have dinner on Friday night, and the purpose of my trip was to agree what they might cover.

Brian commented positively about the prime minister's speech in Northern Ireland, but it was clear that the Irish government was upset by our decision to back the Brady amendment and that, rather than encouraging them to compromise, it had reinforced in their minds the need for a watertight backstop, because it was clear that they could soon be dealing with a different British government that wanted a more distant relationship that, absent a backstop, would mean a hard border. He said there was no appetite for reopening the Withdrawal Agreement, but wanted to know what our proposal was. I ran through the options we had considered, to check whether our assessment of their relative negotiability was accurate. He was dismissive of alternative arrangements ('not on this planet') and of an end date, but seemed less implacably opposed to an exit mechanism in certain situations. He was keen to understand the coalition we were trying to build, and seemed reassured when I said we were not assuming we could get everyone who voted for Brady. We needed to get some Labour MPs, which was why the prime minister was talking about workers' rights and the role of parliament in the next phase, but I explained that we could only get those Labour MPs if we had enough numbers on our own side, which was why we needed some assurances that we couldn't be trapped in the backstop. Our conversation was frank but warm, and it went on well into the night.

I got back to London on the morning of 7 February to discover the prime minister had received two important letters. One was from Jeremy Corbyn, setting out what changes Labour needed in order to back a deal: a customs union, close alignment with the single market, dynamic alignment on rights and protections, clear commitments on participation in EU agencies and agreement on access to the European arrest warrant and shared security databases. The other letter was from some of the soft Brexit contingent in cabinet, and said that in order to avoid resignations at the next scheduled vote, the prime minister needed to confirm that we would hold a second meaningful vote in the week beginning 25 February, and seek an extension if we lost it.

On 7 February, the prime minister was back in Brussels for a meeting with Jean-Claude Juncker and Michel Barnier. Barnier started by warning her that all the member states felt strongly about the backstop – it was about protecting the integrity of the single market. He was ready to return to his original proposal of a Northern Ireland-only backstop with a 'de-dramatised' border. While he was prepared to look at alternative arrangements, they couldn't be a replacement for the backstop. The prime minister wasn't interested in going back to the Northern Ireland-only backstop, but welcomed his offer on alternative arrangements. The backstop was a problem, she argued, because of its indefinite nature. She needed something legally binding that addressed that. Martin Selmayr responded that it would come to an end when we agreed the future relationship – if it had an end date, the UK would have leverage in these negotiations. President Juncker and the prime minister agreed that their teams 'should hold talks as to whether a way through can be found that would gain the broadest possible support in the UK parliament and respect the guidelines agreed by the European Council' and to meet again before the end of February.

She then met with Donald Tusk, but as usual this was less constructive. She wanted Geoffrey Cox to meet Hubert Legal, director general of the European Council's legal service, but Tusk said he was sceptical – 'it is a political problem, not a legal one'. We challenged that: 'You say this isn't a legal problem, but we have a legal question, the answer to which is crucial. What would happen if the UK and EU were unable to agree a future relationship? How long could the backstop endure, given its legal base is Article 50, which is only meant to provide for withdrawal arrangements and not a future relationship?' He and his team had no answer.

Tusk then pushed the prime minister on Jeremy Corbyn's letter. Wasn't that a better route to a majority? No, she replied – any deal with Corbyn would mean the collapse of her government, and he certainly wasn't interested in a coalition. The meeting ended with Tusk repeating what Jeppe had told me: there was no appetite for any additional council, so anything that was agreed would have to be signed off at the March European Council. That wouldn't leave enough time to get the Withdrawal Agreement Bill through parliament before 29 March – shouldn't she be applying for an extension? The prime minister privately knew that was true, but didn't want to discuss this until she'd made some progress on the substance.

The next day, the prime minister went to Dublin for dinner with the taoiseach at Farmleigh House. Based on my meeting with Brian, I advised her to start by talking about the impression her recent visit to Northern Ireland had made on her; then to talk about our strategy for getting the deal through – we weren't assuming that every Conservative would vote for it, but we needed most of them to unlock

Leave-supporting Labour MPs; and then to set out our proposal. Whether because of the more convivial surroundings or our prep work, this was their best meeting by far. One sign of that was that the discussion wasn't just about Brexit – they also talked about restoring devolved government in Northern Ireland and ways to strengthen the UK–Ireland relationship. Though Varadkar didn't sign up to what we were proposing, he wasn't totally hostile and they left with a better understanding of each other's position. Geoffrey Cox was also in Dublin to meet his Irish equivalent and reported back that it was 'not a dead rubber'.

On 18 February, Amber Rudd, Greg Clark, David Gauke and David Mundell came to see the prime minister and told her that if we didn't win a meaningful vote at the start of the following week, there was no chance of leaving with a deal on 29 March. If the prime minister wasn't prepared to say we should seek an extension to avoid no deal, they and others were minded to support Yvette Cooper's amendment that would allow the House to take control of the order paper to prevent no deal. I spoke to Philip Hammond, who was also threatening to resign, and the prime minister received a similar message from a group of junior ministers.

At around this time, it is clear from my diary that the toll of the hours I was working combined with the pressure I was under was beginning to tell on my health. I have no memory of being unwell, but my diary records that I was sent home early on 18 February; that my friend Jason Cummings, who worked in the political team, texted me the next day to say that people were concerned about my health; and that I took a half day off on 20 February. My main memory of this period is of interminable conference calls either of the full cabinet or some sub-group that went round and round in circles. Although everyone could see that we were in a hole, no one could identify a way out.

When I went back in to Downing Street at lunchtime on 20 February, it was to the news that Heidi Allen, Anna Soubry and Sarah

Wollaston had resigned from the Conservative Party, saying they could no longer 'remain in the party of a government whose policies and priorities are so firmly in the grip of the ERG and DUP'. The prime minister was very distressed by this news – the Conservative coalition was beginning to splinter and she felt personally responsible. She wrote a reply to them that thanked them for their service, rebutted the charge that the party was in the grip of the ERG and DUP and expressed the hope that they could continue to work together on issues where they agreed. After Prime Minister's Questions, she flew to Brussels for another meeting with President Juncker. They agreed three areas of work: guarantees regarding the backstop that underlined its temporary nature and gave legal assurance; the role alternative arrangements could play in replacing the backstop in the future; and changes to the political declaration that increased confidence in the future relationship being agreed as soon as possible. He pressed the prime minister on when she would hold a second vote and whether she might need an extension ('I will not tell,' he promised).

On 22 February, senior ministers agreed in a telephone conference call that there was no prospect of holding a second meaningful vote in the week ahead, but that they should commit to holding one by 12 March. The prime minister had promised to report back to the House by 26 February if no meaningful vote had been held by then, so discussion turned to what she would say to reassure the House that we were not going to leave without a deal. It was by now pretty obvious we would need an extension, but she was reluctant to commit to that – it would be less painful to do so after we'd won a meaningful vote. David Lidington advised her that if she wanted to avoid ministerial resignations she needed to promise a subsequent opportunity for the House to stop no deal.

On 24 February, the prime minister flew to Sharm el-Sheikh for an EU–Arab League summit that would give her a chance to meet with a number of senior EU leaders. Donald Tusk asked when she was planning to put the deal to parliament, and she took him through the timetable. This was the first meeting with either Tusk or Juncker where she acknowledged that we would probably need to extend. Tusk raised the issue of June's European elections. The prime minister said she didn't want to hold them, but his team replied that if an extension went beyond the end of June, we would need to do so. That evening she had an informal chat with the Italian prime minister, Giuseppe Conte. There was a pool table next to our table, so while we were waiting for him I had a game. When he arrived, he saw me playing and challenged the prime minister to a match. I don't think she'd ever played before, so improving the prime minister's cue action turned out to be another role of the chief of staff. A misspent youth meant I was better suited to that than giving wardrobe advice.

The next morning, the prime minister had a conversation with Angela Merkel, who was in an unusually expansive mood and reflected on the whole Brexit process: 'David Cameron had this great idea to hold the referendum at the height of the refugee crisis. You should be the last country to leave the EU, because the Irish border makes it so difficult.' On the flight home, we managed to convince the prime minister to join in an alcohol-fuelled game of cards that culminated in deputy private secretary Will Macfarlane spilling beer all over her. It was a side of Theresa May that the media didn't get to see, and it was great to see her relaxing with her closest advisers for a couple of hours, despite the extraordinary pressure she was under.

The next day, the prime minister briefed ministers on the commitments she would make to the House that afternoon to try to persuade MPs not to take control of Commons business from the government. They were: first, that the government would hold a second meaningful vote by 12 March; second, that if the government lost that vote, it would table a motion to be voted on by 13 March asking if the House supported leaving the EU without a deal on 29 March; third, that if the House rejected leaving without a deal, the government would on 14 March bring forward a motion on whether parliament wanted to seek a short, limited extension to Article 50; and fourth, that if the House voted for an extension, the government would seek to agree that extension with the EU and bring forward the necessary legislation to change the exit date in UK law. In addition, the prime minister intended to publish a paper providing an honest assessment of the short-term challenges posed by no deal.

The meeting was notable in a number of regards. First, there was real anger about an article in that morning's *Daily Mail* by Claire Perry and two junior ministers, Richard Harrington and Margot James, in which they said that we needed to extend the Article 50 period, and a similar article Amber Rudd, David Gauke and Greg Clark had written a few days previously. Andrea Leadsom called their behaviour 'despicable'. Second, some minsters were concerned about taking no deal off the table, but David Gauke argued that doing so 'may help get colleagues to vote for a deal'. Jeremy Hunt probably captured the centre ground of the meeting best when he said that what the prime minister was proposing was 'not helpful, but not fatally damaging and the only option we have' if the government wanted to keep control of House business. Finally, in a sign of the damage that persistent leaking was doing to effective government, the attorney general declined to brief his colleagues about his progress in talks with the commission. The prime minister's statement was reasonably well received in the House and did the job: for the moment, the government remained in control of events.

On 6 March, senior ministers had a virtual conference with Olly, Geoffrey Cox and Steve Barclay, who were in Brussels. The news wasn't encouraging. The EU had concluded that we weren't going to win the second vote, so they weren't inclined to make a significant concession. Geoffrey thought what was on offer would only allow 'a nuanced change' in his advice. There were also the first signs we were running out of road politically. Rachel Maclean and Maggie Throup, two naturally loyal parliamentary private secretaries, suggested to me that the prime minister should go if we lost the second meaningful vote. And George Hollingbery, her former PPS and one of her most loyal supporters, told me he thought she was doomed. The next day, she met her whips and Paul Maynard, another loyalist, tearfully told her that she should go.

A couple of days later, the prime minister went to Grimsby and appealed for support from 'those who, like me, voted Remain but believe in honouring the result, and that leaving with a good deal is much better than leaving with no deal and . . . those who voted to leave, but who accept that compromise is necessary if we are bring our country back together'. One of the MPs in the former category was the town's Labour MP, Melanie Onn, who spoke to the prime minister afterwards. She was pleased with what the government was saying on workers' rights, but voting with us was 'not an easy ask' and she needed to know we had enough Conservatives onside that her support would make a difference. The honest answer was that we didn't.

On 9 March, Olly reported back on the legal instrument and supplement to the political declaration that the team had negotiated. The key win was that it confirmed that the EU could not try to trap the UK in the backstop indefinitely. Geoffrey's view was that although the team had 'squeezed the best they could have got', it 'amounts to very little indeed in legal terms; it's marginally useful, but would not shift my legal analysis' because it didn't cover the situation where it proved impossible to agree a future relationship, but not because of bad faith on the EU's part. David Lidington and Steve Barclay shared his view that it was as much as we were going to get, while the chief whip said we were out of time: we had to proceed on Tuesday. We decided to make a unilateral declaration alongside what we had agreed with the EU.

We could obviously declare whatever we wanted, but it would only be of any use if the Commission didn't publicly disagree with our interpretation. The prime minister and Steve Barclay therefore flew out to see President Juncker to discuss the unilateral declaration on 11 March. The meeting was made slightly surreal by the fact that the lights in Juncker's office kept failing. Leo Varadkar had been on the phone to Juncker before we arrived, objecting to a sentence in the declaration which said that 'if it proves not to be possible to negotiate an agreement, the UK records its understanding that nothing in the Withdrawal Agreement would prevent it from instigating an end to its arrangements under the proviso of full compliance with its obligations to avoid a hard border on the island of Ireland'. Varadkar was objecting to the word 'end'. Someone suggested replacing it with 'suspension', but that wasn't enough for the prime minister. Juncker suggested 'disapplication', which was ambiguous and therefore acceptable to both sides. David Lidington was making a statement in the Commons while all this was going on, and the whips had to keep questions coming, in order to give us time to get the documents tabled for the next day's debate.

Jean-Claude Piris, a former director general of the European Council's legal service, tweeted, 'with this the UK has a legal remedy not to be trapped in a customs union with the EU', but Geoffrey Cox didn't agree. His legal advice, on which the vote – and therefore the future of the government – hung, concluded:

> The legally binding provisions of the joint instrument and the content of the unilateral declaration reduce the risk that the United Kingdom could be indefinitely and involuntarily detained within the protocol's provisions, at least in so far as that situation had been brought about by the bad faith or want of best endeavours of the EU . . . It is highly unlikely that a satisfactory subsequent agreement will not be concluded . . . However, the legal risk remains unchanged that if, through no demonstrable failure of either party but simply because of intractable differences, that situation *does* arise, the United Kingdom would have . . . no internationally lawful means of exiting the protocol's arrangements, save by agreement.

The contrast between this dry judgement and his powerful presentation of the balance of political risk in his statement to the House could not have been more stark, but the damage was done and the second meaningful vote was lost, by 391 votes to 242. Thirty-nine Conservatives and one Labour MP who hadn't supported the deal previously voted for it this time round, including David Davis and Graham Brady, but it was nowhere near enough.

Asking for an extension

At the end of the debate, the prime minister confirmed that the government would table a motion to test whether the House supported leaving the European Union without a deal on 29 March. On the government side, it would be a free vote. She told the House:

> I have personally struggled with this choice . . . I am passionate about delivering the result of the referendum, but I equally passionately believe that the best way to do that is to leave in an orderly way with a deal . . . I am conscious also of . . . the potential damage to the Union that leaving without a deal could do when one part of our country is without devolved governance. I can therefore confirm that the motion will read: 'That this House declines to approve leaving the European Union without a withdrawal agreement and a framework on the future relationship on 29 March 2019; and notes that leaving without a deal remains the default in UK and EU law unless this House and the EU ratify an agreement.'

The government published the most sensitive bits of its no-deal planning, in order to inform the debate. Two amendments quickly went down. The first was from Caroline Spelman ruling out no deal in any circumstances. Unless it was prepared to revoke Article 50, parliament couldn't do this, because any extension required the EU's agreement. The second was from Damian Green proposing a wholly unnegotiable variant of the Malthouse compromise. There were mixed views on Damian's amendment at cabinet the next morning, so it was agreed that there would be a free vote on that, too. At an informal meeting just beforehand, Greg Clark raised the question about how we would vote on the main motion if the Spelman amendment was passed – it was clear that a number of ministers were happy to vote down Spelman and vote for the government's motion, but if Spelman passed, voting against the *amended* motion could be interpreted as voting for no deal. No collective decision was taken.

By the time the votes came, Caroline had been persuaded by Greg Clark and co not to move her amendment but Yvette Cooper moved it for her, and it passed by 312 votes to 308. Damian's amendment was roundly defeated, though four cabinet ministers – Andrea Leadsom, Gavin Williamson, Jeremy Hunt and Sajid Javid – voted for it. I told Gavin what I thought about him voting for such nonsense when he popped into the prime minister's office later that evening and was so angry that I had to apologise once I'd calmed down. When it came to the vote on the amended main motion, the chief whip asked Conservative MPs to vote against it. A few junior ministers told Andrew Bowie, the prime minister's parliamentary private secretary, that they were minded to defy the whip. He came to me in a panic and, unable to get hold of the chief whip, I said to tell them to abstain rather than voting against the government. The amended motion passed by 321 votes to 278.

When it became apparent that a number of ministers (including Greg Clark, David Gauke, Amber Rudd, David Mundell and Claire Perry) had abstained, all hell broke loose. We would have lost the vote anyway, but that wasn't the point. The prime minister read the riot act at political cabinet the next morning, supported by the party chairman, the chief whip and the leader of the House of Lords. There was a great deal of anger with those who had abstained, but it turned into quite a cathartic discussion. Those who had abstained expressed regret for the upset they had caused, while pointing out that there had been no discussion of what the whipping would be in that situation. Several said they were prepared to resign but feared that if they did, everyone else who had abstained would follow suit. Michael Gove made a particularly powerful intervention. He had lost dear friends by campaigning for Leave, he said. He had accepted difficult compromises and stayed in government, costing him more friends, because he felt a responsibility to make the referendum decision work. Now relationships in cabinet were beginning to fracture. You can tell when a marriage is going to break up, he said, because when one person speaks, the other rolls their eyes, and that had begun to happen around the cabinet table. After he'd finished speaking, the prime minister said that now the air had been cleared, cabinet needed to stick together and agree a way forward.

There was better news that evening, when 334 MPs – not just a majority, but an absolute majority of those entitled to vote – voted down an amendment which called on the government to use any extension to hold a second referendum. The government's motion, which agreed to seek an extension, noting that it could be a short one to avoid the need for European elections if the deal was approved by the March European Council, passed. However, 188 Conservative MPs voted against it, preferring to leave without a deal, with all the damage that would have done to our economy and our Union.

On 15 March, the chief whip had some potentially game-changing news. We had been trying to agree a package of commitments to get the DUP to reluctantly support the deal, the key elements of which were Great Britain staying aligned with Northern Ireland if the backstop was triggered and giving Stormont a veto on new regulations being added to the backstop. The chief whip reported that they were close to signing up. However, when John Bercow made a statement saying it would be disorderly to bring the same deal for another vote, the DUP trail went cold. Bercow's ruling was the latest in a series of interventions that made the government's job even harder. Rather than apply the standing orders, he saw himself as a servant of the House: if a majority wanted to stop no deal, he was willing to reinterpret the rules to allow them to do it. To be fair to him, on this occasion there was precedent for his ruling, but most people in government had lost all confidence in him. I'd had a good relationship with him when I was a whip and so was softer than most, but even I was beginning to lose patience. He thought he was helping the House avoid a hard Brexit, but he is, in fact, one of the architects of where we have ended up.

Cabinet on 19 March focused on how long an extension we should ask for and, if the EU offered us something different, what we could accept. Nobody wanted a long extension, but there was a contrast between those who had grappled with the detail of what no deal would involve and those who were driven by the politics. After cabinet, the prime minister met Boris Johnson, who wanted her to go back to Brussels and ask for more. If she wanted him to vote for the deal, he said he needed to hear either that she was dumping Chequers or that someone else would be taking over the party leadership. The most startling moment of the conversation was when he asserted that if she'd taken his advice and gone for a distant relationship, Philip Hammond et al would have gone along with it. He didn't seem to have any idea that people on the other side of the argument felt just as strongly as him.

The day before the European Council, the prime minister wrote to Donald Tusk to formally ask for an extension until 30 June. At this point, we made a serious mistake. There's always a danger of Number 10 developing a bunker mentality, but it's a particular risk when you're under siege. We were, quite frankly, exasperated with parliament, which continued to vote down the deal on offer but was incapable of agreeing what it wanted. Someone suggested the prime minister should make a televised statement, in order to put some public pressure on MPs to come to a decision. We started drafting something, and as more people got involved, it got punchier. The prime minister didn't take much persuading and about an hour later, she was outside Number 10, telling MPs to do their job:

> You, the public, have had enough. You are tired of the infighting, tired of the political games and the arcane procedural rows. Tired of MPs talking about nothing else but Brexit when you have real concerns about our children's schools, our National Health Service and knife crime. You want this stage of the Brexit process to be over and done with. I agree. I am on your side.

It made her, and us, feel better. There was a lot of truth to what she said, although we had to take some of the blame for the impasse, and it was essentially the message Boris Johnson went to the country with in December 2019. However, as the chief whip pointed out in no uncertain terms the next morning, politically it was nuts. We couldn't call an election, so we needed to persuade the current House to vote for any deal. MPs were already feeling under huge pressure, and we had just publicly attacked them.

Suitably chastened, we headed to Brussels to seek an extension. Before the council meeting, Donald Tusk told the prime minister that the mood was for an extension to 22 May. She went in and made her pitch for 30 June. The meeting went on for ages, and it was clear that there was a huge row going on, with President Macron in particular pushing for a shorter extension. In the end, the council's offer was 22 May, but only if the Withdrawal Agreement was approved by parliament the following week; otherwise, an extension until 12 April was granted, with an invitation to 'indicate a way forward before this date for consideration by the European Council'. These two dates weren't arbitrary: 12 April was the date by which we would have to confirm if we were holding European elections and 22 May was polling day. After consulting David Lidington, Philip Hammond, Julian Smith and Steve Barclay, the prime minister accepted the offer.

The trouble was, this was neither one thing nor the other. If the

EU had really wanted to force parliament's hand, it should have rejected the request for an extension unless parliament approved the Withdrawal Agreement or agreed a second referendum. As it was, they had left open the possibility of both a no deal Brexit on 12 April and a further extension. The one thing the decision *did* do was focus attention on the withdrawal agreement. We didn't need to win a third meaningful vote; we just had to get parliament to agree that it was happy with half of the deal – given Labour's concerns were with the political declaration, that might be possible.

Back in London the next day, senior ministers considered what to do next. The chief whip said we were facing another chicken-and-egg problem. We wouldn't get more Labour MPs to vote for the deal until we had better numbers on our own side, but it would be hard to get them without the DUP, who didn't want to move until others had done so. Michael Gove argued that we needed to teach our rebels to count and 'show them the instruments of torture' – in other words, what MPs would vote for if they didn't back our deal. Liam Fox took the point – he was against indicative votes, but he could tolerate them as a tactical device. Steve Barclay was realistic: the Letwin amendment that would take control of House business in order to hold indicative votes was going to pass. Did we want to control the process or have it done to us? And did we want indicative votes before or after a third vote? David Lidington had to update the House on 25 March and ministers agreed that he should signal the government's willingness to make time for indicative votes, in an attempt to stop the Letwin amendment passing.

Chequers II

On the morning of 23 March, the prime minister had the idea of inviting the leading opponents of her deal within the Conservative Party to an 'away day' at Chequers. We spent the day arguing about the cast list before settling on the prime minister, David Lidington,

Michael Gove, Steve Barclay, Brandon Lewis, Julian Smith and me from the government; Boris Johnson, Jacob Rees-Mogg, Iain Duncan Smith, Dom Raab and Steve Baker as the opponents of the deal; David Davis, as a senior Brexiteer who had opposed it initially but switched for the second vote; and Damian Green and Alistair Burt from the 'soft Brexit' wing of the party. George Hollingbery texted me to say he was going to tell the prime minister that if she wanted to get the deal through, she needed to indicate that she would stand down.

As we headed to Chequers the next day, I sent a text to attendees:

> By way of context ahead of this afternoon's meeting, the prime minister has to decide by tomorrow morning whether to bring back the deal for a third meaningful vote. The chief whip advises we are likely to lose the Letwin amendment tomorrow. If we don't bring back the deal for a third meaningful vote on Tuesday, or we do but we lose it again, we will then be into indicative votes on Wednesday. The prime minister is very concerned about the consequences of that for the party and the country.

At the start of the meeting, the prime minister, the chief whip and Michael Gove set out what was going to happen. There was a majority in the House to take control of business, legislate to prevent no deal and hold indicative votes that would either back a softer Brexit or a second referendum. The only way out was to call an election, and right now, having failed to deliver Brexit and extended Article 50, we would lose. It no longer mattered who around the table was right about whether no deal was a good or bad outcome; it was no longer an option.

Damian Green and Alistair Burt both confirmed they would not support no deal. Steve Baker accepted there was a risk Brexit might not happen, but said some people would prefer to lose Brexit than accept the deal. Michael Gove countered that this made no sense:

people were worried about the deal because they feared it might lead to the UK being trapped in a customs union, but if they continued to oppose the deal, parliament would definitely trap us in a customs union. Steve replied that he would emigrate if that happened. Iain Duncan Smith said he didn't like to say it, but the debate about what should happen in the next phase of the negotiations was best had through a leadership election. Brandon Lewis replied that a leadership election wouldn't change the parliamentary arithmetic. Jacob Rees-Mogg said that he was minded to support the government next time round, but he was only one vote – we needed the DUP and most of the Conservative Party. He usually spoke in euphemisms, he said, but on this occasion he needed to be more direct: the prime minister had used up all her political capital on this most difficult of issues.

I tried to focus the discussion. We weren't trying to change their minds about the merits of the deal – four of the six opponents had resigned from the government over it, so they clearly felt strongly. The question was, what was now the least bad outcome from their perspective – the deal passing or letting events take their course? It was no good talking about seeking further changes; we were out of time, and parliament was going to take decisions that week. Some of the things we'd previously warned about had happened. If we were right about the rest, it would then be too late to close Pandora's box. We broke at that point for individual discussions. Jacob and Steve both told me that the prime minister should set a date for her departure; IDS said the same thing to her directly. When we reassembled, she said she was grateful for their candid advice, which she would reflect on.

The third vote and aftermath

The next day, Theresa told IDS that she would stand down in time for a new leader to be in place at conference. He said she needed to say this publicly. She also spoke to Arlene Foster, who said the DUP were not yet in a position to support the deal. We'd received worry-ing intelligence that they would prefer a softer Brexit to our deal and were waiting to see where indicative votes led. The prime minister met with Jeremy Corbyn and Keir Starmer and asked them whether Labour might be prepared to support the withdrawal agreement only. Keir replied that they could only do that if there was agreement on the future relationship and a second referendum. 'Couldn't those issues be sorted out during the passage of the Withdrawal Agreement Bill?' I asked. No, he said, because we would have left by then. I was stunned that the shadow Brexit secretary did not understand the basic fact that we would not have left until the Withdrawal Agreement Bill had been passed. That evening, three junior ministers – Steve Brine, Alistair Burt and Richard Harrington – resigned from the govern-ment, in order that they could support Oliver Letwin's amendment that took over control of parliamentary business. The amendment passed by 329 votes to 302. One of the predictions we had made at Chequers had come to pass.

27 March brought a glimmer of positive news: Jacob Rees-Mogg wrote an article in which he said that he was prepared to back the deal 'because the numbers in parliament make it clear that all the other potential outcomes are worse'. The prime minister met with IDS to discuss what to say about her future at the 1922 Commit-tee that afternoon. He said that she was within spitting distance of getting the deal through, but needed to say publicly what she had told him privately. She was willing to sacrifice her premiership for the compromise she believed in, but wanted some guarantee that the deal would go through if she did. They also talked about tim-ing. He wanted the parliamentary part of the leadership election to be complete before the summer recess; she wanted the process to end at conference. Iain was apologetic – he said the whole thing was a 'monstrous business' and he was dealing with 'monstrous people full of ambition'. The prime minister was by this point reconciled to her fate: 'The Conservative Party doesn't let its leaders go gracefully,'

she observed. She then saw Nigel Dodds, who confirmed that there was still a chance that the DUP could support the deal, though he was worried about who would follow her. As the prime minister prepared for the 1922, I warned her parliamentary staff what she was about to say.

The 1922 went well, with a number of MPs announcing that they would now back the deal. But the prime minister returned to a bombshell, when Arlene Foster called to say the DUP would not. That evening, the House voted against every option put to it in the first round of indicative votes.

On 28 March, the prime minister decided that we should ask the House to approve just the Withdrawal Agreement the next day – the day we should have left the EU. While there was movement in our direction as the debate progressed, it was not enough. The prime minister met with a group of Labour MPs – Caroline Flint, Gareth Snell, Rosie Cooper, Emma Lewell-Buck, Melanie Onn, Ivan Lewis, Sarah Champion and Yvonne Fovargue. They wanted to vote for the deal, but they were under pressure from their whips' office and could see that we weren't going to win without the DUP. In the end, the motion was lost by 344 votes to 286. Of the six rebels who had come to Chequers, all but Steve Baker voted in favour. He and the DUP were crucial.

People often ask me who I'm most angry with. I was frustrated with those MPs who wanted to leave without a deal or to overturn Brexit – I thought the former would be catastrophic for our economy and Union and the latter for trust in politics and social cohesion. And I was equally frustrated with the DUP, who seemed to be making a terrible misjudgement – if Theresa went, she would be replaced by someone who would prioritise a hard Brexit over the Union. But it's difficult to be angry with people who stood up for what they believe in. I want people in parliament who stand up for their principles rather than toeing the line. The people who made me really angry were the people who voted against what they believed in for tactical reasons. On our side, there were the cabinet ministers who had campaigned for Remain but were happy to champion the hardest of Brexits because it suited their leadership ambitions. Likewise, there were people who claimed to be worried about the backstop because we could break our international law obligations, but a year later were happy to back Boris Johnson when he said he would do just that. And on the opposition benches, there were good reasons why Labour had opposed the two meaningful votes, but this third vote was purely on the Withdrawal Agreement, which they had no argument with. If they had voted for it, we would have introduced the Withdrawal Agreement Bill and as that went through the House, we would have seen whether there were majorities in favour of staying in a customs union and putting the deal to a confirmatory vote. Labour's argument was that it was clear by then that the prime minister was going soon – and they didn't trust her successor to abide by any deal. That was a legitimate concern, but had they allowed the Withdrawal Agreement Bill to proceed, they could have constrained her successor and they would have been much less vulnerable to the charge that they had blocked Brexit at the election that her successor would have to call, if they wanted to overturn any deal.

Looking back, it is hard to avoid the conclusion that parliament's decision to require a meaningful vote was a major cause of the trouble that followed. The fear that it would not have a say over the deal was misplaced – any deal would have to be put into UK law via a Withdrawal Agreement Bill and its passage would give parliament the opportunity to have its say. The meaningful vote meant we had to agree the whole package in one go, rather than dealing with each issue in turn, and that proved impossible.

On 31 March, the prime minister spoke to her four living predecessors. Tony Blair thought she needed to lead a longer deliberative process, pivoting from 'being the captain of the team to the referee of the process'. He told her that a lot of the people he was speaking to were more sympathetic to her position than she might think.

Gordon Brown argued for some kind of citizens' assembly; he thought the view of the country was less extreme than that of MPs. David Cameron thought she needed to rule out no deal, and his instinct was that a second referendum would be easier for the Conservative Party to accept than a soft Brexit. John Major's main concern was avoiding no deal. She also met the Labour deputy leader Tom Watson and the Labour MPs Peter Kyle and Phil Wilson at her home in Sonning. They pitched the case for a pivot to a second referendum. That was the only way to keep her deal alive, but the prime minister thought it was wrong in principle to ask the question a second time, and had she tried to do so it would have split the party.

On April Fool's Day, parliament held a second round of indicative votes. There was still no majority for anything, although a customs union came within three votes. The next morning, Oliver Letwin made it clear that he would not be organising any more indicative votes; parliament had given up on finding a solution and the ball was back in the government's court.

CHAPTER 20

TALKING TO
THE OPPOSITION

Cabinet met on the morning of 2 April to decide what to do next. The prime minister had scheduled the meeting because she had feared that the government might have a difficult decision to take if the House of Commons had voted for an option that was contrary to government policy. In the event, it had failed to support anything, but that wasn't a cause for celebration – Nick Boles's resignation from the Conservative Party was further evidence of how the impasse was stretching the Conservative coalition to breaking point.

She wanted cabinet to focus on two things. First, was there any chance of ratifying the deal? Winning a meaningful vote wasn't enough – we needed a sustainable majority that would support the Withdrawal Agreement Bill through all its stages. Second, if there was no chance of creating a sustainable majority for the bill, what should we do? She could not support leaving without a deal on 12 April because of the likely implications for the Union, but cabinet needed to understand that any further extension was going to be long (though it could end early if we ratified the deal during the extension), and that if we hadn't ratified by 22 May, we would have to hold European elections. She was not prepared to tell the British people that Brexit was delayed again without a plan for how to resolve it – and in any case, the EU probably wouldn't give us an extension without a plan – so cabinet needed to decide what we would use any extension for. One option cabinet needed to discuss was calling an election, which is why it was initially meeting in political cabinet format. She didn't think this was a viable option, but she wanted cabinet to hear from Brandon Lewis and Mick Davis, the Conservative Party's highly respected chief executive.

Mick calmly set out the reasons why a general election was not an attractive option, ending with, 'I'm not in favour of this option – in fact, I'm implacably opposed.' For once, cabinet was completely united: everyone agreed that we needed to plan for an election because it could be forced on us, but choosing to fight one from our current position would be political suicide. The prime minister then turned to Julian Smith, who said bluntly that he did not see a way to pass the deal in its current form. We needed to amend it in a way that allowed us to attract opposition support, he said, without losing too many from our side. We then ran through the usual unicorns. Liz Truss, Jeremy Hunt, Gavin Williamson, Penny Mordaunt and Sajid Javid wanted to force a choice between deal or no deal. That was superficially attractive, but as others pointed out, the House would never let us pull it off – and even if we did, it wouldn't create a sustainable majority for the Withdrawal Agreement Bill. Andrea Leadsom wanted a managed no deal or a time limit on the backstop, but there was zero prospect of the EU agreeing to either of those things. Chris Grayling thought we should try bringing forward the Withdrawal Agreement Bill, but what would we do if the House voted it down at the second reading? Damian Hinds wondered whether the House would let us organise some kind of preferential vote between no deal, our deal and other options, but would whatever emerged as the first choice have a sustainable majority behind it? And for the first time, some of the cabinet – Jeremy Wright, David Gauke, Caroline Nokes, Karen Bradley and David Lidington – were prepared to contemplate a second referendum as a way to break the impasse.

The three key interventions came from Philip Hammond, Michael Gove and Geoffrey Cox. Philip argued that it was clear we weren't going to get anything more from the EU, we didn't want an election and the House would not allow the government to choose to leave without a deal. The only option, then, was to secure more votes for the deal, which meant either a customs union or a second referendum. He thought a second referendum was less unpalatable, but no deal would have to be one of the options. Michael urged his colleagues to stop thinking about what they wanted and focus on what was achievable. He agreed with Philip that the House would block no deal and that an election was undesirable. We might be able to get something more from the EU, he said, but it seemed unlikely. But he disagreed that a second referendum was the least unpalatable option. After all, the original referendum had not been a therapeutic experience, and the House of Commons would rig the terms of a second one in favour of Remain. The best way forward was to amend the deal and secure Labour votes. Geoffrey spoke towards the end. The discussion about whether to have an election had been like a convention of turkeys who didn't want Christmas, he said. The question was, how could one be avoided? He agreed with Michael: no Brexiteer could contemplate a second referendum, so the only way – unpleasant though it was – was to move our red lines. We should make a big, bold and generous offer to Labour to accept their terms for a deal.

It was political cabinet, so I was sitting at the table and contributed at the end. I said that unless cabinet adopted no deal as the government's policy – and it was clear that hardly anyone thought we should do that – we would have to apply for an extension. But an increasing number of our MPs wanted to leave without a deal. The gridlock was tearing the party apart – if we were going to extend, we had to come up with some way of resolving the issue. Only three credible paths had been suggested: introducing the Withdrawal Agreement Bill, some kind of preferential vote or finding out what changes it would take to get Labour to drop their opposition to the deal.

The meeting broke for lunch, before reconvening as a formal cabinet meeting. The prime minister asked for everyone's views on two questions. Should we adopt no deal as a policy, or should we ask for an extension? And if we asked for an extension, should we use it to introduce the Withdrawal Agreement Bill, hold preferential votes or reach out to Labour? On the first question, only Gavin Williamson and Liz Truss opposed asking for an extension, although several other ministers said they only supported a short one. Michael Gove reminded everyone that the facts didn't care about their feelings. The length of an extension was not in our control, the European elections were a fact and the government had to obey the law. The key point was that we should be able to bring any extension to an end as soon as we had ratified a deal.

On the second question, there was little support for immediately introducing the Withdrawal Agreement Bill, but the cabinet was fairly evenly split better the other two options. Summing up, the prime minister said she didn't like the idea of doing a deal with Labour or preferential voting, but we should try the former first and resort to the latter if a deal couldn't be reached. But she warned the cabinet that either option would only work if it produced a stable majority at all stages of the Withdrawal Agreement Bill. In the case of preferential votes, that would mean committing to abide by the result.

We kept the cabinet in the Cabinet Room, while we drafted a statement for the prime minister, so the decision didn't leak. She told the waiting media:

> Today I am taking action to break the logjam. I am offering to sit down with the leader of the opposition and to try to agree a plan – that we would both stick to – to ensure that we leave the European Union and that we do so with a deal. Any plan would have to agree the current Withdrawal Agreement . . . the EU has repeatedly said that it cannot and will not be reopened. What we need to focus on is our future relationship with the EU. The ideal outcome of this process would be to agree an approach on a future relationship . . . that both the leader of the oppos- ition and I could put to the House for approval . . . However,

if we cannot agree on a single unified approach, then we would instead agree a number of options . . . that we could put to the House in a series of votes to determine which course to pursue. Crucially, the government stands ready to abide by the decision of the House. But to make this process work, the opposition would need to agree to this, too . . . We would want to agree a timetable for this Bill to ensure it is passed before 22 May, so that the United Kingdom need not take part in European parliamentary elections.

Looking back on this crucial cabinet meeting, two things stand out. First, no one suggested the solution that Boris Johnson in the end adopted – accepting the EU's original plan of a partial border between Great Britain and Northern Ireland. I strongly disagree with what he did, but it is a fact that he succeeded where Theresa failed in part because he was prepared to think the unthinkable and cut Northern Ireland and the DUP loose. Second, the outcome of the meeting was not one we had pre-cooked. No one in Number 10 knew that Geoffrey Cox was going to suggest accepting Labour's terms for a deal. We hadn't prepared the party for it, and we weren't prepared ourselves. I was privately sceptical about whether it would work – the momentum in Labour was towards a second referendum. On the other hand, we didn't have a better plan, so I threw myself into it.

Talking to the enemy

The decision to enter talks with Jeremy Corbyn went down like a bucket of cold sick with many Conservatives MPs. Nigel Adams and Chris Heaton-Harris, two loyal junior ministers, resigned the next day. To an extent, MPs' anger was understandable. How could we work with someone who had presided over a rising tide of anti-Semitism in the Labour Party and regularly sided with our country's enemies?

On the other hand, what did they expect the prime minister to do, given the refusal of some of their colleagues to compromise?

Jeremy Corbyn brought shadow DExEU secretary Keir Starmer, shadow business secretary Rebecca Long-Bailey, opposition chief whip Nick Brown, and Seamus Milne and Andrew Fisher from his office (the latter of whom I knew, because he was a Labour activist from my old constituency) to the initial meeting. The prime minister began by setting out what she hoped the talks could achieve: either a deal we could both support or options we could put to the House for a preferential vote, with both sides agreeing to abide by the result, plus a timetable for passing the Withdrawal Agreement Bill, ideally by 22 May. The Labour team were full of questions. They were concerned about workers' rights in the backstop – was reopening the Withdrawal Agreement impossible? Yes, but there might be other ways of addressing that concern. How quickly could we negotiate any changes to the political declaration? That depended on what they were.

The prime minister tried to find out what changes the Labour team were looking for. Keir Starmer referred to customs, broad single market alignment, including a discussion on free movement, workers' rights, environmental protection, a confirmatory vote and the entrenchment of any agreement – given that Theresa had announced that she would be standing down after the first phase of Brexit, they wanted assurance that her successor wouldn't renege on any deal. This package was close to staying in the customs union and single market, which would clearly be unacceptable to the vast majority of Conservative MPs. However, it was clear that there were differences of opinion within the Labour side, just as there were on ours. Seamus Milne had briefed just a few hours earlier that it was Labour policy to end free movement, and it felt like some of the people opposite us were not so wedded to a confirmatory vote. The meeting ended with agreement that the negotiating teams would meet at the Cabinet Office the next day.

Our team was led by David Lidington and included Julian Smith, Steve Barclay, Greg Clark and me, with Olly Robbins providing official support. The Labour team were led by Keir Starmer and included Rebecca Long-Bailey, Seamus Milne and Andrew Fisher. David opened the meeting by acknowledging that this wasn't an easy conversation for either side, given the adversarial nature of our politics. He reassured them that it was a genuine attempt to find a way forward – the prime minister had taken a big political risk by offering to talk. He suggested that we work through each of Labour's asks in turn.

We started with customs. Keir said Labour wanted a comprehensive and permanent customs union. We pointed out that the political declaration effectively committed the government to what the World Trade Organisation would term a customs union, but a novel one that allowed for an independent trade policy. The government had not used the phrase, both because people thought it referred to the existing EU customs union and because the phrase had become toxic for many Conservative MPs. Andrew Fisher asked what our policy would be if we couldn't negotiate that, to which we replied that the default was the backstop, which explicitly was a customs union. Keir argued that the use of the phrase 'customs union' was important.

We moved on to alignment with the single market. Rebecca Long-Bailey said Labour's concerns were about regulatory barriers to trade at the border, workers' rights and environmental standards. Our recent proposals were a welcome step forward, she said, but they were looking for a guarantee that workers' rights would be no less favourable in the UK than the EU, along with some domestic mechanism to enforce them. This was easier territory than customs. Keir sought to broaden the conversation out to wider single market alignment, but the officials present noted the risks of making commitments to align with EU rules without securing any additional market access, which we were unlikely to get.

After lunch, we turned to what assurances we could offer that any deal would stick when Theresa was no longer prime minister. Labour were looking for separate legislation on workers' rights, for the negotiating objectives for the next phase to be put in law and changes to the political declaration. The latter would take time, but they were adamant that at least one of the two documents that made up the deal had to change. We explored whether we could start the Withdrawal Agreement Bill while negotiating changes to the political declaration, or it would be impossible to get all this done by 22 May.

Finally, we turned to a confirmatory vote. Here, Keir said lots of Labour MPs wouldn't support any deal without one, but Steve Barclay was admirably robust: if we'd been prepared to accept a second referendum, we wouldn't be having these talks about how to amend the deal because enough MPs had already made it clear that they would accept the existing deal if we conceded on a referendum. Seamus struck a different tone: was there some way that this issue could be addressed as part of the passage of the bill?

All in all, it had been a good first meeting. Both sides had approached the talks constructively and we'd been able to clear up a few areas where the problem was not that we wanted different things, but that what we both wanted wasn't negotiable. The biggest concerns were customs and the fact that Labour were not in as much of a hurry as we were. We undertook to get back to them the next day with a draft memorandum of understanding based on our discussion.

We spent hours trying to draft this memorandum of understanding. Pizzas were ordered and bottles of wine opened. The ministers who were involved in the talks were nervous about going too far, so Liam Fox was asked to come and serve as a litmus test. In the end, it was agreed that we should get some sleep and reassemble the next day to sign off what we had agreed. However, in the cold light of morning, Julian and Geoffrey decided that they wanted to redraft certain sections. This was the one occasion when stress and sleep deprivation caught up with me, and I absolutely lost it. We were meant to be the ones in a hurry, and yet we were going to be late getting Labour what we'd promised.

We finally got the thing signed off and it was agreed that I should deliver it to Jeremy Corbyn's office. Wary of the cameras outside Number 10, I went through the link door into the Cabinet Office and out on to Whitehall, but there were cameras there, too. Did I have any update on the talks? Thankfully, no one noticed the brown envelope I was carrying that contained our initial offer.

Keir and Rebecca responded frostily later that day, saying that we would need to make a much more significant shift in our position, but on Saturday 6 April they sent a more useful response that set out their concerns. On customs, they felt we had just restated our position; on workers' rights, they wanted changes to be enshrined in domestic law and referred to in the Withdrawal Agreement or a supplement to it; and they emphasised their desire for changes to the Political Declaration. Their response also contained a masterpiece of drafting to cover up the differences within their party on a confirmatory vote:

> There is growing support in parliament – especially in opposition parties – that any deal should be put to a confirmatory vote. Labour has made clear that we would back a public vote for any deal we did not believe protected UK living standards and industry.

The first sentence implied that Labour thought any deal needed to be put to a confirmatory vote; the second that they did not think one would be necessary if the deal protected living standards and industry. Which was it?

Rebecca Long-Bailey was more encouraging about the talks on *The Andrew Marr Show* on 7 April, commenting that the mood had been 'quite a positive and hopeful one'. To try to move things forward, we drafted a short reply to their letter rather than amending the long and technical draft memorandum of understanding. It was explicit that we were 'prepared to seek changes to the political declaration [and] consider a variety of options for how any commitments could be entrenched in UK law'. On customs, we felt that they had misunderstood what we were saying, probably because we had been opaque about it, given the sensitivities on our own side. We clarified that we were offering to secure 'the benefits of a customs union in all scenarios [and] to enshrine this commitment in domestic legislation'.

I had further talks with Andrew Fisher and his team on 8 April. He suggested that it would be helpful if John McDonnell and Sue Hayman were part of their negotiation team and asked if we would therefore add Philip Hammond and Michael Gove to ours. The second round of negotiations took place the next day. Keir said our letter had been helpful and David emphasised that 'the benefits of a customs union in all scenarios' *was* a shift in the government's position. We got into a lot more detail about the environment and the services sector of the economy, where Philip Hammond made the case that staying aligned would not secure much additional market access. It was another constructive meeting, with the only frustrating point coming at the end, when Julian tried to get Labour to commit to a timetable for the Withdrawal Agreement Bill and Keir and John said we needed to make more progress first. They wanted to see draft legislation and changes to the political declaration, which meant it was increasingly unlikely that we could leave by 22 May. The harsh truth was that although Labour didn't particularly want European elections, they didn't have as much to fear from them as we did. Jeremy Corbyn's main concern was resolving everything before their conference, which was likely to shift Labour policy into supporting a second referendum.

Intermission: securing another extension

On the morning of 10 April, the prime minister signed off a revised memorandum of understanding to send to Labour. Given that there was no imminent prospect of introducing the Withdrawal Agreement

Bill, she reluctantly agreed to an Easter recess for the House of Commons. Then we went to Brussels, to try to secure the extension we needed to avoid a no-deal Brexit two days later.

When we got there, Donald Tusk told the prime minister that most of the leaders wanted to offer a longer extension than the 30 June date she had asked for (Tony Blair had contacted me on 6 April and warned that this was likely to be the case). They didn't think our politics would be resolved by then, and they didn't want to have to keep meeting to agree further extensions. However, Tusk was worried about President Macron. He'd had no contact with him in the last twenty-four hours, which was unusual before a European Council. The prime minister replied that although she would prefer 30 June, the key point was that any extension should be terminable if parliament ratified the deal. She was worried that President Macron would be tempted to create another short-term cliff edge, in an attempt to persuade people to vote for the deal. That, she said, would actually encourage some of her colleagues that no deal was within reach. And she could not agree to second-class membership while we remained in the EU – we must retain our full rights and obligations. Tusk sympathised with this, but said that some member states were worried about how her successor might behave.

I wish we had been able to bring every single MP with us to see the humiliating position they had put our country in. The prime minister was invited to address the European Council but then had to wait outside, while the other heads of government deliberated over our country's fate. It turned out the extension that MPs had thought a formality when they rejected the Withdrawal Agreement was nothing of the sort. We waited in the delegation room for a while, before going back to Tim Barrow's residence. We were summoned back to the Europa building in the middle of the night and told that the council's decision was a terminable extension until the end of October, but that Belgium wanted to strengthen the text on the duty of sincere co-operation. The prime minister refused to accept the new text and a compromise was agreed, where the European Council took note of 'the UK's commitment to act in a constructive and responsible manner throughout the extension in accordance with the duty of sincere co-operation'. The prime minister tried to get hold of her most senior ministers to check that they were happy for her to accept these terms, but she could only reach David Lidington, Geoffrey Cox and Michael Gove, all of whom agreed that she should do so.

Back to the negotiating table

We were back in London the next morning, and I met with Andrew Fisher to review our progress. We agreed that we should continue to have meetings of the negotiating teams, but also set up sub-groups to work on particular areas. I also tried to make some progress on the timetable. Could we explore introducing the Withdrawal Agreement Bill once we'd published draft domestic legislation and agreed what changes we would seek to the political declaration, but before we had negotiated them with the EU?

In the third round of negotiations, on 12 April, we discussed a potential solution to Labour's concerns about the lack of dynamic alignment on workers' rights in the backstop. The EU wouldn't re-open the Withdrawal Agreement, but we could put a statutory duty on ministers to enhance protection through the joint committee once the agreement was ratified and get the EU to say publicly that they would agree to such a change. On workers' rights more generally, John McDonnell – who was leading the Labour team in the absence of Keir Starmer – clarified that they would like a bespoke bill and we undertook to get them a draft a week later. From my perspective as the person holding the pen on the draft agreement, the addition of John to Labour's team meant we were getting much clearer steers, and he was much more perceptive about what lay behind some of our language ('There are areas where you deliberately have constructive ambiguity – it's like a composite Labour conference motion'). He was also occasionally amusingly indiscreet, observing drily that 'at every meeting, we're obliged to raise the issue of a confirmatory vote'.

On Monday 15 April, we sent some further papers to Labour, the most important of which was a set of proposed changes to the political declaration. We also got back their latest comments on the draft memorandum of understanding. Customs was still the key problem, with Labour saying they did not believe 'it is either possible or desirable' to negotiate what the government wanted, before concluding, 'We therefore believe that the government should make clear that it is committed to a customs arrangement in the interim.' This was a strange request, because that's exactly what the backstop was. Conservative MPs were refusing to back the deal because they thought we would be stuck in a customs union, while Labour were saying they couldn't back the deal because they were worried we *wouldn't* be in a customs union.

On 17 April, the prime minister had a conference call with the ministers in our negotiating team, plus Geoffrey Cox and Liam Fox, on how to respond. It felt like there were two ways forward: we could offer up some new language on customs or switch to plan B, preferential votes in the House of Commons. The problem with the latter quickly became clear: Liam said that if parliament voted for a standard customs union, he could not support us accepting that, and the chief whip advised that Labour would not be bound by the result either. And the problem with the former plan was articulated by Michael Gove, who said he was sceptical about whether the Labour front bench would do a deal. In the end, the meeting decided to keep trying, but only for lack of a better option.

The political damage this was doing to the party and the prime minister was becoming increasingly clear. A poll conducted on 15 and 16 April showed the Brexit Party on course to get the most votes in the European elections. On 21 April, it was announced that an extraordinary general meeting of the party's most senior activists would consider a motion of no confidence in the prime minister. The party chairman Brandon Lewis told her that morale among activists was 'at the lowest point I've ever known it', with many refusing to campaign for the European elections. And on 23 April, Graham Brady told the prime minister that some members of the executive of the 1922 Committee wanted to change its rules to allow another confidence vote before the twelve-month period was up. He said he and his fellow officers wondered whether she wanted to pre-empt the discussion, either by saying something further about her intentions or by submitting herself to another confidence vote voluntarily? That suggestion met with a pretty punchy response. She'd been told previously that if she announced that she would go once the first phase of Brexit was complete, colleagues would back the Withdrawal Agreement on 29 March, and they hadn't. Why should she say anything further? Graham was sympathetic, but said the situation was ugly and that he feared it was going to get worse. She said she would think about it overnight, but told him the next morning that she was not prepared to name a date.

At a meeting of senior ministers the same day, those who were opposed to talks with Labour – Gavin Williamson, Liz Truss, Chris Grayling and Penny Mordaunt, in particular – made the case for an alternative strategy of bringing forward the Withdrawal Agreement Bill and accepting backbench amendments that united the parliamentary party but were inconsistent with what we had agreed with the EU – essentially 'Brady Mark 2'. However, this wouldn't lead to us leaving the EU because the EU wouldn't accept us unilaterally changing the terms of the deal. Others, including Andrea Leadsom and Julian Smith, favoured a softer version of this strategy, which involved bringing forward the Withdrawal Agreement Bill with some of the things we had agreed with Labour, a package for the DUP and something for Conservative backbenchers on alternative arrangements, and seeing how the House amended the bill. Their argument was that on customs, in particular, it was better for things to be done to us than for us to propose them upfront.

At the fourth round of negotiations later that day, Julian broached this idea with Labour. We could agree some things and amend the Withdrawal Agreement Bill accordingly, he said, but allow the House to resolve the two most difficult issues – customs and a confirmatory vote – during the committee stage of the bill. His view was that the House would probably support Labour's position on customs and our position on a confirmatory vote. John McDonnell seemed interested in this idea.

On 26 April, the prime minister had a teleconference with David Lidington, Steve Barclay, Julian Smith, Michael Gove and Geoffrey Cox. I circulated a memo beforehand that set out six key questions. How much time were we prepared to give the talks, given the political damage, before switching to preferential votes? If we had a deadline, should we tell Labour? If we reached the deadline, should we publish something setting out what we had offered? Doing so would show that we had compromised, but by going public we would be making these concessions without any guarantee of increased support. Were ministers content with our plan for how preferential votes would work? What would we do if the Withdrawal Agreement Bill was rejected at its second or third reading? And finally, was there any plan C we wanted to consider? Steve Barclay had been advocating bringing forward the Withdrawal Agreement Bill without the backstop – that was clearly a dead end, because it wouldn't ratify the deal, but a softer version of this plan involved putting the backstop into a separate bill.

The prime minister said she thought we were reaching the point where we should bring the talks to an end, but wanted to hear everyone's else views. It was a pretty unsatisfactory discussion. Everyone was clear that Labour were, at best, on a much slower timetable than us and, at worst, never going to get over the line, but if neither they nor some members of the cabinet were prepared to commit to abiding by the results of preferential votes, plan B wouldn't work, either. Amending the Withdrawal Agreement Bill so that it was inconsistent with what we had agreed with the EU wouldn't work, and introducing it in its current form without Labour's support risked it being voted down at the second reading. Ministers ultimately agreed to communicate to Labour that our patience was finite and that we needed the bill to get royal assent, ideally by 1 July and certainly by the summer recess.

On 28 April, we had a much better conference call. Senior ministers signed off three things to send to Labour: a table showing what changes to the political declaration we were offering to seek, clauses to be added to the Withdrawal Agreement Bill and draft clauses of a Workers' Rights Bill. The next day we sent these to Labour with a covering letter from David Lidington that suggested that rather than continuing to exchange correspondence, we should focus on the text of the memorandum of understanding, the wording of the changes to the political declaration we were going to seek and the wording of the draft legislation.

We went straight into the fifth negotiating round, and David and I began the meeting by talking about the timetable. Were they saying that we needed to secure changes to the political declaration before the second reading of the Withdrawal Agreement Bill? If they were, that meant the second reading would be after the Whitsun recess, so royal assent wouldn't be until September. That timetable didn't work for us. Once again, there seemed to be differences within their team. Keir said that he had always envisaged that the bill wouldn't be brought forward until the revised deal had been approved, Seamus said all that was needed was proof of movement and John said both sides had a mutual interest in getting this done as soon as was practical.

We then moved on to the substance. Although they had received our two documents just ninety minutes earlier, they had clearly made an impact: we made good progress on a number of issues, and Labour briefed afterwards that 'the talks felt different and more substantive in a way that they didn't last week'. The only worrying sign was on a confirmatory vote; Keir said, 'You can read our politics, just like we can read yours,' but it was difficult to see what we could offer. We received further encouragement after the meeting. Greg Clark had spoken to Len McCluskey, who reported that Corbyn wanted a deal to go through, but without his hands being all over it. Nick Boles, now an independent MP, and the BBC journalist Nick Watt both told me that Labour were now much more positive.

On 30 April, there was a fascinating ministerial discussion. Instead of the usual soft Brexit/hard Brexit factions, the divide was between those ministers who were involved in the talks and some of those who were not involved, who wanted to ditch the talks and give a unicorn a go. Julian introduced the discussion by arguing that 'Brady Mark 2' wouldn't get Brexit done; the choice was between a deal with Labour on customs or a second referendum. Steve Barclay argued that preferential votes wouldn't deliver a stable majority for the Withdrawal Agreement Bill: the question was, could Brexiteers live with a two-stage Brexit, where we left, but not for the kind of future relationship they wanted, at least initially? Michael Gove argued that the choice was between the unpalatable and the disastrous. We were in a race against time to avoid a second referendum – Corbyn didn't want one, but nearly all his potential successors did. And we were only talking to him because we'd tried everything else and 'there are some people who will do anything for Brexit except vote for it'. Alun Cairns made a powerful point at the end of the discussion: he said we should remind those colleagues who were criticising us for talking to Labour that we were only doing it because some Conservatives had spent the last few months voting with them.

The prime minister then had another meeting with Graham Brady, who had – rather bravely – come back for another go at persuading her to name her timeframe. The party was angry, he told her. She had said she would stand down if she got the deal through, but what would she do if she didn't? The prime minister said that if anyone thought she was sitting in Downing Street, trying to avoid getting Brexit done in order to cling on for as long as possible, they really didn't understand her mood. She knew this couldn't drag on beyond the summer recess, but setting a timeframe for when she would go if she didn't succeed might simply encourage some to oppose a deal.

On 1 May, Olly and I met with Andrew Fisher to discuss a new document entitled 'What We've Agreed'. Andrew suggested some changes, but the most interesting part of the discussion concerned whether we were trying to get to a point where Labour supported the Withdrawal Agreement Bill at all stages or merely didn't whip against it. The latter felt more realistic, and would probably still allow us to get the deal through.

In the local elections on 2 May, both main parties lost vote share, seats and councils, a clear sign that the failure to get Brexit done was hurting them. A couple of days later, Iain Duncan Smith publicly called on the prime minister to resign.

On 6 May, we sent the 'What We've Agreed' document to Labour. The next day, the prime minister had a brief meeting with Jeremy Corbyn and emphasised that we needed to introduce the bill the following week if we were going to get it through by the summer. We then had a sixth round of negotiations that focused on customs, the most difficult issue. After the progress we'd made the previous week, this brought us down to earth with a bump. Labour were angry about briefing from our side suggesting we'd reached agreement on certain issues and comments by Jeremy Hunt that he hoped the prime minister would not agree to Labour demands on a customs union. Keir objected to the language on customs in the 'What We've Agreed' document, but I pointed out that we'd lifted it from his letter of 22 April – he was objecting to his own policy. He looked suitably embarrassed, but it was clear that their concern had switched from what would happen if we couldn't negotiate our preferred policy to what would happen if we could – they were worried that they wouldn't be able to pursue their own policy if they won the next election.

When we met again the next day, the picture was mixed. On the plus side, Labour were clear that if they agreed to a deal, they would back the Withdrawal Agreement Bill through all its stages, giving us the sustainable majority that we desperately needed. But Keir was back to arguing that we needed to secure changes to the political declaration before the bill's second reading. Seamus told us afterwards not to attach too much weight to what he had said. Robbie, Olly and I met with Seamus and Andrew on 9 May to try to understand the dynamics on their side. Seamus admitted that 'as time has gone on, a confirmatory vote has become more of a totem'. Robbie asked what their own views were, to which Seamus replied 'Opinions differ.' We took this to mean that he was opposed to one, while Andrew thought Corbyn needed to support one to keep the Labour Party together.

The next day, we were joined by Karie Murphy, the executive director of Jeremy Corbyn's office. She was admirably blunt. We were coming to a point where a decision had to be made, she said. It felt to her like the hokey cokey – we discussed things in the talks before struggling to clear what we'd agreed with others, so the language in the documents we sent back was more nuanced. I was equally blunt: she was right, but we needed clarity from them about what it would take to get them over the line. We had a much better chance of persuading the sceptics on our side if we could present a package in return for which they could be sure we would leave the EU, rather than going to them with one concession after another with nothing as yet to show for it. She replied that the shadow cabinet wouldn't be investing all this time in the talks if they weren't serious about finding a way forward. Seamus recognised that the longer this dragged on, the more polarised everyone became. They understood that we needed to announce something at the following's week business statement (the 1922 executive had asked to see the prime minister immediately after the business statement), but they couldn't be confident they would be in a position to publicly support the second reading by then. Could we explore some other way of moving things forward?

I got back to my desk and wrote a note to the ministers involved in the negotiations, summarising where we had got to, and a longer one to the prime minister and Julian Smith setting out the options.

The ideal option was that we would proceed with the second reading on 22 May based on an explicit deal with Labour, but that seemed unlikely. The second option, if Labour were prepared to commit to a second reading after the Whitsun recess, was to announce the date next Thursday and publish a programme motion demonstrating that we could achieve royal assent by the summer. That might be enough for the 1922 executive. The third option was preferential votes. The fourth option was the high-risk gambit of proceeding with the second reading on 22 May without a deal with Labour.

The weekend papers brought little good news. On the Saturday, Graham Brady called for the prime minister to set a date for her departure. On the Sunday, John McDonnell said the talks were on the brink of collapse because the government was disintegrating, while a poll on voting intention in a general election showed the Brexit Party a single point behind us.

I put the first three of the options to Andrew on Monday 13 May, together with a fourth option of breaking the Withdrawal Agreement Bill into several smaller bills. His preference was for resolving some issues via indicative votes and others during the bill's parliamentary stages. Yvette Cooper, who was under pressure from the Brexit Party in her constituency, issued a statement saying, 'we need the cross-party talks to bring people together to get a workable Brexit deal'. This showed that there were Labour MPs who wanted to vote for a deal – we just needed to find a way of accessing their votes. But time was running out. Andrew Bowie and John Randall, a former deputy chief whip and now a member of the prime minister's policy unit, both came to see me to say the game was up.

That afternoon, we met Labour for the eighth – and final – time. We pushed them hard on the timetable, but they couldn't give us answers without consulting the shadow cabinet. They agreed it would be good to resolve the issue by the summer recess, but they could only help us if they had the numbers.

At a ministerial meeting the next morning, the mood was tetchy.

Liz Truss, who better than anyone exemplified how the gridlock was polarising people's opinions, argued that we were headed for a choice between revoke and no deal and called on the cabinet to make up its mind. Liam Fox argued that an extended implementation period was preferable to an open-ended customs union. Michael Gove passionately urged his colleagues to fight for the compromise we believed in. We needed to take on Nigel Farage – he was a charlatan. If we managed to leave, that would be the end of the Brexit Party. He said Keir Starmer was harder to please than anyone he had ever met – we should set a deadline and make our case. The prime minister, summing up, said that we needed to bring things to a head the week after the Whitsun recess.

Later that day, Theresa met Jeremy Corbyn to inform him of our decision. He reported that that 'noises off' from ministers not involved in the negotiations were making it harder to build trust, to which the prime minister replied that there were similar noises coming from the Labour side. When Nick Brown said that she could get her deal through if she agreed to put it to a confirmatory vote, she wearily replied that if she was prepared to support one, she would have done it weeks ago and saved herself a lot of pain. Our plan was to hold the second reading in the week of 4 June, but we would switch to preferential votes if they preferred. We left them to think about it.

The next day Robbie, Olly and I met with Seamus and Andrew again. Olly reported that his EU counterparts would not approve changes to the political declaration without a clear commitment that this would mean support for the deal. He also warned that time was running out – after the European elections, the commission's authority would drain away. We explored Andrew's preference for resolving some issues via indicative votes and others during the passage of the bill, but when we spoke to Julian afterwards, he had received a conflicting message from Nick Brown, who was opposed to any indicative votes.

On the morning of 16 May, the prime minister met with the 1922 executive. They wanted to meet her in private, but I was called in because they wanted help to draft Graham Brady's statement. It read:

> The prime minister is determined to secure our departure from the EU and is devoting her efforts to securing the second reading of the Withdrawal Agreement Bill in the week commencing 3 June and the passage of that bill and the consequent departure of the UK from the EU by the summer. We have agreed that she and I will meet following the second reading of the bill to agree a timetable for the election of a new leader of the Conservative and Unionist party.

I then met with Seamus and Andrew for the final time. They were now keen on indicative votes – it was the only way they could see to move things forward – but the next day, it was all over. Jeremy Corbyn wrote to the prime minister, saying that he believed 'the talks between us have gone as far as they can'. He gave two reasons: 'while there are some areas where compromise has been possible, we have been unable to bridge important gaps'. Furthermore, he continued, 'the increasing weakness and instability of your government means there cannot be confidence in securing whatever might be agreed between us'.

Had the talks been doomed from the start? Probably. The prime minister had announced by then that she would stand down after the first phase of Brexit was complete, so her authority was eroded. People knew a leadership election was approaching, and some cabinet ministers who hoped to be contenders focused on positioning themselves rather than supporting painful compromises. Labour didn't have any confidence that whoever succeeded her would abide by any deal, and it was pretty clear that Keir Starmer was not prepared to settle for anything that didn't include a commitment to a confirmatory vote.

The more interesting question is whether cross-party talks might have been successful if they had begun earlier. I'm not sure whether the Conservative Party would have let the prime minister try – she only just got away with it in April, when she could point to the fact that she had tried to pass a deal with Conservative and DUP votes three times, without success. But if she had been able to do it, I think an agreement would have been possible. As it was, we came pretty close.

But we didn't try until the last minute, and it didn't work. Labour were probably right that Theresa's successor would have tried to wriggle out of any deal, but a deal would have constrained them. I'm not sure whether the shadow cabinet realised at the time, but they had killed off the last chance for a compromise Brexit. The collapse of the talks meant the end of Theresa's premiership, and her successor was bound to be a hard Brexiteer. I presume they thought they could stop whoever came next from leaving without a deal and then win the subsequent general election. If they did, they were right on the first point, but the latter was a colossal misjudgement – if they had done a deal, it would have been much harder for Boris to portray them as blocking Brexit. Jeremy Corbyn wanted to do it, but Keir Starmer stopped it – it seems fitting that he's now dealing with the consequences.

CHAPTER 21

TIME'S UP

We were in the endgame now. Over the weekend of 18 and 19 May, I worked with JoJo, Robbie and the prime minister's three Brexit advisers, Denzil, Raoul and Ed de Minckwitz, on a paper for a meeting of senior ministers.

We had said that the Withdrawal Agreement Bill would have its second reading in the week of 3 June, but there were decisions to take about content, process and timing. How much of what we had offered to Labour did ministers want to include, and what did they want to do about customs and a confirmatory vote, where we had not been able to reach agreement? How much of what we had offered to the DUP back in March did they want to include? Did they want to include a clause on alternative arrangements to make the package more attractive to Brexiteers? Did they want to hold indicative votes before the Bill's second reading, rather than coming forward with a specific package? When did they want to hold the second reading? The D-Day commemorations ruled out 5 and 6 June, so the choice was either 4 June, which would coincide with President Trump's visit, or 7 June, which the whips didn't like because it was a Friday.

Finally, they needed to think about what they would do if we lost. At that point, there would almost certainly be a majority in parliament for a second referendum: ministers would have to decide whether to accept that, try to leave without a deal in the face of parliamentary opposition or call an election. Given that any of these options would lead to the break-up of the government, we argued 'for putting all our chips on the table now and making the maximum compromise that is acceptable to us, so we can secure second reading'.

When the ministers met, they found it easier to reach agreement on content and process than timing. They rejected indicative votes and decided to put forward a broad package, including what we had offered to Labour and the DUP and a clause on alternative arrangements. On customs, they decided to include in the bill a requirement for a vote to be held to determine the government's negotiating position. However, conscious that this might not secure sufficient opposition support, they also approved a reserve option of putting on the face of the bill a requirement to negotiate an interim customs union, which would be terminable – whichever party won the next election could then pursue their preferred policy.

On a confirmatory vote, they decided that our starting offer should be a debate during the passage of the bill on whether the deal should be subject to one. But again, this might not secure sufficient opposition support, so they also approved a reserve option of adding the requirement to hold such a debate to the bill. Opinions were divided on when to hold the second reading. Some didn't like 4 June because it would mean publishing the package before the European elections and the imminent Peterborough by-election, while others thought the package would leak from cabinet anyway and that delaying to 7 June would mean MPs sitting around with little to do for the first three days after the Whitsun recess. We now needed to get policy clearance for this package from the wider cabinet.

I made my way to the office at the crack of dawn the next morning to work on what the prime minister would present to the cabinet and the speech she would give afterwards. To add an element of farce to proceedings, I couldn't get to Downing Street because of an early-morning rehearsal for the Trooping of the Colour, so I had to abandon my car near Methodist Central Hall and walk.

The chief whip opened the discussion and argued that we needed to be bold. There was no guarantee that it would work, but there was no chance of success if we didn't do something to attract Labour support. It was a pretty scratchy meeting. A narrow majority argued that we had previously under-offered – this was our last chance, and we had to be bold. But for some, even the bare minimum went too far. Andrea Leadsom said she couldn't vote for this bill – having things done to us was one thing, but proposing them ourselves was a step too far. Liz Truss predicted that Labour wouldn't go for it and said that people on our side were moving away from supporting a deal. But her alternatives – the 'Brady Mark 2' unicorn or adopting no deal as a policy – wouldn't work, and the latter would break the government. Chris Grayling said that while he understood what the prime minister was trying to do, he would struggle to support it. David Mundell, normally a loyalist, was unhappy about saying anything about a second referendum, given the precedent that would set in terms of a second Scottish independence referendum. Others could support the minimum package, but not the more forward-leaning options on customs and a confirmatory vote. In her summing up, the prime minister said that cabinet had agreed we should offer a vote between two customs options and parliamentary time for a decision on a confirmatory vote, with neither put on the face of the bill. It probably wouldn't have made any difference to how things turned out, but Jeremy Corbyn had been proved right: the need to keep everyone onside had prevented us from making a bold offer.

The prime minister made her speech setting out the offer at the Embankment Place offices of PwC, which is coincidentally now my main place of work (the venue wasn't my idea, and nor did I have any idea then what I would do when my time at Number 10 came to an end). She said:

> I have tried everything I possibly can to find a way through. It is true that initially I wanted to achieve this predominantly on the back of Conservative and DUP votes. In our parliamentary system, that is simply how you normally get things done. I sought

the changes MPs demanded. I offered to give up the job I love earlier than I would like . . . But it was not enough. So I took the difficult decision to try to reach a cross-party deal on Brexit . . . We engaged in six weeks of serious talks with the opposition, offering to compromise. But in the end, those talks were not enough for Labour to reach an agreement with us. But I do not think that means we should give up. The House of Commons voted to trigger Article 50. And the majority of MPs say they want to deliver the result of the referendum. So I think we need to help them find a way, and I believe there is now one last chance to do that . . . Today I am making a serious offer to MPs across parliament. A new Brexit deal . . . We all have to take some responsibility for the fact that we are in this impasse – and we all have a responsibility to do what we can to get out of it . . . I say with conviction to every MP of every party: I have compromised. Now I ask you to compromise, too.

Carolyn Fairbairn, the director general of the CBI, noted that the prime minister's offer 'provides a way forward' and urged MPs 'finally to find the spirit of compromise that has eluded them so far'. However, that was about the only positive response the speech received.

There was an immediate angry reaction from Conservative MPs. The next morning, David Mundell told me he wanted to see the prime minister, so he could tell her privately that he thought she should stand down. Cabinet ministers began lobbying me not to introduce the bill. A number objected to the inclusion of a clause requiring a debate on a confirmatory vote, when the prime minister had said in cabinet that this would not be included. Responding to her statement in the House of Commons on 22 May, Jeremy Corbyn rather laughably claimed that the deal had not changed, but more accurately observed that the prime minister had lost the authority to deliver. The most damning thing, however, was that the chamber was far from full, and few MPs were turning up to our briefings.

In politics, irrelevance is even more damaging than fierce opposition. The game was up.

Julian, JoJo, Parky and I spoke immediately after the statement and agreed that we had run out of road. I knew I had to do the hardest thing a chief of staff has to do: tell their boss that their time is up. But how to do it? I told her that we had all agreed from the start that the defining purpose of her premiership was to get Brexit done. She had spoken powerfully the previous day about the damage the political impasse was doing to the country. If we had run out of options, didn't we owe it to the country to let someone else try? I think she knew it was time to stand down – she didn't take too much persuading. Some people were lobbying me that she needed to make the announcement that night, but I thought she was entitled to spend a couple of days thinking about what she wanted to say. We decided that she would make the announcement on Friday and stand down as party leader with effect from 7 June, so the leadership election wouldn't start until after President Trump's state visit and the D-Day commemorations.

The next morning, the prime minister gave us an initial steer of what she wanted to say in her statement – something about it being in the national interest for someone else to have a go at getting Brexit done and something to encourage young women to believe they could become prime minister. We also talked about the timing of the leadership election. The prime minister thought it was important that the party had a proper debate about what to do next, and there were some things she wanted to get done on the domestic front before she left Number 10. However, unless we were going to extend the Article 50 period yet again, the new government would need time to resolve the Brexit impasse before the end of October.

In addition, there was a strong case that she should endeavour to hand over to her successor while the House of Commons was sitting, because of a concern that a handover during recess could risk dragging the Queen into political controversy. Constitutionally, the outgoing prime minister's final duty is to advise the Queen who their successor should be – which person is most likely to command a House of Commons majority – which might not be simple this time. First, no party had an overall majority. More worryingly, some Conservative MPs had suggested they would resign the whip if Boris Johnson was elected leader. And if the handover happened when the House was in recess, the Queen would be giving the new prime minister the benefits of incumbency before it could be tested whether they commanded the confidence of the House. These three factors pointed to a handover shortly before the summer recess. The timetable would be decided by the 1922 executive in consultation with the board of the Conservative Party, so I was despatched to talk to Brandon Lewis about the prime minister's preference.

That night, Number 10 was eerily quiet, as if power had already seeped away. JoJo, Keelan and I ordered pizza and stayed late working on the prime minister's statement. The next morning, she informed Graham Brady of her decision. They then had a slightly awkward conversation, where she had to ask him if he was thinking of standing to be her successor – if he was, he couldn't announce the timetable for the contest. He went away to think about it and came back to say that the statement should go out from his vice-chairmen, Cheryl Gillan and Charles Walker.

The prime minister then went outside to formally announce to the waiting cameras that she would be standing down. Rereading the statement two years later, three sections stand out for those who want to understand her. The first focuses on her belief in the value of compromise:

> It will be for my successor to seek a way forward that honours the result of the referendum. To succeed, he or she will have to find consensus in parliament where I have not. Such a consensus can only be reached if those on all sides are willing to compromise. For many years, the great humanitarian Sir Nicholas Winton . . . was my constituent in Maidenhead. At another time

of political controversy, a few years before his death, he took me to one side at a local event and gave me a piece of advice. He said, 'Never forget that compromise is not a dirty word. Life depends on compromise.' He was right.

The second section is an insight into Theresa's motivations:

The unique privilege of this office is to use this platform to give a voice to the voiceless, to fight the burning injustices that still scar our society. That is why I put proper funding for mental health at the heart of our NHS long-term plan. It is why I am ending the postcode lottery for survivors of domestic abuse. It is why the Race Disparity Audit and gender pay gap reporting are shining a light on inequality, so it has nowhere to hide. And that is why I set up the independent public inquiry into the tragedy at Grenfell Tower – to search for the truth, so nothing like it can ever happen again, and so the people who lost their lives that night are never forgotten. Because this country is a union. Not just a family of four nations, but a union of people – all of us. Whatever our background, the colour of our skin or who we love. We stand together.

The final key section is the two-sentence peroration:

I will shortly leave the job that it has been the honour of my life to hold, the second female prime minister but certainly not the last. I do so with no ill will, but with enormous and enduring gratitude to have had the opportunity to serve the country I love.

This combined the two things she most wanted to say – that it had been an honour to serve and that she hoped her example would encourage other women to reach the highest echelons of political life – with something I'd encouraged her to say. Nearly all political careers end in failure, and even those people who get to the top rarely leave at a time of their own choosing. Neither Edward Heath nor Margaret Thatcher enhanced their reputations by their behaviour after leaving office, and Alex Salmond has recently fallen into the same trap. Theresa was entitled to feel angry about the behaviour of some of her colleagues, but that was not her style. Moreover, she wanted to carry on as an MP, so she would have to work with the people who had treated her badly.

She got close to tears when she delivered these last two lines. As usual, I had gone outside to watch the statement live. When she finished and went back into Number 10, I raced into Number 11 and along the corridor to catch up with her. She immediately apologised for getting emotional, and it was at this moment that we had the only argument I can remember us having. I say argument, but it was more me being cross with her for apologising. I had spent over two years encouraging her to show more emotion, to let people see the real Theresa May. No one watching the footage on the television news that night was going to think less of her for being upset about having to stand down from a job she had worked her whole life to get. She listened patiently as I ranted that she shouldn't apologise for being a human being, before gently saying, 'You wait and see. The papers will use those pictures differently because I'm a woman.' And she was right (although I still think the media coverage didn't make the public think any less of her, so I am calling the argument a score draw). If you want to understand why Theresa May avoided showing her emotions, it is because of years of sexist reporting had taught her that men showing emotions are regarded as strong, while women who do the same are regarded as weak.

With the statement done, I went and sat on a bench in the Downing Street garden – I wanted to be on my own for a bit. I've tried in this book to describe the various things I turned my hand to as chief of staff, but if you were writing a job description, the first point would be, 'Keep the prime minister in the job.' That's what Theresa had hired me to do, and I had failed. Ed Llewellyn, David Cameron's chief of staff, sent me a very kind text – he knew all too well what this moment was like. After a while, Helen MacNamara, the director general for propriety and ethics who I'd worked with previously at the Department of Communities and Local Government, came and found me. She sat with me for a while and told me I'd done everything I could. And I had – it just hadn't been enough.

The garden is an oasis of tranquillity in the middle of central London, and my favourite thing about Downing Street. It was a lovely spring day. I sat there for a while, feeling sorry for myself, before realising that it was my job to cheer up the rest of the team – they would be feeling down, too. Besides, we had two months left and the prime minister wanted to make the most of every day. When I got back inside, someone suggested going for drink, so the political team adjourned to a bar in Vauxhall and got smashed.

CHAPTER 22

WHAT CAN YOU ACHIEVE IN TWO MONTHS?

The day after the prime minister decided to stand down as party leader, she assembled her closest advisers and asked us a question: what could we get done in the next two months? Brexit would be for her successor to resolve, but now, for the first time in her premiership, she could focus on domestic policy. She wanted to make the most of every remaining day.

This was typical of Theresa. You would never have guessed that twenty-four hours earlier, she had come to the painful decision that it was time to give up the job she loved. There was no self-pity, recrimination or if-onlys. Instead, she was focused on what she could achieve. It was also exactly what the political team needed: something to battle for over the next few weeks. We wanted to build the best possible legacy for her, and if that meant falling out with a few cabinet ministers who wanted to save any good news for her successor, so be it.

Wish list

We got to work. Some things were ruled out because they would need primary legislation, which there was no time for. We settled on a shortlist of nine things: announce a multi-year education funding plan – essentially, a long-term plan for our schools and further education colleges; publish the Augar review of post-eighteen education; legislate for net-zero greenhouse gas emissions by 2050; establish a

Burning Injustices Commission to continue the prime minister's work in this area after she had left office; improve parental leave; announce a package of measures to improve mental health and reduce the stigma attached to it; publish a cross-government disability strategy; launch a review into what the UK government could do to strengthen the Union; and try to restore devolved government in Northern Ireland. That seemed like enough to be getting on with.

I started lobbying cabinet ministers to ensure we could get collective agreement to our shortlist of policies. Michael Gove was very supportive, and he had some environmental announcements that he said he would appreciate Number 10's support on. The next day I spoke to David Lidington and Julian Smith, who were both as supportive as I'd expected. I also had a conversation with Philip Hammond, who was likely to be the biggest stumbling block – a multi-year funding plan for schools was in tension with what he saw as his legacy of leaving the public finances in the best possible state. He was nakedly transactional: what inducement was the prime minister offering him? He wanted her to legislate to give parliament a lock on no deal. She and I were just as worried about no deal as he was, but for her to introduce such a bill would be contrary to what she had said about Brexit being for her successor to resolve.

On 30 May, the prime minister published the Augar review of post-eighteen education. Its core message was that that the disparity between the 50 per cent of young people attending higher education and the 50 per cent who do not had to be addressed. It included recommendations to strengthen technical education, increase funding for further education colleges, introduce a lifelong learning loan allowance for higher technical and degree level qualifications and reduce the cap on tuition fees to £7,500 a year. Decisions about how to implement these recommendations would fall to her successor, but she observed that it was telling that the debate around the review had concentrated on what it would mean for universities but ignored further education almost completely.

On 3 June, I met with Chris Skidmore to discuss the net-zero announcement. He needed clearance from cabinet colleagues and wanted help chasing up a response from Philip Hammond. Then I saw Penny Mordaunt to discuss parental leave, which she was enthusiastic about; and the disability strategy, where she was more sceptical, because in her experience many of these strategies were never actually implemented. On school funding, Amber Rudd, Jeremy Hunt, Matt Hancock, Jeremy Wright and Chris Skidmore were supportive, while Penny thought it should be left to the next prime minister. David Gauke agreed that it was an area of political vulnerability for the government, but he could understand the Treasury's reluctance to settle another big spending area outside of the spending review and was worried about what it would mean for the Ministry of Justice's budget. He didn't expect to serve in the next government, but felt it was his job to stand up for the department's interests.

I had another chat with Philip, who was even less co-operative. With regards to school funding, he thought it was wrong in principle for the prime minister to make such a big decision on spending after she had announced that she was standing down. I would have had some sympathy with this argument if she was proposing to do something that was controversial within the party, but all the potential leadership candidates agreed that schools needed more funding. And he could hardly argue that the prime minister no longer had the authority to make an announcement on school funding while lobbying her to legislate to block her successor's Brexit plan. He was in a slightly better place on net-zero emissions and parental leave, but it was a tetchy meeting.

The next day was largely taken up with President Trump's state visit, but I managed to speak to Brandon Lewis, Natalie Evans, Rory Stewart, Caroline Nokes, Geoffrey Cox and Steve Barclay. All were supportive on school funding, except Steve, who agreed with the policy, but was unsure whether Theresa or her successor should do it.

D-Day commemorations

On 5 June, we headed to Portsmouth for the commemorations of the seventy-fifth anniversary of the D-Day landings. After a moving service, the prime minister spent about ninety minutes chatting with veterans and their families and posing for selfies. In the end, she and President Macron had to be dragged away for lunch with the heads of government or their representatives from fourteen other countries who fought alongside us on D-Day. Chancellor Merkel was also present, proof that the sacrifices of the D-Day generation had not been in vain: not only did they liberate Europe, but the country they fought against is now an ally.

The prime minister said a few words during the lunch about what the countries represented had achieved and President Trump couldn't help interjecting, 'Except Germany.' At that point, the prime minister fixed him with her stare (for those who have never witnessed this in person, it is as intense as Paddington Bear's 'hard stare') and said, 'Donald, behave.' Prime Minister Trudeau warned Trump, 'You need to be careful with her. Now she's announced she's standing down, she's got nothing to lose.' To give the president some credit, he apologised and was on his best behaviour for the rest of the lunch.

The leaders were in an introspective mood. Chancellor Merkel said it was important that memories of what had happened did not fade when the last of the veterans died. Things might be imperfect now, but history taught us they could be a lot worse. Prime Minister Bettel said that Luxembourg was only a small country, but 5,000 Allied soldiers are buried there. He was a liberal, gay man with Jewish blood, and the presence of far-right parties in many of the countries represented around the table worried him. President Macron said France had made the mistake of humiliating Germany after the First World War, but had not repeated it after the Second, building a new Europe with Germany. The EU was good for Europe and America, he argued – we must continue to work together. Prime Minister Trudeau reflected that his generation had it easy because of the sacrifices of the D-Day generation, but there were many countries around the world who did not share our values. The subtext was clear: the other leaders were worried that the US was drifting away from them at a time when the world was becoming a more dangerous place. They signed copies of a proclamation:

> We commit to work constructively as friends and allies to find common ground where we have differences of opinion and to work together to resolve international tensions peacefully. We will act resolutely, with courage and tenacity, to protect our people against threats to our values and challenges to peace and stability. In this way, we salute the surviving veterans of D-Day and we honour the memories of those who came before us. We will ensure that the sacrifices of the past are never in vain and never forgotten.

Unbeknown to me, they also signed an additional copy, which was given to me as a leaving present a few weeks later and hangs proudly on the wall of my study.

As the discussion drew to a close, the prime minister announced that the last two bottles of 1945 port from the government's collection would now be served. The heads of government and their representatives were served first, followed by their advisers. The only three people in the room who didn't get a glass were me, deputy national security adviser Christian Turner and the prime minister's foreign affairs private secretary Jonny Hall. As the leaders began to leave, the three of us made a dash for the head waiter. Was there any left? Enough for three glasses, fortuitously. Just as we were about to get our well-earned reward, the prime minister spotted us from across the room and insisted on a photo of us caught in the act. There is no more 1945 port left, so you'll have to take my word for it: it was divine.

We spent the afternoon being given a tour of our new aircraft carrier, HMS *Queen Elizabeth II*, before travelling to Normandy for the second stage of the commemorations. The next morning, the prime minister and President Macron inaugurated a memorial on Sword, one of the three beaches where British troops landed on D-Day. We then attended a service in the beautiful Cathédrale Notre-Dame de Bayeux, before another service at the Bayeux War Cemetery. Its grounds were gifted by France to the UK in gratitude for the sacrifices of Commonwealth forces in the liberation of France and are beautifully maintained by the Commonwealth War Graves Commission. After the service, the prime minister was in her element as she mixed with veterans and their families. It was lovely to see her enjoying the job now that the pressure of the last two years had been lifted from her shoulders.

These two days showed how much Theresa had grown into the job as she approached the end of her premiership. While writing this book, I recalled a quote from Tony Blair in which he noted that the paradox of being prime minister is that 'you start at your most popular and least capable, and you end at your least popular and most capable'. She had handled President Trump deftly and demonstrated an empathy with the veterans and their families that would have surprised her critics. On a personal level, they were two of my most memorable days as chief of staff. I have a deep interest in the Second World War, and it was an honour to speak to some of the remarkable men to whom we all owe so much. Their bodies were now old and worn out, but their memories were vivid and their pride in their achievements undimmed.

Back to the grindstone

We returned to London to some good news. We had been competing with Italy to host COP26, the next big international climate change conference, but they had approached us to suggest that we submit a joint bid, with the UK as president. This was a significant coup. A few days later, the prime minister made the formal announcement that we would legislate to achieve net-zero greenhouse gas emissions by 2050. We were the first major economy to do so and this decision, taken just six weeks before the end of her premiership, is probably her most significant legacy.

The hope that we could avoid Brexit altogether during this period turned out to be illusory. On 12 June, Labour's opposition motion sought to take control of House of Commons business, with a view to legislating to provide a lock on no deal. A number of cabinet ministers lobbied to be allowed to abstain, but the prime minister was adamant that the government couldn't be neutral on whether the opposition had control of House of Commons business.

On 14 June, I met with Greg Clark to discuss some of the domestic announcements we were still trying to land. On education funding, he supported a one-year settlement, but thought a multi-year one should be for a new leader. Even more frustratingly, he was resistant to doing something on parental leave. As business secretary, he wanted to do take business with us before making changes in this area, and thought there was insufficient time to do so. When pushed, he was prepared to support a consultation paper, but not one advocating a specific policy.

On 17 June, the prime minister announced the mental health package we had worked up: extra support for schools, local authorities and healthcare services to emphasise the importance of mental health and identify issues before they become critical, plus an overhaul the Mental Health Act, including banning the use of police cells to detain people experiencing mental illness. Paul Farmer, the chief executive of MIND, welcomed 'the sustained momentum from the prime minister to improving support for people with mental health problems'.

The news from Northern Ireland was less positive. We had hoped that the public anger at the murder of Lyra McKee and the failure of their politicians to put aside their differences (Sinn Féin had recently been punished heavily in the recent Irish local elections) would pressure the parties into compromise, but the Northern Ireland secretary Karen Bradley reported that the prospects of restoring devolved government did not look good. Sinn Féin were worried the prime minister's successor might opt for no deal and didn't want to be in government if that happened, while the DUP thought they might get a better deal from the next government.

On 18 June, the prime minister had a meeting with Greg Clark and made some progress on the issue of parental leave. She then had a bilateral with Philip Hammond that went less well. As well as arguing it was inappropriate for her to make an announcement on school funding, he wasn't convinced that more funding was the answer – we already spent more than most of the G7 on education, but got worse results. And he reminded her that he had agreed to the funding for the NHS long-term plan on the basis that it would be the only department to be settled before the spending review – she was going back on that agreement and he'd always thought of her as someone who kept her promises. The prime minister acknowledged that she had agreed that other departments' budgets would be settled as part of the spending review, but on the basis that there would be one this summer. In its absence, we needed to do something now to progress the new national funding formula for schools.

These arguments were little more than a sideshow – Philip was willing to give the prime minister what she wanted if she gave him what he wanted on Brexit. He had three possible solutions: the government could apply for yet another extension; she could agree that if the House of Lords passed a private member's bill that provided a lock against no deal, the government would give time for it to be debated in the Commons; or the government could introduce a business motion on any issue, which could the House could amend to provide time for legislation. The prime minister was adamant that she could not do either of the first two options. It was highly likely that there would be a business motion of some kind over the next few weeks, but she warned that it would be difficult for the government not to whip against any attempt to take control of parliamentary business. It was clear from this meeting that there was no chance of Philip giving us the multi-year funding settlement we wanted, so we decided to focus on a one-year deal.

When I met with him again on 21 June, he was in a tetchy mood. He was resisting the announcement on paternity leave, but relented slightly when I told him where the prime minister had got to with Greg. He was open to a one-year deal on schools, but said it would require the tacit agreement of the final two leadership candidates. I let him know that it looked like we might need some legislation on Northern Ireland, which would give him the business motion he was looking for, but reminded him that the prime minister had not agreed to a free vote.

The prime minister received an update from Rebecca Hogg, her private secretary with responsibility for Northern Ireland, that the Northern Ireland Office thought there was a fifty-fifty chance that the cross-party talks would succeed in restoring devolved government. She wanted to go to Belfast to try to persuade Arlene and Michelle O'Neill, the Sinn Féin leader, to do the right thing, but was advised that it might prove counter-productive.

On 24 and 25 June, she spoke to Jeremy Hunt and Boris Johnson, the final two candidates in the leadership contest, to ask them not to give the DUP the impression that a better deal might be on offer if they waited a few weeks. Beyond the obvious benefits of restoring government to Northern Ireland, she reminded them that it would strengthen their hand in the Brexit negotiations if there were a first minister in place. Her conversation with Boris was one of their warmer interactions. He reassured her that he was 'completely and instinctively on-message' and ended the call by wishing her good luck with the Northern Ireland talks and everything else.

I had yet another meeting with Philip on 24 June. His list of objections had grown – he was now concerned that the proposed Office for Tackling Injustices would increase pressure on public spending. However, the next day we got the fourth major announcement over the line when Justin Tomlinson, the minister for disabled people, announced a cross-government approach to disability. Richard Kramer, the chief executive of Sense, called the announcement 'a significant one for disabled people'.

The clock is ticking

On 3 July, we received the depressing news that there had been no breakthrough in the Northern Ireland talks; we needed to extend the deadline by which an executive had to be formed, or fresh elections would have to be held. Meanwhile, I had a further meeting with Philip and Jonathan Slater, the permanent secretary of the Department for Education, to try to hammer out a funding package for education.

On 4 July, the prime minister gave her last major policy speech. Rather fittingly, it was on the Union, one of the issues that defined her politics. She acknowledged that Brexit was 'a profound constitutional change that is putting political and administrative strains on the Union', but said she was optimistic about its future because of its three core strengths: it doesn't rely on a rigid constitution to hold itself together, but on public support; it involves the pooling of risks and the sharing of rewards; and, perhaps most importantly, it respects different identities:

You can be Welsh and Muslim and British. You can be Glaswegian and gay and British. You might feel more English than British, or vice versa. You do not have to choose. You can be both, or either, or neither. The Union has never been about uniformity.

The answer to the challenge facing the Union did not lie in constitutional change, she argued, and while we must fully respect the devolved governments, we must not forget the duty of the UK government to be a government for the whole country. She announced that she was asking Andrew Dunlop to lead a review into how the UK government could strengthen the Union.

On 5 July, I met separately with Eddie Lister and Ed Jones, one of whom would take over my job when Boris or Jeremy became leader. I wanted to give them the handover that I'd never had and prepare them for what life would be like in the job. I had a final chat with Philip, who was still being difficult about parental leave and the Office for Tackling Injustices.

I then took some time off. When I'd been feeling unwell in February, I'd decided to get away as soon as I could. Easter felt too risky – it was clear even in February that there was a risk of the 29 March deadline slipping – so I booked something in early July, when my kids' schools broke up. When the prime minister announced that the handover of her leadership would be in late July, I offered to cancel it, but she insisted that I go. I had worked hard to get all her shortlist of policies over the line, but I hadn't yet secured the school funding announcement, and felt bad about going away with it outstanding. I'd only been away for a couple of days when the news of the deal Philip was trying to strike leaked to *The Times*. That put an end to it, although it didn't stop the establishment of the Office for Tackling Injustices being announced on 12 July.

I was back in the office on 17 July, just in time for one final Brexit-related row. The House of Lords had amended a piece of Northern Ireland legislation to try to stop the next government proroguing parliament in order to force through a no-deal Brexit. The amendment was defective, so a group of MPs had hatched a plan to correct it. Philip called me late in the evening and asked me to let the prime minister know that he, David Gauke, Greg Clark and Rory Stewart, in addition to at least six junior ministers and a larger group of backbenchers, intended to vote for it. The ministers were prepared to be absent rather than vote for the amendment, if the prime minister would assure them that no action would be taken against them.

I explained to Philip why the government didn't like the amendment (it would drag Northern Ireland MPs back to Westminster every couple of weeks, which was not helpful to the talks), but agreed to pass on his message. I told the prime minister that my sense was that these ministers were under pressure from like-minded backbenchers to vote according to their views and not leave it to others to do the dirty work – my guess was that this time, Philip and co weren't bluffing. She therefore had three choices: she could give all Conservative MPs a free vote, she could agree to slip the ministers in question (permit their absence from the vote) or she could insist that they vote against the amendment. The first would mean an immediate row – it would be seen as a deliberate attempt to constrain the next government. The second would cause a row the next day, when it became apparent that we'd lost the vote because ministers had been slipped. And the third would mean a significant number of ministers either resigning or being sacked. As usual with Brexit, there were no good options.

The next morning, the prime minister asked me to tell Philip that he should do what he thought was right, and she would do what she thought was right in response. She was prepared to tell him that if the amendment passed, the government would not pull the bill, and she was also prepared to offer him a way out. He was at a G7 finance ministers' meeting, a credible excuse for missing a vote if he wanted to stay there. To his credit, he wasn't prepared to take a get-out and leave his colleagues in the lurch. In the event, six ministers who attended cabinet abstained (the four he had warned me about, plus Karen Bradley and Caroline Nokes) and we lost by forty-one votes. The prime minister decided not to fire anyone, but instructed her spokesman to say she was disappointed and was sure her successor would take these things into account when considering who to appoint. It wasn't an edifying end to the Brexit votes we'd faced, but it was probably the least bad way out of an impossible situation.

Resignation honours

The next day, we published the parental leave consultation, our final domestic policy announcement. All that remained was for Theresa to decide whose contribution to recognise in her resignation honours list. She didn't find it easy – she thought David Cameron had honoured too many of his advisers, but now she was in the same position, there were a number of people she wanted to recognise. There is a hierarchy to our honours system – if prime ministers choose to have a list, they are forced to rank people's contribution, which runs the risk of upsetting as many people as you please. In deciding who to recommend for which honour, she was guided by a combination of longevity of service and seniority of role.

Theresa had assumed that I would be keen to get back into the House of Commons and was surprised when I told her I had no intention of doing so. I had loved being the MP for my home town, but the Conservative Party had already chosen a candidate for my old seat and I wasn't interested in being MP for somewhere I didn't know. Even if Croydon Central had been available, I thought Boris Johnson would win the leadership contest and quickly be forced to call an election, and knew I would be uncomfortable with the Brexit policy I'd have to stand on as a Conservative candidate. Once she knew I wasn't going back to the Commons, Theresa told me that she wanted to recommend me for a peerage, which I gratefully accepted.

Postscript

The answer to the question the prime minister had posed on 23 May turned out to be 'Quite a lot.' We had achieved seven of the nine aims on our shortlist. The Johnson government delivered the two that got away, with Julian Smith, who Boris appointed as Northern Ireland secretary, playing a pivotal role in restoring devolved government (which, as I had always suspected, only happened once Brexit was settled). We had also made some other significant announcements: a package on domestic abuse, a new legal duty on public bodies to tackle serious violence and increased protections for consumers. Taken together, they give an insight into the kind of reforming prime minister Theresa May would have been had she managed to get Brexit done.

CHAPTER 23

LEAVING NARNIA

On Tuesday 23 July, the prime minister chaired her final cabinet meeting. She thanked the Number 10 team, the Cabinet Secretary Mark Sedwill and Olly Robbins and the Cabinet Office Europe team. Addressing the cabinet, she said her government had taken important long-term decisions on issues such as NHS funding and achieving net-zero carbon emissions, but it would fall to the next government to defeat Corbynism and to find a way to get Brexit done while keeping the Union together. Whatever roles cabinet ministers might play going forward, whether in government or on the backbenches, she wished them well. David Lidington thanked her on behalf of the cabinet for her resilience, her concern for victims of injustice, her commitment to the Union and for her public service.

Later that day, the result of the Conservative leadership election was formally declared. Boris Johnson had beaten Jeremy Hunt, with 66 per cent of the vote.

My final day in the job started with a first in my time as chief of staff: a media interview. *Today* wanted to talk about Theresa's premiership with someone who could give an insight into her feelings as she prepared to leave office. Robbie was keen that I should do it and so was the prime minister, who waived the restriction in the special adviser code that prevented me from doing media interviews.

At about twenty past seven, I wandered over from Number 10 to College Green, where a host of temporary studios had been erected, to talk to Nick Robinson. There was a certain symmetry to it: I'd been interviewed by him just before the prime minister called me to offer me the job, and I was now speaking to him at the close.

In one of the softest interviews I've ever done, he started by asking how I felt – leaving a job that had occupied every waking moment of my life must be 'an extraordinary wrench'? I replied:

There's a mixture of emotions: pride at what we've achieved, huge frustration at what we weren't able to get done, gratitude to have worked with an amazing group of civil servants and, above all, honour to have had the opportunity to serve the prime minister and our country.

He then turned to how the prime minister was feeling. She had been visibly upset when she announced that she was resigning as leader of the Conservative Party. Was she now more accommodated to the fact that her time was up? I responded that she had accepted her time was up when she announced her decision to stand down, 'but it's a perfectly human thing that when you leave a job where you've got things you've done that you're proud of but haven't done the big thing you were trying to do, of course it's emotional'.

Next he focused on her record: as she left office, she would obviously want to dwell on her achievements. On the day she became prime minister, she spoke about tackling burning injustices – were there things that she had done to address them? I tried to give an honest answer:

There's been progress on a number of issues. A good example is the Racial Disparity Audit that she set up, that has shone a real light on some of the unfairnesses that are there, in terms of the way people from different communities are treated by our public services. And progress on the gender pay gap, on mental health issues. But she would also be honest and say, 'It's not all done, these problems are not all solved.'

Finally, he asked about Theresa May, the person:

> Some people say she lacked the charisma, the power to persuade that prime ministers need. What's the other side of the balance sheet? What don't we see?

I replied:

> As you said, I've given up pretty much every waking hour of my life for the last two years to support her. And the reason that I've done that is because what I see is a person who's absolutely committed to public service. And what I mean by that – it's a trite phrase – is that in politics, there are lots of people who sometimes choose to do the thing that's politically easy for them, but with this PM, I've always known that when there's a difficult decision, she'll do what she believes is right for our country. Now you or I may not agree, your listeners may not agree, but the motivation is to try to do what is in the national interest and, to me, that motivation is a really important thing and one of the reasons why it has been a huge honour to work for her.

After that, it was back to Downing Street for the final morning meeting, where I'd find out what the boss thought about what I'd said. In true Theresa May style, she hadn't listened, although several people had told her I'd been very nice about her.

I left a letter on her desk to tell her how I felt, as we both prepared to leave jobs we loved:

> As the time to leave Number 10 approaches, I wanted to write to thank you for the opportunity to serve as your chief of staff. It has been the greatest honour of my life.
>
> And it has been an honour not just because of the importance of the role, but because of the character of the person I have

served. I have been willing to devote nearly all my waking hours to it because I always knew that you would do what you thought was right for our country rather than what was politically convenient for you. That is an all-too-rare quality in politics today.

You should be proud of what you achieved. You leave Number 10 with debt falling, a record number of people in work and the long-term future of our NHS secured, having made a ground-breaking commitment to net-zero carbon emissions and having taken action to tackle the burning injustices you identified in your first speech. This is not yet a country that works for everyone, but it is a fairer country than the one you inherited, and where injustice persists, you have shone a spotlight on it.

You should be equally proud of the Brexit deal you negotiated, which I continue to believe is the only way to bring the country back together after the divisions of the referendum. It is tough to come to terms with our failure to persuade parliament to back the deal. If you're not already familiar with it, I hope the following quote will be of some consolation. It is from a speech by President Theodore Roosevelt after he left office. This particular passage is known as 'The Man in the Arena' (although in this case, 'The Woman in the Arena' would be more appropriate):

'It is not the critic who counts; not the man who points out how the strong man stumbles, or where the doer of deeds could have done them better. The credit belongs to the man who is actually in the arena, whose face is marred by dust and sweat and blood; who strives valiantly; who errs, who comes short again and again, because there is no effort without error and shortcoming; but who does actually strive to do the deeds; who knows great enthusiasm, the great devotions; who spends himself in a worthy cause; who at the best knows in the end the triumph of high achievement, and who at the worst, if he fails, at least fails while daring greatly, so that his place shall never be with those cold and timid souls who neither know victory or defeat.'

When MPs and journalists talk to me about my job, they often observe that you are a very private person and must therefore be a very difficult person to be chief of staff to. That is the exact opposite of my experience. From the moment you invited me down to Sonning on 10 June, you have been entirely open with me, despite the fact that we didn't know each other very well when I started, and it is that which has allowed me to do the job.

Once again, thank you, prime minister – both for the amazing opportunity you have given me and, more importantly, for what you have done for our country.

Shortly before 11 a.m., we were driven from Downing Street to parliament for her final Prime Minister's Questions. I got in the car first, as usual, so I didn't intrude in the photos as she came out of the building. Her first question was from the Labour MP Ruth Cadbury, who paid tribute to her public service and asked her how she felt 'about handing over to a man who, among many things, is happy to demonise Muslims, is prepared to chuck our loyal public servants and diplomats under a bus, and promises to sell our country out to Donald Trump and his friends?' It must have stuck in the craw a bit as she replied:

I am pleased to hand over to an incoming leader of the Conservative Party and prime minister who I worked with when he was in my cabinet, and who is committed, as a Conservative who stood on a Conservative manifesto in 2017, to delivering on the vote of the British people in 2016 and to delivering a bright future for this country.

Jeremy Corbyn also paid tribute to her sense of public duty, recognised the huge pressure she had been under and wished her a more relaxing time on the backbenches. The niceties over, he then tore into her record. Her reply gives a good insight into her view of politics:

> Let me just say something about my record over the past three years and how I measure it. It is in the opportunity for every child who is now in a better school. It is in the comfort for every person who now has a job for the first time in their life. It is in the hope of every disadvantaged young person now able to go to university. It is in the joy of every couple who can now move into their own home. At its heart, politics is not about exchanges across the despatch box. Nor is it about eloquent speeches or media headlines. Politics is about the difference we make every day to the lives of people up and down this country.

She didn't care for the Punch and Judy knockabout of PMQs any more than she did for set-piece political interviews, wining and dining journalists or recording soundbites for social media. She understood the need for such things, but they weren't parts of the job she enjoyed. What she cared about was getting the decisions that crossed her desk right and getting government to work in the interests of ordinary people.

Ian Blackford from the SNP was more generous, and paid tribute not just to her but also to me:

> At times we have clashed on points of political difference, but equally we have stood together when it has been right to do so, over Salisbury and other threats to the UK's national security. She rightly made sure that opposition leaders were informed at key moments . . . In particular, her chief of staff Gavin Barwell always sought to make sure that I was kept informed of important developments.

To my embarrassment – I was just a few feet away, in the 'box' in the corner of the Commons – the prime minister replied:

> I would also like to take this opportunity to pay tribute to Gavin Barwell, who was a first-class member of this House, a first-class minister, and has been an absolutely first-class chief of staff.

It was a telling indication of my standing in the parliamentary party that while this tribute was greeted pretty warmly on the opposition benches, only about half of my former colleagues joined in – quite a contrast from that first meeting of the 1922 Committee in June 2017.

We had arranged with the Speaker's office for the last question to come from the Mother of the House, Harriet Harman; these two women had between them done more than anyone else to transform their respective parties. In 2016, Harriet had said that Theresa was 'a woman, but no sister', but her view had softened over the last few years and she now paid a warm tribute:

> It is always a historic moment when a prime minister leaves office . . . but the right honourable lady's departure marks another milestone, because although we are on to our seventy-seventh prime minister, she is only the second woman ever to have held that office. She made tackling human trafficking and the horrors of domestic violence a priority at the heart of her government . . . Even the prime minister's harshest critics must recognise her integrity, her commitment to public service and her dedication to this country. Those are qualities that none of us should ever take for granted . . . I thank her for her service as our prime minister and I sincerely wish her all the very best for the future.

Theresa returned the compliment, before looking forward to the next female prime minister:

> I came here in 1997 as one of only thirteen Conservative women . . . I am proud to have played my part in getting more women MPs in this House. I am sure that among the women in this House today, there is a future prime minister – perhaps more than one.

She ended by signalling that she would not follow Tony Blair and David Cameron in standing down as an MP shortly after ceasing to be prime minister, but intended to be an active backbencher:

> Later today . . . I will return to the backbenches. It will be my first time on the backbenches in twenty-one years, so it will be quite a change from standing here at the despatch box. I am told that over the past three years, I have answered more than 4,500 questions over 140 hours in this House . . . In future, I look forward to asking the questions . . . That duty to serve my constituents will remain my greatest motivation.

In a relatively recent innovation, she was applauded as she left the chamber for the last time as prime minister, and that is where my notes end. Once she was back at Number 10, she said her farewells to those she had worked closest with and was clapped from the building, with civil servants and political advisers lining the corridors from her private office to the famous black front door. I slipped out through the door of Number 11 so I could watch her final speech as prime minister live rather than on television.

We'd worked on the draft over the previous twenty-four hours. Theresa was determined not to give the media any more images of her tearing up, so we removed a few lines that made her emotional when she rehearsed it. There were four things she wanted to say. First, to express her best wishes to her successor, for which we borrowed some language from President George H. W. Bush's famous, gracious message to President Clinton: 'I wish him and the government he will lead every good fortune in the months and years ahead; their successes will be our country's successes, and I hope that they will be many.' Second, to express her thanks to those who had supported her and to the British people 'for putting your faith in me and giving me the chance to serve'. Third, to express her hope that 'every young girl who has seen a woman prime minister now knows for sure that there are no limits to what they can achieve'. And finally, to express her intention to stay in politics and her optimism about the future of the country – and in doing so, to end her time as prime minister with the phrase that encapsulated her politics: 'I will continue to do all I can to serve the national interest, and play my part in making our United Kingdom – a great country with a great future – a country that truly works for everyone'.

Speech over, she got into the car with Philip and was taken to Buckingham Palace, where she tendered her resignation to the Queen and recommended Boris Johnson as her successor. I returned to Number 10 for my final job as chief of staff: to make sure the political advisers who were not being kept on by Boris Johnson left the building in the next ten minutes, so that his team could then be brought in, ready for when he arrived from his audience with Her Majesty. Once they had left, I said my final goodbyes. I had spent more time with some of these people than my own family over the previous two years, and a number had become close friends. But beyond those who I had got to know well, there were many other people in Number 10 who had gone out of their way to support me: the duty clerks in private office; the switchboard; the overnight security shift, who would open up the building when I arrived at some ungodly hour; Alison in the cafeteria, who would bring something up to me at the end of her shift if I failed to make it down for breakfast or lunch. Many of these people aren't paid much for what they do, but they are each indispensable in helping Number 10 to function effectively.

I left through the link door to the Cabinet Office rather than the famous front door – it is only the prime minister, and not their staff, who should get that photo opportunity. I strolled through London in the beautiful July sunshine with James Marshall, the now former head of the Number 10 policy unit. As we headed to a pub on the South Bank, where the political team were assembling to drown our sorrows, he remarked that it felt rather like leaving Narnia at the end of one of C. S. Lewis's novels: some of us might return in the future, but others would never come back.

EPILOGUE

So, that's my story. The question is, might it have had a different ending? I set out earlier why it was so difficult to get Brexit done, but were there moments when a different choice would have allowed Theresa to get her deal over the line? Or was the attempt to convince people to compromise on Brexit destined to end in failure?

The strongest contender for a 'what if?' moment is the 2017 election. Had Theresa run a better campaign, one that was centred around the 'country that works for everyone' mantra that encapsulated her politics, and had she avoided the flaws in the manifesto that reinforced voters' concerns about the Conservatives, she would have won well. That would have made the parliamentary arithmetic easier and strengthened her authority, both within the Conservative Party and in the negotiations with the EU. And it would probably have forced the Labour Party to go through the process it is now going through of accepting Brexit, even though they deeply regret it. In this scenario, she would have been able to get Brexit done and I would never have become chief of staff: Nick and Fi would have remained in post and – as Theresa herself told me a few months after I started in Number 10 – I would have been appointed secretary of state for communities and local government in the post-election reshuffle.

A lot of people have asked me how things would have turned out if David Davis hadn't resigned over Chequers. Boris Johnson certainly wouldn't have resigned, but there would still have been significant backbench opposition to the Chequers proposals, and I think it is almost certain that Boris would have resigned over the revised backstop in the autumn of 2018. Ultimately, Brexit was the issue that offered him the chance to become prime minister, and it's hard to imagine an alternative history where he didn't take it.

A more interesting question concerns what would have happened if Geoffrey Cox's written legal advice about the backstop before the second meaningful vote had been as powerful as his oral statement about it to the Commons. A lot of the rebels decided to make it the weathervane that determined how they voted; in the event, it did not give them the reassurance they needed. Had Geoffrey's written advice mirrored his speech from the despatch box, the second meaningful vote would have been much closer, giving Theresa a good chance of winning third time round. She might have been able to get Brexit done, which would have changed the verdict on her premiership, but she would only have had another year or two in the job because by this point she had committed not to lead the party into the next election.

Another key moment was the Speaker's ruling that it would be contrary to the rules of the House for the government to bring the same deal back for another meaningful vote. If John Bercow hadn't made that ruling, I think the DUP would have signed up to a package of measures that would have allowed them to back the deal. And if we had got the DUP over the line, we would have won the third vote. By this point, Theresa had committed to stand down once the first stage of the Brexit negotiations had been completed, but she would have got the Withdrawal Agreement through and the verdict on her premiership would have been different.

Lots of people ask why the DUP behaved as they did. Their refusal to back the deal sealed Theresa's fate, allowing Boris to seize the crown and then sign up to a revised version of the protocol that was less palatable to the DUP than Theresa's deal had been. I put this question to Nigel Dodds in the autumn of 2019. His answer was that the reassurances we offered them were in domestic law, whereas the protocol was international law and they worried that whoever followed Theresa would unpick the domestic reassurances. This was a reasonable concern, but rejecting the deal left them with no protection. When faced with a choice between the Brexit they wanted and the Union, Boris and the ERG were always going to choose Brexit.

What if Labour had backed the Withdrawal Agreement in the third vote? It would have passed and the House would probably have put various negotiating objectives into the Withdrawal Agreement Bill, forcing Theresa's successor to call a general election if they wanted to pursue a more distant relationship with the EU. Labour would have been in a better position to fight that election, not being vulnerable to the charge of blocking Brexit. Keir Starmer is one of the people who stopped this happening, gambling everything on getting a second referendum and he is now having to deal with the electoral consequences.

Finally, what if the EU had compromised a bit more? They gave Boris Johnson a consent mechanism in the Northern Ireland protocol, which means there's a legal route out of it if a majority of the members of the Northern Ireland assembly reject it. That is highly unlikely to happen, but such a mechanism would almost certainly have been enough to get Theresa's deal through. Or what if the EU had played hardball in the run-up to the Article 50 deadline, insisting that they would only grant an extension if the House of Commons backed the deal or decided on a second referendum? That would have forced a straight choice, which we were never able to do.

What-ifs are interesting, but ultimately pointless. So what verdict should we reach on Theresa May and her premiership? In one sense, I'm well qualified to make such an assessment, having worked closely with her and seen her strengths and weaknesses. But I cannot claim to be objective: beyond the admiration I have for Theresa, I owe her the loyalty she showed me.

As I noted in the Introduction, the passage of time will not change the fundamental judgement on her premiership – her key job was to get Brexit done, and she failed. She acknowledged this when she announced that she was standing down as leader of the Conservative Party, saying, 'It is, and will always remain, a matter of deep regret to me that I have not been able to deliver Brexit.'

I've already dealt with the critique that she didn't compromise enough, drawing red lines that boxed her in. The main critique from within the Conservative Party is that she compromised too much and gave in to the EU's demands. David Frost, who negotiated Boris Johnson's deal, claimed that Boris and he came in 'after a government and negotiating team that had blinked and had its bluff called at critical moments'. However, given that the deal he negotiated was 95 per cent his predecessor's work, with the 5 per cent that was new ceding to the EU's original demand for unique arrangements in Northern Ireland, that's some brass neck. It's also untrue. On the day after she announced that she was standing down as leader of the Conservative Party, Oliver Wright, policy editor of *The Times*, wrote:

Mrs May chose to go into the negotiations eschewing the theatrical tub-thumping favoured by David Cameron and other former prime ministers. It is possible that Mrs May's strategy led to a better deal than might have been won by a more confrontational leader. Despite condemnation at home, the agreement on the Irish backstop arguably represented a key climbdown by the EU . . . If anyone shifted on their red lines it was Brussels, not Mrs May. The prime minister won grudging respect from EU leaders who admired her tenacity and fortitude. Mr Juncker told his aides that he watched Mrs May's resignation 'with emotion'. 'Theresa May is a woman of courage for whom he has great respect,' his spokesman said. Michel Barnier . . . praised her 'determination', while Leo Varadkar . . . described her as 'principled, honourable and deeply passionate about doing her best for her country'. These are not mere platitudes.

And it wasn't just the backstop – she also won a key concession on the UK's future relationship with the EU. She was originally offered a binary choice: stay in the single market and the customs union or have a free trade agreement, but with arrangements for Northern Ireland that would mean a partial border within our own country. Theresa succeeded in convincing the EU to consider a new model somewhere between the two. Her problem was that neither of these two negotiating successes won her much credit from many Brexiteers. They didn't like the new backstop any more than the old one, and they didn't want a close relationship with the EU after we'd left. One of Theresa's top priorities was ending free movement – she believed it was the issue that had led millions of people to vote Leave – but although they had been happy to exploit it during the referendum campaign, it wasn't a key issue for many of them. What they cared about was regulatory autonomy, although five years after they persuaded people to leave, they still don't know what they want to do with it.

Theresa pursued a compromise on Brexit because she was a passionate unionist, as were several of the key Brexiteers like Michael Gove and Liam Fox who supported her to the end, but large parts of her party were increasingly indifferent to the Union. In June 2019, YouGov published a poll showing that 63 per cent of Conservative Party members would want Brexit to take place even if it led to Scotland leaving the UK. The same poll showed that 61 per cent wanted Brexit to happen even if it did significant damage to the economy, with 54 per cent wanting it to happen if it led to the destruction of the Conservative Party. The only thing they regarded as more important than Brexit was stopping Jeremy Corbyn from becoming prime minister. It is no wonder Theresa struggled to sell a compromise to people with such views.

There is a second, more subtle critique. Some people concede that her deal might have been better than Boris Johnson's deal for the economy and the Union, but argue that it would never have worked politically; the only way to be rid of Nigel Farage was to deliver a hard Brexit. But this, too, is untrue. Our polling showed that the Chequers proposals only became controversial when Brexiteers started knocking lumps out of them; until then, the key elements tested well with Leave voters. And if the Conservative Party had delivered a Brexit that ended free movement and large annual contributions to Brussels while taking back control of our waters and allowing us to negotiate our own trade deals with other countries, Nigel Farage would have been finished. The Brexit Party only became a political threat when the government failed to leave the EU on 29 March 2019.

If the critiques that Theresa gave in to the EU or that her deal wouldn't have worked politically are absurd, subsequent events have vindicated her compromise. The deal that Boris Johnson managed to get through parliament has led to all the problems that she predicted. The partial border down the Irish Sea that Boris agreed to is causing huge problems for businesses that move goods from Great Britain to Northern Ireland, as well as political unrest, and at the time of writing the deal still hasn't been fully implemented.

David Frost said that, despite all the warnings, the government underestimated the effect of the protocol. Some people may be tempted to believe that – that the prime minister and his team didn't bother to understand what they were signing up to – but it's not true. The truth is that their initial plan was to prorogue parliament and leave without a deal. When that failed, they switched to seeking an election. It would be easier to win an election with 'an oven-ready Brexit deal', so the strategy switched to accepting whatever deal was on offer with a view to wriggling out of it subsequently. The EU have worked out that this is what the government is up to, and are determined to hold the UK to what it signed up to.

Economically, Brexit is a slow puncture – the government is lucky that there will be no sudden crash where the damage is visible, but the Office for Budget Responsibility predicts that our economy will be 4 per cent smaller than it would have been if we hadn't left. That's a bigger long-term impact than COVID-19. And finally, Boris's election as leader of the Conservative Party and his hard Brexit has led to an increase in support for Scottish independence. Scots could see that he wasn't willing to compromise one iota on Brexit to take account of the fact that two of the UK's four nations voted to remain. 72 of the 129 candidates they elected to the Scottish parliament this May stood on a manifesto promising a second independence referendum; 50.1 per cent of the votes for the list seats were for parties that support independence. It looks increasingly possible that Brexit will lead to the break-up of our precious Union, the outcome Theresa was so desperate to avoid. Brexiteers counter that a hard Brexit weakens the economic case for Scottish independence – it would mean customs and regulatory checks when goods move between Scotland and the remnant UK – but they of all people should realise that Scottish independence, like Brexit, is about identity rather than economic forecasts. Indeed, it is another paradox of Brexit that if there is a second independence referendum in Scotland, Boris Johnson and Nicola Sturgeon will each be arguing the exact opposite of what they argued in the Brexit referendum. When it came to Brexit, Boris argued that sovereignty is what matters, whereas Nicola argued that nations are more prosperous and safer when they pool their sovereignty. And yet, when it comes to the future of the United Kingdom, they adopt the opposite positions and expect no one to notice.

The damage Boris's deal has done to our economy and the risk it poses to our Union vindicate Theresa's attempts to find a compromise. If she must take some responsibility for failing to sell it, so must those who refused to meet her halfway and instead attempted to overturn the referendum result.

And if her approach to Brexit has been vindicated, so too has her political strategy. Boris deserves credit for successfully assembling the electoral coalition she was trying to build in 2017, but the strategy was essentially the same. On policy, too, they have much in common. Both are less fiscally conservative than George Osborne or Philip Hammond, believing in higher spending on public services; both believe in levelling up and an active industrial policy; both want to increase house-building; and both believe that action to tackle climate change and improve the environment should be a key part of the Conservative offering. Stylistically, they are very different, but the only policy difference I can see between them, apart from on Brexit, concerns the commitment to spend 0.7 per cent of our GDP on overseas aid and equalities issues.

If Theresa lacked the communication skills that are a prerequisite for a modern prime minister, she possessed many of the qualities that we should look for in one: a willingness to grapple with complex problems, respect for expert advice, resilience, a desire to heal wounds rather than draw dividing lines and, above all, the right motivation for being in politics in the first place. Some of these would have served the country well had she had to contend with the COVID-19 pandemic.

As for me, while those two and a bit years were exhausting and stressful, being chief of staff was the most amazing job I'll ever have. Some people wonder why anyone chooses to get involved in politics – you can earn more and be subject to far less media scrutiny and online abuse elsewhere. While it does require a thick skin, politics touches every aspect of our lives. I can't think of any better vocation than trying to change your local community, your country and the world for the better.

The experience inevitably changed me in a number of ways. First, it left me with some behavioural tics I can't shake. Nearly two years on, I'm still awake by 6 a.m. and find it hard to go more than an hour without checking my phone for emails, WhatsApp messages and texts – much to the amusement of my teenage children who say I need some screen-free time.

Second, working closely with highly talented people who care deeply about the governance of our country left me with an increased respect for the quality and integrity of our senior civil servants. The civil service as an institution isn't perfect – it is too departmentalised, too London-centric and good at giving policy advice to ministers but less effective at programme management. It has made huge strides in terms of gender equality but is less diverse when it comes to ethnicity and class, and the culture of people moving jobs every couple of years prevents the development of subject expertise. In short, I agree with Dominic Cummings that it needs reform, but he should have learned from his time in government that politicians need to take the people who work for an organisation with them if they want to reform it, not threaten them with a hard rain.

Third, it convinced me that politicians should spend less time coming up with new policies to satisfy the media's hunger for news and more time focusing on whether the decisions they've taken have been implemented and, if so, are having the desired effect. Speak to anyone at the coalface and they will tell you that they want policy stability rather than constant changes.

Fourth, I left Number 10 believing less of what I read in the newspapers. If much of what you read about meetings you have been in is, at best, only partially true, it makes you sceptical about everything else you read.

Fifth, my time as chief of staff made me like the EU less, but regret our departure more. I witnessed first-hand the deep-rooted instinct at official level that everything should be sorted out before the elected politicians arrive. But I also saw, for example after the chemical attack in Salisbury, the benefit of being a member of the club. and came to appreciate how the EU is a regulatory superpower, and the rules it makes will continue to affect us even though we've left.

Sixth, it made me less partisan. I find that I now care less about which party someone belongs to and more about their motivation for getting into politics, whether they are prepared to grapple with complexity and whether they try to bring people together or drive them apart.

Finally, and ironically, it made me think advisers are too influential. If I were to do it all again, my first piece of advice to Theresa would be that she should invest more time in her relationships with senior colleagues. The Thatcher ministry was sustained by the support of people like Cecil Parkinson and Norman Tebbit; the Blair ministry by John Prescott and Peter Mandelson; the Cameron ministry by George Osborne and William Hague. Theresa didn't have key lieutenants of this stature around her. Thirty or forty years ago, the House of Commons sat late most nights, but today it only sits late on Mondays. That has helped to make it more family-friendly, but at the expense of ministers spending more time together. At the same time, there has been an explosion in the number of political advisers. They are the people ministers now spend most of their time with, and that's a mistake.

I'm proud of some of the domestic achievements I helped to deliver – the commitment to net-zero carbon emissions, the long-term plan for the NHS, the extra investment in housing and the Race Disparity Audit. I'm also proud of the collegiate atmosphere we built in Number 10, and the way the team stuck together despite huge political pressure. And I'm proud that at heart, I'm still the same boy I used to be. I may have spent two years mixing with presidents and prime ministers, but the cornerstones of my life are still my family and the friends I made as a teenager. They don't treat me any differently now I'm the Lord Barwell PC, former Downing Street chief of staff, and I wouldn't have it any other way.

Would I put myself through it all again? Yes, for the right person. At the moment, I'm unlikely to be asked – and I'm enjoying working with some talented people in the private sector, who also care about solving society's problems. But if the last five or six years have taught me anything, it is that you never know what the future holds.

ACKNOWLEDGEMENTS

If wading through some old memories proved as painful as I had anticipated, the experience of writing this book was much more enjoyable than I'd feared, thanks to the help of a few special people.

I was vacillating about whether to write the book when – in one of life's fortuitous coincidences – I met Diane Banks, the founder of Northbank Talent Management, in the autumn of 2020. She was chairing a socially distanced Bright Blue event on housing policy, and I was one of the guest speakers. We chatted afterwards and I mentioned that I was umming and ahhing about writing about my time in Number 10. She introduced me to one of her colleagues, Martin Redfern, whose contribution to this book cannot be overstated. He helped to develop my vague notion of writing something based on the notes I kept during my time as chief of staff into a book that would simultaneously provide a fly-on-the-wall account of the last two years of Theresa's premiership and an insight into the role of chief of staff and how our country is governed. He also helped me identify Atlantic Books as the perfect publisher. I could not have asked for a better literary agent.

I am also hugely grateful to my editors, Mike Harpley and Nick Humphrey. They didn't complain when I submitted something that was nearly 50 per cent longer than promised, nor at my constant tinkering to try to get things right. Their feedback was invaluable in identifying sections of the initial draft that weren't core to the narrative and sections that needed further explanation, and the whole book – but particularly the two chapters on the Brexit negotiations and the chapter on the failed attempts to get parliament to back Theresa's deal – is much the better for their input.

I am also very grateful to the many people who have shared their recollections of key events or offered comments on all or parts of the book: Theresa herself (though this is not an 'authorised' account – the conclusions are mine alone); David Gauke; Mark Sedwill; Denzil Davidson; Liz Sanderson; a number of other current and former ministers and senior civil servants who prefer to remain anonymous; my friends Atul, Mark, Paul and Peter; and my brother, Richard. Their recollections and comments have been extremely useful in filling gaps in my memory and in helping me think about why things turned out as they did, and how the decisions Theresa took should be seen with the benefit of a few years' hindsight.

Writing this book while continuing to run the business I have set up has necessitated a temporary return to the hours I worked as chief of staff. I am hugely grateful to my wife Karen for her support during this period, as well as for her own comments on the text.

Any errors or omissions are, of course, my own.